June 2–4, 2016
Alexandria, VA, USA

Association for Computing Machinery

Advancing Computing as a Science & Profession

SIGMIS-CPR'16

Proceedings of the 2016 ACM SIGMIS Conference on
Computers and People Research

Sponsored by:
ACM SIGMIS

Supported by:
Howard University, Carnegie Mellon University, Univerität Bamberg, University of Wisconsin-Whitewater, Syracuse University, and Griffith University

**Association for
Computing Machinery**

Advancing Computing as a Science & Profession

The Association for Computing Machinery
2 Penn Plaza, Suite 701
New York, New York 10121-0701

Notice to Past Authors of ACM-Published Articles

ISBN: 978-1-4503-4203-2 (Digital)

ISBN: 978-1-4503-4596-5 (Print)

Additional copies may be ordered prepaid from:

ACM Order Department
PO Box 30777
New York, NY 10087-0777, USA

Phone: 1-800-342-6626 (USA and Canada)
+1-212-626-0500 (Global)
Fax: +1-212-944-1318
E-mail: acmhelp@acm.org
Hours of Operation: 8:30 am – 4:30 pm ET

Printed in the USA

Foreword

It is our great pleasure to welcome you to the annual *Computers and People Research Conference – ACM SIGMIS CPR 2016*. For more than 50 years, ACM SIGMIS CPR has engaged the academic and practitioner communities in understanding the issues related to the information technology (IT) workforce. Increasingly, IT empowers organizations and communities to improve the world around them through positive connection, interaction, and presence. The ways that we engage, understand and communicate around major events in communities, on the national landscape, and in the media has solidified a legitimate role for technology for years to come. As a result, we selected the conference theme of *organizational and social movements enabled by IT.*

The papers, posters and panels within the proceedings address themes related to the recruitment, retention and turnover of IT professionals, demand for their skills and talents, their readiness for the workplace, and topics in IS education and management. This year, several papers, posters and panels specifically focus on organizational and social movements themes related to smart cities, the sharing economy, making Black lives matter, social media collaboration in virtual teams and emerging technologies. We also encourage attendees to attend the keynote presentation entitled "Organizational Design" by Dr. Scott Bernard who currently serves as the U.S. Federal Chief Enterprise Architect at the Office of Management and Budget within the Executive Office of the President. His valuable and insightful talk will guide us to a better understanding of a holistic enterprise architecture framework. We hope these proceedings serve as a valuable reference for computer and people researchers and practitioners in the coming years.

Putting together the *ACM SIGMIS CPR 2016* conference was made possible by the work of many dedicated individuals. We first thank the authors for providing the content of the program, which continues to showcase exemplary work in the field. We are grateful to the program committee who worked diligently in reviewing papers and providing constructive feedback for the authors. In addition, we would like to thank Michelle Kaarst-Brown and Leigh Ellen Potter for organizing this year's doctoral consortium, which provides a glimpse of the exciting research on the horizon. We would like to thank Daniel Manson for his role as the poster session coordinator, Mike Gallivan and Susan Yager for their roles as registration coordinators, and Conrad Shayo, Andreas Eckhardt and Damian Joseph for publicity. Special thanks go to Irene Frawley and April Mosqus at the ACM for their support in coordinating the conference. And to Lisa Tolles and her team from ACM Sheridan Communications Proceedings Service for their work in processing the proceedings in a timely manager. Finally, we thank our sponsor, ACM SIGMIS, and the leadership of Janice Sipior.

We hope that you will find this program interesting and thought-provoking and that the symposium will provide you with a valuable opportunity to share ideas with other researchers and practitioners from institutions around the world.

Allison Morgan
CPR'16 Conference Co-Chair
Howard University, USA

Jeria Quesenberry
CPR'16 Conference Co-Chair
Carnegie Mellon University, USA

Sven Laumer
CPR'16 Program Co-Chair
Otto-Friedrich-University, Germany

Christina Outlay
CPR'16 Program Co-Chair
University of Wisconsin Whitewater, USA

Table of Contents

Panel: Making Black Lives Matter

Session 5.1: Recruitment, Retention and Turnover-2

Session 5.2: IT, Computers and People

Author Index

ACM SIGMIS CPR 2016 Conference Organization

General Chairs: Allison Morgan *(Howard University, USA)*
Jeria Quesenberry *(Carnegie Mellon University, USA)*

Program Chairs: Sven Laumer *(Otto-Friedrich-University, Germany)*
Christina Outlay *(University of Wisconsin Whitewater, USA)*

Poster Session Coordinator: Daniel Manson *(California State Polytechnic University, USA)*

Doctoral Consortium Chairs: Michelle Kaarst-Brown *(Syracuse University, USA)*
Leigh Ellen Potter *(Griffith University, Australia)*

Doctoral Consortium Mentors: Xuefei (Nancy) Deng *(California State University, USA)*
Mike Gallivan *(Georgia State University, USA)*
Indira Guzman *(Trident University International, USA)*
Jo Ellen Moore *(Southern Illinois University Edwardsville, USA)*
Eileen Trauth *(Pennsylvania State University, USA)*
Tim Weitzel *(University of Bamberg, Germany)*

Registration Coordinators: Mike Gallivan *(Georgia State University, USA)*
Susan Yager *(Southern Illinois University Edwardsville, USA)*

Publicity Chairs Conrad Shayo *(Cal State San Bernardino, USA)*
Andreas Eckhardt *(German Graduate School of Management and Law, Germany)*
Damian Joseph *(Nanyang Technological University, Singapore)*

Best Paper Award Committee Deborah J. Armstrong *(Florida State University, USA)*
Andreas Eckhardt *(German Graduate School of Management and Law, Germany)*
Fred Niederman *(Saint Louis University, USA)*
Conrad Shayo *(Cal State San Bernardino, USA)*

Program Committee: Monica Adya *(Marquette University, USA)*
Daniel Beimborn *(Frankfurt School of Finance & Management, Germany)*
Dárlinton B. F. Carvalho *(UFSJ, Brazil)*
Sebastian Duerr *(University of Bamberg, Germany)*
Yogesh Dwivedi *(Swansea University, United Kingdom)*
Andreas Eckhardt *(German Graduate School of Management and Law, Germany)*
Nooredin Etezady *(Nova Southeastern University & IS Consultant, USA)*
Jens Foerderer *(Uni Mannheim, Germany)*
Mike Gallivan *(Georgia State University, USA)*
Saurabh Gupta *(Kennesaw State University, USA)*
Damien Joseph *(Nanyang Technological University, Singapore)*

ACM SIGMIS CPR 2016 Sponsor & Supporters

Sponsor:

Supporters:

HOWARD UNIVERSITY

Carnegie Mellon University

UNIVERSITÄT BAMBERG

UNIVERSITY OF WISCONSIN
WHITEWATER

SYRACUSE UNIVERSITY
School of Information Studies

Virtual World Consumer Behavior

Angie M. Cox
Trident University
5757 Plaza Drive #100
Cypress, CA 90630
001(850)725-2540
Angiecox7@yahoo.com

ABSTRACT

This research will look at consumer behaviors in Virtual Worlds (VW) in order to fill the research gap and build a model to explain why users chose to purchase in VWs. Results from this study will help Information Systems (IS) researchers and game developers understand specific user attributes that may affect their intentions to purchase. With this knowledge IS researchers and developers may have the opportunity to manipulate system components in ways to improve business processes and stimulate profits for businesses. This study will rely on the Theory of Reasoned Action (TRA), Flow Theory and the concept of desire for uniqueness (DFU). The study's data will come from online survey volunteer VW users in one region of the United States testing both the model's measurement tool and hypotheses with Structural Equation Modeling (SEM) with Partial Least Squares (PLS). The validity and reliability and the strength and polarity relationships between the variables (user skill, challenge and DFU; VW shopping attitude, subjective norms (SN); and VW purchase intentions) will be assessed. With the results of the study, suggestions for further research will be made.

Keywords

Theory of Reasoned Action; Flow Theory; Virtual World; Consumer Behavior; Desire for Uniqueness

1. INTRODUCTION

According to Chaturvedi, Dok and Dmevich (2011), Virtual worlds (VW)s comprise a new class of Information System (IS) with simulation, emergent user dynamics and emergent knowledge processes present (Markus, Majchrzak, & Gasser, 2002). This research project looks at consumer behaviors within Virtual Worlds (VW). Spence (2008) used 'Second Life', a popular VW, to determine the way VW goods are purchased but had difficulty understanding why individuals chose to buy things that are only virtual and therefore unable to be used in conventional ways. Guo and Barnes (2011) found VW purchase intentions were affected by intrinsic and extrinsic factors formulated by staged decision making. Other research focused primarily on how to sell products, the workings of the monetary systems but there the information lack data on reasons for buying and behavior patterns of shoppers (Huang, 2011). There still lies a gap in explaining when, how and why VW participants buy VW

SIGMIS-CPR '16, June 2-4, 2016, Alexandria, VA, USA.
ACM 978-1-4503-4203-2/16/06.
http://dx.doi.org/10.1145/2890602.2906192

products. Regardless of the VW product limitations, research shows it is still a multi-million dollars market with an estimated 50 million participants (Bennett, 2008). Further, VWs News (2008a) judged that VW participation could reach a billion users by 2017.

1.1 Problem Statement

There is a knowledge gap regarding shopping in VWs, which is one of the most popular activities in VWs (Animesh et al., 2011). Shopping involves businesses and entrepreneurs marketing products within VWs so the VWs can improve their profits by receiving cuts from these sales.

1.2 Purpose and significance of the study

An IS is a work system whose activities are devoted to capturing, transmitting, storing, retrieving, manipulating and displaying information. (Alter, 2013) Understanding consumer behavior in VWs can help businesses succeed in VW markets. The knowledge can help developers design games in ways to steer users in to making purchases. This knowledge can aid to research and further clarify VW consumers by type, markets and products. Every day, thousands of people spend millions of dollars on goods that exist only within virtual environments (Spence, 2008). The purpose of this study is to explore the behaviors of VW consumers to improve marketing strategies and business decisions. How are businesses selling products and what makes VW participants chose to buy these products? Are VW consumers different from 'normal' shoppers based on their goals and motivations? How can other businesses tap into to VW markets wisely and with minimal risks? How can VW designers, IS researchers and engineers develop programs and tools to stimulate sales? A better understanding of VW consumer behavior is the starting point and begins the study's goals. The research questions of this study are :1.) Are VW user characteristics such as their skill, challenge level and desire for uniqueness (DFU) positively associated with their VW shopping attitude? 2.) Do VW shopping attitudes and subjective norms (SN)s positively relate to VW users' intentions to purchase VW products?

2. CHAPTER II. LITERATURE REVIEW

The TRA has been a popular theory to explain human behaviors. It is states behavior intention comes from a person's attitude and their SNs (Fishbein and Ajzen, 1975). TRA has been used to explain shopping behaviors and online shopping intentions. Pavlou and Fygenson (2006) for instance, did with internet shopping and Chi, Yeh and Yang (2011) used TRA to explain behaviors related to smartphone purchases.

Flow theory is most commonly associated with Csikszentmihalyi (1990). Flow is described as an optimal experience where one is immersed entirely in the situation with great focus and involvement. From Flow theory (Csikszentmihalyi, 1990), this emotional state is determined by two factors: skill and challenge meeting a perfect balance. Researchers differ on the way they operationalize the concept and because of the ambiguity this study looks at the main factors associated with flow (e.g. skill and challenge) for the proposed VW Consumer Behavior model rather than the 'flow state' itself. Flow and its components have helped to explain consumer behavior, user behavior and gaming. Specifically, flow has been used to understand internet use, internet shopping, (Lim, 2014) shopping behaviors, (Wang & Hsiao, 2012) and gaming enjoyment (Holsapple & Wu, 2008).

There are limited amounts of research in VW consumer behavior. VW purchase indications were examined by Guo and Barnes (2009) who found factors influencing VW purchases. The researchers found factors to be things like expectancy, character competency, VW system quality, social influence, virtual item resources, personal real resources, and self-actualization. Jung (2014) looked at VW purchase intentions in terms of consumer goals. Results from this study indicated goals of socializing, creativity, and escape overlapped with the goals of virtual consumption, meaning users had to buy to fulfill their objectives for partnership in VWs.

DFU is the concept to define when, while shopping, some individuals are drawn to products that self-define or set them apart from others. Berger and Heath (2007) found that motivation to show off uniqueness is high when it is perceived to be socially profitable. Some VWs have a huge social component to them. Lynn and Harris (1997) said the extent to which people pursue unusual objects can be influenced by their individual differences regarding the need for uniqueness. Berger and Health (2007) relied on situational cues as the driver of DFU and specific identity.

2.1 Conceptual Framework

This study explains VW consumer behaviors by relying on TRA, Flow Theory, and pervious work associated with VWs user behavior, and the DFU. The framework links VW user's skill and challenge level to their shopping attitudes and SNs; their DFU to their shopping attitudes and then their shopping attitudes and SNs to their intentions to purchase VW products.

2.2 Hypotheses

H1: VW User's Skill and Shopping Attitude
H2: VW User's Skill and Shopping SN
H3: VW User's Challenge Level and Shopping Attitude
H4: VW User's Challenge Level Shopping SNs
H5: VW User's DFU and Shopping Attitude
H6: VW Shopping Attitudes and Intentions to Purchase
H7: VW Shopping SNs and Intentions to Purchase

3. CONCLUSION

As VW popularity grows consumer products may become more important due to the social aspect and game objectives. This will increase the understanding of VW consumer behavior for IS researchers, VW developers and businesses regarding VW consumer behavior. This knowledge can help VWs gain vendors and help businesses to make decisions for VW marketing, advertising and strategizing. It will also fill a research gap by studying VWs as a whole, without concentrating on one specific world.

4. REFERENCES

[1] Chaturvedi, A.; Dolk, D.; and Dmevich, P. 2011. Design principles for Virtual Worlds. *MIS Quarterly, 35*(3) 673-684.

[2] Markus, M.; Majchzrak, A.; and Gasser, L. 2002. A design theory for systems that support emergent knowledge process. *MIS Quarterly, 26*(3)179-212.

[3] Spence, J. 2008a. VWs Research: Consumer Behavior in VWs. *Journal of VWs Research, 1*(2)1941-8477.

[4] Guo, Y., and Barnes, S., 2011. Purchase behavior in Virtual Worlds: An empirical investigation in second life, *Information and Management, 48*(7), 303-312.

[5] Huang, E. 2011. Online experiences and virtual goods purchase intention. *ROC Internet Research, 22*(3), 252-274. DOI 10.1108/10662241211235.

[6] Bennett, J. 2008, July 8. Videos: Why People live a Second LiveNewsweek.

[7] Virtual Worlds News (2008a, June 3). Interview: strategy analytics' Barry Gilbert – 137M Virtual Worlds users now; 1B by 2017. *Virtual World Management.* Retrieved from http://www.virtualworldsnews.com/2008/06/strategy-analyt.html.

[8] Animesh, A.; Pinsonneault, P.; Yeng, S and Oh, W. 2011. An Odyssey into Virtual Worlds: Exploring the impact of Technology and Spatial Environments on Intention to Purchase Virtual Products. *MIS Quarterly, 35*(3), 789-810.

[9] Alter, S 2013. Work System Theory: Overview of Core Concepts, Extensions, and Challenges for the Future. *Journal of the Association for Information Systems, 14* (2): 72–121.

[10] Fishbein, M. and Ajzen, I. 1975. Belief, attitude, intention, and behavior: An introduction to theory and research. Reading, MA: Addison-Wesley.

[11] Pavlou, P. and Fygenson, M. 2006. Understanding and predicting electronic commerce adoption: An extension of the theory of planned behavior. *Management Information Systems Quarterly, 30*(1), 115-143.

[12] Chi, H.; Yeh, H. and Yang, Y. 2011. Applying Theory of Reasoned Action and Technology Acceptance Model to Investigate Purchase Behavior on Smartphone. *Journal of International Management Studies, 6*(3)1.

[13] Csikszentmihalyi, M. 1990. *Flow: The Psychology of Optimal Experience.* Harper and Row. ISBN 978-0-06-016253-5. Retrieved 10 November 2013.

[14] Lim, W. 2014. Understanding the Influence of Online Flow Elements on Hedonic and Utilitarian Online Shopping Experiences: A Case of Online Group Buying. *Journal of Information Systems. American Accounting Association, 28* (2), 287-306. DOI: 10.2308/isys-50773.

[15] Holsapple, C. and Wu, J. 2008. Antecedent s and Outcomes of Flow Experience: An Empirical Study in the Context of Online Gaming. *Journal of International Technology and Information, 17*(3/4), 285.

[16] Jung, L. 2014. A Study of Affecting the Purchasing Intention of Social Commerce. *International Journal of Software Engineering and Its Applications*, 5, 73-84.

[17] Berger, J. and Heath, C. 2007. Where Consumers Diverge from Others: Identity-Signaling and Product Domains. *Journal of Consumer Research, 34*(2), 121–34.

[18] Lynn, M. and Harris, J. 1997. Individual Differences in the Pursuit of Self-Uniqueness through Consumption. *Journal of Applied Social Psychology, 27*(21), 1861–83.

The Use of Weight Loss Apps by Women with Eating Disorders

Elizabeth V. Eikey
The Pennsylvania State University
323 IST Building
University Park, PA 16802
1-949-438-1337
eveikey@psu.edu

ABSTRACT

It is estimated that 20 million females in the United States have an eating disorder, and many more have unhealthy eating behaviors [17, 21]. Two eating disorders that are more common among females than males are anorexia and bulimia nervosa [1]. Approximately 1 in 200 females will develop anorexia nervosa, and 1-3 in 100 will develop bulimia nervosa [13]. The prevalence of these eating disorders has been continuously increasing [21]. While biological and psychological factors play a role in an individual's predisposition and development of eating disorders [5], researchers in psychology have highlighted the sociocultural perspective, which is used to understand how social and cultural factors, such as media, affect an individual's mental processes and behaviors [2]. Much of this research has focused on conventional mass media, such as magazines and television. In recent years, researchers have been calling for more work in understanding the impact of new media, such as online content, on the thin ideal, body image, and eating disorder symptomology [15]. Recent work has shown that online content, such as social media, is associated with poor body image and eating disorders, especially among females [7, 12, 20].

Missing in this research are studies on the impact of weight loss applications ("apps") on eating disorders even though they contain similar content. Weight loss apps are becoming increasingly popular [8]. They allow users to track their calories, exercise, weight, and other factors. Weight loss apps enable and promote dieting, which is a risk for developing an eating disorder [14].

In Human-Computer Interaction (HCI), there has been a great deal of research on apps for diet and/or physical activity [3, 4, 18, 19]. While HCI researchers have focused on designing these apps to promote behavior change, they have largely viewed weight loss app users as having similar needs and have paid little attention to other factors that may influence their app use, such as eating disorders.

However, not all weight loss app users have the same needs or challenges. In order to understand the potential negative effects of these apps and the best ways to address these problems, researchers and designers must understand the various types of users who utilize weight loss apps. One such subgroup is women with anorexia and bulimia nervosa. This is an important user

SIGMIS-CPR '16, June 02-04, 2016, Alexandria, VA, USA.
ACM 978-1-4503-4203-2/16/06.
http://dx.doi.org/10.1145/2890602.2906187

group to study because many females frequently suffer from disordered eating behaviors, and anorexia and bulimia nervosa are most common among females [1, 9]. On one hand, research has shown that people with behaviors indicative of eating disorders use technology to maintain the symptomology of their disorder [11, 16]. On the other hand, technology can also be used to aid in eating disorder recovery [10, 22]. However, there has been little research examining the role of weight loss apps in enabling eating disorders or in supporting eating disorder recovery and maintenance. There may be aspects of weight loss apps that are helpful for eating disorder recovery; however, there may also be aspects that impede user recovery or promote the maintenance of eating disorders. In spite of the popularity of weight loss apps, few studies have considered the role of these apps on women with eating disorders.

My work aims to fill this gap by examining both users' and healthcare providers' perceptions of weight loss apps on women with eating disorders, specifically anorexia and bulimia nervosa. Although the sociocultural perspective views sociocultural influences as contributing to eating disorders, my research aims to examine both the positive and negative aspects of weight loss apps. I use qualitative methods in order to understand how and why women with these eating disorders use weight loss apps.

In my preliminary study, I conducted a qualitative content analysis of users' posts on an online forum associated with a popular weight loss app. Through this study, I found that users with underweight Body Mass Index (BMI) goals have various perceptions of the app's abilities to reduce eating disorder behaviors and to exacerbate eating disorder behaviors. This study showed there are users with eating disorder behaviors utilizing apps intended for weight loss. These findings can shed light on problems with using weight loss apps for eating disorder recovery and the needs of users with eating disorders. Specifically, weight loss apps focus too heavily on weight and calories and allow unhealthy eating plans. For recovery, users with eating disorders want a way to track their eating behaviors and a tailored healthy plan. Prior research shows that many current eating disorder recovery apps lack a way to track these behaviors but also do not make good use of smartphone capabilities [6, 10], which may help explain why users with eating disorders turn to mobile weight loss apps. In my future work, I will explore these concepts further and seek to expand the understanding of not only how these apps are used, but also explain why.

In my main study, I will use think-aloud-inspired exercises and interviews to further examine the role of weight loss apps on young women with a history of anorexia or bulimia nervosa both from a user perspective and a healthcare provider perspective. With users, I will use two data collections methods: 1) think-aloud-inspired exercises and 2) formal semi-structured interviews.

Each data collection method will complement one another but will seek to address different things. For instance, the think-aloud exercise will focus on how the app is used and specific app features. The interview, on the other hand, will focus more on the users' perceptions of the app and seek to answer why they use weight loss apps. For providers, I will conduct formal semi-structured interviews, which will consist of questions about their own and their patients' experiences with weight loss apps and opinions of weight loss app features. The goal of the interviews with providers is to understand their perceptions of weight loss apps on their patients with eating disorders.

Through my research, I aim to make four main contributions. First, my work will provide insight on an understudied area in HCI: users with eating disorders. Specifically, my research will help researchers better understand how weight loss apps affect women with anorexia and bulimia nervosa in positive and negative ways, which will lead to a better understanding of their needs. Secondly, I will make design recommendations for weight loss apps to reduce the potential of promoting eating disorder behaviors and encourage healthy habits. Because weight loss apps may never be suited for eating disorder recovery, this work may lead to design recommendations for eating disorder recovery apps as well. Third, I extend the sociocultural perspective to weight loss apps and encourage HCI and sociocultural researchers alike to consider weight loss apps as an influence on eating disorders. Finally, I will demonstrate how weight loss apps play a role in clinical settings, which may lead to recommendations that providers discuss the use of this technology with their patients in order to aid the diagnostic and treatment process of eating disorders.

Keywords
Mobile weight loss applications; smartphone app; eating disorders; human-computer interaction; users; providers; health; anorexia nervosa; bulimia nervosa

1. ACKNOWLEDGMENTS
I want to thank my committee members and friends for their feedback. This material is based upon work supported by the National Science Foundation (NSF) under Grant No. DGE1255832. Any opinions, findings, and conclusions or recommendations expressed in this material are those of the author and do not necessarily reflect the views of the NSF.

2. REFERENCES
[1] American Psychiatric Association ed. 2013. *Diagnostic and Statistical Manual of Mental Disorders (DSM-5)*. American Psychiatric Publishing.

[2] Ata, R.N. et al. 2015. Sociocultural Theories of Eating Disorders. *The Wiley Handbook of Eating Disorders*. John Wiley & Sons, Ltd. 269–282.

[3] Choe, E.K. et al. 2014. Understanding quantified-selfers' practices in collecting and exploring personal data. *CHI '14* (Toronto, Ontario, Canada, 2014), 1143–1152.

[4] Cordeiro, F. et al. 2015. Rethinking the mobile food journal: Exploring opportunities for lightweight photo-based capture. *CHI '15* (Seoul, Korea, 2015), 1–10.

[5] Culbert, K.M. et al. 2015. Research Review: What we have learned about the causes of eating disorders - A synthesis of sociocultural, psychological, and biological research. *Journal of Child Psychology and Psychiatry and Allied Disciplines*. 56, 11 (2015), 1141–1164.

[6] Fairburn, C.G. and Rothwell, E.R. 2015. Apps and eating disorders: A systematic clinical appraisal. *International Journal of Eating Disorders*. 48, 7 (2015), 1038–1046.

[7] Fardouly, J. et al. 2015. Social comparisons on social media: The impact of Facebook on young women's body image concerns and mood. *Body Image*. 13, (2015), 38–45.

[8] Fox, S. and Duggan, M. 2012. Mobile Health 2012. *Pew Internet & American Life Project*. (2012).

[9] Hudson, J.I. et al. 2007. The Prevalence and Correlates of Eating Disorders in the National Comorbidity Survey Replication. *Biological Psychiatry*. 61, 3 (2007), 348–358.

[10] Juarascio, A.S. et al. 2015. Review of smartphone applications for the treatment of eating disorders. *European Eating Disorders Review*. 23, (2015), 1–11.

[11] Keski-Rahkonen, A. and Tozzi, F. 2005. The process of recovery in eating disorder sufferers' own words: An internet-based study. *International Journal of Eating Disorders*. 37, (2005), 580–586.

[12] Mabe, A.G. et al. 2014. Do you "like" my photo? Facebook use maintains eating disorder risk. *International Journal of Eating Disorders*. 47, (2014), 516–523.

[13] Neumark-Sztainer, D. 2005. *"I'm, Like, SO Fat!": Helping Your Teen Make Healthy Choices about Eating and Exercise in a Weight-Obsessed World*. The Guilford Press.

[14] Neumark-Sztainer, D. et al. 2006. Obesity, disordered eating, and eating disorders in a longitudinal study of adolescents: How do dieters fare 5 years later? *Journal of the American Dietetic Association*. 106, 4 (2006), 559–568.

[15] Perloff, R.M. 2014. Social media effects on young women's body image concerns: Theoretical perspectives and an agenda for research. *Sex Roles*. (2014), 363–377.

[16] Ransom, D.C. et al. 2010. Interpersonal interactions on online forums addressing eating concerns. *International Journal of Eating Disorders*. 43, 2 (2010), 161–170.

[17] Reba-Harrelson, L. et al. 2009. Patterns and prevalence of disordered eating and weight control behaviors in women ages 25-45. *Eating and Weight Disorders*. 14, 4 (2009).

[18] Rooksby, J. et al. 2015. Experience Design for Games Pass the Ball : Enforced Turn - Taking in Activity Tracking. *Chi.* (2015), 2417–2426.

[19] Stawarz, K. et al. 2015. Beyond Self-Tracking and Reminders : Designing Smartphone Apps That Support Habit Formation. *CHI.* (2015), 2653–2662.

[20] Stronge, S. et al. 2015. Facebook is linked to body dissatisfaction: Comparing users and non-users. *Sex Roles*. 73, (2015), 200–213.

[21] Wade, T.D. et al. 2011. Epidemiology of eating disorders. *Textbook in Psychiatric Epidemiology (3rd ed.)*. Wiley. 343–360.

[22] Whitlock, J.L. et al. 2006. The virtual cutting edge: The internet and adolescent self-injury. *Developmental Psychology*. 42, 3 (2006), 407–417.

Teens and Information Quality: An Intersectionality-Based Dissertation in Progress Exploring Fitness Information and Social Media

Kayla M. Booth
The Pennsylvania State University
334 IST Building
University Park, PA 16802
1.814.865.8952
Kmb5445@ist.psu.edu

ABSTRACT

This paper is part of the SIGMIS CPR doctoral consortium, summarizing a dissertation in progress. This dissertation explores how youth, teenagers in particular, search for, evaluate, and create exercise and nutrition information they interact with via social media. This dissertation also employs an Intersectionality lens to examine the ways in which the intersections of race, gender, sexuality, and socio-economic status relate to the ways in which teens make decisions about information online.

CCS Concepts

• **Human-centered Computing→ Collaborative and social computing.**

Keywords

Information quality; social media; youth; health; fitness; qualitative methods

1. INTRODUCTION

Scholars across disciplines have been invested in youth and their online behavior for decades. While there are numerous contexts in which these behaviors are examined, one of the most heavily studied is health. While there are a myriad of topics and subtopics that fall under "health information," a 2015 study from researchers at Northwestern University [4] suggests that fitness and nutrition are the most popular health-related topics teens search for online. This phenomenon is particularly interesting given that exercise and nutrition-centered pages and profiles are increasingly common across social media platforms. While this content is easily accessible, diverse and interactive [1], the lack of traditional gatekeepers and the ability for any user to upload content provides a landscape worthy of examination. Scholars also point out that the sheer volume of fitness information available via social media makes it difficult for users to discern between healthy and disordered content [1][3]. This exploration is of particular importance given that the same 2015 study [4] indicates that nearly a third of teens alter their behavior based on the information they interact with online.

When exploring the ways in which young people interact with information online, researchers at the Youth and Media Lab at The Berkman Center for Internet & Society at Harvard University suggest taking a "youth-oriented" approach [2]. This approach includes examining the holistic process in which youth interact with information, including how they search for, evaluate, and create their own content online. This dissertation seeks to employ this process-oriented approach, as well as exploring the ways in which multiple identity characteristics intersect and relate to the ways in which young people assess the fitness information they interact with via social media. The research questions guiding this dissertation are:

RQ1: How do youth search for and evaluate the quality of fitness information they interact with via social media?

RQ2: How do young people's online content creation relate to their search and evaluation processes?

RQ3: How do the intersections of multiple identity characteristics (age, race, gender, sexuality, and socioeconomic status) relate to their search, evaluation, and content creation processes

2. METHODOLOGY

This dissertation takes an interpretive epistemological approach to addressing these questions. Semi-structured interviews were conducted with 30 teens ages 13-18. Fifteen participants were recruited from urban charter schools and fifteen were recruited from suburban public schools, all within in the United States. The interview questions were informed by Gasser et al.'s Youth-Oriented Information Quality Framework [2], as well as an Intersectionality approach. The questions were constructed not only to explore the ways in which identity characteristics related to search, evaluation, and creation, but also to explore the subjective meanings, values, and experiences young people associated with their information processes.

3. ACKNOWLEDGMENTS

Special thanks to my committee members: Dr. Eileen Trauth, Dr. Lynette Yarger, Dr. Michael McNeese, and Dr. Karen Keifer-Boyd.

4. REFERENCES

[1] Carrotte, E. R., Vella, A. M., & Lim, M. S. 2015. Predictors of "Liking" Three Types of Health and Fitness-Related Content on Social Media: A Cross-Sectional Study. *Journal of Medical Internet Research, 17*(8), e205. http://doi.org/10.2196/jmir.4803

[2] Gasser, U., Cortesi, S., Malik, M., & Lee, A. 2012. Youth and digital media: From credibility to information quality.

SIGMIS-CPR'16, June 2–4, 2016, Alexandria, VA, USA.
ACM 978-1-4503-4203-2/16/06.
DOI: http://dx.doi.org/10.1145/10.1145/2890602.2906190

Berkman Center for Internet & Society. Retrieved April 10, 2014 from http://ssrn.com/abstract=2005272

[3] Syed-Abdul S, Fernandez-Luque L, Jian WS, Li YC, Crain S, Hsu MH, Wang YC, Khandregzen D, Chuluunbaatar E, Nguyen PA, Liou DM. 2013. Misleading Health-Related Information Promoted Through Video-Based Social Media: Anorexia on YouTube. J Med Internet Res; 15(2):e30

[4] Wartella, E., Rideout, V., Zupancic, H., Beaudoin-Ryan, L., Lauricella, A. 2015. Teens, Technology, and Health: A National Survey. Center on Media and Human Development, School of Communication, Northwestern University. http://cmhd.northwestern.edu/wp-content/uploads/2015/05/1886_1_SOC_ConfReport_TeensHealthTech_051115.pdf

Increasing Physical Activity In Seniors Using Emerging Technology: Identifying Adoption Barriers and Enablers

Jake Araullo
IDEA Lab, Griffith University
Kessels Rd, Nathan 4111
QLD, Australia
jake.araullo@griffithuni.edu.au

ABSTRACT

This paper summarises an in-progress dissertation that explores emerging technologies that promote physical activity and senior communities. This research work will undertake three case studies with the aim to identify the barriers and facilitators to the adoption of emerging technologies that promote physical activity in a senior cohort. This work identifies these barriers to technological adoption in the hopes that future commercial and research work is able to increase the uptake of emerging technologies for promoting physical activity in seniors.

Keywords

Emerging Technology; Seniors; Physical Activity; HCI; Human Factors;

1. INTRODUCTION

Ageing population growth across the Western world due to increased life expectancy and medical treatments is a major challenge to public health systems, particularly moving forward. In ageing populations, the leading cause of death is no longer chronic disease, but instead degenerative diseases and age related illnesses.

Increasing physical activity in senior populations has a litany of health benefits within this community, however inactivity levels in this population continue to rise. Emerging technologies that exploit new modalities of interaction and physicality present a compelling opportunity for further exploration in this area. Attitudes to emerging technology adoption, physical activity and behaviour change must be identified.

2. METHODOLOGY

A qualitative approach is appropriate in the research to gain "the experience of individuals, captured in its "lived" form, with a minimum of pre-planned, imposed structure" [1]: necessary to understand the contextual factors of technological adoption and motivational factors in a specific community.

An interpretivist paradigm is appropriate as it "emphasizes human interpretation and understanding as constituents of scientific knowledge" [2]. Interpretivist work is "much less likely to be led astray by preconceived notions that stem from inappropriate generalizations" [3] but conversely may "suggest solutions that are not appropriate for cases other than their own" [3]. This research completed in this study will directly address the concerns of a specific community and the context around which those concerns can be satisfied. As such, the findings of this work should be generalizable to other senior populations of similar parameters, being externally valid.

The primary data collection method of this research will be three case studies. The Health Action Process Approach model [4] has guided case study design in this work, allowing the identification and assessment of components of the health-behaviour change process at various points (pre/intra/post intervention). This also allows the identification of how emerging technology affects that process, including individual's attitudes towards that technology.

A pilot study has commenced. This study is to trial and validate the ability of the study design to infer accurate findings relevant to the research outcomes.

3. RESEARCH OUTCOMES

The research outcomes of this work are focused on identifying barriers and facilitators to technological adoption in this group. We do not aim to increase activity in seniors directly, instead focusing on the early adoption of this technology. This will allow the practical adoption of strategic information system implementations that can create meaningful social change in this in area, not just on a micro, but macro, level.

While many studies have attempted to increase senior physical activity with emerging technology, to date there has been no strong focus on quantifying adoption barriers and enablers in this area. This work will produce:

1. An exhaustive set of quantified barriers and facilitators to the adoption of technology to boost physical activity in seniors, particularly regarding emerging technologies.

2. Best practices for information system design for designers to adhere and refer to when working with emerging technologies and senior populations, with particular regard to motivation and physical activity.

3. A comprehensive outline of facilitators and inhibitors to consider when implementing emerging technologies with the goal of increasing physical activity in seniors.

4. Empirical and case-study driven evidence to support all findings, allowing structured and evidence-based creation of future technological artefacts in this area.

4. REFERENCES

[1] Bowman, M., Debray, S. K., and Peterson, L. L. 1993. Reasoning about naming systems. *ACM Trans. Program. Lang. Syst.* 15, 5 (Nov. 1993), 795-825. DOI= http://doi.acm.org/10.1145/161468.16147.

SIGMIS-CPR '16, June 02-04, 2016, Alexandria, VA, USA
ACM 978-1-4503-4203-2/16/06.
http://dx.doi.org/10.1145/2890602.2906185

[2] Ding, W. and Marchionini, G. 1997. *A Study on Video Browsing Strategies*. Technical Report. University of Maryland at College Park.

[3] Fröhlich, B. and Plate, J. 2000. The cubic mouse: a new device for three-dimensional input. In *Proceedings of the SIGCHI Conference on Human Factors in Computing Systems* (The Hague, The Netherlands, April 01 - 06, 2000). CHI '00. ACM, New York, NY, 526-531. DOI= http://doi.acm.org/10.1145/332040.332491.

[4] Tavel, P. 2007. *Modeling and Simulation Design*. AK Peters Ltd., Natick, MA.

[5] Sannella, M. J. 1994. *Constraint Satisfaction and Debugging for Interactive User Interfaces*. Doctoral Thesis. UMI Order Number: UMI Order No. GAX95-09398., University of Washington.

[6] Forman, G. 2003. An extensive empirical study of feature selection metrics for text classification. *J. Mach. Learn. Res.* 3 (Mar. 2003), 1289-1305.

[7] Brown, L. D., Hua, H., and Gao, C. 2003. A widget framework for augmented interaction in SCAPE. In *Proceedings of the 16th Annual ACM Symposium on User Interface Software and Technology* (Vancouver, Canada, November 02 - 05, 2003). UIST '03. ACM, New York, NY, 1-10. DOI= http://doi.acm.org/10.1145/964696.964697.

[8] Yu, Y. T. and Lau, M. F. 2006. A comparison of MC/DC, MUMCUT and several other coverage criteria for logical decisions. *J. Syst. Softw.* 79, 5 (May. 2006), 577-590. DOI= http://dx.doi.org/10.1016/j.jss.2005.05.030.

[9] Spector, A. Z. 1989. Achieving application requirements. In *Distributed Systems*, S. Mullender, Ed. ACM Press Frontier Series. ACM, New York, NY, 19-33. DOI= http://doi.acm.org/10.1145/90417.90738.

Coping with the Dark Side of IT Usage: Mitigating the Effect of Technostress

Christoph Weinert
Otto-Friedrich University Bamberg
An der Weberei 5, 96047 Bamberg
christoph.weinert@uni-bamberg.de

1. INTRODUCTION

Besides productivity gains, IT usage also contains a dark side regarding threatening IT-events [8]. These IT-events and the resulting negative user responses lead to IT discontinuance [7]. However, in response to these threatening IT-events individuals might perform coping behaviors to handle the negative IT-events and preserve IT usage [2–4]. As the research stream on the dark side of IT usage originates quite recently, the findings on how coping behavior might reduce these consequences are limited. However, it is essential to comprehend how individuals cope with negative IT-events to defend IT usage, and hence protect and increase the return on the enormous amount of money organizations invest in IT products and applications. To counteract the dark side of IT usage and hence safeguard the use of and the investment in IT, the present study focuses on coping behavior, which might alleviate IT-events and their consequences. Therefore, the present research aims to answer the research question: *How coping behavior can mitigate the threatening IT-events, and its consequences?*

2. RESEARCH BACKGROUND
2.1 TECHNOSTRESS

Technostress is stress perceived when using IT and should be understood as an umbrella term, which comprises users' perceptions of IT-events and their responses to these IT-events, which are called strains [11]. IT-events are technology-related stimuli perceived by the individuals [1]. User responses are the response towards the IT-event and can be psychological, physiological, and behavioral. *Psychological user responses* include emotional responses to the IT-event and has been interpreted as emotional exhaustion in prior technostress literature [1, 11]. *Physiological user responses* include bodily responses to IT-events such as cardiovascular, biochemical and gastrointestinal symptoms [9]. *Behavioral responses* include behavioral responses to the IT-event, such as poor task performance [11].

2.2 COPING THEORY

Coping behavior manages taxing demands. Coping encompasses two cognitive appraisal processes. In the first, threat appraisal, users evaluate the potential adverse consequences of being attacked by IT. It represents the extent how dangerous an individual perceives the IT-event. The second, coping appraisal, assesses the individual's ability to handle the perceived IT-event [5]. The perception of the IT-event activates the coping appraisal in which users evaluate available action options and decide what they can do to cope.

SIGMIS-CPR '16, June 02-04, 2016, Alexandria, VA, USA
ACM 978-1-4503-4203-2/16/06.
http://dx.doi.org/10.1145/2890602.2906189

Coping appraisal evaluates the abilities of the individual to avoid threatening IT-events [5]. Based on the strengths of the IT-event (threat appraisal) and the individual's ability to handle the IT-event (coping appraisal) each individual selects a coping behavior. Individuals rely on these two cognitive processes to adopt the two major coping behaviors: problem-focused coping (PFC) or emotional-focused coping (EFC).

2.3 PRIOR WORK

Several investigations show that the perception of so-called IT-events, which are external stimuli, that can be sourced directly in the IT (e.g., new IT implementations) as well as grounded in the usage of IT (e.g., IT complexity) [8] lead to different user responses. For example, Galluch et al. [4] investigate how IT-enabled interruptions influence physiological and psychological user responses.

Besides the user responses, the basic Coping Model of User Adaption (CMUA) and Technology Threat Avoidance Theory (TTAT) and numerous other examinations show that individuals who perceive an IT-event are going to two cognitive appraisal processes (e.g. [2, 5]): threat and coping appraisal. Both appraisal processes lead to the determination of coping mechanisms in terms of PFC and EFC [3]. Bala and Venkatesh [2] develop a model of technology adaptation behaviors and state that adaptation behaviors are an essential linking mechanism between IT-events and job outcomes such as job performance. They identified different technology adaptation behaviors which are performed based on the appraisal of the IT-event. Their results show that adaptation behaviors influence job performance and job satisfaction.

Summing up, based on the previous literature it can be concluded that IT usage leads to several negative **IT-events**, which directly impulse different **user responses** and causes a **cognitive appraisal** process of the IT-event. User responses and cognitive appraisal, in turn, lead to two different **coping behaviors**: PFC and EFC. Performing coping behavior increases **IT usage behavior** and in turn, several **job outcomes** such as performance or satisfaction (see Figure 1).

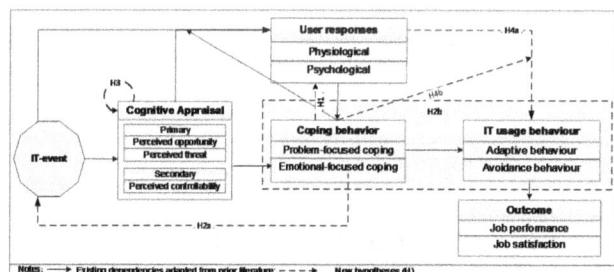

Figure 1: Coping model

3. HYPOTHESES DEVELOPMENT

As prior coping literature is limited, the coping model (see Figure 1) contains several shortcomings, which have not been investigated so far. To manifest these deficiencies more precisely several hypotheses are developed in the following.

Literature shows that IT-events lead to psychological responses such as emotional exhaustion or emotions and physiological responses such as bodily arousal [3, 4]. However, no investigation focuses on coping behavior that aims to reduce such user responses. According to the literature, coping behavior in terms of PFC is supposed to change the situation by reducing the IT-event, and emotional-focused coping is meant to mitigate the negative emotions tied to the IT-event [5]. Seeking emotional or instrumental support might reduce psychological and physiological responses (H1).

Coping behavior manages taxing demands. If individuals receive too many emails and perceive email-overload as threatening IT-event, they actively do something to reduce the amount of emails by prioritizing or deleting them such that the IT-event itself is eliminated (H2a).

Literature shows that coping behaviors, either emotional- or problem-focused, are strategies to reduce the perceived IT-event (i.e., seeking social support or venting), whereas adaptive or avoidance IT usage behaviors are adjusted behaviors while perceiving the IT-event, without any actions against the IT-event itself. Hence, it is assumed that coping and adaptive behaviors are distinct patterns of behavior (H2b)

Several investigations in psychology show a habituation process towards user responses. IT-events lead to a psychological response [1], which might decrease when the same IT-event is repeatedly presented since individuals learn to filter out bad stimuli, mitigating the effect of the IT-event on psychological responses (H3)

Previous investigations indicate that the perception of IT-events and the resulting user responses increase the intention to stop using IT [7]. As individuals might behave differently when they are emotionally or physiologically aroused, the emerging user responses might influence IT usage behavior in the way that individuals perform either adaptive or avoidance behavior (H4a). When user responses influence IT usage behavior, the question arises how coping behavior can mitigate this effect. As coping behavior in terms of social support from peers might reduce user responses, the relationship between user responses and IT usage behavior might be moderated by PFC and EFC behavior (H4b).

Table 1: Proposed hypotheses

H1: Coping behavior reduces psychological and physiological user responses.
H2a: Coping behavior reduces the perception of the IT-event.
H2b: Coping behavior reduces IT-events and the resulting user responses, whereas adaptive or avoidance behavior refers to an adjusting IT usage behavior, without an effect on the IT-event itself.
H3: Individuals cope by habituating towards the IT-event such that the psychological and physiological user responses will be diminished.
H4a: Psychological and physiological user responses directly influence IT usage behavior.
H4b: The effect of psychological and physiological user responses on IT usage behavior is moderated by coping behavior in the way that the effect of user responses on IT usage behavior is alleviated.

4. EXPECTED IMPLICATIONS

As usage of IT does not only lead to productivity gain but also involves a dark side, which threatens the investments of organizations and burdened individuals [10], the investigation of coping behavior which might reduce these issues or prevent them from occurring might reveal novel insights. By conducting the examination, the findings are expected to extend prior literature.

The validation of H1 might extend existing literature [11] in the way that the results show how different coping mechanisms reduce psychological and physiological user response. Furthermore, it is intended to analyze whether PFC or EFC is more efficient by reducing negative user responses, which might extend existing coping literature [4]. Additionally, by this examination, it is aimed to extend neuroIS knowledge [6] by providing a neurobiological explanation why individuals respond to IT-events with increased sweat secretion.

The validation of H2a and H2b might extend prior research by distinguishing coping behavior and adaptive usage behavior [2]. Additionally, the results of this examination might extend existing literature regarding IT usage behavior. It might also contribute to coping literature [3, 4] by showing insights how coping behavior reduces or eliminates IT-events. As this examination focuses on the special group of IT professionals, it might extend findings regarding the perception of IT-events and its consequences among this group.

Prior coping literature concentrates on the evaluation of the IT-event and on coping behavior, which actively counteracts IT-events and its responses [4, 5], whereas the present research proposes that the repeated exposure to the IT-event results in habituation, which in turn, lowers user responses without active coping behavior. Also, this research might provide insights why individuals continue using an IT even though its threatening nature. Hence, it is expected to contribute to the adoption literature focusing on discontinuance usage [7].

The results might extend prior literature [3] by investigating the effect of psychological and physiological user responses on IT usage behavior. Also, the findings might contribute to coping literature by revealing insights how coping behavior in terms of PFC and EFC moderates the relationship between psychological as well as psychological user responses and IT usage behavior [2, 8].

5. REFERENCES

[1] Ayyagari, R., Grover, V., and Russell, P. 2011. Technostress: Technological Antecedents and Implications. MIS Quarterly 35, 4, 831–858.

[2] Bala, H. and Venkatesh, V. 2015. Adaptation to Information Technology. A Holistic Nomological Network from Implementation to Job Outcomes. Management Science, Forthcoming.

[3] Beaudry, A. and Pinsonneault, A. 2010. The Other Side Of Acceptance: Studying The Direct And Indirect Effects Of Emotions On Information Technology Use. MIS Quarterly 34, 4, 689-A3.

[4] Galluch, P. S., Grover, V., and Thatcher, J. B. 2015. Interrupting the Workplace: Examining Stressors in an Information Technology Context. Journal of the Association for Information Systems 16, 1, 1–47.

[5] Liang, H. and Xue, Y. 2009. Avoidance of information technology threats: a theoretical perspective. MIS Quarterly 33, 1, 71–90.

[6] Liang, T.-P. and vom Brocke, J. 2014. Special Issue: Neuroscience in Information Systems Research. Journal of Management Information Systems 30, 4, 7–12.

[7] Maier, C., Laumer, S., Weinert, C., and Weitzel, T. 2015. The effects of technostress and switching stress on discontinued use of social networking services. A study of Facebook use. Information Systems Journal 25, 3, 275–308.

[8] Ortiz de Guinea, A. and Webster, J. 2013. An Investigation of Information Systems Use Patterns: Technological Events as Triggers, the Effect of Time, and Consequences for Performance. MIS Quarterly 37, 4, 1165–1188.

[9] Riedl, R. 2013. On the Biology of Technostress. Literature Review and Research Agenda. DATA BASE for Advances in Information Systems 44, 1, 18–55.

[10] Tarafdar, M., D'Arcy, J., Turel, O., and Gupta, A. 2015. The Dark Side of Information Technology. MIT Sloan Management Review 56, 2, 61–70.

[11] Tarafdar, M., Tu, Q., and Ragu-Nathan, T. S. 2010. Impact of Technostress on End-User Satisfaction and Performance. Journal of Management Information Systems 27, 3, 303–334.

Early Career Experiences of IT Professionals

Tenace Setor
Nanyang Technological University
Singapore
tenacekw001@ntu.edu.sg

ABSTRACT

Considerable IT research has examined issues pertaining to IT careers and outcomes. Prominent among this stream of research are studies that have examined IT human capital endowments as determinants of IT career success and mobility patterns of IT professionals as they traverse career paths. According to Joseph, Boh, Ang and Slaughter's analysis of 500 IT professionals drawn from the National Longitudinal Survey for Youth 1979 cohort dataset, IT career paths are more diverse than the traditional view of technical vs managerial career paths. The career histories of IT professionals revealed three distinct career paths i.e. IT careers, Professional Labor Market (PLM) and Secondary Labor Market (SLM). IT professionals who took the IT and PLM career paths enjoyed more career success in terms of pay received relative to those who took the SLM route.

Other studies have examined determinants of IT career success. Drawing on human capital theories, Ang, Slaguhter and Ng (2002) and Levina and Xin (2007) find that IT compensation is directly related to human capital endowments such as education and experience. Mithas and Krishnan (2008) added to this stream of research by examining how much firms pay for MBA education held by IT professionals and IT-related experience such as firm-specific experience. They find that firms value MBA education and IT experience at other firms relative to firm-specific experience.

A common theme that runs through the stream of research examining IT careers and IT career outcomes (Ang et al., 2002; Joseph, Boh, Ang, & Slaughter, 2012; Levina & Xin, 2007; Mithas & Krishnan, 2008), is that the studies draw on samples of IT professionals in the mid-to late careers. Mid-to late IT career professionals are well endowed with IT-related experiences known to play a pivotal role in determining IT career outcomes. In situations where IT professionals may not be well endowed with IT experience, the literature is however silent on what human capital attribute replaces IT experience and how that attribute influences career outcomes. Such is the situation for early career IT professionals.

Early career IT professionals have less experience in the IT labor market and as such may not be endowed with much IT-related experiences required to move the needle on career success

measures such as compensations and wages. So what influences career outcomes of early career IT professionals? A few studies have explored the career outcomes of early career IT professionals. These include studies by Joseph (2008) which investigates the role career-based college experiences play in IT students' choice of IT as a career; and Choudhury et al (2010) which examines IT careers camp as an intervention strategy to increase IS enrollment in colleges.

Although these studies focus on early IT careers, we still do not have clear idea of what human capital attribute influences early career success and early career mobility or persistence in IT. The paucity of research examining pertinent issues in early IT careers affords me the opportunity to embark on a research agenda which focuses on the career outcomes and experiences of early career IT professionals. Specifically, I seek to address the following research questions pertaining to what indicates human capital endowment of early career IT professionals; and career outcomes of human capital endowments of early career IT professionals:

1. What human capital attributes influence early entry into the IT labor market?

2. What is the value of formal IT training to early career IT professionals?

3. What human capital attributes of early career IT professionals influence IT career persistence?

I propose a three-essay dissertation in examining the research questions stated above. A three-essay approach will enable the researcher to set modular research objectives in solving an overarching research problem.

REFERENCES

[1] Ang, S., Slaughter, S., & Ng, K. Y. (2002). Human Capital and Institutional Determinants of Information Technology Compensation: Modeling Multilevel and Cross-Level Interactions. *Management Science, 48*(11), 1427–1445.

[2] Joseph, D., Boh, W. F., Ang, S., & Slaughter, S. A. (2012). The Career Paths Less (or More) Traveled: A Sequence Analysis of IT Career Histories, Mobility Patterns, and Career Success. *MIS Quarterly, 36*(2), 427–452.

[3] Levina, N., & Xin, M. (2007). Research Note—Comparing IT Workers' Compensation Across Country Contexts: Demographic, Human Capital, and Institutional Factors. *Information Systems Research, 18*(2), 193–210. http://doi.org/10.1287/isre.1070.0121

[4] Mithas, S., & Krishnan, M. S. (2008). Human Capital and Institutional Effects in the Compensation of Information Technology Professionals in the United States. *Management Science, 54*(3), 415–428. http://doi.org/10.1287/mnsc.1070.0778

SIGMIS-CPR'16, June 2–4, 2016, Alexandria, VA, USA.
ACM 978-1-4503-4203-2/16/06.
DOI: http://dx.doi.org/10.1145/10.1145/2890602.2906186

Keynote: Organizational Design

Scott A. Bernard
Federal Chief Enterprise Architect
Office of Management and Budget
Executive Office of the President
sabernar@syr.edu

ABSTRACT

Dr. Scott Bernard will speak on the topic of *organizational design* and his experiences with and approach to integrating strategic, business, and technology planning for large/complex organizations using a holistic enterprise architecture framework.

CCS Concepts

• **Social and professional topics ~ Management of computing and information systems** • **Social and professional topics ~ Computing organizations**

General Terms

Management, Design, Human Factors

Keywords

Organizational Design; Strategic Value; Organizational Planning; Enterprise Architecture; IT Profession; Management

1. BIOGRAPHY

Scott Bernard currently serves as the U.S. Federal Chief Enterprise Architect at the Office of Management and Budget within the Executive Office of the President. He has over thirty years of information technology management experience in the public, private, military, and academic sectors and has held executive positions as a Chief Information Officer, Chief Enterprise Architect, Chief IT Security Officer, and owner of a management and technology consulting firm.

Dr. Bernard has also served since 1998 as a part-time Professor of Practice on the faculty of Syracuse University's School of Information Studies where he developed a number of new courses, helped to launch the university's first executive doctorate program in IT management, developed a graduate certificate in E-Government with the Maxwell School of Public Administration, and co-founded a university-wide center for cybersecurity studies. Since 2005, he has served as a senior lecturer at Carnegie Mellon University's School of Computer Science, with the Institute for Software Research where he developed an executive education program in enterprise architecture. Dr. Bernard founded the Journal of Enterprise Architecture in 2005 and served as its Chief Editor until 2010. In 2004, he wrote the first textbook on enterprise architecture which features the EA^3 Cube ™ Framework that is currently being used to integrate strategic, business, and technology planning by corporations and government agencies around the world, as well as being featured in a number of university curricula and training programs on enterprise architecture, strategic planning, capital planning, program management, cybersecurity, and organizational design. Dr. Bernard was elected by peers to the Enterprise Architecture Hall of Fame in 2012.

Dr. Bernard earned his Ph.D. in Public Administration and Policy at the Virginia Polytechnic Institute and State University; a master's degree in Business and Personnel Management from Central Michigan University, a master's degree in Information Management from Syracuse University, and a bachelor's degree in Psychology from the University of Southern California. He is a graduate of the United States Naval War College, and earned a Chief Information Officer Certificate and an Advanced Program Management Certificate from the National Defense University. Dr. Bernard is also a former career naval aviator who served on aircraft carriers and with shore squadrons, led IT programs, and was the Director of Network Operations for the Joint Chiefs of Staff at the Pentagon.

SIGMIS-CPR'16, June 2–4, 2016, Alexandria, VA, USA.
ACM 978-1-4503-4203-2/16/06.
DOI: http://dx.doi.org/10.1145/2890602.2890628

The Potential of Emerging Technology for Social Change

Leigh Ellen Potter
IDEA Lab, Griffith University
Kessels Rd, Nathan 4111
L.Potter@griffith.edu.au

Lewis Carter
Idea Lab, Griffith University
Kessels Rd, Nathan, 4111
L.Carter@griffith.edu.au

Jake Araullo
IDEA Lab, Griffith University
Kessels Rd, Nathan 4111
jake.araullo@griffithuni.edu.au

Michelle L. Kaarst-Brown
School of Information Studies
Syracuse University, NY USA
Mlbrow03@syr.edu

ABSTRACT

The purpose of this panel is to explore the potential for emerging technology to engender social change. Technology is transformative, and has already seen innovative application in business and industry, and of course in relation to society and social networking. We will discuss the current state of 'emerging technology', and several perspectives of considerations with emerging technologies and society. We will describe some current applications of emerging technology in a range of fields, in order to identify the potential for emerging technology to support social change. Our goal is to open discussions about opportunities for emerging technology, and practical applications or approaches to how these opportunities can be exploited.

CCS Concepts

Human-centered computing~Collaborative and social computing

Keywords

Emerging Technology; social change; innovation

1. INTRODUCTION

The term 'emerging technology' is used in a range of fields to indicate a new tool or technique within an environment. For the purposes of this panel, emerging technology is defined as a technology that has transformational potential for business, industry or society, regardless of the age of the technology itself; is not yet widespread; and may be emerging in one context, yet established in another (transplanted). Emerging technology is associated with a degree of ambiguity, generated by its emergent nature and the fact that it is not yet established [10]. This problem has been experienced with the traditional diffusion of older technologies, however, we are not seeing a reduction in the radical potential of capabilities and implications.

The Internet of Things has seen mainstream technologies used in new ways, and the advent of new technologies connecting and interacting. There are emerging technologies such as the Leap Motion controller, Microsoft Kinect, Myo gesture control

armband, VTTs InTouch technologies and others providing new ways for people to use and interact with their computers.

Interest in the application of gamification methods, particularly within mobile applications and devices, in relation to emerging technologies is growing [3, 7]. Shortcomings have been identified, particularly in relation to motivation, habit creation and the application of design approaches when interacting with these new technology artefacts [1]. We have new technology, however the innovative application and potential for this technology has not been fully explored.

We tend to think of emerging technologies as following a standard developmental or diffusion pattern. However, every technology has its own "s" or developmental and diffusion life cycle in different industries, countries, and societal groups. We see this in research on early versus late adopters [9], aging and older adults [2], and in studies of aboriginal or Native American communities where social structures and power relationships can be disrupted by new technologies [11]. As we see increasingly heterogeneous social groups and sub-cultures in local and global society with different needs and goals, we may need to think not only about the potential of new technologies, but also how established technologies in one setting, may challenge social structures in another. At the same time, there is a presumption that with social media, audiences are becoming more homogeneous, when in fact, globalization and socio-economic, educational, generational, and other factors increase the likelihood of heterogeneous audiences for both emerging and transplanted technologies.

These new devices and new methods of interaction may provide an opportunity to improve societies and the lives of the communities within these societies, however, there are risks along with potential rewards. The questions to be answered are, "What can we achieve, and how can we achieve it?"

The aim of this panel is to explore innovative practices and approaches for the design and application of emerging technologies, and their potential for supporting social change. We will discuss examples of work currently underway in this area, and seek to generate discussions regarding the potential for emerging technology application, and ideas for future directions.

2. OVERVIEW OF PRESENTATIONS

Leigh Ellen Potter will discuss user experience when interacting with emerging technology. These technologies often enable new interaction mechanisms through the use of innovative device capabilities [8]. Established interaction mechanisms may not work effectively with these emerging technologies, affecting the user experience. Consideration of the user experience when designing emerging technology to support social change is vital. She will describe work currently underway in the Idea Lab, such as Seek and Sign [6].

Lewis Carter will discuss a project exploring design conventions for the emerging head mounted virtual reality devices, such as the Oculus Rift and the HTC Vive. Virtual reality comes with its own strengths and weaknesses, and these must be taken into account when designing applications to produce the best possible experience for players. Lewis will discuss research exploring the application of design techniques that maximize the new capabilities offered by emerging technologies.

Jake Araullo will discuss the application of wearable technology for motivating senior citizens to be more active. Opportunities are present for emerging technologies to promote and engage seniors in physical activity. There is a potential for wearables to support social change in this area, in terms of boosting quality-of-life, core health, self-efficacy and autonomy in this growing segment of the population. Jake will discuss research in this area, including the potential and limitations of emerging technology when working with seniors.

Michelle Kaarst-Brown will share a cultural analysis technique used as part of an "anticipatory design" approach engaged in *before* beginning development of a digital heritage preservation system for the Choctaw Nation of Oklahoma. She applied the theory of archetypal "IT Cultures" [4, 5] to engage a sample of culturally respected tribal elders. Unlike traditional requirements analysis, the goal was to better understand cultural concerns and anticipatory design considerations in advance of any developmental efforts for this "'new' technology opportunity for the Choctaw." A key finding was the importance of "situated symbolism" to distance from the technological features to engage in design considerations that could affect social change.

3. PRESENTERS

Leigh Ellen Potter is a lecturer in the School of Information and Communication Technology, Griffith University in Australia, and the Director of the Idea lab – Innovative Design and Emerging Application. Her industry background in business analysis and user experience informed her PhD research, exploring the attributes of IT professionals, and what draws them to the industry. Her research interests include user centred design and usability, and emerging technology. She is team lead for several research projects through the Idea lab.

Lewis Carter is a PhD Student at Griffith University in Australia. He has a degree in Software Engineering with Honours, and has a strong interest in game design. His research looks at consumer virtual reality and how current game design principles need to adapt to better suit the technology. He has completed a research project identifying preliminary design heuristics for this type of VR technology. Lewis works with the Idea lab, and is currently project lead for the development of a gaming application for consumer virtual reality technologies.

Jake Araullo is a PhD Candidate at the Griffith University Idea Lab. He has a degree in Software Engineering with Honours. Jake's research area is around promoting physical activity in seniors using emerging technologies. In the past, Jake has worked in startup environments and in research, and has studied best usability practices with emerging technologies such as Leap

Motion and Oculus Rift. Emerging technology provides novel interaction opportunities and Jake's research attempts to harness this, with the aim of creating macro-level positive change in physical activity for older populations.

Michelle Kaarst-Brown is an Associate Professor at the School of Information Studies, Syracuse University. Much of her recent research has been in partnership with practitioners in government, industry, and education. Drawing upon prior management and consulting experience, her research studies how social, cultural, knowledge and generational factors influence IT governance, the IT workforce, and technology adoption. Dr. Kaarst-Brown has published in a number of top academic and business journals including MIS Quarterly, IT&P, the Journal of Strategic Information Systems, and MIS Quarterly Executive. She serves as a Senior Editor for MIS Quarterly Executive.

4. REFERENCES

[1] Bice, M.R., Ball, J.W. and McClaran, S. 2015. Technology and physical activity motivation. *International Journal of Sport and Exercise Psychology*. (Apr 2015), 1–10.

[2] Birkland, J.H. and Kaarst-Brown, M.L. 2012. It's All a Matter of Choice: Understanding society's expectations of older adult ICT use from a birth cohort perspective. *Cultural Attitudes towards Technology and Communication (CATaC)* (Aarhus, Denmark, 2012).

[3] Buttussi, F. and Chittaro, L. 2010. Smarter Phones for Healthier Lifestyles: An Adaptive Fitness Game. *IEEE Pervasive Computing*. 9, 4 (Oct. 2010), 51–57.

[4] Kaarst-Brown, M.L. 2005. Understanding an Organization's View of the CIO: The role of assumptions about IT. *MISQ Executive*. 4, 2 (2005), 287–301.

[5] Kaarst-Brown, M.L. and Robey, D. 1999. More on Myth, Magic and Metaphor: Cultural Insights into the Management of Information Technology in Organizations. *Information Technology and People*. 12, 2 (1999), 192–217.

[6] Korte, J., Potter, L.E.C. and Nielsen, S.H. 2015. An experience in requirements prototyping with young deaf children. *Journal of Usability Studies*. 10, 4 (2015), 195–214.

[7] Madeira, R.N., Costa, L. and Postolache, O. 2014. PhysioMate - Pervasive physical rehabilitation based on NUI and gamification. *2014 International Conference and Exposition on Electrical and Power Engineering (EPE)* (Oct. 2014), 612–616.

[8] Potter, L.E., Araullo, J. and Carter, L. 2013. The Leap Motion controller. *Proceedings of the 25th Australian Computer-Human Interaction Conference on Augmentation, Application, Innovation, Collaboration - OzCHI '13* (Adelaide, Australia, Nov. 2013), 175–178.

[9] Rogers, E. 2003. *Diffusion of Innovation*. Simon and Schuster.

[10] Rotolo, D., Hicks, D. and Martin, B. 2015. What Is an Emerging Technology? *Research Policy*. 44, 10 (2015), 1827–1843.

[11] Roy, L. and Raitt, D. 2003. The impact of IT on indigenous peoples. *The Electronic Library*. 21, 5 (2003), 411–413.

Toward Building a Mobile App Experience to Support Users' Mobile Travel Needs

Chad Schaefer
University of Wisconsin - Whitewater
800 West Main Street
Whitewater, WI 53190
SchaeferCW24@uww.edu

Users' reliance on mobile devices has grown tremendously in recent years. For travelers in particular, the use of mobile travel (hereafter, referred to as "mtravel") apps has been increasingly important in order to check the status of hotels, convert currencies, and provide convenience when traveling away from home. Examples of such applications used for travel purposes include hotel/motel apps, airline apps, location-based services such as maps, and travel tools such as translators, currency converters, etc.

In this research, we sought to learn more about the types of uses international and domestic travelers have for mobile applications. As a result, we looked at prior literature based on three categories: travel and hospitality applications, evaluating mobile applications, and mobile application usability. With this knowledge, our aim was to develop and evaluate a multi-purpose travel application to meet the needs of frequent travelers with need for multiple types of travel-related information. For our purposes, we considered a multi-purpose travel application to be one that provides multiple travel-related functions for a user, without requiring the use of separate applications for separate functions.

Prior research on mtravel applications has focused on topic such as users' motivation to download apps (Mo Kwon et al, 2013), features that determine app usefulness and desirability (i.e., Chung et. al 2015), and types of mtravel app users (Eriksson, 2014). Tourist apps process information in six different information flows including: (1) Information search, (2) Information request, (3) Information provision, (4) Initiate online transaction, (5) Initiate offline action, and (6) Push notification. Each individual user has a different idea of what is relevant to him or her (Burgess et al., 2012). Overall, users are more likely to download an application that is fun and simple to use rather than downloading an app in order to receive promotional information. The ability for customers to have constant access to the internet and mobile apps allows them to use an application to create value at any time (Coussement and Teague, 2013), such as looking at an existing reservation or looking up reviews for a hotel. Additionally, location-based information and applications are most desired by both business and leisure travelers, followed by

communication-based innovations and hotel-services-based innovations (Verma et al., 2012).

After conducting the preliminary literature review, we identified several areas to focus on for our research. This included looking at different mtravel applications to determine what functionality they currently provide, identifying additional functionality desired, by users, and learning what methods have been used to evaluate apps in the past. Our goal was to determine whether users want a multi-purpose travel application that has the ability to provide a variety of information to the users, what functions should be included. Finally, our wish was to employ relevant usability techniques as recommend by prior research to effectively evaluate the design of the app. Collectively, accomplishing these goals would contribute to prior literature's call to identify (and remove) barriers that prevent users from using Internet and mobile services for travel purposes (e.g., Eriksson, 2014).

To gather potential users' mtravel usage and preferences, we created and distributed an online survey. we sent the survey to a convenience sample of international and graduate students of a public University located in the Midwestern United States. Despite the relatively young age of the population (mostly undergraduate students), we believed this sample was appropriate due to the high likelihood that international students had traveled within the past year, if for no other reason, to travel to and from the University. Also, this younger population was likely to have and use their mobile device for applications frequently. The survey included both quantitative and open-ended qualitative questions.

For the purpose of our survey and our study, we defined a travel application as any existing mobile tourism application that contains defined content, OR using devices with networking capabilities that access tourist content via wireless network coverage (Kenteris, Gavalas, & Economou, 2009). The purpose of this survey was to get a better idea of what individuals would look for if they were going to download and use a travel application. Gathering such information would help us to determine what type of travel applications were popular and look for a relationship between the number of candidates using the applications and the features that it provides. Since all applications can be significantly different, it is important to look at what individuals are looking for in an application and then determine what other applications can do in order to incorporate these features within their apps. Specifically, we addressed the following research question:

1. What features were most desired by potential mtravel app users?

SIGMIS-CPR'16, June 2-4, 2016, Alexandria, VA, USA.
ACM 978-1-4503-4203-2/16/06.
http://dx.doi.org/10.1145/2890602.2906193

2. What travel needs do different types of users want mtravel apps to meet?

We sent the survey to a convenience sample of 262 students, of which 47 responded for a response rate of 17.9%. Of the respondents, 45% (n=21) were male, while 55% (n=26) were female. Ages of the respondents ranged from 18 to 52 years, with the average age of respondents as 27.04 years (mode = 21 years). Of the respondents, 100% (n=47) own a smartphone or a tablet that allow for surfing of the web and installation of mobile applications. 70% (n=33) of the respondents reported their race as White/Caucasian and non-Hispanic, 2% (n=1) Black/African-American and non-Hispanic, 6% (n=3) Hispanic, 15% Asian or Pacific Islander, 2% (n=1) Native American, and 2% (n=1) other. Within the past year, 66% (n=31) of respondents said they had traveled outside of the country and 91% (n=43) said they had traveled domestically.

In order to identify the desired features, the survey included open ended questions to determine what type of travel apps respondents currently use and what features they would like to see in a travel app. Of the respondents, 79% (n=37) of the respondents said they currently have/use a mobile travel app, including maps, hotel, airlines, trip planning and other apps like currency converters, weather, translators, and public transportation systems. The top three reasons for using mtravel apps included finding a way around town (73%), providing real-time flight information (64%), and planning and booking travel (62%). The least common reasons to use a travel app included seeing unit measurement types (7%), and being able to check electric plug types (2%).

The top three features desired by respondents are being able to see food or attraction lists and reviews (87%), seeing the predicted weather conditions for the destination (82%), and translating between languages (60%). The bottom three features include finding products needed to be purchased for a trip (36%), viewing a summary comparing differences between two countries (33%), and sharing information through email or social media (29%).

Based on the information we uncovered from the data collected and prior works, we designed a prototype of an mtravel app that included some of the features listed by survey respondents. We created a travel app that can be used by individuals interested in traveling abroad on business or leisure. The primary purpose of the app is to function as a multi-purpose app that will be used by mtravel users that fall into the "all-rounders" category (Eriksson, 2014) and to provide some offline access to information. We also wanted the app to meet the effectiveness criteria identified by multiple prior studies, such as ease of use, visual appeal, constant access, and other key factors. Based on our survey, we also wanted the app to provide as many of the desired features listed by potential users as possible. Though our main goal for the app was to support international travelers, we also wanted the app to include features related to domestic travel, where possible.

We provide a description of the app and describe our plans for next steps.

ACKNOWLEDGEMENTS
My thanks to the Research Scholars program of the College of Business and Economics at the University of Wisconsin – Whitewater.

REFERENCES
[1] Anne Coussement, M. and Teague, T.J., 2013. The new customer-facing technology: mobile and the constantly-connected consumer. *Journal of Hospitality and Tourism Technology*, 4(2), pp.177-187.

[2] Burgess, S., Sellitto, C., & Karanasios, S. (2012). A Model of ICDT Internet Flows on Mobile Devices for the Travel and Tourism Consumer. *Tourism Analysis*, 17(6), 705–719. http://doi.org/10.3727/108354212X13531051127140

[3] Chung, N., Han, H., & Joun, Y. (2015). Tourists' intention to visit a destination: The role of augmented reality (AR) application for a heritage site. *Computers in Human Behavior*, 50, 588–599. http://doi.org/10.1016/j.chb.2015.02.068.

[4] Eriksson, N., 2014. User categories of mobile travel services. *Journal of Hospitality and Tourism Technology*, 5(1), pp.17-30.

[5] Kenteris, M., Gavalas, D. and Economou, D., 2009. An innovative mobile electronic tourist guide application. *Personal and ubiquitous computing*, 13(2), pp.103-118.

[6] Mo Kwon, J., Bae, J. (Stephanie), & Blum, S. C. (2013). Mobile applications in the hospitality industry. *Journal of Hospitality and Tourism Technology*, 4(1), 81–92. http://doi.org/10.1108/17579881311302365

[7] Verma, R., Stock, D., & McCarthy, L. (2012). Customer Preferences for Online, Social Media, and Mobile Innovations in the Hospitality Industry. *Cornell Hospitality Quarterly*, 53(3), 183–186. http://doi.org/10.1177/1938965512445161.

Providers' Perceptions of the Impact of Weight Loss Apps on Users with Eating Disorders

Elizabeth V. Eikey
The Pennsylvania State University
323 IST Building
University Park, PA 16802
1-949-438-1337
eveikey@psu.edu

ABSTRACT

It is estimated that 30 million people in the United States have an eating disorder, and many more have unhealthy eating behaviors [5]. In addition to being psychological in nature, eating disorders are a social problem driven by the mass media promotion of the "thin ideal" [6]. More researchers have recognized the importance of studying technology on users' body image and eating behaviors [1, 4, 8, 9, 13]. Despite their popularity, few studies have considered the impact of health applications ("apps") for weight loss on users with disordered eating behaviors. To begin to address this understudied area, I consider eating disorder treatment providers' perceptions of these apps. Some researchers have urged providers to be aware of the existence, possibilities, dysfunctions, and impact of technology in relation to eating disorders [23, 110]. Yet few studies consider providers' perceptions of weight loss apps and how they think about them when diagnosing and treating eating disorder patients.

My work aims to explore this gap by examining providers' perceptions of weight loss apps (i.e., MyFitnessPal[1]) on users with eating disorders. In this preliminary pilot study, I interviewed four healthcare providers who work with patients with eating disorders to better understand if and how they discuss weight loss apps with their patients and the role of weight loss apps in reducing or exacerbating eating disorder behaviors. My work is guided by two primary research questions:

RQ1: What are providers' perceptions of health apps in relation to eating disorders?
RQ2: What elements or features of weight loss apps may reduce or exacerbate eating disorder behaviors?

Research has shown that people with behaviors indicative of eating disorders use technology both to maintain their unhealthy habits and to reduce them [7, 10]. Prior studies have found that some technologies, especially those that facilitate social support, can be beneficial to users with eating disorder behaviors [2, 15]. However, many online weight loss and fitness communities either overtly or subtly promote eating disorders, and this negatively affects users who are trying to address their eating disorder issues [12, 14]. A great deal of research has sought to explain how pro-eating disorder communities and social media negatively impact

users' body image and eating behaviors [1, 3, 4, 8, 9, 11, 13]. Little work has considered the impact of weight loss apps in relation to eating disorders.

This research highlights future areas of study and gives providers a basis for discussing weight loss app use with their patients. By uncovering ways weight loss apps impact eating disorder behaviors and getting experts' (i.e., providers) opinions of weight loss apps, we will be able to provide other researchers and developers design recommendations to create better weight loss apps as well as provide clinical recommendations.

Dieting behaviors are a risk factor for developing an eating disorder [78, 99], and weight loss apps promote dieting behaviors. Healthcare providers are encouraging their patients to track their diet and exercise behaviors using these types of apps in order to create tailored health plans. These apps may be promising; however, more research is needed to understand in what ways weight loss apps can help and harm users, especially those with eating disorders.

ID #	Role	Experience	Do some patients discuss using weight loss apps?	If patients do not bring it up, do you?
ID1	Instructor, dietician, and has masters in counseling	N/A	Y	Y – only teens though
ID2	Registered dietician; community health educator	5.5 years; 9 months	Y	N
ID3	Physician	6 years	Y	N
ID4	Nurse Practitioner for adolescent medicine and eating disorders	3 years	Y	N

Table 1. Participant information and answers to app use

Table 1 shows the role and experience of each participant as well as whether or not they discuss weight loss apps with their patients. Of the four providers we interviewed, they all expressed concerns about the use of weight loss apps by their patients with eating disorders. While these results are very preliminary and I have not yet interviewed enough participants to reach data saturation, a few noteworthy things stand out and will have to be further examined in the full study.

Some users may initially utilize a weight loss app to lose weight in a healthy way. However, over time, some of these users develop eating disorders because these apps emphasize the thin ideal and a heavy focus on numbers related to calorie intake,

---

[1] https://www.myfitnesspal.com/

SIGMIS-CPR '16, June 02-04, 2016, Alexandria, VA, USA.
ACM 978-1-4503-4203-2/16/06.
http://dx.doi.org/10.1145/2890602.2906194

expenditure, and weight instead of actual health. For instance, ID3 explained how weight loss apps can first be used a tool for healthy weight loss that goes too far:

"Apps for weight loss and physical activity tracking are concerning for people who appear predisposed to eating disorder or have early signs. A significant portion of eating disorders start with "healthy" weight loss that just never stops. And many of these apps reinforce the thin ideal, the idea that one can gain health/happiness/success by losing weight. An app that focuses on health behaviors, increasing fitness, attending to other aspects of health (e.g. sleep, emotions, relationships) could be far less worrisome and potentially helpful to everyone." [ID3]

Secondly, providers felt that weight loss apps can trigger and feed into eating disorders by focusing too heavily on the numbers and data around calories and weight as well as the need for control associated with eating disorders. Additionally, apps act as a constant reminder of how to lose weight even if the user is already at a healthy or below healthy weight. ID2 expressed worry over the data-driven aspects of weight loss apps and how those can exacerbate eating disorder behaviors:

"I think they can be triggering initially and then can feed the eating disorder. It can be triggering because it causes them to acutely focus on weight, weight loss, and food whereas maybe they thought about it before but didn't always have set numbers put with anything or something telling them, this is what you are allotted in order to lose weight. It can the facilitate the eating disorder, especially anorexia." [ID2]

Lastly, although only one provider was explicitly discussed competition, it is an important aspect of weight loss apps that may not be as prevalent in traditional diet tracking methods (e.g. paper diaries). Because weight loss apps often have progress visualizations that encourage users and even rewards them to eat below their daily calorie allotment, users may compete with themselves and with the app to eat less.

The preliminary results suggest users with eating disorders are using weight loss apps. From a providers' perspective, these weight loss apps may exacerbate eating disorder behaviors by focusing too heavily on the numbers associated with calories and weight loss and not nutrition and healthy behaviors. While providers express concern over the use of these apps, providers do not always include discussions of weight loss apps with their patients. Features of weight loss apps may be able to be redesigned to focus more on healthy behaviors. For instance, users could be rewarded for adding healthy fats to their diets. In clinical settings, providers need to start to discuss the use of weight loss apps with their patients and with other providers in order to better understand how these apps may contribute to the development and maintenance of eating disorders. In my future work, I plan to interview more providers and also users regarding their perceptions around the impact of weight loss apps on users with eating disorders.

Keywords
Mobile health apps; weight loss apps; eating disorders; healthcare; clinical; providers; qualitative methods

1. ACKNOWLEDGMENTS
This material is based upon work supported by the National Science Foundation (NSF) under Grant No. DGE1255832. Any opinions, findings, and conclusions or recommendations expressed in this material are those of the author and do not necessarily reflect the views of the NSF.

2. REFERENCES
[1] Andsager, J.L. 2014. Research directions in social media and body image. *Sex Roles*. 71, (2014), 407–413.

[2] Bowler, L. et al. 2012. Eating disorder questions in Yahoo! Answers: Information, conversation, or reflection? *ASIST 2012* (Baltimore, Maryland, 2012).

[3] Csipke, E. and Horne, O. 2007. Pro-eating disorder websites: Users' opinions. *European Eating Disorders Review*. 15, (2007), 196–206.

[4] Fardouly, J. et al. 2015. Social comparisons on social media: The impact of Facebook on young women's body image concerns and mood. *Body Image*. 13, (2015), 38–45.

[5] Get the facts on eating disorders: 2015. *https://www.nationaleatingdisorders.org/get-facts-eating-disorders*. Accessed: 2015-11-11.

[6] Hesse-Biber, S. et al. 2006. The mass marketing of disordered eating and Eating Disorders: The social psychology of women, thinness and culture. *Women's Studies International Forum*. 29, 2 (2006), 208–224.

[7] Keski-Rahkonen, A. and Tozzi, F. 2005. The process of recovery in eating disorder sufferers' own words: An internet-based study. *International Journal of Eating Disorders*. 37, (2005), 580–586.

[8] Mabe, A.G. et al. 2014. Do you "like" my photo? Facebook use maintains eating disorder risk. *International Journal of Eating Disorders*. 47, (2014), 516–523.

[9] Meier, E.P. and Gray, J. 2014. Facebook photo activity associated with body image disturbance in adolescent girls. *Cyberpsychology, Behavior, and Social Networking*. 17, 4 (2014), 199–206.

[10] Ransom, D.C. et al. 2010. Interpersonal interactions on online forums addressing eating concerns. *International Journal of Eating Disorders*. 43, 2 (2010), 161–170.

[11] Sharpe, H. et al. 2011. Review Pro-eating disorder websites: facts, fictions and fixes. *Health (San Francisco)*. 10, 1 (2011), 34–44.

[12] Stover, C.M. 2014. *Elements of a Sensibility: Fitness Blogs and Postfeminist Media Culture*. The University of Texas at Austin.

[13] Stronge, S. et al. 2015. Facebook is linked to body dissatisfaction: Comparing users and non-users. *Sex Roles*. 73, (2015), 200–213.

[14] Tiggemann, M. and Zaccardo, M. 2015. "Exercise to be fit, not skinny": The effect of fitspiration imagery on women's body image. *Body Image*. 15, (2015), 61–67.

[15] Whitlock, J.L. et al. 2006. The virtual cutting edge: The internet and adolescent self-injury. *Developmental Psychology*. 42, 3 (2006), 407–417.

Encouraging Minority and Low-Income Girls to Pursue Computing through Inclusive Technology Camps

Danielle Sherman
University of Wisconsin - Whitewater
800 West Main Street
Whitewater, WI 53190
ShermanDJ10@uww.edu

ABSTRACT

It is no secret that there exists a great disparity between the percentages of women compared to men in any computing-related field. Traditionally, women have composed 12 to 15% of undergraduate students enrolled in computer degree programs in North America (http://cra.org/resources/taulbee-survey/). From 2000-2014, the percentage of first-year undergraduate women interested in majoring in computing declined 7% (https://www.ncwit.org/resources/numbers). As of 2014, women represented only 26% of the computing workforce. Minority women represent even less. Further actions and research need to do be done to learn what will help inspire this population, and the population of low-income women, to pursue computing as a hobby and potential career.

Quite a lot of focus has been paid in recent years on attracting more women to IT careers. There are multiple reasons why it would be beneficial to have greater gender diversity in the male-dominated computing profession. For example, a team with a more diverse membership is found "to produce better solutions to problems than do homogenous teams" [4]. While this illustrates the importance of including more women in IT, it's also important to draw women from different perspectives. These perspectives include (but are not limited to) minority and low-income women. The problem is, it appears that a large part of the research data we currently have regarding women in computing-related fields represents middle class white girls and women, or does not take race, class, and other demographics factors into account when drawing conclusions.

A handful of studies have focused on computing "interventions," or short camps, that introduce computing concepts in a fun and engaging way to a diverse group of girls [1][2][3][5][6]. Results of these efforts have not come to fruition quite yet; out of the women who earned computing related bachelors degrees in 2013, a combined total of 22% were African-American (11%), Hispanic (9%), American Indian/Alaskan Native (0%), and multi-racial,not Hispanic (2%) women (http://cra.org/resources/taulbee-survey/). More targeted efforts are needed on both local and national levels to encourage minority and low-income girls to pursue an interest in computing-related fields. One way of doing this is to provide role models to show how computing is feasible and fun.

GoldieBlox, a girl-focused toy company, has created an African American and Latina girl action figure in hopes to encourage young girls to get excited about STEM (http://time.com/4098641/goldieblox-ad-ruby-rails-action-figure/). More research needs to be done to reveal whether there exists a difference in values between ethnicities and income levels, and how those differences could determine, for example, the methods we should use when designing intervention programs targeting girls from different demographic groups.

The purpose of our research study is to expand upon the learnings obtained from the limited research that has been published in this area as well as enhance the outreach efforts made at our own university. Our university currently conducts 1-2 day girls only summer computing camps for middle and high school girls. Like a large portion of the existing research in this area, our past camps have consisted of girls residing close to the campus (in mostly suburban and rural towns) who are also homogenous in terms of race, ethnicity, and financial need. Especially noteworthy for our geographic area is the large Native American / Alaskan Native population, relative to some other parts of North America. Despite this high population, we have not recruited a significant number of girls to our program.

By partnering with a local branch of a national youth focused afterschool and community support organization, we developed a program to broaden our reach to minority and low-income girls from an area that has not traditionally been represented in our camp enrollments. Up to 30 middle school and high school girls were invited to attend one day workshops on different computing related topics. During the workshops, the girls complete a survey that enables us to gauge the girl's interest and experience in computing related activities. After the day's events, the girls complete an assessment activity that tests their knowledge of what they learned that day. The information that we gather during the workshops will help gain insight on how to effectively go about closing the gender gap in computing, specifically focused on minority and low-income girls.

Beyond workshop content, our program includes additional support for unique circumstances encountered when working with our target demographic [3]:

- The community partner would coordinate communication between the camp faculty and the girls attending, including collecting parental consent as needed.

SIGMIS-CPR '16, June 02-04, 2016, Alexandria, VA, USA.
ACM 978-1-4503-4203-2/16/06.
http://dx.doi.org/10.1145/2890602.2906195

- Camp and/or community partner staff would provide transportation for any campers who might need it.
- A make up camp day would be scheduled for campers who could not attend as planned, due to babysitting, work, or other family obligations.
- Camps would be greatly overbooked to accept more girls than the available capacity, since the dropout rate for prior programs can be as high as 50%, often due to need for the prior three items above.

One workshop included in our program consists of building a game using the tool Scratch. To spark girls' interest in a subject at a younger age, it is important to make the learning process relatable to what interests your subject, rather than focusing solely on the technical details (http://scratched.gse.harvard.edu/guide/). Making this workshop event consist of mostly hands on exercises (with minimal lecture) should enable us to spark creativity and excitement by making the design process a group activity. We do this by showcasing Scratch's capabilities through presentation and exploration (http://scratched.gse.harvard.edu/guide/). Below is a working agenda for the event:

Sign-in, welcome and survey	
Ice breaker	Ask the group questions to get them engaged with the day's topic Connect the girls' answers to careers that are gaming and graphic design related
Scratch Intro	Introduce Scratch by showing the Scratch intro video created by the website Showcase a game that I created and use aspects of that game to give the girls ideas of what kinds of games they could make
Scratch Tutorial	Describe the concept of drag-and-drop coding Go through several tutorials with the group (step-by-step) to help them understand the concept of drag-and-drop coding
Lunch	
Scratch worktime	Offer the group links to tutorials to help get them started or let them start from scratch on their own project
Presentations	Allow students who wish to present approximately 3-5 minutes to showcase their projects to the entire group
Extend Beyond	Give the students resources to take home (handout or website link)

Table 1. Build a Game with Scratch workshop agenda

The first event included an hour-long lecture about web development and the Internet, which included a few hands-on exercises. Although it was effective in teaching the concepts (the girls answered almost all of the event's follow up questions correctly), it appeared as if most of the participants were bored. To avoid the effect boredom could have on their future interest in computing, we are splitting up the next event into smaller sections. This will hopefully help harness the girls' attention spans and keep the event lively and moving forward (http://ideas.time.com/2012/10/02/why-lectures-are-ineffective/).

REFERENCES

[1] Denner, J. (2011). What Predicts Middle School Girls' Interest in Computing? International Journal of Gender, Science and Technology, *3*(1).

[2] Marlino, D. & Wilson, F. (2006). *Career expectations and goals of Latina adolescents: Results form a nationwide study*, in Denner, J., & Guzman, B. (eds.) Latina Girls: Voices of Adolescent Strength in the U.S. (pp. 123-140). New York, NY: New York University Press.

[3] Outlay, C. (2016 forthcoming). Targeting Underrepresented Minority and Low-Income Girls for Computing Camps: Early Results and Lessons Learned. *The Journal of Computing Sciences in Colleges*, 31(4).

[4] Ramsey, N. and P. McCorduck (2005). Where are the Women in Information Technology? Report of Literature Search and Interviews Prepared for the National Center for Women & Information Technology.

[5] Scott, K. A., & White, M. A. (2013). COMPUGIRLS' Standpoint Culturally Responsive Computing and Its Effect on Girls of Color. Urban Education, 48(5), 657-681.

[6] Scott, K., & Zhang, X. (2014). Designing a Culturally Responsive Computing Curriculum For Girls. International Journal of Gender, Science and Technology,6(2), 264-276.

From "Weight Loss Tips" to "Fastest Exercise to Get Abs:" How Teens Search for Fitness Information Across Social Media Platforms

Kayla M. Booth
The Pennsylvania State University 334 IST Building
University Park, PA 16802
1.814.865.8952
Kmb5445@ist.psu.edu

ABSTRACT

This paper summarizes a poster which presents a segment of initial findings from a dissertation in progress entitled, "Teens and Information Quality: An Intersectionality-Based Exploration of Youth and Their Information Behavior Surrounding Fitness Information and Social Media." Below is an outline of the research problem, this study's approach, and its key contributions:

There are a myriad of ways in which teenagers in the US are using social media, ranging from connecting with peers to searching for health information. According to a 2010 study conducted by Pew Research Center, 31% of teens have looked online for "health, dieting, or physical fitness information" online [2]. Just four years later, researchers at the same center found that 65% of internet users perceived their internet and cellphone use to have increased their knowledge about health and fitness [3].

In conjunction with traditional search engines, teens are also using social media to search for fitness content. This is noteworthy because users often use the health information they find to influence their offline behavior. Searching for fitness information via social media has potential benefits in that it makes diverse, enriching content available to those who cannot afford or access medical professionals, personal trainers, or nutritionists. Conversely, some scholars have found social media to contain disordered content that makes it difficult for users to distinguish between healthy and unhealthy information [4]. For example, some content advocates for anorexia as a lifestyle choice rather than a serious medical condition. This problem space is compounded by the notion that teens searching for fitness information via social media encounter and interact with results beyond traditional text. As Gasser et al. (2012) point out, we know relatively little about how users, youth in particular, search for videos, images, and graphics [1]. This preliminary work takes a youth-oriented perspective to explore how youth are searching for fitness information via social media and how their search and interaction processes differ across various platforms.

SIGMIS-CPR '16, June 02-04, 2016, Alexandria, VA, USA.
ACM 978-1-4503-4203-2/16/06.
http://dx.doi.org/10.1145/2890602.2906196

This particular poster presents initial findings to the research questions:
RQ1: How do youth search for fitness information via social media?
RQ2: How do teens' choice of search strategies differ across various social media platforms when it comes to health information?

These questions (and subsequent findings) are significant in two regards. The first is from an Information Systems (IS) perspective. The question of how users, particularly those who are considered vulnerable, are searching for health information has historically been a scholarly topic of interest in the field. This study seeks to build on existing literature to move towards new trends by looking at how young people alter their search strategies across different social media platforms (Instagram, YouTube, Pinterest, Facebook, etc.). Similarly, it also explores how teens search for information in formats beyond traditional text results; it examines how search strategies change depending on whether the user desires text, graphics, pictures, or video results.

The second sphere of importance lies in the public health sphere. Teenagers are particularly vulnerable to poor body image and are searching for fitness information in spaces that, while beneficial in terms of low economic cost, are not monitored by healthcare professionals (i.e. traditional "gatekeepers"). This creates a unique problem space in that teens tend to be highly experienced with social media, far more so than their adult counterparts, but less knowledgeable about crucial health information. By exploring the considerations and values teens have while searching for high-stakes information, we can build better design-based and educational interventions.

The data for this study was collected via 30 semi-structured interviews with teens ages 13-18. Fifteen of these interviews took place at urban charter schools, 15 at suburban public high schools. The interview questions were informed by Gasser et al.'s (2012) Youth-Oriented Information Quality Framework [1]. During each interview, each participant led a "walk-through" in which they discussed how they choose which platform to use and demonstrated how they use each platform via iphone. I recorded screenshots of each search and audio recorded their descriptions. These audio recordings were later transcribed and analyzed according to Gasser et al.'s (2012) framework. Finally, I engaged in open coding of emergent themes that were not covered by the aforementioned framework. The poster created for this conference includes select screenshots from these interviews to demonstrate how teens' strategies differ across platforms.

While this work is preliminary, it provides potential insight into the factors teens consider when **choosing where and how to search** for information via social media. These results begin to explore **how and why young people are using different platforms** to search for health related content. Similarly, this study also provides a potential starting point for a deeper analysis in terms of **how teens search for and interact with various forms of information**, ranging from videos to infographics to images and photographs.

This work offers a unique perspective by emphasizing and prioritizing the values and voices of young users. By exploring the factors and processes young people consider and enact, rather than what adults expect of them, we can better develop curriculum, policies, and designs that benefit them.

CCS Concepts
• **Human-centered Computing→ Collaborative and social computing.**

Keywords
Information quality; social media; youth; health; fitness; qualitative methods

1. ACKNOWLEDGEMENTS
Special thanks to my committee members: Dr. Eileen Trauth, Dr. Lynette Yarger, Dr. Michael McNeese, and Dr. Karen Keifer-Boyd.

2. REFERENCES
[1] Gasser, U., Cortesi, S., Malik, M., & Lee, A. 2012. Youth and digital media: From credibility to information quality. Berkman Center for Internet & Society. Retrieved April 10, 2014 from http://ssrn.com/abstract=2005272.

[2] Lenhart, A., Purcell, K., Smith, A., Zickuhr, K. 2010. Social Media & Young Adults http://www.pewinternet.org/2010/02/03/social-media-and-young-adults/

[3] Purcell, K., Rainie, L. 2014. Americans Feel Better Informed Thanks to the Internet. http://www.pewinternet.org/2014/12/08/more-information-yields-more-learning-and-sharing/

[4] Syed-Abdul S, Fernandez-Luque L, Jian WS, Li YC, Crain S, Hsu MH, Wang YC, Khandregzen D, Chuluunbaatar E, Nguyen PA, Liou DM. 2013. Misleading Health-Related Information Promoted Through Video-Based Social Media: Anorexia on YouTube. J Med Internet Res; 15(2):e30

Investigating the Role of Top Management and Institutional Pressures in Cloud Computing Adoption

Elston H. Steele
Trident University
Elston.steele@trident.edu

Indira R. Guzman
Trident University
Indira.guzman@trident.edu

ABSTRACT

While cloud computing adoption is on the rise, barriers continue to play a critical role in delaying the progress of some cloud computing adoption efforts. In 2010 the United States federal government launched the 'Cloud First' policy which requires government agencies to consider the adoption of cloud computing when the solution is secure, reliable and cost effective (Kundra, 2010). Unfortunately, cloud computing adoption among federal agencies has been sluggish. This study investigates pressures asserted to facilitate cloud computing adoption. Although a vast amount of literature exists, very few studies empirically investigate cloud computing adoption from an institutional perspective in concert with top management support. This study aims to fill the gap where the literature is lacking concerning the adoption of cloud computing by federal agencies.

Keywords

Cloud Computing; Top Management; Institutional Theory

1. PROBLEM STATEMENT

Cloud computing is a new information technology which offers organizations advantages such as scalability, flexibility, reliability, and cost savings through the use of software and platform applications, processors, storage, and other compute resources hosted in an external environment accessible via the internet. Despite the advantages, cloud computing adoption among U.S. federal agencies has been sluggish. Persistent struggles to take advantage of cloud computing technology prevents agencies from reducing maintenance costs of existing infrastructure, eliminating duplicative IT systems supporting similar business processes, and dedicating more time to core business processes. In response to this problem, this study proposes to investigate the supporting role of top management of cloud computing adoption and impact of institutional pressures in cloud computing adoption by federal agencies.

Previous studies on cloud computing primarily focused on organizational factors affecting adoption and employed the use of several theories to investigate these factors. For example, Bhattacherjee and Park (2013) used migration theory to investigate the behavioral intentions and other drivers that facilitated end-users' abandonment of their existing technology in favor of migrating to cloud computing. Incorporating the Social Exchange Theory into the Technology Acceptance Model, Obeidat and Turgay, (2013) formulated and validated the

SIGMIS-CPR '16, June 02-04, 2016, Alexandria, VA, USA.
ACM 978-1-4503-4203-2/16/06.
http://dx.doi.org/10.1145/2890602.2906197

Technology Trade Theory (Triple T) in their empirical analysis of factors affecting cloud adoption initiatives by IT executives. However, none of these studies looked at the influence of institutional pressures and the role of top management on cloud computing adoption. Liang et al.(2007) studied the impact of external institutional pressures on the degree of usage of enterprise resource planning (ERP) systems. This study extends their study by testing adapting their framework in the context of cloud computing adoption.

2. STUDY FRAMEWORK

2.1 Institutional Theory

Institutional theory has been applied in the field of information systems by several researchers (Zheng et al., 2013, Basaglia et al., 2008, and Liang et al., 2007). Institutional theory views the social world as significantly comprised of institutions – rules, practices, and structures that set conditions on action. Neo-institutional theory, emerged with the seminal works of Meyer and Rowan (1977) and DiMaggio and Powell (1983). A central tenant of neo-institutional theory asserts that organizations and organizational actors seek to gain legitimacy through the process of homogeneity to ensure their survivability. Homogeneity in organizational fields occurs as the result of institutional isomorphic changes within organizational environments. DiMaggio and Powell (1983) introduce three isomorphism mechanisms as a compelling means to influence an organizational actor to resemble another organizational actor subjected to the same environmental circumstances. It is expected that each isomorphic mechanism will have a significant role in cloud computing adoption.

Coercive Isomorphism

Coercive Isomorphism is formal and informal pressures and cultural expectations exerted on organizations by superior organizations upon which they depend (DiMaggio and Powell, 1983). Teo et al. (2003) found that coercive pressures significantly influenced organizations' intention to adopt financial exchange data interchanges (FEDI). Thus the following hypothesis is presented:

H1: Coercive pressures will have a positive association with the intention to adopt cloud computing.

Normative Isomorphism

DiMaggio and Powell (1983) suggest that sharing norms of adoption innovation facilitates consensus which increases the strength of these norms and their influence on organizational behavior. The following hypothesis is provided:

H2: Normative pressures will have a positive association with the intention to adopt cloud computing.

Mimetic Isomorphism

The imitation or modeling of an organization after another organization deemed successful within the institutional environment as a result of mimetic pressures enables decision makers to minimize experimentation costs and avoid risks that are borne by early adopters (Teo et al., 2003). Since cloud computing is a relatively new technology, it has the characteristics of uncertainty, ambiguity, and misunderstanding. Hence the following hypothesis:

H3: Mimetic pressures will have a positive association with the intention to adopt cloud computing.

2.2 Top Management Support
Top management support has been acknowledged considerably in the IS literature (Lin, 2010). Drawing on the work of Lin (2010) this study operationalizes top management support as the degree to which top management understands the importance of cloud computing adoption and the extent to which top management is involved in cloud computing adoption. The involvement and participation of top management, such as the CEO and CIO, in managing IT and committing resources to cloud services illustrates the degree of importance placed on cloud computing. Zheng et al. (2013) found that top management had positive and significant influence on the allocation of IT human resources and financial resources which lead to the intention to adopt technology. Hence, it is essential that top management assess the needs of its employees and build strong ties to fulfil those needs, thus ensuring needed training and education for deploying cloud strategies and manage expectations for cloud adoption.

H4a: Higher top management support mediates the effect of institutional pressures on the intention to adopt cloud computing.

3. METHODOLOGY
This study will employ a quantitative, non-experimental, correlational design. A cross-sectional design will be used to collect data at one point in time via an on-line survey.

The population for this study includes federal agencies located in the military district of Washington, D.C. that are components of the Department of Homeland Security (DHS). The unit of analysis for this study is at the organizational level and a stratified sampling technique will be used. At random, samples will be chosen from the list of CIO's, CFO's, and IS Managers within the study population.

This study will use previously used items measuring specific variables adapted for this study.

Table 1. Operationalization of variables

Variable	Role	Adapted from
Intention to Adopt Cloud Computing	Dependent Variable.	Teo et al. (2003).
Coercive Pressures	Independent Variable.	DiMaggio and Powell, (1983).
Normative Pressures	Independent Variable.	DiMaggio and Powell, (1983).
Mimetic Pressures	Independent variable	DiMaggio and Powell, (1983).
Top Management Support	Mediating variable.	Liang et al., (2007).

This study aims to fill the gap where the literature is lacking concerning the adoption of cloud computing by federal agencies. Preliminary results will be presented at the Conference.

4. REFERENCES
[1] Bhattacherjee, A. and Park, S.C. (2013). Why end-users move to the cloud: a migration-theoretic analysis. *European Journal of Information Systems.*

[2] DiMaggio, P., and Powell, W.W. (1983). The iron cage revisited: institutional isomorphism and collective rationality in organizational fields. *American Sociological Review, Vol. 48*(2), pp. 147-160.

[3] Fischer, E.A. and Figliola, P.M. (2013). Overview and issues for implementation of the federal cloud computing initiative: implications for federal information technology reform management. *Congressional Research Service,* 7-5700, R42887.

[4] Government Accountability Office (2012). Information technology reform: progress made but cloud computing efforts should be better planned. (GAO Publication No. 12-756). Washington, D.C.: United States Government Printing Office.

[5] Liang, H., Saraf, N., Hu, Q., and Xue, Y. (2007). Assimilation of enterprise systems: the effect of institutional pressures and the mediating role of top management. *MIS Quarterly, Vol. 31*(1), 59-87.

[6] Lin, H-F. (2010). An investigation into the effects of IS quality and top management support on ERP system usage. *Total Quality Management, Vol. 21*(3), 335-349.

[7] Low, C., Chen, Y., and Wu, M. (2011). Understanding the determinants of cloud computing adoption. *Industrial Management and Data Systems, Vol. 111*(7), pp. 1006-1023.

[8] Mell, P. and Grance, T. (2009). The NIST definition of cloud computing. United States Department of Commerce.

[9] Meyer, J.W., and Rowan, B. (1977). Institutionalized organizations: formal structure as myth and Ceremony. *American Journal of Sociology, Vol. 83*(2), pp. 340-363.

[10] Mignerat, M., and Rivard, S. (2009). Positioning the institutional perspective in information systems research. *Journal of Information Technology, Vol, 24.*

[11] Obeidat, M.A., and Turgay, T. (2013). Empirical analysis for the factors affecting the adoption of cloud computing initiatives by information technology executives. *Journal of Management Research, Vol. 5*(1).

[12] Scott, W.R. (1987). The adolescence of institutional theory. *Administrative Science Quarterly,* 493-511.

[13] Teo, H.H., Wei, K.K., and Benbasat, I. (2003). Predicting intention to adopt interorganizational linkages: an institutional perspective. *MIS Quarterly, Vol. 27*(1), 19-49.

[14] Zheng, D., Chen, J., Huang, L., and Zhang, C. (2011). E-government adoption in public administration organizations: integrating institutional theory perspective and resource-based view. *European Journal of Information Systems, Vol. 22.*

What is missing for trust in the Cloud Computing?

Teofilo Branco Jr.
University of Minho
Department of Information Systems
Campus Azurém Guimarães Portugal
(+351) 253510319
teofilotb@hotmail.com

Henrique Santos
University of Minho
Department of Information Systems
Campus Azurém Guimarães Portugal
(+351) 253510319
hsantos@dsi.uminho.pt

ABSTRACT

This article deals with an analysis of some contracts Cloud Computing on the questions involved in the security of their environment. The objective of this study is to evaluate if the content of the contracts for the provision of IT services platforms in Computer Cloud includes, at present, the clauses necessary to transmit trust in relation the safety. The services must comply with the recommendations and with the security standards to convey reliability. Also is necessary to make indications about security's requirements in their contracts. This study analyzed through in a literature review, the standards and the recommendations proposed by groups of research and Cloud Computing regulatory entities and made a comparison with the contractual clauses published on the web by some suppliers of Cloud IT platforms. A comparison of these contracts with the recommendations of respected entities in the area of the security for consumption of this type of service shows that there is still a lot to improve in these agreements to clarify the aspects of the safety in a transparent way.

Keywords

Cloud Computing; Information Security; Cloud Provider Contracts; Platform as a Service (PaaS); Service Level Agreements (SLA)

1. INTRODUCTION

Several IT companies offer services of Cloud Computing (CC). This technology promises advantages such as reduction of customer costs with IT infrastructure in exchange for simpler and more specialized solutions. Thus, the clients can focus their efforts on their end activity while the highly skilled companies can provide better services of IT through a client portfolio that can provide them with resources to consolidate their business [3].

However, several issues related to security and quality of service provision has raised discussions in academia and reflections in the business community about the risks involved in adopting this model of service at this time [9]. One concern in this regard relates to the establishment of a trust relationship between contractors and providers of this service by establishing Service Level Agreements (SLA) and the feasibility of audits to verify the delivery of these services [14]. It should be possible to create

SIGMIS-CPR '16, June 02-04, 2016, Alexandria, VA, USA.
ACM 978-1-4503-4203-2/16/06.
http://dx.doi.org/10.1145/2890602.2890605

ways of measuring metrics related to these clauses so that the providers and the consumers can check their interests and their obligations [2].

We evaluate some contracts that are applied to the platform service (PaaS) in CC environment by some of the leading companies in the industry to verify the issues related to the information security.

2. THE CONCERNS OF SECURITY IN THE CC ENVIRONMENT

Cloud Computing (CC) still presents challenges; particularly regarding distrust of users put their data on computers that do not have control. The Internet presents itself as a hostile environment, and it becomes critical when you have sensitive data traveling between terminals and servers Cloud [11].

In this sense, there is a growing concern about security. The standard of interest varies from compliance with regulations to the issue of safety in dealing with end users [4].

It is important to recognize that security is a cross-sectional aspect of architecture that spans all layers of the reference model, ranging from physical security to application security. Therefore, the security in CC raises concern not only in the purview of cloud providers, but also involving consumers and other players involved [10].

The CC beyond the traditional safety standards has yet to adopt security measures for the environment itself [5].

Regarding the characteristic of the CC environment, some vulnerabilities are from services that are provided i.e. self-service on-demand network access to any IT platform, sharing resources, rapid elasticity, and measured service [7].

Compared with traditional IT systems, where an organization has control over the whole stack of computing resources and the entire life cycle of systems, CC providers and CC consumers must act collaboratively to design, build, deploy, and cloud-based operating systems. Security must be shared responsibility. Is need security controls to determine which party can best implement the safety requirements. This analysis should include analysis and considerations that different models of services imply varying degrees of control over providers and consumers. The CC providers must protect what has been secured in service level agreements (SLA), and customers should also ensure the fulfillment of their responsibilities [10].

Customers should not rely blindly on allegations of the provider on the robustness and security of your cloud environment, and should be clarified all the details of the adopted policies regarding the technologies employed. The organization shall investigate the

CC provider, requesting information on all relevant and significant points to consider in CC [12].

Still in this subject, one of the challenges is to develop mutual auditing templates for agreements management (SLAs), so that may be established a trust between the partners, thus consolidating the use of this environment through a formal relationship, involving the relevant legal responsibilities [5].

3. THE CONTRACTUAL TERMS OF SOME OF THE PaaS PROVIDERS

A service-level agreement (Service Level Agreement - SLA) is a contract between a supplier of IT services and a customer specifying in general and often contain measurable terms of what services the client will pay. Service levels are set at the beginning of any hiring ratio of IT services and are used to measure and monitor the performance of a vendor supplier [1].

In the majority of contracts in CC do not expressly mention the issues related to the safety of the environment and their consequences about possible disasters. Only the issues of the availability services are referenced. Metrics that represent the performance and availability of each of the services are listed in SLA clauses. In general, each service has their calculation formulae the contracts just contain forms of compensation for unavailability of any service through a corresponding time credit.

There is no a standardization of common nomenclatures by contractual arrangements between all companies. In general, the metrics used in contracts are made available by own providers and the customers must consult the providers about their performance of their offers. Each contract has proprietary metrics.

Regarding the possibility of monitoring or audit, service providers Microsoft Azure [6] and IBM [8] allow the customer chooses to hire a third party to perform the control. However, Microsoft's Azure contract [6] limits the scope of restricting the number of these companies through a list of accredited companies that the customer can hire. The others companies do not allow auditing or external monitoring by limiting the use of a monitoring tool of its property, for which the customer even paid for their use. The SLA provided by Salesforce Company [13] does not mention technical clauses, only about terms involving financial issues such as payments and deadlines by the contracting client.

4. CONCLUSIONS

This study suggests us to examine the reliability of CC technology from the perspective of what is required to ensure a safe environment and how it can be formally guaranted by contractual clauses (SLAs).

Regarding regulatory bodies, it is clear that these are developing in-depth studies, but many of them are not consolidated yet. Many of the proposed standards are still in development or under review. On the other hand, from the perspective of CC providers, the primary focus is the commercial, as shown by the clauses dealing with billing services and regarding the issue of availability of the environment. On the latter, some compensation given to the client for a possible unavailability of the environment is through discounts on future rates over the coming months.

For aspects of confidentiality and integrity, some vendors omit or do not address explicitly and transparent forms of verification and the implications that providers are subject. Another fact that stands out is how to monitor services, often by the use of metrics

and measurement tools imposed by CC own service providers. The omission in some security requirements in SLA agreements proposed by providers leads to the conclusion that even the CC environment is not reliable because there are no guarantees about the safety and quality of services explicitly in the contracts.

It can be concluded that the contracts of the CC service providers should be more transparent and more specifics to clarify the issues surrounding the security and to define the pertinent responsibilities in the business relationship with their clients.

5. ACKNOWLEDGMENTS

Our thanks to ALGORITMI CENTER - The research unit of the School of Engineering - University of Minho - Portugal to support this publication.

6. REFERENCES

[1] Armbrust, M. et al. 2009. Above the clouds: A Berkeley view of cloud computing. *University of California, Berkeley, Tech. Rep. UCB.* (2009), 07–013.

[2] Buyya, R. et al. 2009. Cloud computing and emerging IT platforms: Vision, hype, and reality for delivering computing as the 5th utility. *Future Generation Computer Systems.* 25, 6 (Jun. 2009), 599–616.

[3] Buyya, R. et al. 2011. *Cloud Computing: Principles and Paradigms.* John Wiley and Sons.

[4] Che, J. et al. 2011. Study on the Security Models and Strategies of Cloud Computing. *Procedia Engineering.* 23, (2011), 586–593.

[5] Chen, Y. et al. 2010. *What's new about cloud computing security.*

[6] Contrato de Nível de Serviço do Microsoft Azure: 2015. *http://azure.microsoft.com/en-us/support/legal/sla/.*

[7] Grobauer, B. et al. 2011. Understanding Cloud Computing Vulnerabilities. *IEEE Security & Privacy Magazine.* 9, 2 (Mar. 2011), 50–57.

[8] IBM Cloud Services Agreement IBM Cloud Service Description : IBM Bluemix: 2014. *http://www-03.ibm.com/software/sla/sladb.nsf/pdf/6605-01/$file/i126-6605-01_06-2014_en_US.pdf.*

[9] Jensen, M. et al. 2009. On Technical Security Issues in Cloud Computing. *Cloud: 2009 Ieee International Conference on Cloud Computing* (2009), 109–116 ST – On Technical Security Issues in Clou.

[10] Liu, F. et al. 2013. NIST Cloud Computing Security Reference Architecture. *NIST Special ....* 500, 299 (2013), 1–204.

[11] Mirashe, S.P. and Kalyankar, N. V 2010. Cloud Computing. *Communications of the ACM.* 51, 7 (2010), 9.

[12] Mouratidis, H. et al. 2013. A framework to support selection of cloud providers based on security and privacy requirements. *Journal of Systems and Software.* 86, 9 (Sep. 2013), 2276–2293.

[13] Salesforce - Professional Services Agreement: 2013. *http://www.salesforce.com/company/legal/agreements.jsp.*

[14] de Vaulx, F. et al. 2015. Cloud Computing Service Metrics Description. *Nist Special Publication.* 500, 307 (2015), 24.

An Enhanced Visualization Tool for Teaching Monoalphabetic Substitution Cipher Frequency Analysis

Matthew D. Sprengel
California State Polytechnic University, Pomona
3801 West Temple Ave.
Pomona, CA 91768
mdsprengel@cpp.edu

Jason M. Pittman
California State Polytechnic University, Pomona
3801 West Temple Ave.
Pomona, CA 91768
jmpittman@cpp.edu

ABSTRACT

Information Systems curricula require on-going and frequent review [2] [11]. Furthermore, such curricula must be flexible because of the fast-paced, dynamic nature of the workplace. Such flexibility can be maintained through modernizing course content or, inclusively, exchanging hardware or software for newer versions. Alternatively, flexibility can arise from incorporating new information into curricula from other disciplines. One field where the pace of change is extremely high is cybersecurity [3].

Students are left with outdated skills when curricula lag behind the pace of change in industry. For example, cryptography is a required learning objective in the DHS/NSA Center of Academic Excellence (CAE) knowledge criteria [1]. However, the overarching curriculum associated with basic ciphers has gone unchanged for decades. Indeed, a general problem in cybersecurity education is that students lack fundamental knowledge in areas such as ciphers [5]. In response, researchers have developed a variety of interactive classroom visualization tools [5] [8] [9].

Such tools visualize the standard approach to frequency analysis of simple substitution ciphers that includes review of most common, single letters in ciphertext. While fundamental ciphers such as the monoalphabetic substitution cipher have not been updated (these are historical ciphers), collective understanding of how humans interact with language has changed. Updated understanding in both English language pedagogy [10] [12] and automated cryptanalysis of substitution ciphers [4] potentially renders the interactive classroom visualization tools incomplete or outdated.

Classroom visualization tools are powerful teaching aids, particularly for abstract concepts. Existing research has established that such tools promote an active learning environment that translates to not only effective learning conditions but also higher student retention rates [7]. However, visualization tools require extensive planning and design when used to actively engage students with detailed, specific knowledge units such as ciphers [7] [8].

Accordingly, we propose a heatmap-based frequency analysis visualization solution that (a) incorporates digraph and trigraph language processing norms; (b) and enhances the active learning pedagogy inherent in visualization tools. Preliminary results indicate that study participants take approximately 15% longer to learn the heatmap-based frequency analysis technique compared to traditional frequency analysis but demonstrate a 50% increase in efficacy when tasked with solving simple substitution ciphers. Further, a heatmap-based solution contributes positively to the field insofar as educators have an additional tool to use in the classroom. As well, the heatmap visualization tool may allow researchers to comparatively examine efficacy of visualization tools in the cryptanalysis of mono-alphabetic substitution ciphers.

SIGMIS-CPR'16, June 02-04, 2016, Alexandria, VA, USA.
ACM 978-1-4503-42032/16/06.
http://dx.doi.org/10.1145/2890602.2890613

1. REFERENCES

[1] CAE Team (2014). National centers of academic excellent in information assurance/cyber defense (IA/CD) knowledge units. Retrieved from http://bit.ly/1OWjFL5

[2] Davis, G.B., Gorgone J. T., Couger, J. D., Feinstein, D. L., & Longenecker, H.E. (1997). Model curriculum and guidelines for undergraduate degree programs in information systems. Retrieved from http://bit.ly/1GvBRcV

[3] Maybury, M. T. (2015). Toward Principles of Cyberspace Security. In *Cybersecurity Policies and Strategies for Cyberwarfare Prevention*, (1-12). Hershey, PA: Information Science Reference, an imprint of IGI Global.

[4] Mishra, G., & Kaur, S. (2015, January). Cryptanalysis of Transposition Cipher Using Hill Climbing and Simulated Annealing. In *Proceedings of Fourth International Conference on Soft Computing for Problem Solving* (pp. 289-298). Springer India.

[5] Schweitzer, D., & Baird, L. (2006). The design and use of interactive visualization applets for teaching ciphers. In *Proceedings of the 7th IEEE Workshop on Information Assurance, 21*(23). 69-75. doi: 10.1109/IAW.2006.1652079

[6] Schweitzer, D., & Boleng, J. (2009). Designing web labs for teaching security concepts. *Journal of Computing Sciences in Colleges, 25*(2), 39-45

[7] Schweitzer, D. & Brown, W. (2007). Interactive visualization for the active learning classroom. ACM SIGCSE Bulletin, 39(1). 208-212.

[8] Schweitzer D., Baird L., Collins M., Brown W., Sherman M. (2006). GRASP: A visualization tool for teaching security

protocols. In *Proceedings of the 10th Colloquium for Information Systems Security Education.*

[9] Schweitzer D., Collins M., Baird L. A. (2007). Visual Approach to Teaching Formal Access Models in Security. In *Proceedings of the 11th Colloquium for Information Systems Security Education.*

[10] Sim, T.; Janakiraman, R. (2007). Are digraphs good for free-text keystroke dynamics? In *Computer Vision and Pattern Recognition, 2007. CVPR '07. IEEE Conference on, 17*(22). 1-6. doi: 10.1109/CVPR.2007.383393

[11] Tatnall, A. (2000). Innovation and change in the Information Systems curriculum of an Australian University. (Doctoral dissertation, Central Queensland University)

[12] Venezky, R. L. (1967). English orthography: Its graphical structure and its relation to sound. *Reading Research Quarterly*, 75-105. Retrieved from http://www.jstor.org/stable/747031?seq=1#page_scan_tab_c ontents

A Plan to Improve Learning of Requirements Elicitation in an IS Curriculum

Jeremy D. Ezell
James Madison University
Harrisonburg, VA 22853 USA
ezelljd@jmu.edu

Diane Lending
James Madison University
Harrisonburg, VA 22853 USA
lendindc@jmu.edu

S.E. Kruck
James Madison University
Harrisonburg, VA 22853 USA
kruckse@jmu.edu

Thomas W. Dillon
James Madison University
Harrisonburg, VA 22853 USA
dillontw@jmu.edu

Jeffrey L. May
James Madison University
Harrisonburg, VA 22853 USA
mayjl@jmu.edu

ABSTRACT
In this paper, we present our plan to integrate requirements elicitation concepts and learning assessments into an Information System curriculum. Both contemporary research and practitioners have noted deficiencies in the abilities of entry-level IT consultants to effectively evaluate new information system needs in business environments. Thus, the ability to professionally and effectively elicit new IS requirements adds significant value to students seeking an IS degree.

CCS Concepts
• Social and professional topics~Information systems education • Social and professional topics~Systems development • Software and its engineering~Requirements analysis

Keywords
Requirements Elicitation; Systems Development; IS Curriculum

1. PROJECT PLAN
We began a multiyear project to improve our teaching and student learning of requirements elicitation. The methodology for curriculum improvement is based upon Fulcher et al [1]. A baseline assessment of the curriculum is needed prior to curriculum changes and subsequent reassessment to ensure improvement goals are met

To carry out the assessments, we first developed an assessment rubric built upon the vital skills and abilities we identified as necessary for IS professionals. During spring semester 2015, we developed an assessment rubric for requirements elicitation. The rubric was developed and grounded using 1) informative interviews with experts and 2) sample requirements elicitation interviews conducted by students as an assignment.

Based on this rubric, we conducted a baseline evaluation in two sections of a Systems Analysis and Design course. Student groups were given a homework assignment to elicit requirements and develop a prototype. They elicited requirements by interviewing a faculty member who role played a client.

Additional faculty members were then trained and independently evaluated each student group using the assessment rubric.

We then converted each rubric dimension into measurable objectives based on Bloom's taxonomy of learning. Bloom's taxonomy represents the individual's cognitive process on a continuum of increasing cognitive complexity, from remembering to creating [2]. We mapped activities across the current curriculum and found many gaps between needed and actual student exposure to elicitation concepts. Actionable course improvements were developed and measureable objectives for each course were then created by aligning the requirements elicitation rubric with the cognitive domain of Bloom's taxonomy. The faculty members who taught each individual course developed and planned the activities within each course in order to fit the scaffolding.

Our faculty began teaching using the revised activities during the fall 2015 semester. In spring 2016, we will reassess student learning using the rubric developed at the beginning of this project and hope to show significant improvements.

2. IMPLICATIONS
IS curriculums have included instruction of requirements elicitation concepts and noted its importance to students. One implication of our project is the application of aspects of Bloom's taxonomy to this complex skillset in order to move the student from a passing knowledge to a more applicable mastery of requirements elicitation. By developing an assessment rubric grounded in subject-matter expertise and structured according to the progressing cognitive levels as defined by Bloom, our project presents a structured manner for assessing the ability of the IS student to engage in effective requirements elicitation.

3. REFERENCES
[1] Fulcher, K. H., Good, M. R., Coleman, C. M., and Smith, K. L. Dec. 2014. A simple model for learning improvement: Weigh pig, feed pig, weigh pig. (Occasional Paper No. 23). Urbana, Il: University of Illinois and Indiana.

[2] Anderson, L. W. and Krathwohl, D. R. 2001. *A taxonomy for learning, teaching, and assessing: a revision of Bloom's taxonomy of educational objectives.* New York, NY: Longman.

SIGMIS-CPR'16, June 2–4, 2016, Alexandria, VA, USA.
ACM 978-1-4503-4203-2/16/06.
DOI: http://dx.doi.org/10.1145/2890602.2890621

The Dual-sided Effect of Project Failure on IT Professionals

Christoph Pflügler
Technical University Munich
Chair for Information Systems
Boltzmannstrasse 3
85748 Garching / Germany
christoph.pfluegler@in.tum.de

Manuel Wiesche
Technical University Munich
Chair for Information Systems
Boltzmannstrasse 3
85748 Garching / Germany
wiesche@in.tum.de

Helmut Krcmar
Technical University Munich
Chair for Information Systems
Boltzmannstrasse 3
85748 Garching / Germany
krcmar@in.tum.de

ABSTRACT

The effects of project failure on IT professionals have not received much attention in IT research. A failed project evokes negative emotions and therefore could trigger turnover, which has negative influences from the perspective of IT human resource management. However, the failure of IT projects could also have positive influences as professionals might learn from the failed project. This paper focuses on analyzing this dual-sided effect of project failure on IT professionals. We develop hypotheses that will be tested with a large data set from an IT service provider in future research. We expect to contribute to theory by analyzing whether project failure triggers turnover and by analyzing whether IT professionals learn from failed projects and perform better in the future.

Keywords

Project Failure; Learning; Turnover

1. INTRODUCTION

IT projects have a quite high failure rate. According to a report by The Standish Group [42], the rate of unsuccessful projects is higher than 60% and has not significantly decreases over the past decade, although the maturity of the IT market has increased [30; 32]. It is estimated that IT project failures create cost of $3 to $6 billion every year [19; 34].

Most of the literature on IT project failure has concentrated on identifying factors that lead to failure (e.g. Cerpa and Verner [4], Keil [17], Pankratz and Basten [28], Yeo [45]). The focus has mostly been on how to prevent it and therefore project failures have been seen as something negative [10].

Failed projects not only have a financial impact, but also have negative effects on the project members. They create negative emotions, which could be a shock event that triggers turnover based on the unfolding model of voluntary turnover [20; 36]. This relationship has not yet been analyzed. Turnover is problematic for IT organizations, as it is difficult to find a replacement due to the high demand for skilled IT professionals [39; 43]. Additionally, turnover creates high costs [5; 40; 41].

However, IT research has not yet focused on the possibility that project members might learn from failed projects and leverage these learnings in future projects. Learning on the organizational level has been considered by Ewusi-Mensah and Przasnyski [8], but they did not focus on individual project members. However, there are studies in management literature that focused on learning from failure on the individual level [35-38].

As it can be seen, project failure has a dual-sided effect on IT professionals from the perspective of IT human resource management. On the one hand, it could lead to turnover of IT professionals, which has negative effects, but on the other hand, professionals might learn from the failed project. This has not yet been analyzed in IT literature. Therefore, we pose the following research question:

What is the relationship between project failure and turnover as well as learning from failure on the individual level?

We plan to answer this question with a unique data set from an IT service provider, called ALPHA. They granted us access to data from its internal project controlling and human resource management systems. We gained extensive data on all 36,413 projects conducted by ALPHA between January 1995 and April 2014 and on all 8,180 IT professionals that worked for ALPHA during that time period.

The remaining sections of the paper are structured as follows. First, we present background information on learning from failed projects as well as on turnover of IT professionals. This is followed by the development of the hypotheses that will be analyzed in future research. We then outline our dataset in detail und present the planned analysis approach. Finally, the expected contributions are discussed and the paper ends with a conclusion.

SIGMIS-CPR '16, June 02 - 04, 2016, Alexandria, VA, USA
Copyright is held by the owner/author(s). Publication rights licensed to ACM.
ACM 978-1-4503-4203-2/16/06...$15.00.
DOI: http://dx.doi.org/10.1145/2890602.2890610

2. THEORETICAL BACKGROUND

2.1 Learning from Failure

Project failure can be divided into project management failure, where the project fails to meet cost, time or quality, and into product failure, where the outcome of the project fails to meet the expectations [3; 28; 42]. As previously mentioned, quite a significant share of IT projects fail which creates high costs [19; 34; 42].

Most of the literature on IT project failure has concentrated on identifying factors that lead to failure (e.g. Cerpa and Verner [4], Keil [17], Pankratz and Basten [28], Yeo [45]). This focus on hindering project failure creates a negative view. However, a failure might not always be a total loss and offers the opportunity to learn from it [8; 10].

For instance, Ewusi-Mensah and Przasnyski [8] argue that organizations should keep record of their failed projects and try to understand what went wrong. According to Grainger, McKay and Marshall [10], project failures should be considered in a broader context, as the learning from a failure could be the reason for a subsequent successful project. However, the mentioned studies focus on the organizational level and did not consider the learning from project failure on the individual level.

Learning from failure on an individual level has been analyzed in management literature [35-38]. It has been found that failure evokes negative emotions, but depending on how individuals cope with these emotions leads to learning [35-38]. Members of the failed project start thinking about different actions that could have been taken and their influence on the project [38]. By doing so they develop capabilities and knowledge about how to react in similar situations in future projects [7; 38].

2.2 Turnover of IT professionals – The Unfolding Model of Voluntary Turnover

Turnover is defined as "voluntarily leaving an IT job for an alternative IT job with a different employer" [15]. Turnover is problematic for IT organizations, as it is difficult to find a replacement due to the high demand in the IT labor market [39; 43]. Additionally, turnover creates high costs through recruiting and training, but also through the disruption of organizational processes [5; 40; 41]. There are several studies that estimate these costs to be between 90% and 700% of the annual salary of an IT professional [1; 18].

The unfolding model of voluntary turnover after Lee and Mitchell [20] is a theory that has gotten more popular in recent turnover research [2]. It focuses on the decision process of turnover and argues that a shock event often acts as a trigger. Shock events can either be (1) positive or negative, (2) expected or unexpected and (3) originate on the organizational or personal level [21]. Several decision paths that can be taken by IT professionals have been proposed by Lee and Mitchell [20].

This kind of turnover theory has been mentioned by several IT as well as general turnover related literature reviews as a possible area for future research [2; 13; 16]. According to Joseph, Ng, Koh and Ang [16] IT turnover research should focus on understanding events that trigger turnover.

Recent IT turnover literature has employed and contributed to the unfolding model of voluntary turnover. Niederman et al. [27] have found additional decision paths that are especially relevant to the IT domain. Mourmant and Gallivan [23] focused on the influence of personality on taking different decision paths. There are a few studies that employed the unfolding model of voluntary turnover to analyze the turnover of IT professionals that have the aim of founding an own company [24-26].

3. HYPOTHESES

The aim of this article is to examine the dual-sided effect of project failure on IT professionals.

A project failure could be a shock event after the unfolding model of voluntary turnover of Lee and Mitchell [20]. It has been shown that project failures evoke negative emotions, such as frustration, disappointment, depression, anger or doubts about one's work [35-38]. These emotions should be strong enough to trigger the decision processes of turnover. Employing the categorization of Lee and Mitchell [20], a project failure is a shock that is (1) seen negatively by the individual, (2) mostly unexpected, as individuals normally do not expect the failure at project start, and (3) originates on the organizational level. Therefore we formulate the following hypothesis:

H1: Project failure increases the probability of turnover among the members of the team that worked on the project.

A project failure enables members of the project to learn from the failure to improve their knowledge for future projects [8; 35-38]. It has even been claimed that the possibility to learn from failure is higher than from success [29; 31]. The reason for this is that a success does not attract enough attention to think about the causes for this positive outcome [7]. Project members of a failed project can leverage their gained knowledge and tend to conduct on average more successful projects regarding budget, time and quality in the future [38]. Therefore, the following second hypothesis is formulated:

H2: Team members that have experienced a project failure conduct more successful projects in the future.

4. METHOD

4.1 Data Sample

In order to examine these hypotheses, we extracted data from the internal project controlling and human resource management systems of a large German IT service provider, which is called ALPHA due to non-disclosure reasons. Directly accessing quantitative data from internal systems is not subject to recall bias, which could be a problem in case studies and surveys [9; 14]. ALPHA granted us access to all 36,413 projects conducted between January 1995 and April 2014. Additionally, we collected information on all of its 8,180 IT professionals that worked during that time period for ALPHA.

We collected information about each project such as the project profitability, the contract type, the team size, the number of interactions with a client as well as within an industry, the business climate based on a recognized index, the project start, the project size, the industry of the client and the project duration. To link each IT professional to the projects, we extracted the information which professional worked how many hours for which project on which day. Detailed Information about the yearly performance review, the planned and attended trainings, the home base, the educational background, the organizational unit, the job level, the recruitment date and the turnover date of the IT professionals have as well been collected.

4.2 Measures and Planned Data Analysis

For analyzing the described hypotheses, we created subsets of the previously described overall dataset. The measures of these subsets are described in table 1 and 2. We plan to analyze the hypotheses H1 and H2 with the two described subsets. As turnover is a dichotomous variable, H1 will be analyzed with a logistic regression model. H2 will be analyzed with an ordinary least squared regression model.

Table 1. Measures for analyzing H1

Dependent variable	• **Turnover**: This information has been directly extracted from the human resource management systems and therefore allows the analysis of actually occurred turnover, which is an under-researched area [16; 22].
Independent variables	• **Project failure experienced**: Projects with a high negative profitability and a certain amount of loss are used as a proxy for this measure, because they can be seen as a failure for ALPHA. This measure captures whether team members have experienced a project failure in the past. • **Control variables**: Several factors that have been found to influence turnover are employed as control variables, such as age, gender, organizational tenure, training and educational background [16; 22].

Table 2. Measures for analyzing H2

Dependent variable	• **Project profitability**: This measure has been extracted from the project controlling systems of ALPHA.
Independent variables	• **Project failure experienced**: Projects with a high negative profitability and a certain amount of loss are used as a proxy for this measure, because they can be seen as a failure for ALPHA. This measure captures whether team members have experienced a project failure in the past. • **Control variables**: Research on ITO vendor profitability has revealed several factors that have an influence on profitability, such as project size, duration, team size, client knowledge, industry knowledge [12; 33]

5. EXPECTED CONTRIBUTION

We expect to contribute to theory and practice in various ways. According to Joseph, Ng, Koh and Ang [16] the unfolding model of voluntary turnover and the identification of shock events has not yet received much attention in IT turnover literature. In recent years, it has gotten more popular and has been employed by several studies [23-27], but they did not focus on project failure as a possible shock event.

An expected practical contribution is that project failure could trigger turnover and that IT managers should intervene to prevent the turnover of key IT professionals. It has been shown, that retention actions should be taken rather quickly, because professionals that experienced a shock tend to leave faster than professionals with a low satisfaction [21].

Another theoretical contribution will be the understanding of project failure as a learning opportunity for IT professionals. This has not received much attention in IT literature. We expect to shed light into the relationship between project failure and learning from this failure of IT professionals.

IT professionals should be carefully selected for risky projects. Professionals that already have a low organizational commitment and high levels of stress could be indirectly forced into turnover. Additionally, learning from failure should not always be experienced by the same people, because otherwise they do not have the opportunity to exploit their learnings in less riskier projects.

After analyzing the described hypotheses, future research could analyze the underlying relationships in more detail. This could be done with explorative qualitative studies. An interesting research topic could be to analyze how employees could learn from project failures without having to be a member of the failed project. Additionally, the personality of the IT professionals could be taken into account, which has been found to significantly influence job outcomes [6; 11; 44]. Shepherd, Haynie and Patzelt [36] suggest that employees differently cope with failures.

6. CONCLUSION

Project failure has mostly been considered as a negative event in IT literature. We extend this view and argue that failure could have a dual-sided effect. It should increase the probability of turnover among the members of the project, but on the other hand the project members have the opportunity to learn from the failure and increase their contribution to the performance of future projects. We expect to shed light into these relationships through the outlined future research.

7. REFERENCES

[1] Allen, D.G., Bryant, P.C., and Vardaman, J.M. 2010. Retaining Talent: Replacing Misconceptions with Evidence-Based Strategies. *The Academy of Management Perspectives* 24, 2, p. 48-64.

[2] Allen, D.G., Hancock, J.I., Vardaman, J.M., and McKee, D.l.N. 2014. Analytical mindsets in turnover research. *Journal of Organizational Behavior* 35, S1, p. 61-86.

[3] Baccarini, D. 1999. The Logical Framework Method for Defining Project Success. *Project management journal* 30, 4, p. 25-32.

[4] Cerpa, N. and Verner, J.M. 2009. Why did your project fail? *Communications of the ACM* 52, 12, p. 130-134.

[5] Chang, C.L.-H. 2010. The study of the turnover of MIS professionals - The gap between Taiwanese and US societies. *International Journal of Information Management* 30, 4, p. 301-314.

[6] Clark, J.G., Walz, D.B., and Wynekoop, J.L. 2003. Identifying exceptional application software developers: A comparison of students and professionals. *Communications of the Association for Information Systems* 11, 1, p. 137-155.

[7] Eisenhardt, K.M. and Martin, J.A. 2000. Dynamic capabilities: what are they? *Strategic management journal* 21, 10-11, p. 1105-1121.

[8] Ewusi-Mensah, K. and Przasnyski, Z.H. 1995. Learning from abandoned information systems development projects. *Journal of Information Technology* 10, 1, p. 3-14.

[9] Gefen, D., Wyss, S., and Lichtenstein, Y. 2008. Business Familiarity as Risk Mitigation in Software Developmen Outsourcing Contracts. *Management Information Systems Quarterly* 32, 3, p. 531-551.

[10] Grainger, N., McKay, J., and Marshall, P. 2009. Learning from a Strategic Failure. In *Proceedings of the Twentieth Australasian Conference on Information Systems* (Melbourne, Australia).

[11] Hall, D.J., Cegielski, C.G., and Wade, J.N. 2006. Theoretical Value Belief, Cognitive Ability, and Personality as Predictors of Student Performance in Object-Oriented Programming Environments. *Decision Sciences Journal of Innovative Education* 4, 2, p. 237-257.

[12] Hoermann, S., Hlavka, T., Schermann, M., and Krcmar, H. 2014. Determinants of vendor profitability in two contractual regimes: An empirical analysis of enterprise resource planning projects. *Journal of Information Technology* advance online publication, p.

[13] Holtom, B.C., Mitchell, T.R., Lee, T.W., and Eberly, M.B. 2008. Turnover and Retention Research: A Glance at the Past, a Closer Review of the Present, and a Venture into the Future. *The Academy of Management Annals* 2, 1, p. 231-274.

[14] Josefek, R.A. and Kauffman, R.J. 2003. Nearing the threshold: An economics approach to pressure on information systems professionals to separate from their employer. *Journal of Management Information Systems* 20, 1, p. 87-122.

[15] Joseph, D., Ang, S., and Slaughter, S.A. 2015. Turnover or Turnaway? Competing Risks Analysis of Male and Female IT Professionals' Job Mobility and Relative Pay Gap. *Information Systems Research* 26, 1, p. 145-164.

[16] Joseph, D., Ng, K.-Y., Koh, C., and Ang, S. 2007. Turnover of information technology professionals: a narrative review, meta-analytic structural equation modeling, and model development. *Management Information Systems Quarterly* 31, 3, p. 547-577.

[17] Keil, M. 1995. Pulling the plug: Software project management and the problem of project escalation. *Management Information Systems Quarterly*, p. 421-447.

[18] Kochanski, J. and Ledford, G. 2001. "How To Keep Me" - Retaining Technical Professionals. *Research Technology Management* 44, 3, p. 31-38.

[19] Krigsman, M. 2012. Worldwide cost of IT failure (revisited): $3 trillion Retrieved 20.01.2016, from http://www.zdnet.com/article/worldwide-cost-of-it-failure-revisited-3-trillion/

[20] Lee, T.W. and Mitchell, T.R. 1994. An alternative approach: The unfolding model of voluntary employee turnover. *Academy of Management Review* 19, 1, p. 51-89.

[21] Lee, T.W., Mitchell, T.R., Holtom, B.C., McDaneil, L.S., and Hill, J.W. 1999. The unfolding model of voluntary turnover: A replication and extension. *Academy of Management Journal* 42, 4, p. 450-462.

[22] Lo, J. 2015. The information technology workforce: A review and assessment of voluntary turnover research. *Information Systems Frontiers* 17, 2, p. 387-411.

[23] Mourmant, G. and Gallivan, M. 2007. How personality type influences decision paths in the unfolding model of voluntary job turnover: an application to IS professionals. In *Proceedings of the 45th Annual Conference on Computers and People Research*, ACM, 134-143.

[24] Mourmant, G., Gallivan, M.J., and Kalika, M. 2009. Another road to IT turnover: the entrepreneurial path. *European Journal of Information Systems* 18, 5, p. 498-521.

[25] Mourmant, G. and Voutsina, K. 2010. From IT Employee to IT Entrepreneur: the Concept of IT Entrepreneurial epiphany. In *Proceedings of the Thirty First International Conference on Information Systems* (St. Louis, Missouri).

[26] Mourmant, G. and Voutsina, K. 2012. What should I understand?: The concept of shift of understanding, a quote-based analysis. In *Proceedings of the 50th Annual Conference on Computers and People Research*, ACM, 49-60.

[27] Niederman, F., Sumner, M., Maertz, J., and Carl, P. 2007. Testing and extending the unfolding model of voluntary turnover to IT professionals. *Human Resource Management* 46, 3, p. 331-347.

[28] Pankratz, O. and Basten, D. 2013. Eliminating Failure by Learning from It–Systematic Review of IS Project failure. In *Proceedings of the Thirty Fourth International Conference on Information Systems* (Milan, Italy).

[29] Petroski, H. 1985. *To Engineer Is Human: The Role of Failure in Successful Design*. St. Martin's Press, New York.

[30] Pflügler, C., Wiesche, M., and Krcmar, H. 2015. Are we already in a mature ITO market? A longitudinal study on the effects of market maturity on ITO vendor project performance. In *Proceedings of the Thirty Sixth International Conference on Information Systems* (Fort Worth, Texas).

[31] Popper, K.R. 1959. *The logic of scientific discovery*. Hutchinson, London.

[32] Schermann, M., Dongus, K., Yetton, P., and Krcmar, H. 2016. The role of Transaction Cost Economics in Information Technology Outsourcing research: A meta-analysis of the choice of contract type. *The Journal of Strategic Information Systems* (In Press, Corrected Proof), p.

[33] Schermann, M., Lang, M., Hörmann, S., Swanson, E.B., and Krcmar, H. 2014. When Does Learning Pay Off? The Relationship of Organizational Learning and ITO Vendor Profitability. In *Proceedings of the Thirty Fifth International Conference on Information Systems* (Auckland, New Zealand).

[34] Sessions, R. 2009. *The IT complexity crisis: Danger and opportunity*. ObjectWatch.

[35] Shepherd, D.A. and Cardon, M.S. 2009. Negative emotional reactions to project failure and the self-compassion to learn from the experience. *Journal of Management Studies* 46, 6, p. 923-949.

[36] Shepherd, D.A., Haynie, J.M., and Patzelt, H. 2013. Project failures arising from corporate entrepreneurship: Impact of multiple project failures on employees' accumulated emotions, learning, and motivation. *Journal of Product Innovation Management* 30, 5, p. 880-895.

[37] Shepherd, D.A., Patzelt, H., Williams, T.A., and Warnecke, D. 2014. How does project termination impact project team members? Rapid termination,'Creeping death', and Learning from failure. *Journal of Management Studies* 51, 4, p. 513-546.

[38] Shepherd, D.A., Patzelt, H., and Wolfe, M. 2011. Moving forward from project failure: Negative emotions, affective commitment, and learning from the experience. *Academy of Management Journal* 54, 6, p. 1229-1259.

[39] Streim, A. and Pfisterer, S. 2014. In Deutschland fehlen 41.000 IT-Experten Retrieved 01.09.2015, from https://www.bitkom.org/Presse/Presseinformation/Pressemitt eilung_1704.html

[40] Sumner, M. and Niederman, F. 2003. The Impact of Gender Differences on Job Satisfaction, Job Turnover, and Career Experiences of Information Systems Professionals. *Journal of Computer Information Systems* 44, 2, p.

[41] Thatcher, J.B., Stepina, L.P., and Boyle, R.J. 2002. Turnover of information technology workers: Examining empirically the influence of attitudes, job characteristics, and external markets. *Journal of Management Information Systems* 19, 3, p. 231-261.

[42] The Standish Group. 2013. *Chaos Manifesto 2013 - Think Big, Act Small*.

[43] Thibodeau, P. 2012. IT jobs will grow 22% through 2020, sas U.S. Retrieved 01.09.2015, from http://www.computerworld.com/article/2502348/it-management/it-jobs-will-grow-22--through-2020--says-u-s-.html

[44] Wiesche, M. and Krcmar, H. 2014. The relationship of personality models and development tasks in software engineering. In *Proceedings of the 52nd Annual Conference on Computers and People Research* (Singapore, Singapore), ACM, 149-161.

[45] Yeo, K.T. 2002. Critical failure factors in information system projects. *International Journal of Project Management* 20, 3, p. 241-246.

Big Data and Analytics Leaders: the Changing Role of CIO

Vincenzo Morabito
Management & Technology
Department
Università Commerciale Luigi
Bocconi
Via Roentgen, 20136 Milano, Italy.
vincenzo.morabito@unibocconi.it

Gianluigi Viscusi
CDM-MTEI-CSI
École Polytechnique Fédérale de
Lausanne (EPFL)
ODY 1 16 (Odyssea)
Station 5-1015 Lausanne,
Switzerland.
gianluigi.viscusi@epfl.ch

Marinos Themistocleus
Department of Digital Systems
University of Piraeus
150 Androutsou Street, 18532,
Piraeus, Greece.
mthemist@unipi.gr

ABSTRACT

This article investigates the changing role of the Chief Information Officer (CIO) at organizational level with regard to the rise of Big Data and Big Data analytics as a potential source of innovation and competitive advantage. The paper aims to provide a theoretical contribution to the research stream on the topic, by further exploring the emergent properties and understandings related to the role of CIO. As a consequence of the need to adopt advanced technologies, the CIO has been named to master the current unheard information growth for business innovation. To this end we present the results of a qualitative research based on grounded theory carried out on data concerning CIOs of medium and large companies from different industries in the Italian market. Finally, a substantive theory and categories are discussed, showing the role of generation gap and power of new entrants as well as of project and execution excellence on the making of identity and recognition of the CIO as relevant at the time of Big Data analytics.

Keywords
Big Data; Analytics; CIO; Grounded theory

1. INTRODUCTION

The increasing relevance of Big Data and its impact on firms, individuals and governments is fueling a growing number of streams of research in the analytics field as well as in management of information systems [10, 15, 21, 25, 29]. From the point of view of the economic system, there is a clear and relevant growth of investments, both from the public and the private side.

As an example, the European Commission and the Big Data Value Association - a non-profit, industry-led organization comprising Universities, Research Centers, and Companies – have recently agreed upon a public-private partnership (PPP) aiming to raise €2.5 billion over five years in Big Data investments [13]. The objective is to focus and sustain public, private and academic research efforts on Big Data innovations in fields such as energy, health, production processes, leveraging and concentrating

SIGMIS-CPR '16, June 02-04, 2016, Alexandria, VA, USA.
© 2016 ACM. ISBN 978-1-4503-4203-2/16/06...$15.00
DOI: http://dx.doi.org/10.1145/2890602.2890619

Horizon 2020 support on common priorities in order to strengthen the European Big Data community. The envisioned benefits deriving from the Big Data transformation include 100,000 new data-related jobs in Europe by 2020, 10% lower energy consumption, better healthcare outcomes and increased productivity in industrial machinery. When Chief Information Officers (CIOs) talk about Big Data and analytics the diverse backgrounds, industrial contexts and business strategies seem to result in fragmented opinions and diverging points of view, ranging from an incremental innovation approach to a perceived era of disruption and transformation, with different levels of focus on investment significance, technological issues and emerging value streams. Notwithstanding the interest by practitioners for the role and actions of the CIO for Big Data and Big Data analytics [2, 5, 8], academic research on their impact on the changing role of the CIO [28] are still dependent on more general issues such as, e.g., sources of power and influence [20, 23], the perception of its value by the top management and relationship with other executives [24] or the of the contribution of the IT function in organizations [19]. Thus, in this article we aim to provide a theoretical contribution to this research stream by further explore the emergent properties and understandings related to the impact of Big Data and Big Data analytics on the role of the CIO. To this end, we present the results of a qualitative research based on grounded theory carried out on data concerning CIOs of medium and large companies from different industries in the Italian market.

The paper is structured as follows. We first analyze the literature background, further motivating the research focus of this study. Then the research method is presented, followed by the results of the coding activities as a more specific discussion of the results of the analysis. The final part of the paper presents the conclusions of this study and defines the needs for further research on the topic.

2. BACKGROUND AND MOTIVATIONS

The article by Applegate and Elam [3] on the changing role of CIO, which was published by MISQ in 1992, has formed one of the main motivations for this work, being the CIO a central subject and reference at practitioner level for the research on information systems strategy [26]. Back in late 80s and early 90s there were big changes and challenges in the business, technological and political environment including the Internet revolution and on-line businesses, the massive use of computers at global level, the automation and integration of business processes and the digitalization. As a result, all these challenges had an impact and reshaped the role of CIOs, e.g. CIOs have become more powerful figures [3]. The last few years we have experienced another wave of transformation of the business, social, national and international environment mainly due to the mass production of data. According to Baesens et al. [4] the advanced technologies that have been used the recent years have led to the production of the 90% of the data in world. This indicates a radical change and a big challenge for CIOs which will lead to a big impact [10]. Given that the Internet revolution and the digitalization empowered the role of CIOs in organizations, it will be really interesting to investigate and understand the changing role of CIOs in the Big Data and analytics era. Yet, besides technical or practitioners oriented publications and contributions from fields like computer science and engineering, our interest was in understanding how the topic have been discussed and investigated by the information systems scholars.

Thus, for the purpose of this research we conducted an extensive literature review based on established review methodologies like, for example, those proposed by [11] and [6]. Based on these methodologies we reviewed the literature and we search on books, journals, conference proceedings and working papers, that were published during the last six years, using libraries and database search engines like AISel, IEEE Xplore, Science Direct, ProQuest and Google Scholar. The search was carried out from 15th June to 15th September 2014 first on all the aforementioned sources, yet with a specific attention devoted to the AIS Basket of eight Journals which includes European Journal of Information Systems (EJIS), Information Systems Journal (ISJ), Information Systems Research (ISR), Journal of Information Technology (JIT), Journal of Management Information Systems (JMIS), Journal of Strategic Information Systems (JSIS), Journal of the Association for Information Systems (JAIS), and MIS Quarterly (MISQ).

The period considered is from 1st January 2008 to 1st September 2014. While according to Forbes contributor Gil Press [1] the first use of the terms 'Big Data' in a magazine as the Communications of the ACM date the August 1999, we have chosen to start the literature review the same year of the article by Chris Anderson, The End of Theory: The Data Deluge Makes the Scientific Method Obsolete [32], at the crossroads of what would have been considered the key questions and challenges of Big Data and analytics in the subsequent years. As for the keywords, due to the specific interest on the relationship between the topics of CIO, Big Data and analytics from a managerial rather than technical perspective we have used the following preliminary set: CIO, Big Data, CIO AND Big Data, CIO AND Big Data AND Analytics. Furthermore, keywords as "Analytics" alone and "Business Intelligence" have been discarded because, however producing high numbers of papers, they resulted from a preliminary analysis too domain specific, IT artifact related, and not focused on IT unit or CIO role issues.

It is worth noting that the papers resulting from the query "CIO AND Big Data AND Analytics" are actually a subset of the "CIO AND Big Data" query. Thus, the sample of cited papers considered is 303 (262 from the AISEL library, including four of the AIS basket of eight journals, and 37 from a subset of the AIS basket, including only six journals). Besides keywords, a specific attention has been provided to the articles citing the seminal contribution by Applegate and Elam [3] (forward searches). The analysis of the selected 303 papers shows that the vast majority of the articles considered mainly focus on Big Data and in few cases on Big Data and Analytics. In addition to this, the literature review on the aforementioned set of the 303 articles depicts that the term 'CIO' was reported mainly in the keywords and introduction, thus not really considering it a core subject neither for dedicated empirical research nor for developing substantive or mid-range theories. This led us to the conclusion that the topic (CIO, Big Data and Analytics) and its implications is still unexplored and has yet to be assessed, providing scope for timely and novel research.

3. RESEARCH METHOD

In this article we investigate the changing role of CIO at organizational level with regard to the rise of Big Data using a grounded theory approach [9, 18, 33] that allows collecting empirical data and analyzing them in order to come up with the proposition of a new theory [27]. In particular, the audio documents, transcripts, and memos from the workshops and the interviews have been analyzed following the three steps of grounded theory as in the Barney Glaser perspective, that are open, selective, and theoretical coding [17, 33]. Yet, the study aims to produce a substantive theory for the specific domain, which may allow an understanding of the impact Big Data and Analytics on the role of CIO, also by the meaning provided to them by the executives involved in transformation initiatives [34].

Thus, while the Glaser perspective provides a rigorous approach to the data analysis, abduction allows pursuing the most plausible explanation [9]. Consequently, the approach to grounded theory followed in this article is worth to be positioned in a pragmatist stance towards reality and theoretical sensitivity, acknowledging knowledge exists in the form of coping mechanisms, not once-and-for-all-time truths [7], rather in the difference between positivist and interpretivist perspectives. As for this issue, it is worth noting that the literature review discussed in the previous section, on the one hand, made worth pursuing the development of a substantive theory on the becoming of the CIO facing Big Data and Analytics initiatives; on the other hand, it has contributed to generate the sensitivity further increased in the data collection phase. Actually, the literature review has provided a general perspective on the substantive area for the initial decisions in theoretical sampling for the subsequent "back and forth" between data and concepts [17].

Finally, in order to avoid the forcing of data in preconceived concepts, the knowledge obtained through the literature review has been considered as data worth analyzing in the theory generation process.

3.1 Data collection

From March 2012 to July 2014, senior IS executives from large corporations headquartered in Italy have been involved in ten workshops made up of thirty (30) participants each [22]. The workshops, organized under the umbrella of a research program on the digitalization of business (Table 1 shows the demographics for the participants to the program), have been held as focus groups moderated by two of the authors, while the other authors assisted as participants.

The workshops, all held in English, have been focused on topics such as Big Data, Big Data and analytics, the impact of these trends on the role of the CIO, the organization of IT unit, and the overall changes on IT governance. The workshops structure encompasses a first introduction to the topic by an expert, both from academia or consultancy.

Table 1. Companies per industry with revenues and average number of employees

Industry	Number of Companies	Revenue (in millions €)		Employees	
		Average	Range	Average	Range
Financial Services	32	118640	62,3 - 849000	16094	110 - 166000
Constructions	1	-	-	12000	12000
Consumer Products	5	2133	1100 - 4000	50875	3500 - 172000
Health Services/Pharmaceuticals	2	1073	745 - 1400	77250	55000 - 99500
ICT	5	566	12 - 987	8710	50 - 27000
Utilities	8	18208	270 - 80535	31638	697 - 145000
Petroleum, Chemicals and Plastics	3	43607	3821 - 115000	43050	7149 - 78000
Manufacturing	5	27218	5800 - 87000	72313	1250 - 215000
Transportation/Aerospace	4	7400	2000 - 17300	33067	5200 - 75000
Media/Entertainment/Recreation	2	1680	385 - 2974	4678	1855 - 7500
Fashion/Luxury	2	3965	730 - 7300	37800	2200 - 73400
Telecommunications	4	9885	2392 - 23407	23567	2707 - 76560
Tourism	1	50	50	400	400
Total	**74**				

Table 1 shows the number of companies represented by the executives participating at the workshops in nearly two years. Financial services, including banking and insurance, where the main industry represented followed by utilities and manufacturing.

Table 2. IS Budget for the companies considered for the intensive interviews

Industry	# Companies	IS Budget (in millions)		
		<50 €	50-199 €	>200 €
Financial Services	3	1	2	0
Health Services/Pharmaceuticals	1	1	0	0
Utilities	1	1	0	0
ICT	1	1	0	0
Petroleum, Chemicals and Plastics	2	0	1	1
Manufacturing	2	1	0	1
Transportation/Aerospace	1	1	0	0
Fashion/Luxury	2	1	0	1
Telecommunications	1	0	1	0
Total	**14**	**7**	**4**	**3**

The companies, having different IS budget, were not only medium and large local organizations, but also representatives or branch of corporations active at European as well as global level. Along the workshops, on the basis of theoretical sampling interviews have been carried out on CIOs and IS executives of companies pertaining to a subset of industries from the ones participating to the workshops (Table 2).

As shown in Table 3 (which aims to replicate what shown by [3]), also in this case financial services is the main industry considered and the executives provenance is nearly equally distributed, being 40 executives internally hired with regard to the 34 coming from outside the company. It is worth noting that the background of the IS executives of the companies considered for the informational interviews see a prevalence of them having an IS background (32 executives), that is routed in discipline such as management of information systems, engineering or computer science, against 22 executives with a business background, that is routed in economics, management or accounting, and 20 having a hybrid background for education or experience. Among the population of 74 interviewees, on the basis of theoretical sampling 18 informants have been then selected for intensive interviews for the analysis presented in what follows, being also participants to the workshops. The interviews conducted in the October-December 2014 period were mainly open-ended or made up of a limited number of questions (max 5) in order to obtain reach material, avoiding the imposition of preconceived concept on it at the data collection step of the research activity [9].

Table 3. Background and provenance of the IS executives of the companies considered for the intensive interviews

Industry / Background	Internal Hire			External Hire			
	IS	Business	Hybrid	IS	Business	Hybrid	Total
Financial Services	8	6	4	5	7	5	**35**
Health Services/Pharmaceuticals	1	1	0	0	0	0	**2**
ICT	0	0	1	0	0	1	**2**
Utilities	0	2	2	1	3	1	**9**
Petroleum, Chemicals and Plastics	1	1	0	2	1	0	**5**
Manufacturing	5	0	0	1	0	0	**6**
Transportation/Aerospace	1	0	0	0	0	1	**2**
Telecommunications	3	1	3	2	0	1	**10**
Fashion/Luxury	0	0	0	2	0	1	**3**
Total	**19**	**11**	**10**	**13**	**11**	**10**	**74**

4. RESULTS

In what follows the results of the research are discussed for each of the grounded theory coding activities mentioned in previous section, that are *open coding*, *selective coding*, and *theoretical coding*. Finally, a substantive theory is discussed, emerging from the data analysis and the interpretation by the authors. The theory pertains to the phenomenon [33], that in our case is the changing role of CIO with regards to Big Data and analytics.

4.1 Open and selective coding

The open coding activities have been carried out bottom-up, line by line, and at sentence level. The initial coding by one of the authors resulted in 78 codes. Another author has carried out a second round of coding, leading to a set of 60 codes. Then, a common session of analysis followed, leading to the identification of 54 open codes to be worth used in the selecting coding activity. Table 4 shows a set of considered codes with related excerpt from the transcript.

At this stage there are yet topics and discourses emerging as related to the rise of Big Data and analytics that are worth to be commented. The first issue is the connection, by some of the informants, of the phenomenon and its potential impact as innovation to a generalization of the problem of the IT evolution and professionalism to a generation gap, where the lack of critical thinking in the new breed of IT staff as well as the orientation towards reuse of available solutions and *bricolage* are seen by the informants as a limit (see the code *Uncritical and ready-made oriented youth* in Table 4). Whereas, it is worth noting that these characteristics are actually considered at the state of the art as typical of the new tech entrepreneurs and startups, designing applications services exploiting and making accessible the data deluge connected to the hype on Big Data and analytics [30, 31]. However, another codes allows to see another discourse related to the generation gap:

"in Italy there is a generational change which tends to zero... It is clear that from this point of view to take up the challenge of innovation and make structural changes is extremely complicated" (Code – Generational change problem).

Table 4. Open codes example and related excerpt from the transcripts

Excerpt from the transcripts	Open code
the IT one is a world which is struggling to keep pace with innovation not so much in technology but in the mindset... I see young people who think they get everything ready, do not have the mindset to question and to think in an innovative way.	Uncritical and ready-made oriented youth
What we are seeing is that in reality marketing and IT are really getting closer and closer in terms of realization... this is the real trend that we are seeing.	Marketing and IT convergence
When we talk about innovation, we begin to say "innovation is the mobile", " innovation is the internet banking", but is this innovation? This is a channel, this is not innovation	Confusion between channel and innovation
And about Europe because I think the culture is different. For instance, in Italy the penetration of iPhone is quite high, but it Is only used to discuss and talk. A population of certain age uses it...	Culture
Now analytics is industrialized, but when will it finish? It already happened with dot com bubble. What is the percentage of analytics that was industrialized.	Same old story
if the CIO has two levels above him, this is a problem, so innovation must begin, I think, first of all in the composition of the Board.	Distance from the CEO

Furthermore, other codes show the emphasis by some interviewees on the potential risk of exchanging innovation means with the ends (see, e.g., the code *Confusion between channel and innovation* in Table 4) or the fear of another potential "bubble" related to the ecosystems of technology innovation emerging with Big Data and analytics (see, e.g., the code *Same old story* in Table 4). Besides these issues, another stream of discourse emerging from the coding activity is related to the relevance of the context where the innovation takes place (*In Italy it is forbidden to geolocalize employees.* Code - Contextual and institutional factors) and the actions should be developed (see, e.g., again the code *Culture* in Table 4). This issue is also related to the characteristics of the managerial culture as in what follows:

"Globalization is good if you can leverage on the scale, but if you are an Italian company that's not directly linked to computers. We have to find the right way for digital transformation." (Code - *Globalization and local context*) "...but if when I have to design my service instead of asking the supplier and consultant I ask the user, yet this is a paradigm shift" (Code - *Ask the customer not the consultant*).

Finally, are worth mentioning the discourses about the relationship with other units and executives interested in Big Data and analytics (see the code *Marketing and IT convergence* in Table 4) as well as the position of the CIO with regard to the CEO (see the code *Distance from the CEO* in Table 4).

Once completed the open coding activities, the subsequent clustering and grouping tasks for selective codes resulted in the set shown in Table 5. Considering for example *Abstraction of technology from reality*, this code is one of the available open codes (*"we are in a market where is clear, in technology, ...where nobody is making a relationship with reality anymore"*), which, however, allows to include different facets of abstraction related to the phenomenon of Big Data and analytics. For example, it allows to describe the above mentioned claimed characteristics of the generation gap (see the code *Uncritical and ready-made oriented youth* in Table 5), in terms of level of abstraction - in this case a narrow IT specialization and focus on artifacts (software rather than hardware). The latter presents an homology with the argued confusion between means and ends of technology innovation, focusing once again, for example, on the intelligence or the storage artifacts than on the use for it (see, e.g., the code *Confusion between channel and innovation* in Table 5). Finally, the *Abstraction of technology from reality* encompasses another dimensions emerging from open coding, which refers to *Unmeasured markets* (see the open code in Table 5):

"There is this industry where analytics are completely hidden... The objective here is not to create a business, but to create a company, place it on the stock, find somebody who buys it."

Here the abstraction is related to the views available on some financial markets, products, and operations, that can be challenged by the adoption of Big Data analytics, for example, providing access to information at different level of granularity or improving with a consequent increase in transparency.

4.2 Theoretical coding

At this stage the selective codes identified are further elaborated and connected to each other. To this end, the first step consisted in associating them to the family codes identified in literature. Also in this case we opted for a choice among the ones proposed by Glaser [15, 16, 31], in particular, codes referring to *causes* and *conditions*, sociocultural *frames* of understanding, *process* and *strategy*. The result of the association provides the connection between family codes, selective codes and open codes. For example, *Abstraction of technology from reality* and *IT mindset* codes are worth to be considered under the *causes* family, while *Industrialized analytics* impact and *Transformation* are concerned with *frames* for the discourses on the impact of Big Data analytics on the CIO and IT unit as we know it.

Table 5. Themes and major categories

Themes	Major Categories	Selective Codes	Open Codes
Generation gap impact on mindset and IT profession	Cultural shift	Abstraction of technology from reality	Uncritical and ready-made oriented youth; Confusion between channel and innovation; Unmeasured markets
		IT mindset	Age, Young versus old; Looking at toys rather than business; Decrease in IT professionalism
		Continuous change	Compliance with business models; Mindset challenges to IT innovation; Ask the customer not the consultant
		Globalization and local context	Culture; Italian management difference; Contextual and institutional factors; Generational change problem; Reference to tacit knowledge
Diversity of the CIO role	Identity and recognition	Distance from the CEO	CEO commitment and approval; CIO participation to the board of directors
		CIO role and behavior	CIO and other executives collaboration; IT support to exploration of business opportunities
The centrality of marketing and human resources	Power of new entrants	Commoditization of IT	Cost cutting; Cost focus
		Difference of Big Data Analytics	Marketing and IT convergence;

			Link digital campaigns with their effects; Business-to-Business (B2B); Disclosure and privacy; Structured marketing processes
Measure and control as CIO tools	Project and execution excellence	Sourcing of capabilities	Full outsourcing as partnership; outsourcing under the IT control; Innovation spaces and groups
		Project assessment easiness	Always on budget, always on time; Performance; Evaluation based on Key Performance Indicators (KPIs); Effort and money
		New way to innovate business	Business processes; Data Integration and centralization; Lack of profits; Service; Disclosure and privacy; Legal Framework; Security
Questioning the novelty of Big Data and analytics innovation	Uncertainty about innovation	Industrialized analytics impact	Same old story; Fear and bubble risk; IT management as repetition of questions and topics; Investments
		Transformation	Resistance of hierarchies against project orientation; Unrealistic C-level

The association between coding families and selective codes allow us to consider the latter as subcategories with properties inherited from their coding families. Consequently, we decided to carry out a further conceptualization based also on the memos written during the workshops and the interviews to identify major categories that abstract from the selective codes, however integrating them and their properties (see Table 5).

Figure 1 shows the resulting major categories, which are *Cultural shift*, *Identity and recognition*, *Powers of new entrants*, *Project and execution excellence*, and *Uncertainty about innovation*. It is worth noting that these categories may encompass selective codes from different families as in the case of *Cultural shift*, having two *causes*-related codes (*Abstraction of technology from reality* and *IT mindset*) and two *conditions*-related codes (*Continuous change* and *Globalization and local context*). Major categories are now considered as substantive codes, for they are generated from and, thus, pertain to the domain of investigation [17, 33].

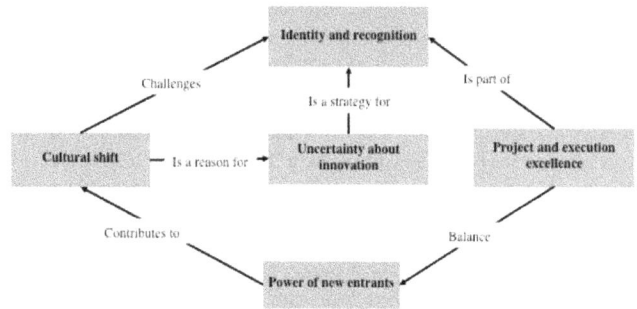

Figure 1. Diagram relating categories

The above discussed intermediate classification step allows having more properties for the identification of the relationships between the diverse major categories as shown in the diagram of Figure 1. Considering, for example, *Cultural shift*, it challenges the *Identity and recognition* of the CIO, where "challenges" refers to the fact that the former category is a *cause* for the latter (because of the *Abstraction of technology from reality* and *IT mindset* codified discourses) and it emerges from *conditions* such as the ones codified by *Continuous change* and *Globalization and local context*. Following the same ratio, *Cultural shift* is a reason for the argued *Uncertainty about innovation* coming from Big Data and analytics, the latter category being a – defender or analyzer oriented - strategy for framing *Identity and recognition*. As a traditional expertise of the CIO, *Project and execution excellence* is part of the strategy for *Identity and recognition*, while balancing the *Powers of new entrants*, such as, e.g., the Marketing or Human resource executives. The *Powers of new entrants* finally contributes to the *cultural shift* as condition and part of the process leading to *Identity and recognition*.

5. DISCUSSION OF THE RESULTS

The joint consideration of Big Data and analytics is a relatively recent development, particularly, within the domain of management of information systems (MIS). Analyzed at the state of the art often from a technological perspective, when their impact is considered on the CIO, the main executive profile representative of MIS within companies, the topic emerges as yet pretty unexplored. This argument motivates the choice for carrying out the grounded theory presented in previous sections. The focus on CIO and IS executives of companies acting in a specific country (Italy, in our case), while providing elements of a substantive theory for the context, it requires further theoretical sampling [18] for an increased generality of the theory, for example considering similar groups in other countries for a certain area such as, e.g., the ones within the European Union, first.

Furthermore, a parallel and alternative path for further theoretical sampling may concern a narrow focus on single industries in the Italian market.

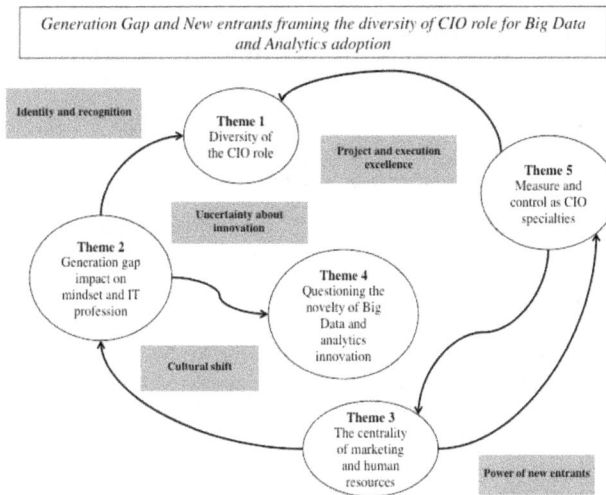

Figure 2. Substantive theory diagram

Notwithstanding the actual limitations in terms of scalability and generalization of the research results, Figure 2 shows a diagram for the substantive theory [33], mapping the substantive categories to some identified emerging themes related to the impact of Big Data and analytics on the role of the CIO. The substantive theory insights can be associated to the statement "*Generation Gap and New entrants framing the diversity of CIO role for Big Data and Analytics adoption*". Consequently, the four themes we have identified are strictly dependent on the substantive categories as for their definition and relationship to each other (the latter is represented by arrow, where a direction of the impact is provided). Thus, while the Theme 1 (*Diversity of the CIO role*) emerges as having a certain centrality with regards to three of substantive categories (*Identity and recognition, Uncertainty about innovation, Project and execution excellence*), the chain of evidence that moves from open coding to theoretical coding through selective coding points out that causes and conditions for Theme 1 are worth to be analyzed with regards to themes related to *Cultural shift* and *Power of new entrants*. These are associated to the Theme 2 (*Generation gap impact on mindset and IT profession*) and Theme 3 (*The centrality of marketing and human resources*). Also, Theme 4 (*Questioning the novelty of Big Data and analytics innovation*) is worth investigating in relationship to conditions for Theme 2. Finally, Theme 5 (*Measure and control as CIO specialties*) is worth considering for an investigation on strategies and processes for *identity and recognition* of the role of CIO as well as balancing the *power of new entrants*, such as marketing and human resource executives.

6. CONCLUSION

The rapid changes in the volume, variety, velocity, veracity, validity and volatility of data and the recent developments in the algorithms and technologies that are used to collect, share and analyze data have resulted in new challenges for business and CIOs. In an attempt to further investigate the state of the art on the role of CIOs in recent years, we have carried out a literature review that has shown a little consideration for the role of CIOs in relation to Big Data and Analytics. The limitations of the literature led us not to propose any items of conceptualization (e.g. research questions, model etc.). Instead, in an attempt to better understand the changing role of CIO in the Big Data and Analytics era, this study employs a grounded theory research approach in order to let the data speak. In doing so, we conducted workshops and interviews and around 300 participants attended ten workshops in a period of 27 months.

The analysis of the data was conducted using open coding, selective coding, and theoretical coding. Based on the data discussion presented in the previous sections we suggest that in the case of the Italian market the main factors emerging from the rise of Big Data and Big Data analytics refer to *cultural shift in IT mindset and professionalism* related to a *generation gap* and the *power of new entrants*, specifically marketing and human resource executives. These issues challenges the identity and the recognition of the role of the CIO and the IT within organizations, with a consequent strategy of questioning the novelty of Big Data and Big Data analytics as well as their potential in terms of innovation. The data let emerge also the relevance of project and execution excellence as building blocks for the definition of the changing identity and recognition by the CEO and other executives. Under this perspective, Big Data and Big Data analytics seem to provide a basis for using, e.g., key performance indicators as conversations tool for making evident the value of IT, thus, balancing the contribution of new entrants in the IT innovation leadership arena, such as, e.g., the above mentioned marketing and human resource executives. The resulting substantive theory and categories may provide a contribution focused to Big Data and Big Data analytics to the literature on the changing role of CIO, showing, for example, the relevance of project and execution excellence in the current transition [28] or on the evaluation by CEO and other C-managers [24]. Finally, the research allows to emphasize the challenges related to the generation gap in framing the identity of the CIO and the IT at organizational and corporate level, arguing for the need for further research on IT organization behavior and models allowing an appropriate absorption of skills and capabilities by the IT [14], such as, e.g., the one of data scientists [12] in domains where persist diverse cultural orientations and mindset legacies.

7. ACKNOWLEDGMENTS

The authors thank Nadia Neytcheva who greatly assisted with the research and supported the authors in the data collection activities.

8. REFERENCES

[1] Press, G. 2013. A Very Short History Of Big Data. *http://www.forbes.com/sites/gilpress/2013/05/09/a-very-short-history-of-big-data/#178ca51455da*. Accessed: 2016-04-05.

[2] Akella, J., Marwaha, S., and Sikes, J. 2014. How Cios Can Lead Their Company's Information Business. *McKinsey on Business Technology*. 33, Spring (2014).

[3] Applegate, L.M. and Elam, J.J. 1992. New Information Systems Leaders: a Changing Role in a Changing World. *MIS Quarterly*. 16, 4 (1992), 469–490.

[4] Baesens, B., Bapna, R., Mardsen, J., Vanthienen, J. and Zhao, J. 2014. Transformational Issues of Big Data and Analytics in Networked Business. *MIS Quarterly*. 38, 2 (2014), 629–630.

[5] Biesdorf, S., Court, D. and Willmott, P. 2013. Big Data: What's Your Plan? *McKinsey Quarterly*. (2013).

[6] Brereton, P., Kitchenham, B.A., Budgen, D., Turner, M. and Khalil, M. 2007. Lessons from applying the systematic literature review process within the software engineering domain. *Journal of Systems and Software*. 80, 4 (2007), 571–583.

[7] Bryant, A. 2009. Grounded Theory and Pragmatism: The Curious Case of Anselm Strauss. *Forum Qualitative Sozialforschung / Forum: Qualitative Social Research*. 10, 3 (2009).

[8] Buhl, H.U. 2013. Interview with Martin Petry on "Big Data." *Business & Information Systems Engineering*. 2, (2013), 101–102.

[9] Charmaz, K. 2006. *Constructing grounded theory: a practical guide through qualitative analysis*. Sage Publications.

[10] Chen, H., Chiang, R.H.L. and Storey, V.C. 2012. Business Intelligence and Analytics: From Big Data to Big Impact. *MIS Quarterly*. 36, 4 (2012), 1165–1188.

[11] Cooper, H.M. 1988. Organizing knowledge syntheses: A taxonomy of literature reviews. *Knowledge in Society*. 1, 1 (1988), 104–126.

[12] Davenport, T.H. and Patil, D.J. 2012. Data Scientist : The Sexiest Job Of the 21st Century. *Harvard Business Review*. October (2012).

[13] European Commission and data industry launch €2.5 billion partnership to master Big Data: 2014. *http://europa.eu/rapid/press-release_IP-14-1129_en.htm*.

[14] Francalanci, C. and Morabito, V. 2008. IS integration and business performance: The mediation effect of organizational absorptive capacity in SMEs. *Journal of Information technology*. 23, (2008), 297–312.

[15] Gillon, K., Aral, S., Lin, C.Y., Mithas, S. and Zozulia, M. 2014. Business analytics: Radical shift or incremental change? *Communications of the Association for Information Systems*. 34, (2014), 287–296.

[16] Glaser, B.G. 2005. *The Grounded Theory Perspective III: Theoretical coding*. The Sociology Press.

[17] Glaser, B.G. 1978. *Theoretical Sensitivity: Advances in the Methodology of Grounded Theory*. The Sociology Press.

[18] Glaser, B.G. and Strauss, A.L. 1967. *The Discovery of Grounded Theory: Strategies for Qualitative Research*. Aldine.

[19] Guillemette, M. and Paré, G. 2012. Toward a New Theory of the Contribution of the It Function in Organizations. *MIS Quarterly*. 36, 2 (2012), 529–551.

[20] Karpovsky, A. and Galliers, R. 2012. Sources of Power and Cio Influence and Their Impact: An Explorative Survey. *International Conference of Information Systems* (2012).

[21] Lavalle, S., Lesser, E., Shockley, R., Hopkins, M.S. and Kruschwitz, N. 2011. Big Data, Analytics and the Path From Insights to Value. *MIT Sloan Management Review*. 52, 2 (2011).

[22] Liamputtong, P. 2011. *Focus Group Methodology - Principles and Practice*. SAGE.

[23] Lim, J., Han, K. and Mithas, S. 2013. How Cio Position Influences Information Technology Investments and Firm Performance. *International Conference on Information Systems (ICIS2013)* (2013).

[24] Manfreda, A. and Indihar Štemberger, M. 2013. The impact of top management support on the perceived IS value – should we focus on the partnership? *UK Academy for Information Systems Conference* (2013).

[25] Marton, A., Avital, M. and Blegind Jensen, T. 2013. Reframing Open Big Data. *ECIS 2013* (2013).

[26] Merali, Y., Papadopoulos, T. and Nadkarni, T. 2012. Information systems strategy: Past, present, future? *Journal of Strategic Information Systems*. 21, 2 (2012), 125–153.

[27] Miles, M.. and Huberman, A.. 1994. *Qualitative data analysis: An expanded sourcebook*. SAGE Publications.

[28] Ragowsky, A., Licker, P., Miller, J., Gefen, D. and Stern, M. 2014. Do Not Call Me Chief Information Officer, but Chief Integration Officer. A Summary of the 2011 Detroit CIO Roundtable. *Communications of the Association for Information Systems*. 34, (2014).

[29] Tamm, T., Seddon, P. and Shanks, G. 2013. Pathways to Value from Business Analytics. *International Conference of Information Systems (ICIS2013)* (2013).

[30] The Economist 2014. *A Cambrian Moment - Special Report Tech Startups (January 18th 2014)*.

[31] The Economist 2010. Data, data everywhere. *Special Report: Managing information*.

[32] Anderson, C. 2008. The End of Theory: The Data Deluge Makes the Scientific Method Obsolete. *http://www.wired.com/2008/06/pb-theory/*. Accessed: 2016-04-05.

[33] Urquhart, C. 2013. *Grounded Theory for Qualitative Research - A Practical Guide*. SAGE Publications.

[34] Walsham, G. 1993. *Interpreting information systems in organizations*. Wiley.

Is It All About Awareness? People, Smart Cities 3.0, and Evolving Spaces for IT

H. Patricia McKenna
AmbientEase
#541, 185-911 Yates Street
Victoria BC, CANADA V8V 4Y9

mckennaph@gmail.com

ABSTRACT

The purpose of this paper is to explore contemporary understandings of the smart city movement in relation to information technology (IT) transformations, specifically emerging aware technologies and the use of social media in urban spaces. Faced with rapid urban growth, cities are responding by innovating themselves to address the associated and unprecedented challenges and opportunities. This paper is significant in that it reaches across interdisciplinary domains, to shed light on awareness and the smart cities phenomena. The theoretical perspective for this work draws on material-discursive practices, practice theory, and a performative perspective in relation to IT transformations, smart cities, and awareness. The research design for this study employs an exploratory case study approach, a minimally viable social media space, and multiple methods of qualitative and quantitative data collection and analysis. This paper focuses on two levels of analysis, the individual and the social, in contemporary urban environments. Anecdotal evidence from informal conversations conducted in parallel with this study supports further data analysis, comparison, and triangulation. Key findings are discussed in terms of awareness in relation to experiences of contemporary urban spaces based on the constructs of noticing, sensing, sharing, and smartness. The major contributions of this work include: further development of the research literature for awareness and for IT transformations in relation to smart cities; development, operationalization, and advancing of a conceptual framework for awareness in smart cities; and the identification of future directions for smart cities practitioners and researchers.

Keywords

Aware technology; Awareness; Human geography; IT; Material-Discursive practice; Performative perspective; Practice theory; Smart city; Social media, Transformation

1. INTRODUCTION

The rapid growth of cities is posing enormous challenges and opportunities for urban areas and for society globally. Gil-Garcia,

SIGMIS-CPR '16, June 2–4, 2016, Alexandria, VA, USA.
Copyright is held by the owner/author(s). Publication rights licensed to ACM.
ACM 978-1-4503-4203-2/16/06...$15.00.
DOI: http://dx.doi.org/10.1145/2890602.2890612

Pardo, and Nam [1] point to the interplay between emerging technology, social, and organizational elements including "governance and citizen participation" as critical to the generation of "innovative smart initiatives" as a response. Smartness in relation to 21st century cities is understood to be multi-dimensional in nature [2] where cities are seen as being on a continuum of involving many individuals across the city, focused on initiatives designed to improve livability [1].

Using the constructs of noticing, sensing, sharing, and smartness, this paper looks at the smart cities phenomena in terms of awareness and how use of social media and aware technologies is shifting the ways people interact and collaborate together in urban environments.

The purpose of this paper is to explore contemporary understandings of the smart city phenomena in relation to information technology (IT) transformations, specifically emerging aware technologies and the use of social media in urban spaces. As such, this paper is significant in that it reaches across interdisciplinary domains to shed light on awareness and the smart cities phenomena. The theoretical perspective for this work draws on material-discursive practices, practice theory, and a performative perspective in relation to IT transformations, smart cities, and awareness. Included also are elements of the human geographies perspective, contributing understanding to evolving IT and information and communication technologies (ICTs) spaces as innovation in relation to civic engagement.

The research design for this study employs an exploratory case study approach, a minimally viable social media space, and multiple methods of qualitative and quantitative data collection and analysis. This paper focuses on two levels of analysis, the individual and the social, in contemporary urban environments. Anecdotal evidence [3], [4] from informal conversations conducted in parallel with this study supports further data analysis, comparison, and triangulation. Content analysis is employed inductively to gather insights from individuals across the city. Deductive coding and analysis is also used during content analysis, drawing upon terms emerging from the research and practice literature.

In developing a theoretical perspective for this work, a review of the literature is presented focusing on IT transformations, smart cities, and awareness. A conceptual framework for awareness in smart cities is developed, operationalized, and advanced.

Key findings are presented in terms of awareness in relation to the four research questions and corresponding propositions, followed by a discussion; key contributions are outlined along with the identification of future directions for practitioners and researchers; and limitations and mitigations are described followed by a conclusion.

2. Theoretical Perspective

In addressing the challenge raised by the title of this paper – *Is it all about awareness?* – this paper employs several theory types [5] in exploring awareness in 21st century cites. As such, the theoretical perspective for this work draws on material-discursive practices [6], practice theory [7], and a performative perspective [8] in relation to a review of the research and practice literature focusing on IT transformations, smart cities, and awareness.

Orlikowski uses a sociomateriality [9] approach to identify established and emerging perspectives on technology in the information management literature, as – absent presence, exogenous force, emergent process, and more recently, entanglement in practice. Of particular importance to this work is an entanglement perspective amenable to "contemporary forms of technology and organizing that are increasingly understood to be multiple, fluid, temporary, interconnected, and dispersed" [9]. For contemporary technology and organizing, Orlikowski [9] identifies the need to "study the dynamic and multiple sociomaterial (re)configurations as these are performed in practice."

Feldman and Orlikowski [7] point to the value of the practice lens for "analyzing social, technological, and organizational phenomena." Of particular importance to this paper is the value of practice theory in terms of "the capacity to offer important practical implications for practitioners" and the potential for "theoretical generalizations."

Schultze and Orlikowski [8] identify the importance of a performative perspective as offering "powerful insights for understanding" social media and other digital spaces that "involve multiple, complex, and emergent sociomaterial configurations in practice." A performative lens enables the viewing of everyday life "as constituted by fluid, dynamic, multiple, and emergent phenomena" focusing "more on how humans and technologies are interrelated in practice" [8]. As such, this paper extends the use of performative practice to social media and smart cities. For Orlikowski and Scott [6], the importance of material-discursive practices, as in, materialization and performativity, is that it serves as a reminder "that the world is always in the process of becoming: it is enacted in practice."

In summary, this multi-theory approach supports analysis, the use of propositions for exploration of the research questions, and the use of action oriented constructs.

2.1 Information Technology Transformations

Orlikowski [10] advanced a perspective on organizational transformation that "proposes change as endemic to the practice of organizing" and as such, is "enacted through the situated practices of organizational actors as they improvise, innovate, and adjust their work over time." Using a practice lens, Orlikowski [10] seeks to accommodate the needs of contemporary organizations around "flexibility, self-organizing, and learning." Anderson and Ackerman Anderson [11] define developmental change as improvement; transitional change as replacing what is; and transformational change as "far more challenging" for two reasons. First, in transformational change "the future state is unknown" and emerges through "trial and error as new information is gathered." Second, transformational change operates at the "personal levels of mindset, behavior and culture" requiring early and ongoing involvement because "the future state

is so radically different." Harmsen and Molner [12] point to the "multidimensional and complex interplay" of 21st century enterprise transformations from a socio-technical perspective. Ashkenas [13] defines transformation as "a portfolio of initiatives, which are interdependent or intersecting" as distinct from change management that focuses on a "few discrete, well-defined shifts" in an organization. For Ashkenas [13] the goal of transformation is "to reinvent the organization and discover a new or revised business model." As such, transformation is "more unpredictable, iterative, and experimental" involving "a process of discovery" with considerably "higher risk" and no guarantee of success. Ashkenas [13] points to the need for transformational leadership capabilities consisting of "more flexible and dynamic coordination of resources, stronger collaboration across boundaries, and communication in the midst of uncertainty."

Concerned with the spatial practices of everyday life, De Certeau [14] presents a dynamic depiction of the city as "a place of transformations and appropriations" that is "the object of various kinds of interference but also a subject that is constantly enriched by new attributes." Ibrahim, Adams, and El-Zaart, [15] discuss transformation models and challenges for smart sustainable cities (SSCs) highlighting Brownfield and Greenfield approaches. The Brownfield approach is based on the application of a model for existing cities and the Greenfield approach uses a model for creating cities from scratch.

2.2 Smart Cities

The rapid growth of cities is posing wicked challenges and opportunities for society, motivating the need for cities to innovate themselves in a variety of ways [1]. Goodspeed [16] proposes moving beyond urban cybernetics to address instead, wicked problems. What Goodspeed [16] claims to be "a jumble of definitions of a smart city" that "has emerged in the scholarly literature" along with "a confusing jumble of theory" is perhaps suggestive of the interdisciplinary nature of smart cities, along with evolving understandings. The jumble observed by Goodspeed gives further rationale for the use of a practice lens "to see and value the complexity and dynamics" of "contemporary realities as multiplicity, transience, and dispersion" as in, the messiness of everyday life. It is worth noting the work emerging from the UrbanTheoryLab including that of Brenner and Schmid [17] and Salgueiro [18] on contemporary urban theorizing around a rethinking of where the urban begins and ends.

Greenfield [19] is critical of the smart cities movement, claiming that an emphasis is placed on technology over people in the development of initiatives and solutions. Utopian and dystopian perspectives on smart cities are presented in the research literature [20], [21], [22], [23]. Townsend [22] identifies three key concerns in the smart cities literature as: – the buggyness of software driven systems; the brittleness of systems that may not be highly adaptive, responsive, or resilient; and the issue of privacy, as in, being bugged by a surveillance society. It is important to note that Jacobs [24] observed that, "people's love of watching activity and other people is constantly evident in cities everywhere." As such, Jacobs identified the critical role of 'watching' in the city, making the connection between city surveillance and city safety. It could be argued that aware technologies may support people to keep an eye on spaces in their neighborhoods, as part of daily practices and activities.

Hollands [21] describes the trend of cities increasingly "becoming a backdrop to corporate advertising and the privatisation of public spaces." Pointing to Harvey's [25] notion of a transformation in city governance from managerial welfare to urban entrepreneurialism, Hollands notes the concern with cities capitalizing on the smart city movement. Highlighting alternatives, the work of Hill [26] and de Waal [27] are described by Hollands [21] in terms of the importance of "people and citizens." Hollands [21] provides examples of community projects involving people and social media, highlighting the "right to use the technology" and the "right to shape the city using human initiative and technology for social purposes."

Cohen [28] identifies three generations or waves of the smart city where 1.0 focused on the technology driven smart city; 2.0 became city driven; and the current or third wave as Smart Cities 3.0 involving people in the city in co-creation. Cohen sees promise in a combination of all three waves or generations, advising that "cities must move from treating citizens as recipients of services, or even customers, to participants in the co-creation of improved quality of life."

Emphasizing the importance of people in the urban ecosystem, Mone [29] claims that new smart cities are beginning to emerge, based on the joint efforts of "academics, civic leaders, businesses, and individual citizens working together to create urban information systems." Vander Veen [30] points to the importance of the people component of smart cities, claiming that, "a truly smart and connected city begins with people who are smart and connected" as "places where ideas, infrastructure and technology intersect."

2.3 Awareness

Orlikowski [31] identified the importance of awareness as "the first and critical thing" in the context of transformation at the level of work practices. However, Orlikowski added that "it's not awareness alone, it's always awareness and action, the willingness to act on that awareness." Scharmer [31] links Orlikowski's work on awareness with that of "Arthur, Varela, Rosch, Bortoft, and Nan" pointing to the research territory of "how our quality of awareness changes the quality of what we enact."

Kaptelinin and Nardi [32] identify awareness as a human attribute, adding that, "technologies that beckon us are not merely carriers of information in systems, but potentially transformative artifacts capable of providing people with diverse new cognitive, emotional, social, aesthetic, and physical experiences." As such, the interweaving of people and technology is advanced by Kaptelinin and Nardi, in the notion of 'acting with technology.'

In the context of computer-supported collaborative work (CSCW), Dourish and Bellotti [33] state that, "awareness information is always required to coordinate group activities, whatever the task domain." Dourish and Bellotti [33] note that with information sharing, whether in a mode encompassing synchronous, asynchronous, or semi-synchronous, the "workspace becomes a persistent space in which collaborators can interact," supportive of active or passive awareness. Concerned with privacy issues from a technical perspective in ubiquitous systems, Bellotti and Sellen [34] developed a design framework in response that also served to "elucidate the delicate balance that exists between awareness and privacy."

It is worth noting that Jacobs [24] articulated the importance of visibility on a city and community level. And it is on visibility, awareness, and accountability that Erickson and Kellogg [35] focus in the development of socially translucent systems to support graceful "communication and collaboration among large groups of people over computer networks." Erickson and Kellogg

[35] advance the idea of technologies with windows instead of walls, so as to "mesh with human behavior" at "individual and collective levels." The translucence afforded by windows allows "users to 'see' one another, to make inferences about the activities of others, to imitate one another," supporting the potential for "new social forms" to emerge.

Gu, Riboni, and Hu [36] articulate awareness in terms of context awareness through pervasive computing encompassing the three areas of personal awareness, social awareness, and urban awareness. Scholl [2] notes that the smart cities movement is not new and has been developing over the past decade. Yet, in terms of awareness, Brandt [37] points to a kind of obliviousness in the United Kingdom where "nearly 100 percent" of people "do not notice smart cities growing around them." However, the adoption and use of mobile and aware technologies in the form of smartphones and wearable devices is widespread [38], [39], extending even to a type of Fitbit for the city [40]. Paradoxically perhaps, smartphones, fitness devices, and other technologies are aware-enabled with location, presence, and other types of real-time tracking and data gathering features [41]. Biocchi et al. [41] outline an architecture for "citizens using their own capabilities integrated with ICTs" to "collaboratively constitute a large-scale socio-technical superorganism to support collective urban awareness and activities." Beginning with a story about human sensing and pulse-taking of the city, Fine [42] articulates urban digitization as a way of leveraging the pulse of the city. Fine [42] points to the importance of critical factors such as, trust and privacy, in the handling of data, as determinants for the uptake of digital solutions by cities.

For the purposes of this study, constructs related to awareness include noticing, sensing, sharing, smartness, and spaces, with descriptions for each provided in sections 2.3.1 to 2.3.5.

2.3.1 Noticing
Conceptualizing linkages between action, awareness, and experience in the city gives rise to the importance of noticing. From a human geography perspective, Laurier [43] "seeks variously to discover, uncover, and reveal what members of society take for granted" in order to reveal what are "seen but unnoticed features of the world."

2.3.2 Sensing
Lévy [44] points to elements such as mobility, multi-dimensionality of the senses (multi-sensorial sensors), and technology-enabled bodily movement "through immaterial vectors" giving rise to a vast potential for reach and influence so that humans "are not reducible to the size of their bodies."

2.3.3 Sharing
Dourish and Bellotti [33] identified the importance of sharing for awareness, interaction, and collaboration in that, "an awareness of the activity of others" provides "a context for your own activity" and through information sharing, the "workspace becomes a persistent space in which collaborators can interact."

2.3.4 Smartness
Gil-Garcia, Pardo, and Nam [1] refer to smartness as encompassing an "array of phenomena in cities and other urban environments" and as "public sector innovation in urban contexts."

2.3.5 Spaces
Dourish, Adler, Bellotti, and Henderson [45] maintained that "the media-space world *is* the real world" and as such, "it is a place

where real people, in real working relationships, engage in real interactions." Scharmer et al. [46] refer to "spaces of innovation" and identify three types of space as co-sensing, co-inspiring, and co-enacting. Williams, Robles, and Dourish [47] place an emphasis on urban experience and users embedded as actors in the global networks of interactions and flows.

Lévy et al. [44] explore the space of the Internet in relation to urban spaces and Beaude [48] identifies the digital world of the Internet as a real space "where an increasing portion of our practices, exchanges and lives take place." As such, Beaude describes the Internet as an "essentially spatial innovation" where space is not eliminated but is created in new ways. Pointing to geolocation and other aware technologies, Beaude describes the accelerated and complex hybridization of material and immaterial spaces. Vander Veen [30] refers to the capacity to "transform society from one that goes online to one that exists online." This conceptual shift in understandings of the entanglement of material and immaterial resources sheds light on the Internet as a contemporary space "to be invented, again and again" [48].

Lévy et al. [44] claim that people are themselves spaces while referring to their activities as spatialities. With the Internet of Things (IoT) where everything is connected everywhere and data is increasingly generated autonomously by our things, Vander Veer [30] looks to people "to make the most of data" and to "make it meaningful."

In summary, complex urban and global issues give rise to the need for greater awareness of urban environments and aware technologies in order to understand and leverage the potential for smart cities as mechanisms for innovating in support of 21st century society. As such, this exploration of awareness and smart cities uses a multi-theory approach and multiple awareness-related constructs in responding to four key research questions.

Research Questions

Q1: Does noticing contribute to awareness in contemporary urban environments?

Q2: Does sensing, as in, feeling the pulse of the city, contribute to awareness in contemporary urban environments?

Q3: How is the relationship between aware people and aware technologies manifesting in social media and other spaces in contemporary urban environments?

Q4: What form does smartness take, as in, aware people and aware technologies, in contemporary urban environments?

This study is operationalized using the constructs of noticing, sensing, sharing, smartness, and spaces enabling exploration of the four research questions. The following four propositions will be tested, corresponding to each of the research questions.

Propositions

P1: Noticing contributes to greater awareness in the city;

P2: Sensing and feeling the pulse and vibrancy of urban environments contributes to greater awareness in the city;

P3: Social media and other digital interactions foster the potential for new and emerging relationships for sharing based on aware people and aware technologies in urban spaces;

P4: Smartness as the interweaving of aware technologies and aware people takes multiple and diverse forms in the city and urban spaces.

Based on the theoretical perspective for this study, this paper advances a conceptual framework for awareness in smart cities as presented graphically in Figure 1. The physical/material, aware technologies and social/media co-exist, informing and contributing to smart cities, IT transformations, and awareness at any moment in time. On a theoretical level, a combination of material-discursive practices, practice theory, and a performative perspective contribute to process, practice, and research. Action is enabled through noticing, sensing, sharing, in smartness enables spaces, supportive of awareness, IT transformations, and smart cities

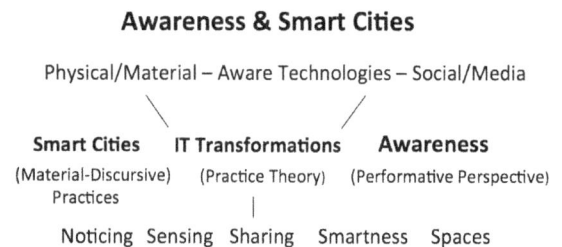

Figure 1. Conceptual framework: Awareness in smart cities.

This conceptual framework for awareness and smart cities guides exploration of the research questions.

3. Methodology

The research design for this study employs an exploratory case study approach [49]. Quantitative and qualitative data collection techniques are used involving survey (closed-ended) and use experience activity for the former and interview and open-ended survey data for the latter. Qualitative data are analyzed using content analysis.

This study spans a 7-month timeframe from mid 2015 into 2016, across multiple cities of small to medium to large sized populations, mostly in Canada but also extending to northern Europe. Interest and involvement was sought from individuals 18 years of age or older. In parallel with this study and beginning 5 months earlier, anecdotal evidence was gathered over a 1-year period through informal individual and group discussions with people across the city.

The methodology is described in more detail in sections 3.1 to 3.3 in terms of the process used; the evidence collected using mixed methods; and the types of data analysis conducted.

3.1 Process

Individuals across the city were randomly invited to participate in the study by registering online. Registration involved sharing minimal, optional demographic data including age and urban location and self-identification in one or more of the six urban categories (e.g., business, city official, community member, educator, student, or visitor). Once registered for the study, participants were then assigned an anonymous alpha-numeric identifier, given access to three additional webpages, and invited to engage with their particular city through noticing, idea generation, and sharing using the minimally viable webspace containing social media elements, or imagined use of the same. Follow-up semi-structured interviews and an online survey with a combination of closed and open-ended questions were used to explore the research questions identified for the study. In parallel with this study, anecdotal evidence was gathered from individuals across the city during informal individual and group discussions.

50

3.2 Sources of Data

Multiple methods of qualitative and quantitative data collection were used for this study including real-time tracking of content generation, in-depth interviews, and an online survey. Participants were invited to contribute content to the social media webspace in terms of what they notice about the city as well as ideas for the city. In real time, content becomes available for others to view and interact with and participants can contribute as much and as often as they like. In parallel, anecdotal evidence was gathered from individuals across the city during informal individual and group discussions. From an organizational perspective, Jemielniak and Krzyworzeka [3] make the case for grounded anecdotal evidence, noting that it is especially valid for a range of purposes including innovation. Cubitt. [4] argues that "the power of anecdote is to bring us to the absolute specificity of experience" forcing "us to confront the materiality of people, things, and events" in order to understand that "the human cannot be separated from the technical, physical, or organic environments."

3.3 Data Analysis

Content analysis is employed inductively to gather insights emerging from individuals across the city. Deductive coding and analysis is also used during content analysis, drawing upon terms from the research literature. Two levels of analysis are used in this paper – the individual and the social, in contemporary urban environments. Anecdotal evidence from informal conversations gathered in parallel with this study supports further data analysis, comparison, and triangulation [50]. Overall, data were analyzed for an n=16, spanning all age ranges from individuals in their 20s to those in their 70s and a gender representation of 55% male and 45% female.

4. Findings

Key findings from this study are summarized in Table 1 in terms of the four propositions and the awareness-related constructs.

Table 1. Awareness in the city: Noticing, sensing, sharing & smartness

	Constructs Explored	People-Technologies-Cities
P1	Noticing as awareness	People, Business, City services, Cleanness, Climate, Homelessness, Interactions, Mobility, Objects, Spaces
P2	Sensing as awareness	Multi-sensorial, Dynamic, Arts, Culture, Electric, Multi-modal travel, Safety, Vibrant
P3	Sharing as awareness – Social/media interactions	Access, App, Back channel, Connectivities, Multi/Media-purpose spaces, Ownership
P4	Smartness as awareness – Aware people/technology	Awareness, Balance, Enhance/Hinder, Navigate, Connect, Safety, Sensors

In sections 4.1 to 4.4 the awareness-related constructs of noticing, sensing, sharing, and smartness are explored in relation to people and their experience of technology-infused cities and urban spaces.

4.1 Noticing as Awareness

A postsecondary educator in an urban agglomeration of the city of Victoria noticed first, "the unhurried and quiet way" that "people appear to share and engage with each other" as they seek out "the amenities provided by the urban space." Notice was also made of "the sounds of the fountain as I walk to work." This matters because the fountain "provides a touchstone for people in the area" that brings "people out" and "causes people to go, did you see that, look at how neat that is." The fountain was described as a fun space encouraging people to talk to each other, connect, and slow down. Thinking about what engages people in the city, reference was made to the "conscious things" that governments, organizations, and communities do, including the housing, the coffee shops, the restaurants, the things that encourage people to come out and "because we've blended it all together it's exciting."

A community member in Toronto noticed how coming together is amplified by the positioning of jumbotron screens outside of sports events, where the city experiments with the creation of temporary informal spaces in support of social activities and connection in the city.

An individual in the technology business sector in the Greater Victoria area was concerned with noticing "how easy it can be to get from point A to point B," Another observed that "outside is actually becoming inside" in a city because "the buildings are getting so tall and its getting so congested" it seems that "you almost have a roof over your head even though you're outside." And an engineering student looks for "an opportunity maybe for making the city a little smarter" and "I hope to change people's minds so they follow a more green way."

In the city of Ottawa, a community leader notices the "overnight and morning warmth" concerned that this may be an indicator of "changing climate" with "unclear outcomes."

In a small to medium-sized city in Finland, an educator notices "a lot of snow and snow removal services working reliably" and this is important because "it helps me in my short commute" by bicycle to the "workplace and back."

Several educators reported that they notice "the homeless situation" and the state of the city in terms of "how clean it is." Another notices the architecture and aesthetics. And another states, "I like to look at people's faces" because "I like to see if they are happy, if they're friendly, how they are going to maybe interact with me." A city councilor commented on the importance of "people coming together from across sectors to work on things collaboratively, in hubs." Hubs were described as looking like "neighborhood village centers and sometimes a coffee shop." Referring to ad hoc, pop-up events, an urban placemaker commented that, "we like to do those to demonstrate how a space can change" and to "look at any given space and analyze what's working and what isn't and what could improve it."

4.2 Sensing as Awareness

Commenting on the experience of the city, a postsecondary educator stated that, "an urban setting is dynamic." Acknowledging that a city "can have its ups and downs" it was noted that, "overall it is vibrant" and "spending time in the energy" of the city "is just electric." Regarding what contributes to the pulse of the city, the educator stated that it is "the people, first and foremost the people, the way that people walk and talk and engage each other, the coffee shops, the businesses, all those things" encompassing "people and daily goings on." Asked about body awareness in the city, the educator responded by saying that there are "so many clues and cues as you walk, its everything from the visual to the sensual to the smell, all of your senses."

A city councilor in a small to medium-sized city observed that "vibrancy is created by people and connections between people." The councilor added that, "the way that comes to life" is through "arts and culture, sitting and having a coffee discussing the city and things you're passionate about." Further, it was noted by the councilor that a vibrant city is "a place where you get to know your neighbors" and learn about and celebrate "what you have in common and what is different." Critical to the pulse and vibrancy of the city, commented the councilor "is people interacting with each other and with their surroundings because its creating activity."

Multi-modal transportation was identified by a community member in a large Canadian metropolitan area, as a way of sensing the pulse of the city. For example, "you're not just moving one way, you're walking, a lot of times I'll ride my bike somewhere and I'll park my bike and jump on a streetcar and the subway." Commenting on the pulse of the city, a postsecondary educator in Finland spoke of the rhythm of the city connected with the academic cycles. The city filling with students and how "the nightlife is bustling with energy" was mentioned along with "walking on the streets" and the special events and exhibitions throughout the summer months and the outdoor activities generally, including the open-air gym.

From the perspective of an individual in the technology business sector, the importance of touch, the "flesh space" and "those open air meeting spaces" were emphasized, as activity increasingly moves away from "bricks and mortar" spaces.

Using sample questions from Anderson's [51] body intelligence scale (BIS), adapted for the purposes of this study to the city, study participants were invited to self-assess on the three BIS sub-scales: energy body scale (EBS), comfort body scale (CBS), and inner body scale (IBS). On a scale of 1 (disagree) to 5 (agree), 50% of respondents rated themselves at 4 for EBS and 50% at 5; for CBS and IBS, 100% of assessments were at 5.

4.3 Sharing as Awareness & Relationship

A community member shared the idea of "social financing for community centres in new communities" as infrastructure that would "stop sprawl, build community" and provide "many places for people."

An educator shared the idea of a "mobile cloud-based app to capture and share insights, feedback, and knowledge" as a simple, cost efficient" mechanism for "instant awareness." The app is intended for "business, design, infrastructure, learning, safety, sport, and tourism."

In the case where a respondent opted not to share ideas for the city, upon further probing, a concern with the ownership of ideas was revealed.

The example of using social media at a conference where a speaker also includes a screen with Twitter feeds was viewed by an educator as a challenge, commenting that, "I was more engaged with the social space of the TwitterVerse than the social space of the convention and the person doing the speaking" giving rise to the question, "why am I there?"

Social media was viewed by a city councilor as beneficial in being able to, "definitely create discussion and connections" and "more particularly, to extend conversations on issues and ideas." Unsure whether social media "enhances the vibrancy of a city," the councilor added that, "it enhances the personality of a city on the Internet" through Facebook and Twitter followers, and "makes it all more accessible." While social media "can facilitate conversations" the councilor stated that, "it can't replace people coming down to City Hall."

Where a sports event attracts thousands of people inside and half the number again in a free, open space set up outside the event by the city, "that was bringing a city together" commented a community member, adding that it is "exciting and fun to see."

The example of a blog as social media was described by an urban placemaker where a particular post about 'library boxes' triggered unexpected interest and interactivity, resulting in Twitter activity, Google mapping, new connections, engagement and participation, and video sharing.

4.4 Smartness as Awareness in Urban Spaces

An educator remarked that, "awareness is a more appropriate word" than smartness "because it allows you to see technology as an affordance to living in our communities differently, not better, but differently." Further, smartness was interpreted as scary. Instead, it was suggested that for the city, "we need to make it a more engaging space" adding that, "I love technology, I want my technology, but I come back to" the need for "that balance, and I don't know what the balance is."

A city councilor stated that smartness, as in smartphones, can enhance and hinder in that, "it can enhance when it's allowing for more connectivity in terms of face-to-face connections." The councilor added that smart devices "cannot replace face-to-face, knowing the name of your neighbor, and being able to talk to them when you see them, in any way that's meaningful" and "you don't want it to be a substitute in any way for that physical connection." Further, commented the councilor, "it is important to think of technology as a tool that will allow people to connect to each other and to their surroundings" and "when you're looking down at your phone you're not connected to the people around you and you're not connected to your surroundings."

A community member in Toronto claimed to be usually ahead of the curve in adoption and uptake of new technologies but acknowledged this not to be the case with aware technologies. This individual stated that, "the smart city thing or that predictive aspect of technology has got me on edge a little bit." Further, it was suggested that, for the most part, people "have no interest" or awareness "about the concept of smart cities." Shock was expressed at how quickly technologies such as drones and driverless vehicles are being adopted and adapted for use.

An urban placemaker spoke of "ways to animate a space," providing the example of a city parkade with embedded sensor technology that "plays different sounds as you go up based on where you are in the stairwell" and the "lighting changes."

In a small to medium-sized urban area in Finland, an educator commented that, "one thing I really like about the city is that it's compact." This is important because, "in terms of logistics" it enables one to "move very quickly." It was also noted that investments in technology elements are evident in "smart construction, including lights" aiding flows of traffic and pedestrians.

Navigation in the city was articulated by a community member in terms of "a need for location" and the feeling that "I have to count on myself to get around." This is because "I don't feel like I can rely on other people" so "it is more a matter of self-reliance" in that, "if I can't do it then I don't want to go there."

Pointing to agile, adaptive examples of leveraging existing infrastructure to advance new ways of doing things, an individual in the tourism sector referred to the Uber travel movement as "piggybacking on someone else's infrastructure in a way that is win win." An individual in the technology business sector pointed to the importance of adopting a "smart city thought process" as a "wonderful thing that connects all the pieces," as in, "people, community." Articulated by another educator, "lets spend less time *finding* the connection" and more time "actually *making* it."

5. Discussion

A discussion of findings is organized into the three key theme areas of multi-purpose/modal spaces and awareness; extended and entangled smartness; and IT transformations and smart cities, presented in sections 5.1 to 5.3.

5.1 Multi-Purpose/Modal Space & Awareness

The importance of creating multi-purpose spaces in the city was highlighted in terms of transportation, housing, and public spaces in support of improved awareness of what works for people in the city.

The extending of conference, town hall, sports, arts and culture, and other event spaces as ad hoc, temporary, and experimental environments enabled with social media, aware, and other multi-modal technologies contributed to unexpected and desirable interactions, connections, collaborations, opportunities, and spaces for awareness and action. The example of the challenge raised by Twitter during a conference event took a turn when the participant realized that the social media space of Twitter extended the conference beyond itself. It was observed that, "you've got 500 people at a conference but you've actually got 5000 that are participating in that conference through the Twitter feed." The educator concluded that "it's a fabulous idea and I think it adds great richness particularly when that conversation" is moderated and compiled to record "what really took place," making it, "not just fun, but I think very meaningful." Similarly, the initial concern by a city councilor with technology being an inadequate substitute for face-to face interaction shifted when the councilor recalled that, "we held our first interactive e-Town Hall and we were able to get feedback from people sitting at home who were watching the live stream video." This led the councilor to observe that "not only did we have a packed house in person and also, an overflow room, we also had hundreds of people at home watching the video, tweeting, sending direct messages that we could respond to." Becoming aware of the multi-modality of spaces, people, and technology in the city, the councilor noted that this e-Town Hall enabled "an interactive experience that makes the city more real for those people."

The compactness of the city identified in a small to medium sized urban area in Finland accommodates multiple modes of transport including cycle lanes, walkability, and pedestrian spaces, characteristic of smart cities. In support of awareness, "in terms of the infrastructure," the comment was made that, "when you need it, it is there, that's for sure." The large urban area of Toronto includes similar compactness along with multi-modal and multi-directionality, enabling rapid, adaptive city mobility under and above ground.

5.2 Extended & Entangled Smartness

The case of the community member emphasizing the importance of self-reliance in navigating around the city, not wanting to rely on the assistance of others, opens possibilities for an awareness of people and technology acting together to navigate, get around, and feel safe. The "musical railing" in the city parkade, as part of "art in public places" supported by the city, provides an example of collaborations extending across multiple sectors in support of local technology, arts, culture, and cross-sector urban collaboration, characteristic of smart cities. A city councilor is quoted as saying the musical railing is "designed to ensure that civic parkades are safe and welcoming" pointing to safety, engagement, cultural, and other benefits.

While technology was initially viewed as a tool on the one hand and not a replacement for the physical and face-to-face interaction, it is worth noting that a city councilor eventually pointed to the importance of "online tools that will be designed for youth to create, to bring them into some sort of online public" as part of a youth engagement strategy.

This interweaving of people, interaction, and technology in the city is perhaps taken for granted and less often thought about and discussed. Where Fine [42] proposes urban digitization solutions, findings from this work may assist in figuring out how the multi-sensorial capabilities of people might inform, enrich, and enhance pulse-taking in the city. Further, findings from this work serve to confirm the words of Orlikowski [31] who stated that, "I don't think people are aware of their institutional contexts", extending the context in this case, to urban spaces. The work of Beaude [48] is also valuable in assisting to understand the Internet, social media, and other so-called virtual spaces as an *innovation of space* and as such, an extension of real space for work, interactivity, social activities, and civic engagement.

5.3 IT Transformations & Smart Cities

IT transformations in the context of smart cities, involving aware people and aware technologies, contribute more broadly to the concept, pushing beyond organizations into the urban and global spheres.

The question that was raised in the title of this paper – *Is it all about awareness?* was perhaps answered in part by Orlikowski [31] many years ago in the assertion that "awareness is the first and critical thing." Orlikowski [31] added that awareness must be accompanied by action because "it is what people do that makes the difference." This is where the importance of the context comes in, provided by the subtitle of this paper – *people, smart cities 3.0, and evolving spaces for IT.* This subtitle may constitute in part what Kaptelinin and Nardi [32] refer to as "the technologies that beckon us" in terms of "providing people with diverse new cognitive, emotional, social, aesthetic, and physical experiences," in the form of the emerging smart cities 3.0 space. This subtitle also extends to Orlikowski's [9] calling for a "perspective of entanglement" for "temporally emergent sociomaterial realities." And this subtitle also responds to what Schultze and Orlikowski [8] refer to as computing that involves "multiple, complex, and emergent sociomaterial configurations in practice" that is manifesting in smart cities 3.0.

For smart cities to be smart and to work for people, the interactive dynamic of people-technologies-cities must be present, as in smart cities 3.0. As revealed from the findings of this paper, balance is important, calling into play what Scharmer et al. [46] refer to as "the quality of awareness" taking into account the tangible (e.g., walking) and the intangible (e.g., experience), extended here to urban spaces. In an age of aware technologies, smart cites 3.0 provide an opportunity for people to become more aware, be supported to act on their awareness, and be more integrally involved in smarter urban initiatives.

Orlikowski [31] pointed to the riskiness associated with acting on awareness because "people are concerned about the consequences of changing the status quo." Smart Cities 3.0 provide the opportunity for co-creation involving technology-cities-people and what Orlikowski [31] described as the necessary requirements for awareness to happen, as in, "a supportive environment that allows people to engage in experimentation and reflection" accompanied by "a conversation about alternatives." Smart cities 3.0 also afford meaningful involvement, possibly responding to the IT transformation challenges identified by Anderson and Ackerman Anderson related to "personal levels of mindset, behavior and culture" [11]. Indeed, given the nature of the wicked challenges confronting smart cities, it could be argued that not acting may pose greater risks than acting.

Awareness is explored in this paper in terms of the emerging topic of people's awareness of IT space in what may seem to be the booming smart cities movement. It is worth noting that smart cities are advanced by Habitat III, the United Nations Conference on Housing and Sustainable Urban Development [52] as part of a series of issue papers, one of which also focuses on inclusive cities [53]. Quality of life, access, complexity, openness, and rights figure strongly in these papers along with the generation of awareness.

Guided by the conceptual framework for awareness in smart cities (Figure 1), findings in this paper support and affirm all four propositions pertaining to noticing, sensing, sharing, and smartness in the city.

In summary, an understanding of smartness in contemporary urban environments is dynamic, overlapping, evolving, and adaptive. Smartness is integrally related to awareness of both people and technologies. It is not just aware technologies that possess sensing and data generation capabilities but also people with their multi-sensorial, multi-directional capabilities. Becoming more aware of, and more fully activating and utilizing human multi-sensorial capabilities, contributes to the people dimension of smart cities. With this increased awareness, people then become more prepared to work together in new types of relationships with each other and with aware technologies in co-creating contemporary and future cities. Smart cities 3.0 provide the supportive environment enabling awareness and action involving people – technologies – cities in a co-creative dynamic.

6. Contributions and Future Directions

This work makes a contribution in several ways. First, the theoretical perspective of material-discursive practices, practice theory, and a performative perspective is advanced to complement and enrich understandings of IT transformations, smart cities, and awareness; second, a conceptual framework is developed, operationalized, and advanced for awareness in smart urban environments; third, this work contributes to the research literature across multiple domains including awareness and IT transformations in smart cities; and fourth, opportunities for future initiatives are identified for practice and research focusing on awareness, action, and aware technologies in urban contexts.

Based on study findings, this paper makes recommendations for both practice and research going forward in terms of awareness, IT transformations, and smart cities.

6.1 Future Directions for Practice

Awareness & Action: The awareness-related activities of noticing, sensing, sharing, and smartness are action-oriented and designed for practical use in urban spaces. As such, these activities can be incorporated into smart city initiatives to foster greater awareness, engagement, and participation.

Awareness & IT Transformations: More comprehensive awareness involving an interweaving of aware people and aware technologies contributes to the potential for emerging understandings and opportunities for IT transformation initiatives in the context of smart cities. Incorporating more comprehensive awareness into smart cities 3.0 initiatives invites new directions for practitioners.

6.2 Future Directions for Research

Awareness & Smart Cities Conceptual Framework: The awareness in smart cities conceptual framework is intended for developers, planners, community members, researchers and all those concerned with smarter people and smarter cities. As such, the framework will benefit from further use, testing, and development with the potential to open new opportunities for research and practice.

Awareness & Smart Cities Research: While the use of aware technologies is well advanced as a component of information and communication technologies (ICTs) in the context of smart cities, this work highlights the importance of human awareness and action, as an area that may be lagging, requiring further research and opening new challenges and opportunities for smart cities.

Theory Development for Smart Cities: Insights emerging from this paper offer opportunities to contribute to contemporary urban theory, to IT transformation theorizing for smart cities, and to smart cities theorizing in relation to awareness.

7. Limitations and Mitigations

The small sample size for this study is mitigated by the in-depth and rich detail collected from a variety of individual across small to medium to large cities. Challenges presented by the minimally viable nature of the social media webspace were mitigated by information and guidance shared during the inquiry portion of the data collection interview. While anecdotal evidence may be viewed as a limitation in some research spaces, its utilization in this study of awareness in everyday urban life serves to further validate and contribute rigor through enabling additional analysis, comparison, and triangulation.

8. Conclusion

This paper presents an exploration of awareness in relation to information technology (IT) transformations focusing on aware technologies in the context of contemporary understandings of the smart city phenomena. The use of a city-focused social media space provides a mechanism for action and engagement using noticing, sensing, sharing, and smartness as proxies for awareness. This work sheds light on the interweaving of human awareness and aware technologies in 21st century urban environments. As theorized in this paper, engaging in awareness-related activities in the city contributes to greater awareness in urban environments and in new spaces afforded by social media and other emerging and aware technologies. In turn, this awareness contributes to the potential for people to become co-creators in the third wave or generation of the smart cities movement, referred to as smart cities 3.0.

A framework for awareness in smart cities is developed, operationalized, and advanced in this paper and will benefit from further use, testing, and development by researchers and practitioners. Future directions for practice are identified in relation to *action and awareness* and *awareness and IT transformations*. Future directions are identified for research in relation to the *awareness and smart cities framework*; *awareness and smart cities research*; and *theory development for smart cities*.

The key **take away** from this work is the critical human element of awareness, enabled by smart cities 3.0 thinking that is supportive of co-creative spaces for action.

This interdisciplinary paper engages with both practice and research and will be of interest to a diverse readership including: urban planners and developers, IT and ICT developers and transformers, policymakers, city officials, researchers, human geographers, and anyone concerned with innovating new spaces, relationships, and understandings for working together on aware, vibrant, sustainable, and livable cities.

REFERENCES

[1] Gil-Garcia, J. R., Pardo T. A., and Nam, T. 2016. A comprehensive view of the 21st century city: Smartness as technologies and innovation in urban contexts. In J. R. Gil-Garcia, T. A. Pardo, T. Nam, T. (Eds.) *Smarter as the New Urban Agenda: A Comprehensive View of the 21st Century City*. Switzerland: Springer. Public Administration and Information Technology Series, Volume 11, 1-19.

[2] Scholl, H. J. 2016. Foreword. In J. R. Gil-Garcia, T. A. Pardo, T. Nam, T. (Eds.) *Smarter as the New Urban Agenda: A Comprehensive View of the 21st Century City*. Switzerland: Springer. Public Administration and Information Technology Series, Volume 11, viii.

[3] Jemielniak, D., and Krzyworzeka, P. 2012. Grounded anecdotal evidence: Understanding organizational reality through archetypes in organizational humorous tales. *Standing Conference on Organizational Symbolism*. Providence, RI (USA), 13-14 April. Retrieved 21 March 2016 from https://depot.ceon.pl/bitstream/handle/123456789/305/In%20Suport%20of%20Anectodal%20Evidence-conference.pdf?sequence=1&isAllowed=y.

[4] Cubitt, S. 2013. Anecdotal evidence. *NECSUS: European Journal of Media Studies*. Retrieved 21 March 2016 from http://www.necsus-ejms.org/anecdotal-evidence/.

[5] Gregor, S. 2006. The nature of theory in information systtems. *MIS Quarterly*, 30(3): 611-642.

[6] Orlikowski, W. J., and Scott, S. V. 2015. Exploring material-discursive practices: Comments on Hardy and Thomas' Discourse in a material world. *Journal of Management Studies*, 52(5): 697-705.

[7] Feldman, M. S., and Orlikowski, W. J. 2011. Theorizing practice and practicing theory. *Organization Science,* 22(5): 1240-1253.

[8] Schultze, U., Orlikowski, W.J. 2010. Research commentary – Virtual worlds: A performative perspective on globally distributed, immersive work. *Information Systems Research* 21 (2010): 810-821.

[9] Orlikowski, W. J. 2009. The sociomateriality of organizational life: Considering technology in management research. *Cambridge Journal of Economics,* 34(1): 125-141.

[10] Orlikowski, W. J. 1996. Improvising organizational transformation over time: A situated change perspective. *Information Systems Research*, Special issue on Information Technology and Organizational Transformation, 7(1): 63-92.

[11] Anderson, D., and Ackerman Anderson, L. 2010. What is transformation, and why is it so hard to manage? Durango, CO: Being First Inc. Retrieved 29 March 2016 from http://www.beingfirst.com/resource-center/pdf/SR_WhatIsTransformation_v3_101006.pdf

[12] Harmsen, F., and Molnar, W. A. 2013. Perspectives on enterprise transformation: A sociological meta-model for transforming enterprises. *Proceedings of the 15th IEEE International Conference on Business Informatics (CBI13)*, Vienna, Austria.

[13] Ashkenas, R. 2015. We still don't know the difference between change and transformation. *Harvard Business Review*. Retrieved 27 March 2016 from https://hbr.org/2015/01/we-still-dont-know-the-difference-between-change-and-transformation

[14] De Certeau, M. 1984. *The practice of everyday life.* Berkeley, CA: University of California Press.

[15] Ibrahim, M., Adams, C., and El-Zaart, A. 2015. Paving the way to smart sustainable cities: Transformation models and challenges. *Journal of Information Systems and Technology Management (JISTEM)*, 12(3): 559-576.

[16] Goodspeed, R. 2015. Smart cities: Moving beyond urban cybernetics to tackle wicked problems. *Cambridge Journal of Regions, Economy and Society*, 8(1): 79-92.

[17] Brenner, N., and Schmid, C. 2015. Towards a new epistemology of the urban? *City*, 19(2-3): 151-182.

[18] Salgueiro Barrio, R. 2015. What world? Reframing the world as one city: A review of the exhibition "City of 7 billion. A constructed world." UrbanTheoryLab. Retrieved 30 March 2016 from http://www.urbantheorylab.net/site/assets/files/1170/exhibition_review_def_utl.pdf

[19] Greenfield, A. 2013. *Against the smart city: The city is here for you to use* (Book 1). Seattle, WA: Amazon Digital Services.

[20] Hollands, R. G. 2008. Will the Real Smart City Please Stand Up?: Intelligent, progressive or entrepreneurial? *City: Analysis of Urban Trends, Culture, Theory, Policy, Action*, 12(3): 303-320.

[21] Hollands, R. G. 2016. Beyond the corporate smart city?: Glimpses of other possibilities of smartness. *In:* Marvin, S, Luque-Ayala, A, and McFarlane, C, (Eds.) *Smart Urbanism: Utopian vision or false dawn?*. London, UK: Routledge, pp.169-185.

[22] Townsend, A. 2014. *Smart cities: Big data, civic hackers, and the quest for a new utopia.* New York, NY: W.W. Norton.

[23] Marvin, S, Luque-Ayala, A, and McFarlane, C, (Eds.). 2016. *Smart Urbanism: Utopian vision or false dawn?* London, UK: Routledge, pp.169-185.

[24] Jacobs, J. 1961. *The death and life of great American cities.* New York, NY: Random House.

[25] Harvey, D. 1989. From managerialism to entrepreneurialism: The transformation in urban governance in late capitalism. *Geografiska Annaler, Series B, Human Geography*, 71(1): 3-17.

[26] Ampatzidou, C. 2013. *Smart cities vs smart citizens: PBL expert meeting on smart cities with Dan Hill.* The Mobile City. Rotterdam, The New Institute. Retrieved 20 March 2016 from http://themobilecity.nl/2013/11/01/smart-cities-vs-smart-citizens/

[27] De Waal, M. 2013. *The city as interface: How new media are changing the city.* Rotterdam: NAI Uitgevers/Publishers Stichting.

[28] Cohen, B. 2015. The three generations of smart cities. *FastCompany Exist.* Retrieved 15 September 2015 from http://www.fastcoexist.com/3047795/the-3-generations-of-smart-cities.

[29] Mone, G. 2015. The new smart cities. *Communications of the ACM,* 58(7): 20-21.

[30] Vander, Veen, C. 2015. Without smart, connected people there are no smart cities. *GovTech, FutureSturcture.* Retrieved 14 September 2015 from http://bit.ly/1B9FbWO.

[31] Scharmer, C. O. 1999. *Awareness is the first and critical thing: Conversation with Professor Wanda Orlikowski.* Cambridge, MA: MIT, Sloan School of Management.

[32] Kaptelinin, V., and Nardi, B. 2006. *Acting with technology: Activity theory and interaction design.* Cambridge, MA: The MIT Press.

[33] Dourish, P. and Bellotti, V. 1992. Awareness and coordination in a shared workspaces. In *Proceedings of the ACM Conference on Computer-Supported Cooperative Work (CSCW '92,* Toronto, Canada, Oct. 31–Nov. 4), M. Mantel and R. Baecker, Eds. ACM Press, New York, NY, pp. 107–114.

[34] Bellotti, V., and Sellen, A. 1993. Design for privacy in ubiquitous computing environments. In G. de Michelis, C. Simone, and K. Schmidt (Eds.), *Proceedings of the Third European Conference on Computer-Supported Cooperative Work,* 13–17 September 1993, Milan, Italy ECSCW '93, pp. 77-92.

[35] Erickson, T., and Kellogg, W. A. 2000. Social translucence: An approach to designing systems that support social processes. *ACM Transactions on Computer-Human Interactions,* 7(1): 59-83.

[36] Guo, B., Riboni, D., and Hu, P. (Eds.). 2014. *Creating Personal, Social, and Urban Awareness through Pervasive Computing.* Hershey, PA: IGI Global.

[37] Brandt, J. 2015. Oblivious in the UK? Nearly 100 percent do not notice smart cities growing around them. *SmartGridNews.* Retrieved 14 September 2015 from http://bit.ly/1VVmyfu.

[38] Smith, A. 2015. *US Smartphone Use in 2015.* Washington, DC: Pew Research Center. Retrieved 21 October 2015 from http://pewrsr.ch/19JDwMd.

[39] Pew Research Center. 2014. *The Internet of Things will Thrive by 2025.* Washington, DC. Retrieved 21 October 2015 from http://pewrsr.ch/TsoFyI.

[40] Apperley, I. 2015. Wellington as a smart city: The array of things (Fitbit for a city).*Whatisitwellington: ICT from the Edge of the World.* Retrieved 21 October 2015 from http://bit.ly/1ZYakYr.

[41] Bicocchi, N., Cecaj, A., Fontana, D., Mamei, M., Sassi, A., and Zambonelli, F. 2013. Collective awareness for human-ICT collaboration in smart cities. *2013 Workshop on Enabling Technologies: Infrastructure for Collaborative Enterprise,* IEEE, pp. 3-8.

[42] Fine, D. 2014. Urban digitization and the pulse of cities. In *Re-imagining Urban Mobility.* Geneva, CH: New Cities Foundation.

[43] Laurier, E. 2013. Noticing. In R. Lee, N. Castree, R. Kitchin, V. Lawson, A. Paasi, C. Philo, S. Radcliffe, S. M. Roberts, and C. W. J. Withers (eds.), *The Sage Handbook of Human Geography,* Volume 1. Newcastle, UK: Sage, pp. 250-272.

[44] Lévy, J., Beaude, B., Poncet, P., Noizet, H., Laurent-Lucchetti, B., Bahrani, F., Maitre, O., Bataille, T., Tiphine, L., Yan, L., Tursic, M., and Rommany, T. 2015. EPFLx: *SpaceX Exploring Humans' Space: An Introduction to Geographicity.* Massive Open Online Course (MOOC), edX, Fall.

[45] Dourish, P., Adler, A., Bellotti, V., and Henderson, A. 1996. Your place or mine? Learning from long-term use of audio-video communication. *Computer Supported Cooperative Work (CSCW),* 5(1): 33-62.

[46] Scharmer, C. O., Arthur, W. B., Day, J., Jaworski, J., Jung, M., Nonaka, I., and Seng, P. M. 2002. *Illuminating the blind spot: Leadership in the context of emerging worlds.* Cambridge, MA: McKinsey-Society for Organizational Learning (SoL) Leadership Project (1999-2000).

[47] Williams, A., Robles, E., and Dourish, P. 2009. Urbane-ing the city: Examining and refining the assumptions behind urban informatics. In M. Foth (Ed.), *Handbook of research on urban informatics: The practice and promise of the real-time city* (pp. 1-20), Hershey, PA: Information Science Reference. doi:10.4018/978-1-60566-152-0.ch001

[48] Beaude, B. 2015. Internet: A unique space of coexistence. In J. Lévy et al., *EPFLx: SpaceX Exploring Humans' Space: An Introduction to Geographicity.* Massive Open Online Course (MOOC), edX, Fall.

[49] Yin, R. K. 2014. *Case study research: Design and methods.* Fifth edition. Los Angeles, CA: Sage.

[50] Trochim, W. M. K. 2006. The qualitative debate. *Research Methods Knowledge Base.* Retrieved 20 October 2015 from http://www.socialresearchmethods.net/kb/qualdeb.php

[51] Anderson, Rosemaire. 2006. Body Intelligence Scale: defining and measuring the intelligence of the body. *The Humanistic Psychologist,* 34(4): 357-367.

[52] UN. 2015. *Habitat III Issue Papers, 21 – Smart cities.* United Nations Conference on Housing and Sustainable Urban Development. New York, NY: UN-Habitat, UNDP, and ITU.

[53] UN. 2015. *Habitat III Issue Papers, 1 – Inclusive cities.* United Nations Conference on Housing and Sustainable Urban Development. New York, NY: UN-Habitat, UNDP, and ITU.

Promoting Physical Activity in Seniors: Future Opportunities with Emerging Technologies

Jake Araullo
IDEA Lab, Griffith University
Kessels Rd, Nathan 4111
jake.araullo@griffithuni.edu.au

Leigh Ellen Potter
IDEA Lab, Griffith University
Kessels Rd, Nathan 4111
L.Potter@griffith.edu.au

ABSTRACT

High levels of physical inactivity that are trending upwards in the population present significant health challenges, particularly in seniors. Opportunities are present for emerging technologies to promote and engage seniors in physical activity, leading social change in this area, with a goal to boost quality-of-life, health, self-efficacy and autonomy in this growing segment of the population. Attitudes to emerging technology adoption, physical activity and behaviour change must be identified. This will allow the practical adoption of strategic information system implementations that can create meaningful, macro-level impacts in this in area of senior physical activity, as well as inform strategies and best practices for designers of information technology systems in this developing area.

Keywords

Human Factors; Design; Experimentation; Performance

1. INTRODUCTION

The growth of ageing populations across the Western world due to increased life expectancy and medical treatments is "one of the major public health challenges in the 21st century" [51]. In ageing populations, the leading cause of death is no longer chronic disease, but instead degenerative diseases and age related illnesses. Physical activity has been found to have health benefits across all age demographics, but is particularly valuable in senior (65+) populations, where physical activity has been associated with prolonged cognitive and physical abilities and higher quality of life [53], as well as reducing load on public health systems [29].

The senior population is more sedentary than their younger counterparts, and interventionist attempts to increase physical activity levels in this group with technologies have had inconsistent results and have not focused on the creation of long-term health habits and behaviour change [20, 54, 59].

Technology has the potential to assist with physical activity interventions, through interactive and real time information that can be gathered and shared. A range of new technologies, such as wearable technology, fitness technology, and interactive apps are

SIGMIS-CPR '16, June 2–4, 2016, Alexandria, VA, USA.
Copyright 2016 ACM. ISBN 978-1-4503-4203-2/16/06...$15.00.
DOI: http://dx.doi.org/10.1145/2890602.2890616

readily accessible, and may be useful in addressing the exercise and motivational challenges experienced by the senior population. However, in the area of physical activity "research on persuasive technology has not been focusing on seniors" [13].

This paper explores current literature regarding physical activity and senior populations, and then examines emerging technologies and the issues related to emerging technologies in this context. We will explore the intersection between health-related emerging technologies and senior populations; exploring work that has been completed to date regarding boosting senior physical activity using technology and emerging technology. Finally, the goal of this work, we will explore opportunities and research questions for future study in this area. Identifying this research gap will allow future work to identify how emerging technology can promote physical activity in seniors, allowing future technology to actively and effectively shape the critically important physical activity habits of seniors.

2. METHODS

We present a topical exploration and presentation of literature review findings, appropriate here considering the interdisciplinary subject matter under review [64]. This literature review applied Boell and Cecez-Kecmanovic's hermeneutic framework [11] to review process, acknowledging that formulating a literature review based on our subject matter was "fundamentally an understanding process" [11]. We must thoroughly understand our problem (senior inactivity) and have an understanding of background factors determining why this is the case. Similarly, in order to frame future directions for this area of research, we explore and understand emerging technologies prior to analysing current work and literature in this area, particularly work geared towards boosting senior physical activity.

A strictly systematic literature review was inappropriate in this case, as such would provide a limited cross section of specific problem area knowledge, potentially leading to limited understanding of background issues or the importance of the problem itself. Additionally, interchangeable terminology is this developing field makes a systematic review problematic and limits the iterative and continuing nature that a hermeneutic literature review allows [11].

3. HEALTH AND PHYSICAL ACTIVITY

Health is defined by the World Health Organization (WHO) as the "state of complete physical, mental and social well-being and not merely the absence of disease or infirmity". Many governments adopt this definition directly, including both Australia and the United States [5, 61]. Reflecting on the physicality of these definitions, The Australian Department of Health recognises the contribution of physical activity to overall health, stating: "Being physically active and limiting your sedentary behaviour every day is essential for your health and well-being" [6].

With physical activity critical to health, it is also important we understand what physical activity is. Being physically active is "exercise for fitness, recreation, or sport which caused a moderate increase in heart rate or breathing" [5]. Physical activity is movement that raises energy above a resting or basal level [61]. Physical activity can be walking, swimming, gardening or any activity which requires active body movement.

3.1 Physical Activity Recommendations

Both the Australian and United States Government's physical activity guidelines recommend at minimum 150 to 300 minutes of moderate intensity physical activity per week for adults aged under 65. In children at least 60 minutes of moderate activity per day is recommended [6, 61]. The United Nations' Global recommendations on physical activity for health prescribe the same amounts [66].

While the above recommendations are generally applicable to seniors (for the purposes of this work, those aged 65 years and over), there are additional health considerations in this subgroup. Physical activity is critical to the overall health and quality of life of older populations, and considering unique health constraints regarding ability, fragility and other health factors that may impact physical activity, it is critical that seniors are provided a tailored set of physical activity guidelines [53]. The most tangible recommendation, among several, is: for those aged 65 years and over 30 minutes of activity per day is advised as a minimum [52]. Generally US, Australian and WHO guidelines recommend seniors attempt as much physical activity as they are able to at their current capabilities [6, 61, 66].

3.2 Physical Inactivity

There have been numerous studies conducted across the world that are indicative of general and worldwide trends of increased physical inactivity. The Australian Bureau of Statistics (ABS) conducted a comprehensive set of professional interviews with adults in approximately 15,600 Australian households. It was found that 70% of Australian adults did not meet the minimum physical activity recommendations. Exercise level results from the 'Australian Health Survey: First Results, 2011-12' are depicted in Table 1. 65.82% of Australian adults aged 18-65 partook in little to no exercise in the week prior to the survey being conducted.

Table 1. Derived from ABS Australian Health Survey: First Results, 2011-12, Table 11.1 [5].

Physical Activity and Exercise Amount (adults 18-64)	
Sedentary or Low	65.82%
Moderate	21.00%
High	13.14%

ABS figures also indicate that Australian adults aged 65 years and over became more sedentary than non-senior adults (Table 2). Less than half of Australian adults over the age of 65 reach the minimum recommendation of 150 minutes of physical activity. One third of this inactive population is entirely sedentary [53]. The ABS survey indicates that the number of seniors who performed low or no exercise was 11.2% higher than 18 to 64

year olds. Likewise, the percentage of those who performed moderate and high amounts of exercise dropped 0.9% and 10.4%, respectively, compared to 18 to 64 year olds [5].

Table 2. Derived from ABS Australian Health Survey: First Results, 2011-12, Table 11.1 [5].

Physical Activity and Exercise Amount (adults 65 years +)	
Sedentary or Low	77.03%
Moderate	20.10%
High	2.78%

An external study of available government activity data of countries, where said data was sufficiently available (United States, UK, Brazil, China, India [46]) spanning significant timeframes, collated and analysed available information to identify trends in energy exertion levels in physical activity and inactivity levels worldwide. This analysis showed a drop in worldwide physical activity over the past several decades since 1960, however more sharply since 1995. Additionally, the data indicates a consistent and sharp rise in number of hours spent sedentary per week since the late 1990s [46]. One limitation of this work is that few less-developed countries have adequately had physical activity trends studied, and they are generally found to be more physically active than high-income countries [23].

3.3 Reasons for Higher Physical Inactivity

A clear and consistent deficit in the physical activity level of adults in Australia and around much of the world is evident, and as such it is necessary to examine the causes of high inactivity. There has been considerable academic disagreement when identifying definitive causes of increased physical inactivity. Broadly, the United Nations' Global recommendations on physical activity for health found that poor health habits, such as inactivity, were impacted by three major factors: "population-ageing, rapid unplanned urbanization, and globalization" [66].

The drop in physical activity has been associated with the industrial revolution and the subsequent decrease in physically demanding professions, combined with increased worker efficiency [23]. Ladabaum argues that the primary cause for increased inactivity was the decrease in physical activity conducted during leisure time as by-product of busier work and social lives [31]. This study appears to propose an association between low leisure time physical activity and obesity in adults. Ladabaum also found dramatic increases in the number of adults who reported no leisure time physical activity between 1988 and 2010: from 19.1% in 1988 increasing to 51.7% in women, and from 11.4% in 1988 increasing to 43.5% in men.

However, Bassett et al. directly rebukes Ladabaum's study, instead arguing that leisure time physical activity has remained the same (at least in the United States) however the levels of actual energy expended during these times has decreased [8]. Bassett associates this drop in energy expenditure with transport, cleaning and occupational efficiencies which are less physically demanding on individuals. Ng found, similar to Bassett when examining worldwide trends (United States, UK, Brazil, China, India), that the metabolic equivalent (MET – the energy expended performing a task), in tasks like transport, cleaning and occupation had fallen, while the time spent performing those tasks remained fairly stagnant [46].

3.4 Importance of Physical Activity

With smoking and physical inactivity now roughly equivalent as causes associated with estimated number of worldwide deaths per year [1], it is critical that the importance of physical activity is comprehensively understood.

There have been dramatic findings regarding the toll of physical inactivity on worldwide health levels. Estimates have examined the burden of physical inactivity on the contraction of non-communicable diseases. It was found that by decreasing physical inactivity by 10% to 25%, between 533,000 and 1.3 million deaths could be prevented per year. Additionally, worldwide life expectancy would rise by approximately 0.68 years [36].

Worldwide societal changes, particularly in the adoption of more sedentary behaviours and lifestyles, and thus lessening amounts of physical activity have been marked as a major contributor to the obesity epidemic [25]. Sedentary behaviour in adolescents is often continued into adulthood and has the likelihood to contribute to the development of numerous health issues including obesity and cardiovascular disease as lifelong health problems [56].

One study found that adults undertaking a normal amount of exercise, even when overeating, didn't see a large increase in fat development. While a second group, examined in the work, who were also overeating but significantly more inactive did see increasing fat development [30]. Inactivity, not caloric intake being a larger contributor to fat development has been reiterated by other work in this area, with the suggestion that physical activity more significantly minimised risks of cardiovascular disease (CVD) rather than reduced caloric intake [3].

Physical inactivity causing and exacerbating health concerns (such as CVD) has been found to place direct burden on public health systems, estimates placing "annual direct health-care costs … from US\$28.4 to \$334.4 per head in Australia, UK, and Switzerland" [29].

Healy et al. found positive associations between time spent sedentary and waist size, as well as an association between increased physical activity and decreased likelihood of obesity [26]. Maher contradicts Healy et al., finding that sedentary lifestyles alone did not positively associate with obesity in adults. However, moderate-to-vigorous physical activity did have an inverse association with adult obesity, but "total sedentary time was not associated with increased risk of obesity" [42].

While the health toll of physical inactivity on the general population is evidently significant, this is even more true for those aged 65 and older [52].

3.5 Senior Health and Physical Activity

Seniors will "achieve at least short-term gains in health from behaviour change" by increasing physical activity levels [52]. Those who are more physically active in older populations have lower risk of "bowel cancer, stroke, ischaemic heart disease" [52], "all-cause mortality, coronary heart disease, high blood pressure, stroke, type 2 diabetes, colon cancer, breast cancer, a higher level of cardiorespiratory and muscular fitness, healthier body mass and composition, and a biomarker profile that is more favourable for the prevention of cardiovascular disease, type 2 diabetes and the enhancement of bone health" [66].

As we have identified, seniors are generally more sedentary than the general population. Many seniors also do not just maintain, but gain weight until their mid-70s [52], potentially leading to some of the aforementioned health concerns.

Maintaining a high quality of life becomes important in older age. Studies of older communities found seniors who met walking goals had a higher reported quality of life than those who did not [27]. In separate work, quality of life was self reported to be lower in seniors who had lower levels of functional fitness and self-sufficiency [38]. Physical activity boosts functional autonomy in older populations, making it a crucial component of being able to live independently and autonomously as a senior long term [61].

Besides quality of life, increased physical activity in older adults has also been found to support maintained cognitive function and reductions in depression levels [18].

3.5.1 Senior Physical Activity Factors

A numbers of factors have been determined which inform and shape the physical activity habits of seniors. Three main groups of motivators emerge regarding older adults and physical activity: the desire for social affiliation, continuing lifelong fitness habits from before retirement and finally, a sense of purpose and challenge [9].

Amotivation in the attitudes of seniors towards physical activity was found to be a product of a lack of self-efficacy and little recognition of tangible outcomes by participants. One theory posited that explaining the physiological and psychological benefits to older populations may decrease amotivation levels when considering physical activity. There is scope for further study regarding "relationships between the value attached to exercise and the fulfilment of innate psychological needs" [63] such as those defined by motivational theories like self-determination-theory.

Examining a broad cross section of research found that developing autonomous extrinsic motivation (motivators influenced by external factors) helped develop the more desirable intrinsic motivation (powerful motivation from within, for the sake of enjoyment) towards physical activity [60]. A high presence of autonomous motivational activities helped build long term sustained motivation in the area of physical activity.

When exercise is prescribed alongside personalised goal-setting and monitoring, adherence to these physical activity directives were more likely to be successful over broad physical activity directives alone [39].

3.5.2 Social Factors

The importance of environment, built and social, has ramifications for physical activity in older populations: older males are more active than older females [12, 40] and access and locality of community facilities are positively associated with physical activity participation [40]. Booth et al. [12] examined the effect of social and community support on the physical activity habits of Australians over 60. Those who reported higher levels of self-efficacy, access to walking routes and parks, or having a physically active partner or friends were positively associated with physical activity participation, "suggesting that a social environment in which physical activity is a common occurrence may be an important influence" [12].

As discussed above, "walkability, social support, and self-efficacy" [17] were consistently and significantly positively associated with physical activity throughout the literature. Likewise, strong social networks with others who were also physically active have been consistently identified as a strong influence on the physical activity habits of an individual [12, 17].

Social isolation was identified as a possible barrier to physical activity participation in older adults; specifically for older individuals with less than three friends [65].

The type of physical activity to be engaged in has been found to influence the willingness of older individuals to participate, along demographic splits. For example, younger seniors preferred sport and organised activities, older participants preferred lower intensity activities. Additionally, women and men displayed preferences towards different physical activities [58]: walking and gymnastics for women, and more structured and competitive sports, such as cycling and tennis for men.

It is now evident that inactivity in the senior age group can increase the risk of a multitude of health concerns, over other age groups [52]. How the aforementioned factors (social and otherwise) converge with the use of emerging technologies to promote physical activity has not yet been comprehensively explored or catalogued, and this research opportunity still exists. Emerging technologies facilitate innovative interactions, and may present avenues to boost physical activity in the senior cohort in ways that have not yet been explored by traditional means.

4. EMERGING TECHNOLOGY

Emerging technologies are those which have transformational potential in their field, or those which have the ability to define a new industry entirely [19]. These are new technologies in their own right, or those which incrementally emerge "from the convergence of existing technologies" [55]. The locale, cultural climate and context of the application of a technology may define it as emerging [22]. Technology may be considered emerging in particular domains (such as medicine or education) but be a mature, stable technology in domains where application or innovation of the technology is more widespread [55].

4.1 Emerging Technologies for Physical Activity

Emerging technologies that assist in promoting physical activity have been explored and applied in limited capacities academically, however interest and work in this area is growing particularly in the areas of gamification and mobile applications [16, 41]. This limited body of academic work does present shortcomings, especially around motivation, habit creation and designing for cutting edge technology [10, 13].

One smartphone fitness game, attempts to leverage the benefits of the outdoors and open air, while being aware (via sensors) of the user's heart rate and ideal exercise intensity. Researchers found that this game increased motivation and ability in their participants who were jogging to avoid injury [16].

Another research project has developed a cushion in an attempt to measure sedentary behavior, and prompts a user to stand after protracted periods of inactivity [7].

Virtual reality has been experimented with as an innovative method for promoting increased physical activity in unsupervised physiotherapy rehabilitation environments [41], however at present very little academic work has been undertaken regarding the ability for virtual reality interventions to influence physical activity levels [44].

4.2 Wearables

Wearables are a specific example of emerging technologies, using "electronics and computers that are integrated into clothing and other accessories that can be worn comfortably on the body"

(Wright & Keith, 2014). They are "any body-worn computer that is designed to provide useful services while the user is performing other tasks" [57]. This focus on secondary use may be too limiting, excluding wearable technologies such as virtual or augmented reality which are worn technologies that take primary not secondary user focus. Despite wide availability in consumer markets, wearables are still emerging technologies, having significant transformational potential, but without enough established utility or design standards to yet warrant mass mainstream adoption [37].

Wearables have a strong presence in the health and fitness technology space, with products such as Fitbit, Jawbone, Apple Health, Google Fit, Apple Watch, Misfit Shine and others tracking various body measurements including steps, sleep, heart rate, distance travelled and individual types of exercise. Often physical activity trackers are accompanied by software that allows users to set physical activity goals and prompts them to work towards said goals. However, it has been speculated that the mere physical presence of a physical activity tracker may act as a visual reminder and cue for individuals wearing them to partake in physical activity [10].

Design standards and best practices are still being actively established and critically analysed in the area of wearable technology [4, 28], and it has been argued they are not yet compelling standalone mass-market products, instead primarily smartphone companion devices [37].

Wearable and emerging technologies present the opportunity not only for unique interaction, but for unique design and adoption challenges. In order to explore avenues to increase senior physical activity using emerging technology we must first explore technological adoption barriers, particularly in senior populations.

5. TECHNOLOGY ADOPTION BARRIERS

Technology adoption is the process that commences with a "user becoming aware of the technology, and ending with the user embracing the technology and making full use of it" [50].

Individual factors that have been found to weigh heavily on a person's decision to adopt technology are self-efficacy and perceptions of poor technological quality [32]. When considering emerging technologies that encouraged physical activity, additional barriers merge. One example, in an augmented reality game encouraging participants to run, was initial hesitation to actually engage physically with the game (through running). This initial unfamiliarity with the interaction modality with the game was outweighed by positive factors such as team competitiveness, and the participants did run and successfully played the game [32]. Designers of systems that encourage physical activity and exercise must therefore consider not only the challenge–skill imbalance but also other potential disturbance factors.

5.1 Senior Technology Adoption Barriers

The adoption of technology in senior populations is informed by a number of factors, such as: "value, usability, affordability, accessibility, emotion, confidence, independence, compatibility, reliability, social and technical support, and cost" [34].

Older populations have been found to value not only the technology product's features alone, but also the support (both technical and social) ecosystems that accompany them, as well as the utility and social latitude and stature that owning and using such a product may provide them [35].

With increases in technological capability, and decreases in cost, many older people are exposed to technology via assistive technologies [62], which makes their example valuable in considering technological adoption within the senior population. This exposure does not necessarily mean acceptance. One factor contributing to senior assistive technology abandonment is the amount to which products have traditionally been clinically, not personally, designed [49]. Assistive technologies often do not consider the changing (potentially increasing) needs of older users as they continue to age [48]. Factors that caused older users to abandon assistive technology were not appealing to "different individual learning needs, a lack of capacity building, a need for social interaction and a lack of trust in the technologies" [48].

One successful example of technology adoption has been smartphone technology. A comprehensive review of the literature determined that contextual, sociological, techno-economic, psychological, personal and ageing-specific factors all contributed towards acceptance of these devices [47]. Nikou proposes an acceptance model of technology based on this work. Health and ageing specific factors have been reaffirmed by other literature [45], with disability, illness or infirmity having the ability to reduce technological adoption barriers in older populations.

One noteworthy barrier to technological adoption by seniors, particularly around health and activity technology, was the perception that those types of technology implied some level of illness or infirmity for adults of an older age, a strong negative connotation [67].

5.1.1 Tangible Advantage

Seniors and older adults have consistently been found to be hesitant and resistive to technology when they fail to identify tangible benefits and outcomes for themselves [54, 67]. This included scenarios where seniors had not previously been exposed to technology and were encountering it for the first time [45]. Sookhai et al. used Fitbits in a senior population to monitor vital signs. While most participants were initially hesitant or hostile to technology, when participants believed and could identify that the addition of the Fitbit would be directly beneficial to their health they were more receptive to the technology. Ultimately, one of the most significant barriers to technological adoption by aged populations is that they "need to be convinced of value" [21].

A number of general concerns and considerations of senior populations emerge in regards to adoption of technology. Social and technical support are viewed as critical by older populations, in order to find value in a product. Accessibility and the ability for technology to provide and reinforce autonomy and independence, made product adoption more likely. Competence and self-efficacy using a piece of technology were highly valued in technology used by seniors. Finally, self-image, or perceived self-image was a strong consideration: the ability of a piece of technology to raise social standing, and conversely, the ability for technology to associate an individual with infirmity and ill health. There is however an opportunity for future work to quantify senior attitudes towards emerging technologies comparative to traditional (desktop, laptop etc) technologies, particularly in relation to emerging technologies.

6. EMERGING TECHNOLOGY AND PHYSICAL ACTIVITY FOR SENIORS

The health consequences of physical inactivity are amplified in the senior community. Downwards trends of adults meeting

recommended physical activity targets make intervention to fix this issue paramount, particularly considering seniors are more sedentary than the rest of the population.

Considering the very high inactivity level of seniors, new interventions and methods of increasing physical activity must be considered. Emerging technologies present new, innovative, often physically driven ways to interact with computers and may offer opportunites to reverse inactivity trends in senior populations.

6.1 Work to Date

The current limited body of work in the area of improving senior physical activity with emerging technology has primarily focused around observation, intervention, exergames and identifying reasons for physical inactivity. Interventionist work that has introduced emerging physical activity tracking technology into senior populations has had mixed results.

One study used Fitbits in a non-white senior population with the goal of educating seniors about their vital signs. The study found increased awareness of and involvement with health concerns among the population, however did not find a consistent increase between pre and post study exercise levels. In fact, the 7% of study participants who exercised 6 or more days per week fell to 0% [54].

Another small trial on a homogenous (upper-class white) group of seniors used technology to take various body measurements and a Fitbit to measure steps over 8 weeks. While participants experienced a slight increase in self-efficacy as well as "the desire to live an active lifestyle", the author acknowledges the limitations of this work and the need for further study. This work did not attempt to identify barriers to technological adoption and the development of health and fitness routines in these groups [33].

One work that yielded positive results on physical activity outcomes in an older population was an intervention on almost 500 seniors, promoting physical activity using technology as part of a larger package of intervention tools. Pedometer technology was introduced to seniors as part of a larger set of written materials, basic exercise equipment and telephone coaching. Sedentary time fell in participants by the end of the six-month intervention. These results are promising and provoke further questions regarding the roles that emerging technology can play as a component operating alongside other factors in an individual's physical activity space [15].

When examining current approaches to increasing senior physical activity, it becomes clear that barriers to adoption of emerging technologies are not clearly understood or sufficiently developed to design interventions that will produce consistent results.

There have been other types of technological interventions regarding emerging technology for physical activity that have not specifically focused on raising physical activity levels. A system for monitoring the activity of the elderly indoors harnessed emerging technologies such as RFID and Fitbit activity trackers to record and send away activity levels of seniors while maintaining privacy and a level of non-intrusiveness [59]. An inspection of the literature examined senior health around falling and the role of technology and exercise-based-games (exergames) in balance training. This did not concern itself with overall physical activity levels, motivation or routine, instead finding that emerging technologies may be able to facilitate improved balance training for seniors moving forward [20]. Other related works in this area have explored classifying different types of physical activity using pulse rates [2] and the design of a future fitness MOOC (Massive Open Online Course) [14].

There has been some research conducted in involving seniors in developing video games, particularly exergames. Seniors respond positively to illustrations, metaphor, real-world similarities and physical affordances [43]. Comprehensive literature review showed that Wii-based exergames had positive impacts on "cognition, physical function, and psychosocial outcomes in older adults" [18]. There has been work towards designing Exergames with NUIs in clinical rehabilitation settings, with the specific goal of reaching minimum physical activity targets. However this work, in it's infancy, is as-yet inconclusive [24].

While exergames paired with emerging technology appear to hold potential regarding seniors performing physical activity, there has been little work regarding acceptance of these systems by the senior population, as currently "research on persuasive technology has not been focusing on seniors" [13]. Social factors such as inclusion and competition were found to have positive motivational and persuasive traits in exergames. Issues have been identified when games were not initially developed for the senior population, and later targeted to that group. Exergames have been perceived as too fast, having too much negative feedback and being technologically unfamiliar and confusing. [13].

6.2 Current Issues and Future Work

The primary issue identified in this work has been the large deficit of physical activity in senior populations over the age of 65. Increased health risks of physical inactivity in this population make it imperative that this issue is addressed. Innovative emerging technologies offer initial promise in creating positive physical activity change in seniors, however work to date is sparse, garnering inconsistent results or not focusing on persuasion [13, 33].

There has, to date, not been concerted and focused work into improving the long-term health prospects of senior populations through the creation of routine physical activity habits, nor have barriers to the adoption of emerging technologies in this area been sufficiently quantified. While the literature has identified a number of barriers to technological adoption among older populations, the specific challenges that motivational physical activity emerging technologies present are not yet clear, due to their, by definition, emerging nature.

Further work must examine the motivational factors of seniors undertaking physical activity facilitated through technology. Known factors when considering physical activity in seniors include: the desire for social support and acceptance, tangible benefit of product, continuation of lifelong habits, a sense of purpose and genuine autonomously motivated enjoyment of physical activity. However, how these motivational factors may be influenced, enhanced or diminished through the introduction of technology, particularly emerging technologies, is not yet known.

Current academic work into senior exergames focuses primarily on the introduction and observation of exergames in senior populations, with little regard for acceptance and the creation and reinforcement of physical activity habits over time, rather, simply focusing on cursory measurements of physical activity quantity.

Introduction of emerging technologies such as physical activity trackers to senior populations have not consistently raised physical activity levels in senior samples as hypothesised in current works, and in fact decreased activity during more than one work. Further research must be conducted to understand why these results differed. Some work, while focusing on raising physical activity in adults with technology, do not consider the unique needs of a senior population [10]. Additionally, no intervention-based studies have focused on the presence of adoption barriers, nor system success in these contexts.

With the goal of increasing long-term, sustained physical activity levels in seniors, we must be able to not only accurately measure physical activity in individuals, but comprehensively be able to determine adoption barriers to applied emerging technologies, be able to methodically determine what makes technology successful and accepted in this community, and we must be able to quantify the effect technology has in shaping experience and change in physical activity habits.

Larger, longer-term, comprehensive studies have shown that technology-based interventions can produce promising results and provoke further questions regarding the roles that emerging technology can play as a component operating alongside other factors in improving an individual's physical activity levels.

There is a compelling case for further research into opportunities for emerging technologies, such as wearables, virtual reality, augmented reality and others, to be adopted and used by seniors at a macro level, rather than current, micro intervention type levels – creating larger social change in the area of physical activity.

Research questions identified from this exploration of the literature that warrant further investigation are:

1. What are the attitudes of seniors towards technologies particularly designed to increase physical activity?

2. How do the attitudes of seniors towards emerging technologies differ from their attitudes towards traditional technology?

3. What barriers to adoption exist in seniors in relation to emerging technologies designed to promote physical activity?

4. How do external factors influence senior adoption of emerging technologies for promoting physical activity?

5. What strategies can we implement to overcome these barriers, thus promoting and facilitating habitual physical activity in seniors using emerging technology?

This area presents new challenges for designers of information technology systems. HCI and UX must consider designing not just for a population that has distinct needs and attitudes regarding accessibility and technology, but also, designing information technology systems to motivate physical activity in a group often with physiological constraints.

Avoiding the increased burden on public health systems borne from the twin factors of an ageing population and the health concerns of physical inactivity in seniors is a significant societal concern moving forward. Work to identify emerging technologies to boost physical activity in seniors, and working to identify and eliminate barriers to adoption of said technologies in senior populations will have meaningful and compounding ramifications towards creating significant social change into the future.

7. REFERENCES

[1] Addy, D. 2012. The importance of physical activity. *Archives of Disease in Childhood.* 97, 11 (Nov. 2012), 979–979.

[2] Ahmed, M.U. and Loutfi, A. 2013. Physical activity classification for elderly based on pulse rate. *Studies in Health Technology and Informatics.* 189, (2013), 152–157.

[3] American Physical Therapy Association 2014. Rise in Obesity More About Inactivity Than Caloric Intake. *PT in Motion.* 6, 11 (Dec. 2014), 48.

[4] Araullo, J. and Potter, L.E. 2014. Experiences Using Emerging Technology. *Proceedings of the 26th Australian Computer-Human Interaction Conference on Designing Futures: The Future of Design* (New York, NY, USA, 2014), 523–526.

[5] Australian Bureau of Statistics 2013. Australian Health Survey: First Results, 2011-12. Australian Bureau of Statistics.

[6] Australian Government Department of Health Population Health Division 2014. Make your move – Sit less Be active for life! Australian Government Department of Health.

[7] Barua, D. et al. 2013. Viewing and Controlling Personal Sensor Data: What Do Users Want? *Persuasive Technology.* S. Berkovsky and J. Freyne, eds. Springer Berlin Heidelberg. 15–26.

[8] Bassett, D.R. et al. 2015. Trends in Physical Inactivity. *The American journal of medicine.* 128, 5 (Jan. 2015), e21.

[9] Beck, F. et al. 2010. A theoretical investigation of the development of physical activity habits in retirement. *British Journal of Health Psychology.* 15, 3 (Sep. 2010), 663–679.

[10] Bice, M.R. et al. 2015. Technology and physical activity motivation. *International Journal of Sport and Exercise Psychology.* 0, 0 (2015), 1–10.

[11] Boell, S.K. and Cecez-Kecmanovic, D. 2014. A Hermeneutic Approach for Conducting Literature Reviews and Literature Searches. *Communications of the Association for Information Systems.* 34, (Jan. 2014), 257–286.

[12] Booth, M.L. et al. 2000. Social–Cognitive and Perceived Environment Influences Associated with Physical Activity in Older Australians. *Preventive Medicine.* 31, 1 (Jul. 2000), 15–22.

[13] Brox, E. et al. 2011. Exergames for elderly: Social exergames to persuade seniors to increase physical activity. *2011 5th International Conference on Pervasive Computing Technologies for Healthcare (PervasiveHealth)* (May 2011), 546–549.

[14] Buchem, I. et al. Wearable Learning for Healthy Ageing through Creative Learning: A Conceptual Framework in the project "Fitness MOOC"(fMOOC).

[15] Burke, L. et al. 2013. Physical activity and nutrition behavioural outcomes of a home-based intervention program for seniors: a randomized controlled trial. *International Journal of Behavioral Nutrition and Physical Activity.* 10, 1 (2013), 14.

[16] Buttussi, F. and Chittaro, L. 2010. Smarter Phones for Healthier Lifestyles: An Adaptive Fitness Game. *IEEE Pervasive Computing.* 9, 4 (Oct. 2010), 51–57.

[17] Carlson, J.A. et al. 2012. Interactions between Psychosocial and Built Environment Factors in Explaining Older Adults' Physical Activity. *Preventive medicine.* 54, 1 (Jan. 2012), 68–73.

[18] Chao, Y.-Y. et al. 2015. Effects of Using Nintendo Wii™ Exergames in Older Adults A Review of the Literature. *Journal of Aging and Health.* 27, 3 (Apr. 2015), 379–402.

[19] Day, G.S. et al. 2004. *Wharton on managing emerging technologies.* John Wiley & Sons.

[20] van Diest, M. et al. 2013. Exergaming for balance training of elderly: state of the art and future developments. *Journal of NeuroEngineering and Rehabilitation.* 10, (Sep. 2013), 101.

[21] Ehrenhard, M. et al. 2014. Market adoption barriers of multi-stakeholder technology: Smart homes for the aging population. *Technological Forecasting and Social Change.* 89, (Nov. 2014), 306–315.

[22] Halaweh, M. 2013. Emerging Technology: What is it? *Journal of Technology Management & Innovation.* 8, 3 (2013), 108–115.

[23] Hallal, P.C. et al. 2012. Global physical activity levels: surveillance progress, pitfalls, and prospects. *The Lancet (British edition).* 380, 9838 (Jul. 2012), 247–257.

[24] Hasselmann, V. et al. 2015. Are exergames promoting mobility an attractive alternative to conventional self-regulated exercises for elderly people in a rehabilitation setting? Study protocol of a randomized controlled trial. *BMC Geriatrics.* 15, (Sep. 2015), 108.

[25] Hawley, L. et al. 2010. A social cognitive approach to tackle inactivity and obesity in young Australians. *Journal of Business Research.* 63, 2 (Feb. 2010), 116–120.

[26] Healy, G.N. et al. 2008. Objectively Measured Sedentary Time, Physical Activity, and Metabolic Risk The Australian Diabetes, Obesity and Lifestyle Study (AusDiab). *Diabetes Care.* 31, 2 (Feb. 2008), 369–371.

[27] Hörder, H. et al. 2012. Health-related quality of life in relation to walking habits and fitness: a population-based study of 75-year-olds. *Quality of Life Research.* 22, 6 (Sep. 2012), 1213–1223.

[28] Jensen, M.M. and Mueller, F. "Floyd" 2014. Running with Technology: Where Are We Heading? *Proceedings of the 26th Australian Computer-Human Interaction Conference on Designing Futures: The Future of Design* (New York, NY, USA, 2014), 527–530.

[29] Kohl 3rd, H.W. et al. 2012. The pandemic of physical inactivity: global action for public health. *The Lancet.* 380, 9838 (Jul. 2012), 294–305.

[30] Krogh-Madsen, R. et al. 2014. Normal physical activity obliterates the deleterious effects of a high-caloric intake. *Journal of Applied Physiology.* 116, 3 (American Physiological Society 2014), 231–239.

[31] Ladabaum, U. et al. 2014. Obesity, Abdominal Obesity, Physical Activity, and Caloric Intake in US Adults: 1988 to 2010. *The American Journal of Medicine.* 127, 8 (Aug. 2014), 717–727.e12.

[32] Laine, T.H. and Suk, H.J. 2015. Designing Mobile Augmented Reality Exergames. *Games and Culture.* (Feb. 2015), 1555412015572006.

[33] Lebron, J. et al. 2015. Activity tracker technologies for older adults: Successful adoption via intergenerational telehealth. *Systems, Applications and Technology Conference (LISAT), 2015 IEEE Long Island* (May 2015), 1–6.

[34] Lee, C. 2014. Adoption of Smart Technology Among Older Adults: Challenges and Issues. *Public Policy & Aging Report.* 24, 1 (Mar. 2014), 14–17.

[35] Lee, C. and Coughlin, J.F. 2015. PERSPECTIVE: Older Adults' Adoption of Technology: An Integrated Approach to Identifying Determinants and Barriers. *Journal of Product Innovation Management.* 32, 5 (Sep. 2015), 747–759.

[36] Lee, I.-M. et al. 2012. Effect of physical inactivity on major non-communicable diseases worldwide: an analysis of burden of disease and life expectancy. *The Lancet.* 380, 9838 (Jul. 2012), 219–29.

[37] Lee, M. and Lee, M.R. 2015. Beyond the Wearable Hype. *IT Professional.* 17, 5 (Sep. 2015), 59–61.

[38] Les, A. and Gaworska, M. 2011. Quality of life and functional fitness of the elderly. *Biomedical Human Kinetics.* 3, (2011), 57.

[39] Levkoff, S. et al. 2001. *Aging in good health: multidisciplinary perspectives.* Springer Pub.

[40] Lim, K. and Taylor, L. 2005. Factors associated with physical activity among older people—a population-based study. *Preventive Medicine.* 40, 1 (Jan. 2005), 33–40.

[41] Madeira, R.N. et al. 2014. PhysioMate - Pervasive physical rehabilitation based on NUI and gamification. *2014 International Conference and Exposition on Electrical and Power Engineering (EPE)* (Oct. 2014), 612–616.

[42] Maher, C.A. et al. 2013. The independent and combined associations of physical activity and sedentary behavior with obesity in adults: NHANES 2003-06. *Obesity.* 21, 12 (Dec. 2013), E730–E737.

[43] Marques, J. et al. 2013. Senior-driven design and development of tablet-based cognitive games. (Jan. 2013), 133–138.

[44] Mitchell, L. et al. 2012. The effect of virtual reality interventions on physical activity in children and adolescents with early brain injuries including cerebral palsy. *Developmental Medicine & Child Neurology.* 54, 7 (Jul. 2012), 667–671.

[45] Nayak, L.U.S. et al. 2010. An application of the technology acceptance model to the level of Internet usage by older adults. *Universal Access in the Information Society.* 9, 4 (Feb. 2010), 367–374.

[46] Ng, S.W. and Popkin, B.M. 2012. Time use and physical activity: a shift away from movement across the globe. *Obesity Reviews.* 13, 8 (Aug. 2012), 659–680.

[47] Nikou, S. 2015. Mobile technology and forgotten consumers: the young-elderly. *International Journal of Consumer Studies.* 39, 4 (Jul. 2015), 294–304.

[48] Olphert, W. et al. 2009. Process requirements for building sustainable digital assistive technology for older people. *Journal of Assistive Technologies.* 3, 3 (2009), 4–13.

[49] Ravneberg, B. 2012. Usability and abandonment of assistive technology. *Journal of Assistive Technologies.* 6, 4 (2012), 259–269.

[50] Renaud, K. and van Biljon, J. 2008. Predicting Technology Acceptance and Adoption by the Elderly: A Qualitative Study. *Proceedings of the 2008 Annual Research Conference of the South African Institute of Computer Scientists and Information Technologists on IT Research in Developing Countries: Riding the Wave of Technology* (New York, NY, USA, 2008), 210–219.

[51] Shumaker, S.A. et al. 2008. *Handbook of Health Behavior Change (3rd Edition).* Springer Publishing Company.

[52] Sims, J. et al. 2006. National physical activity recommendations for older Australians: Discussion Document. Australian Government Department of Health and Ageing.

[53] Sims J et al. 2010. Physical activity recommendations for older Australians. *Australasian Journal on Ageing.* 29, 2 (Jun. 2010), 81–87 7p.

[54] Sookhai, L. et al. 2015. Intergenerational activity tracker program: Impact with health related outcomes on older adults. *Systems, Applications and Technology Conference (LISAT), 2015 IEEE Long Island* (May 2015), 1–7.

[55] Srinivasan, R. 2008. Sources, characteristics and effects of emerging technologies: Research opportunities in innovation. *Industrial Marketing Management.* 37, 6 (Aug. 2008), 633–640.

[56] Starkoff, B.E. et al. 2014. Sedentary and Physical Activity Habits of Obese Adolescents. *American Journal of Health Education.* 45, 6 (Oct. 2014), 335–341.

[57] Starner, T. 2014. How Wearables Worked their Way into the Mainstream. *IEEE Pervasive Computing.* 13, 4 (Oct. 2014), 10–15.

[58] Stiggelbout, M. et al. 2008. Entry correlates and motivations of older adults participating in organized exercise programs. *Journal of Aging and Physical Activity.* 16, 3 (Jul. 2008), 342–354.

[59] Tan, T.-H. et al. 2014. Indoor activity monitoring system for elderly using RFID and Fitbit Flex wristband. *2014 IEEE-EMBS International Conference on Biomedical and Health Informatics (BHI)* (Jun. 2014), 41–44.

[60] Teixeira, P.J. et al. 2012. Exercise, physical activity, and self-determination theory: A systematic review. *International Journal of Behavioral Nutrition and Physical Activity.* 9, 1 (Jun. 2012), 78.

[61] United States Department of Health and Human Services 2008. Physical Activity Guidelines for Americans. United States HHS Office of Disease Prevention and Health Promotion.

[62] Vichitvanichphong, S. et al. 2014. Assistive Technologies for Aged Care: Supportive or Empowering? *Australasian Journal of Information Systems.* 18, 3 (Nov. 2014).

[63] Vlachopoulos, S.P. and Gigoudi, M.A. 2008. Why don't you exercise? Development of the Amotivation Toward Exercise Scale among older inactive individuals. *Journal of Aging and Physical Activity.* 16, 3 (Jul. 2008), 316–341.

[64] Webster, J. and Watson, R.T. 2002. Analyzing the Past to Prepare for the Future: Writing a Literature Review. *MIS Quarterly.* 26, 2 (2002), xiii–xxiii.

[65] Willey, J.Z. et al. 2010. Social Determinants of Physical Inactivity in the Northern Manhattan Study (NOMAS). *Journal of Community Health.* 35, 6 (Jun. 2010), 602–608.

[66] World Health Organization 2010. *Global recommendations on physical activity for health.*

[67] Young, R. et al. 2014. "Willing but Unwilling": Attitudinal barriers to adoption of home-based health information technology among older adults. *Health Informatics Journal.* 20, 2 (Jun. 2014), 127–135.

The Sharing Economy: Studying Technology-Mediated Social Movements

Jonathan P. Allen
University of San Francisco
School of Management
San Francisco CA 94121 USA
+1 415 4226570
jpallen@usfca.edu

ABSTRACT

The *sharing economy* is a term used to describe an IT-fueled, rapidly growing social movement around collaborative consumption. This movement has the potential to significantly affect economic opportunity and broader culture. In this research-in-progress paper, we pose as a key question: how does technology mediation of the sharing economy movement change over time? What explains this change, and what difference does technology mediation make? We draw upon the concepts of technology mediation, and computerization movements, in two comparative industry case studies: car sharing, and room sharing. We outline future research steps, and begin the process of critically examining the role of IT in social movement mediation. Is the sharing economy likely to create positive new economic alternatives? Or is it simply another strategy to intensify the role of global finance in everyday life, and fuel the high rates of growth demanded by venture-backed technology startups?

Keywords
Sharing economy; technology mediation; computerization movements; comparative case studies

1. INTRODUCTION

The *sharing economy* is a commonly used term to describe a social movement based on peer-to-peer sharing of assets, including cars, rooms, toys, clothes, and tools [3][4][7][12]. Variations of the sharing economy concept include *collaborative consumption*, emphasizing the replacement of market-based consumption with more community-based alternatives [3][11], and the *gig economy*, emphasizing the more informal and temporary employment relationships created by the sharing economy [6].

The sharing economy, as originally defined by Botsman and Rogers [4], is based on an excess capacity of goods, a critical mass of people willing to share their goods with peers, trust between strangers, and a belief in the value of sharing with others. The excess capacity refers to assets owned by community members that are currently under-utilized, such as a spare bedroom that often sits empty, a car that is only used a few hours a day, or a power tool that might only be used a few times by its owner.

The movement associated with the sharing economy is a complex mixture commercial and non-commercial forces. It includes a significant environmental, anti-consumption aspect, based on access to goods when needed, rather than individual ownership [11][12]. It also incorporates the notion of community self-organization, of peers coming together to share their goods for the greater benefit of all [4][7]. At the same time, the sharing economy includes more consumerist notions of greater convenience and lower prices, and a vision of *micro-entrepreneurship*, or individuals being able to go into business for themselves [4]. The movement tries to hold together parties ranging from anti-consumption greens, to the venture capitalists backing multi-billion dollar startups such as Uber and AirBnB.

As evidenced by the massive participation in the sharing economy so far, and the significant investment it has attracted, this movement has the potential to affect the broader economy and society. Because the sharing economy is dependent on internet-based platforms, there are important questions to answer about the role of information technology (IT) in creating and maintaining these new peer-to-peer relationships.

In this research-in-progress paper, we pose as a key question: how does technology mediation of the sharing economy movement change over time? What explains this change, and what difference does technology mediation make? We draw upon the concepts of technology mediation, and computerization movements, in two comparative industry case studies: car sharing, and room sharing. We outline future research steps, and begin the process of critically examining the role of IT in social movement mediation. Is the sharing economy an occasion for technology to contribute to the greater good, and create positive alternatives to current forms of consumption and service provision? Or will technology play the role of further intensifying existing market-based relationships, such as temporary work, low wages, and stock market winnings for the already wealthy? How does technology make a difference in complex social movements?

2. THEORETICAL CONCEPTS
2.1 Technology Mediation
The main research question of this study—how technology mediation of the sharing economy movement changes over time—is framed in terms of the concept of *mediated technology* and mediation theory. The sharing economy depends on interpersonal relationships, mediated through a peer-to-peer network, in order to function [4][7]. While early visions of the sharing economy have assumed a peer-to-peer network provides a neutral mechanism for building interpersonal trust, others have noted important differences between how platforms mediate online relationships [9].

Technology mediation theory highlights the different types of *relations* between humans, technology, and the outside world, different potential *points of contact* between humans and technologies, and the *types of influence* exerted on human beings by technology [15]. Relations can be analyzed as hermeneutic ones, where a technology platform claims to offer a true representation of the world, or as background relations, when contextual information is influential for interaction but perhaps not engaged consciously. Points of contact include direct interactions with interfaces, but also how visions of appropriate use and material infrastructure choices shape human encounters with technology. Types of influence in platforms can vary in terms of their visibility and force. Coercive influences openly demand compliance, whereas persuasive or seductive influences try to more subtly influence human interactions.

According to this perspective, sharing platforms play an active role in building and shaping trust relations. For example, Keymolen [9] discusses how design choices about which information can be shared (e.g., who can review what), the openness of code and management, the business model of the platform company, and interactions with government regulations (local and national) can potentially mediate interpersonal trust relationships.

The mediation of exchanges between peers is part of a larger, and somewhat unexpected, transformation of e-commerce more generally. Despite predictions that electronic marketplaces would become more transparent, fully informed, and frictionless with digital technology, an increasing number of producer-consumer relationships are in fact highly mediated by search engines, social media, review sites, and others using opaque algorithms and business models rife with potential conflicts of interest [1]. Technology mediation theory, or something close to it, is likely to be useful in untangling these complex socio-technical configurations.

2.2 Computerization Movements
The sharing economy depends on the rapid creation of a critical mass of participants, and a level of commitment and trust that goes beyond regular commercial transactions [4][7]. For these reasons, *computerization movements* appear to be an appropriate concept for understanding the evolution of platform mediation over time.

A computerization movement perspective views technology design, adoption, and use as a social movement [5]. Sustained social movements depend on activities such as political opportunity scanning, appropriate cultural framing, mobilization, and the holding together of coalitions [13]. Recent works highlight some of the advantages that a computerization movement perspective brings to societal-level questions about IT [2][8].

The sharing economy is a complex mixture of communitarianism, ecological sustainability, consumer convenience, entrepreneurship, and high-tech startup growth. The computerization movement concept can help explain changes in platform mediation, through the interplay of technology development, social visions, and business practices over time.

Linking the dynamics of social movements to specific technology mediations will hopefully increase explanatory power over using each of these concepts separately. In particular, we highlight how different sharing economy platforms either become more similar over time (i.e., converge) or maintain their unique approaches to technology mediation.

3. INDUSTRY CASE STUDIES
Two industry case studies have been chosen as a starting point for the research: car (or ride) sharing, and room sharing, both in the United States. These two cases have attracted the most investment, and the highest number of service providers, of any sharing economy models to date.

3.1 Car Sharing
In the United States, two sharing economy platforms have come to dominate car sharing, or ride sharing. It is primarily a story of platform convergence from very different starting points. Lyft started its life as Zimride, a site where people could virtually hitch-hike with other drivers. Uber, by contrast, began as a limousine service featuring easy availability and payment through a smartphone [10].

Over time, these platforms have converged to become more alike. They have added mediations such liability insurance, real time location of drivers, and variable pricing at roughly the same times, and are branching into related services such as deliveries. Some differences remain in their mediation of peer-to-peer relationships, such as the inclusion of tipping in Lyft, and a more strict driver removal process in Uber based on user reviews.

Few of the pure, non-venture backed sharing platforms have been able to survive the growth of Uber and Lyft. Far from providing a neutral peer-to-peer interaction, these car sharing platforms have evolved very specific forms of mediation in response to the dynamics of sharing economy movement.

3.2 Room Sharing
Room sharing platforms in the United States have had a somewhat different evolution. One platform, AirBnB, has attracted the majority of new sharing economy investment and interactions. The dynamic is somewhat different, in the sense that existing platforms for vacation rentals, as represented by the HomeAway family of companies (now owned by Expedia), were already established in a closely related space. There has been some platform convergence between these two, particularly in terms of ease of listing and ease of payments, but they still maintain separate emphases and identities, with HomeAway focusing more on professional property managers versus the new entrants with AirBnB [14]. The two platforms can face similar regulatory issues, for example restrictions on short term rentals. In addition, the world's largest travel platform, Priceline, has now entered the room sharing business through its booking.com site.

Unlike the car sharing case, room sharing has preserved platforms that mediate relationships in unique ways. Craigslist continues to provide room rental connections, from the standpoint of a very different business model, and very different processes for guaranteeing trust and quality. Couchsurfing is another platform that retains a unique form of mediation for room sharing. While business and regulatory pressure led Couchsurfing to re-incorporate itself from a non-profit to a for-profit social company, it continues to mediate relationships between room providers and guests in a uniquely non-commercial way.

4. NEXT STEPS
For this research-in-progress, comments on the conceptual framework and case studies are particularly welcome. As of now, these are the planned next steps:

- Rich descriptions of the industry case studies, with particular attention to the contextual factors identified in the computerization movements literature.
- Identification of the key dimensions of platforms used to mediate the sharing economy movement.
- Identify empirical data sources on platform outcomes—what difference does it make if mediation takes one form vs. another?
- Begin the critical analysis of sharing economy platforms. Is the sharing economy providing a positive, pro-social set of new economic arrangements? Or is it achieving something else?

5. REFERENCES

[1] Allen, J. P . Social informatics and business reform. In P. Fichman and H. Rosenbaum, Eds. *Social Informatics: Past, Present, and Future*. Cambridge Scholars Publishing, Newcastle, UK, 183-196.

[2] Barrett, M., Heracleous, L., and Walsham, G. 2013. A rhetorical approach to IT diffusion: Reconceptualizing the ideology-framing relationship in computerization movements. *MIS Quarterly*, 37,1, 201-220.

[3] Belk, R. 2014. You are what you can access: Sharing and collaborative consumption. *Journal of Business Research*, 67, 1595-1600.

[4] Botsman, R. and Rogers, R. 2010. *What's Mine is Yours: The Rise of Collaborative Consumption*. HarperBusiness, New York, NY.

[5] Elliott, M. S., & Kraemer, K. L. Eds. 2008. *Computerization Movements and Technology Diffusion: From Mainframes to Ubiquitous Computing*. Information Today, Inc.

[6] Gardiner, L. 2015. Does the gig economy revolutionise the world of work, or is it a storm in a teacup? Accessed October 23, 2015. http://www.economist.com/blogs/freeexchange/2015/10/gig- economy.

[7] Hamari, J. Sjöklint, M. and Ukkonen, A. 2016. The sharing economy: Why people participate in collaborative consumption. *Journal of the AIS*, forthcoming.

[8] Hara, N., and Huang, B. Y. 2011. Online social movements. *Annual review of information science and technology*, 45, 1, 489-522.

[9] Keymolen, E. 2013. Trust and technology in collaborative consumption. Why it is not just about you and me. In *Bridging Distances in Technology and Regulation*, R. Leenes and E. Kosta, Eds. Wolf Legal Publishers, Oisterwijk, Netherlands, 135-150.

[10] Macmillan, D. Tech's fiercest rivalry: Uber vs. Lyft. Accessed October 15, 2015. http://www.wsj.com/articles/two-tech-upstarts-plot-each- others-demise-1407800744.

[11] Piscicelli, L. Cooper, T. and Fisher T. 2015. The role of values in collaborative consumption: Insights from a product-service system for lending and borrowing in the UK. *Journal of Cleaner Production*. 97, 21-29.

[12] Schor, J. 2010. *Plenitude: The new economics of true wealth*. Penguin Press, New York, NY.

[13] Tarrow, S. G. 2011. *Power in Movement: Social Movements and Contentious Politics*. Cambridge University Press, New York, NY.

[14] Tripping.com. 2015. VRBO vs. Airbnb. Accessed October 15, 2015. https://www.tripping.com/industry/rental-companies/vrbo-vs-airbnb.

[15] Verbeek, P.-P. 2015. Beyond interaction: A short introduction to mediation theory. *Interactions*. (May-June 2015), 26-31.

Empowering Deep Thinking to Support Critical Thinking in Teaching and Learning

Hisham Al-Mubaid
University of Houston-Clear Lake
2700 Bay Area Blvd.
Houston, TX 77058
+1(281)283-3802
hisham@uhcl.edu

Ahmed Abukmail
University of Houston-Clear Lake
2700 Bay Area Blvd.
Houston, TX 77058
+1(281)283-3888
abukmail@uhcl.edu

Said Bettayeb
University of Houston-Clear Lake
2700 Bay Area Blvd.
Houston, TX 77058
+1(281)283-3857
bettayeb@uhcl.edu

ABSTRACT

This research describes learning activities and techniques that improve deep and critical thinking among students. Critical thinking is considered an ultimate goal in MIS education; and learners who reach critical thinking level can achieve the highest learning goals and outcomes. Critical thinking and English communication are considered the two most essential competencies in the 21st century. Therefore, universities have invested significantly in understanding, promoting, and delivering critical thinking in education. Moreover, the learning and education research has invested extensively in critical thinking. In this research, we present and discuss seven learning activities and techniques that initiate deep thinking and promote critical thinking in teaching and learning in order to achieve high level of quality learning. The main focus of this work is in the higher education setting at the level of colleges and universities. We discuss and explain seven learning activities, with examples and tools that will help increase the level of thinking and improve higher order thinking and critical analysis. The presented techniques and examples can be easily applied and adapted into any discipline to help increase and improve higher order thinking among the learners. The preliminary evaluation results are very encouraging.

Keywords

Critical Thinking, Deep Thinking, Quality Teaching

1. INTRODUCTION

The thinking process is a mental process that results in performing certain processing steps by the brain to estimate, induce, or deduce a desired result or decision for a given problem or decision task [1, 10, 17, 21, 22]. It sometimes involves a high level mental activity to reach a reasonable solution, decision, or convergence acceptable to the mind. The formal definition states that critical thinking is the mental process of actively and skillfully conceptualizing, applying, analyzing, synthesizing, and evaluating information to reach an answer or conclusion [10, 17].

SIGMIS-CPR '16, June 02-04, 2016, Alexandria, VA, USA
© 2016 ACM. ISBN 978-1-4503-4203-2/16/06...$15.00
DOI: http://dx.doi.org/10.1145/2890602.2890606

In education, critical thinking can be viewed as one of the most important goals, because when they reach critical thinking level, learners can achieve the utmost learning outcomes. Critical thinking, along with English communication, were recognized as the two most essential competencies in the 21st century [11, 25, 26]. Therefore, critical thinking in education is of utmost importance and universities have invested significantly in understanding, promoting, and delivering critical thinking in education. Moreover, the learning and education research has invested extensively in critical thinking. In this research, we make an attempt to discuss techniques and thoughts that improve deep thinking and promote critical thinking in teaching and learning in order to achieve the highest levels of quality learning. In engineering disciplines, in particular, critical thinking is given special importance due to its significance in improving problem solving skills and its relationships to creative thinking and creativity [27].

In its simplest form, critical thinking can be viewed simply as *deep thinking* that can yield better solution or improved decision [1, 11, 25, 26, 27]. This will enable the process of critical thinking to be the process that leads to creativity in thinking and can be viewed as thinking and reasoning at its full strength. Also, in this context, deep thinking can be manifested as a higher level mental process and more focused thinking and reasoning. It can be experienced, for example, when the learner considers the problem from multiple points of view. In this paper we rely on this perception to leverage the concept of deep thinking in higher education settings to reach the level of critical thinking. Specifically, we show that, with certain simple steps, learners can exert and apply some important phases of critical thinking that help them reach their utmost learning outcomes from a given learning task. We attempt, in this paper, to explain *deep thinking* and *critical thinking* in higher educational setting with relatively mature learners. To encapsulate the discussion of critical thinking in a more practical way, we can cast the practical scenario that, in critical thinking (CT), the mental process is performed *twice* on the same task in which the second time includes a more extensive mental activity to produce another, perhaps improved, solution or decision.

The second iteration of the mental process to solve the same problem or decision task is more tiring than the first one and it represents, to some extent, a deep thinking process. Moreover, this second iteration may lead to the first step in critical thinking, see Figure 1. Actually, it is considered a *deep thinking* process because the learner exerts deeper and more extensive brain activity in the reasoning process. In this research, we are interested in how to employ and utilize simple techniques and activities to improve the thinking process and the mental activity of the learners in a given learning task. In other words, we investigate how to teach and offer students the means to exercise and apply *deeper* thinking in their everyday learning tasks so as to reach the level of critical thinking. Moreover, injecting deep thinking activities in teaching and education is one of the goals of this research aimed at achieving the highest level of quality and analytical thinking among the students. The presented techniques have been evaluated moderately in a number of educational settings and the results are encouraging, and in many situations, impressive outcomes obtained.

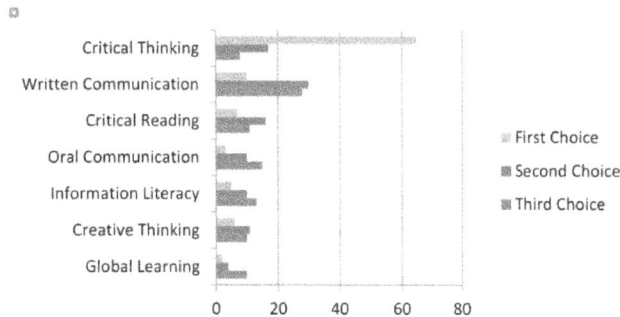

Figure 1: Results of study conducted by University of North Carolina UNC that includes 2822 responses in which *Critical Thinking* was identified as the most essential competency recommended for the UNC system-wide core [25].

2. RELATED WORK

In the academic domain, the interest in critical thinking started few decades ago and continued to progress and increase as a part of research on learning and education. In general, the concept of critical thinking is a very old concept and the interest in it started a long time ago. In the past few decades, however, we started experiencing more attention in integrating, augmenting, and applying critical thinking in education in many content areas and in various branches of science. It has been found that critical thinking is very crucial for delivering quality learning in any subject and content area. Therefore, the learning and education research has invested extensively in critical thinking [4,5,8,9.22]. Also, promoting and applying critical thinking into online education is of particular importance due to the high pace and wide spread of online education with the Internet revolution.

In a research study about critical thinking by Paul, Elder, and Bartell [20], it was shown that an overwhelming majority (89%) of university faculty claim that the promotion of critical thinking is a primary objective of their instruction. However, only 19% could define critical thinking and 77% had little, limited or no conception of how to reconcile content coverage with the fostering of critical thinking [20]. Another study by Bruning (2005) explains the role of critical thinking in online learning environments [7].

In general, three requirements are needed for critical thinking:
− The learner understands the problem (questions, or concept) deeply so that he/she can be close to a highly reasonable solution or answer.
− The educator believes that the learner has gained a complete understanding of the problem or concept.
− The learner has enough information that can be synthesized, arranged, and evaluated to reach high level of mental process of reasoning about the given concept.

Besides, the process of critical thinking can be seen as having two components: the first component includes a set of information and belief generating and processing skills. The second component

involves the habit, based on intellectual commitment, of using those skills to guide behavior [8].

CriticalThinking.net defines critical thinking as "reasonable reflective process of thinking focused on deciding what to believe or do" [9]. In Saade et al. [24], critical thinking is a type of a cognitive ability that has a special importance in decision making and judgment processes. Some of the direct and tangible goals for the learner include: getting an in-depth understanding of the problem or concept, initiating and engaging in quality discussion of the concept among students, and being able to develop different approaches to the solution. MacKnight [17] proposes certain tools and strategies for applying critical thinking skill development in the online education settings. In that article, MacKnight emphasizes on collaborative learning, reflection, peer editing, and monitored online discussions [17].

One of the closest projects to this work is the work of Saade et al. (2012).

They present the work and results of applying critical thinking in virtual learning environments. In that project, Saade et al. present and discuss a web-based course to assess critical thinking.

The assessment is conducted to identify which is the most important part for achieving and promoting critical thinking [24]. Their results indicated the significance of interactivity in what students perceived to be critical thinking oriented versus online material as a resource [24].

In addition, in a study conducted by University of North Carolina UNC [25] that collected a total of more than 2800 responses (of which, 58% tenured and tenure-track faculty, 22% non-tenure-track faculty, 6% academic administrator, and 8% academic staff) *Critical Thinking* along with *Written Communication* were identified as the two most important competencies recommended to UNC system-wide core [25].

As also can be seen in Figure 2, critical thinking has an impact on improving problem-solving skills, creative thinking, creativity, and other important competencies [11].

List of 21st-century competencies
• Creativity/innovation;
• **Critical thinking;**
• Information literacy;
• **Problem solving;**
• Decision making;
• **Flexibility and adaptability; learning to learn**
• Research and inquiry;
• **Communication;**
• Initiative and self-direction;
• Productivity;
• Leadership and responsibility;
• **Collaboration**
• ICT operations and concepts;
• Digital Citizenship;
• Media literacy;

Figure 2: List of competencies in the 21st century from [11]. The most essential skills are in boldface

Elements of Critical Thinking: Paul and Elder [21] summarize the elements of critical thinking, or elements of thought as follows:
  1. All reasoning has a *purpose*
  2. All reasoning is an attempt to figure something out, to settle some *question*, to solve some *problem*
  3. All reasoning is based on *assumptions*
  4. All reasoning is done from some *point of view*
  5. All reasoning is based on *data, information* and *evidence*

6. All reasoning is expressed through, and shaped by, *concepts* and *ideas*
7. All reasoning contains *inferences* or *interpretations* by which we draw *conclusions* and give *meaning* to data
8. All reasoning leads somewhere or has *implications* and *consequences*

Boris and Hall [6] studied critical thinking in a group of graduate students using an online discussion based environment. Students were asked to self-reflect and interact with others using a weekly set of questions. The authors report a significant positive change in critical thinking among the graduate students after they were exposed to Garrison et al. [13] Practical Inquiry Method and asked to use it on a self-directed basis for classroom interaction and dialogues.

In [12], Friston has analyzed brain functions from the free-energy perspective and suggest that the brain functions work to optimize some constant metric, such as the expected reward or expected utility.

Anderson [2] has argued that the college experience should include ways for students to develop creativity within and also outside the formal classroom. Further investigation into the relationship between creativity and critical thinking was carried out by Baker et al. [3]. They argue that although not identical, these two concepts are closely related.

3. CRITICAL THINKING: Activities and Techniques

In this research, we are interested in leveraging and applying critical thinking in the various educational settings where we have a teaching-learning model [12,19,26]. We start with the deep thinking approach to instigate extensive and higher level mental activity for a given learning/thinking problem. We relate the critical thinking process with the learning process as the learning process is a task that requires certain mental activity and thinking or reasoning process to be performed by the brain (*to encode and store the learnt knowledge*). In general, we consider problem solving process is a learning task. A student learns a great deal from solving problems of an assignment in a math course. In the normal model of thinking, the mental activity is performed to produce an acceptable solution to the problem at hand. On the other hand, deep thinking, or deeper level of mental activity, starts when the learner attempts to find another solution, justify, or analyze the first solution. That is, proposing and developing a new solution approach is a key aspect of deep thinking. In normal educational settings, this level of deep thinking is not reached since the normal mental activity produces a good enough solution that makes sense and acceptable to the learner. Therefore, certain simple techniques are needed to instigate the start thinking deeply so as to reach the critical thinking level. One common technique is to ask the student to propose a new solution approach or to solve a given problem in three different ways. In the next section, we present activities and techniques for initiating deep thinking and promoting critical thinking among students in higher educational settings. We evaluated these techniques and the preliminary results are very encouraging.

3.1 Learning Activities to Promote Critical Thinking

In traditional higher education, the levels of learning activities are mostly determined by their difficulty. A learning activity is a task which is a part of the course context and involves some learning and gaining knowledge; and that includes problem-solving assignments, quizzes, exams, discussion groups, and class exercises. There are individual differences among students based on which learning is attained from one activity more than the other. The interest of this work in this paper is in the different ways of injecting deep and critical thinking activities and techniques in the various learning activities. For example, a hard homework assignment may not involve deep thinking or critical analysis as expected when compared to some other simpler tasks that involves deep thinking. We present and explain the following seven learning activities and how and why critical thinking is involved or utilized in these activities:

1: Produce multiple solutions to a given learning problem.
2: Solve problem *P* without using method *m*.
3: Explain the differences between the two methods m_1 and m_2 for problem *P*.
4: Design criteria to distinguish between and compare two concepts.
5: Find the mistake in a given solution, or statement, for a given concept.
6: Recap the most important points in a given topic.
7: Summarize a given subject or story.

Learning Activity 1:
- Producing multiple solutions to a given learning problem: In a Computer Science introductory programming course, an assignment problem asks the learner to write a program in two different ways.

Example: Write a program to produce the *Fibonacci* sequence of *n* numbers where *n = 25*. That is, the program will print the first 25 numbers in Fibonacci sequence (e.g., 0 1 1 2 3 5 8 ..etc). Normally, the professor had in mind several solution approaches for this program (also fairly advanced and brilliant computing students can think of several methods) including: −using simple loop, − using recursion, and − using dynamic programming. Usually a student thinks of a simple loop as follows:

Method 1:
```
n = 25
f0 = 0
f1 = 1
print f0  f1
for i = 1 to n-2
    t = f0
    f0 = f1
    f1 = f1 + t
    print f1
end-for
```

and here is the second approach (using recursion):

Method 2:
```
n = 25
for i = 1 to n
   print Fib(i)
end-for

Function Fib( n ):
   if n = 0 return 0
   if n = 1 return 1
   Else
     Return Fib(n-1)+Fib(n-2)
End-Function
```

In tasks such as this, when the student solves this problem with the first method the brain has exercised only the first iteration of the mental activity with no deep thinking or extensive mental activity applied. To instigate and initiate deep thinking and more extensive mental process the learner should think about and propose a different solution method for this problem.

Learning Activity 2:

- Solve problem $\mathscr{P}$ without using method m. In this case, method m is the direct and straight forward way to solve problem $\mathscr{P}$ without exerting any deep thinking. Quality thinking at a deeper level will start when the learner tries to reason about and think of another method for this problem.

  Example: Write a program (or algorithm) to find the result of this multiplication {123*456} without using the multiplication * operator.

Learning Activity 3:

- Explain the differences between the two different methods $m1$ and $m2$ for solving problem $\mathscr{P}$. The learner in this case is required to explain the logic (rationale) behind the two methods ($m1$ and $m2$) for solving problem $\mathscr{P}$. This is an ideal case when the learner straightforwardly can solve the problem with the two methods. However, deep thinking starts when the learner thinks about the logic behind the two methods rather than just solving the problem with these two methods. In [18], Noris argued that when students provide rationale or justification of their choice of solution, they validate their CT [18].

  Example: The instructor might ask: We discussed in the class two different methods (e.g. *Dijkstra* and *Bellman-Ford*) to solve the shortest path problem. Explain clearly the differences between these two methods. In this activity, a learner uses analytical thinking and deep analysis to produce a good answer. Another example: In an undergraduate data structures class, students are asked to differentiate between *quicksort* and *heapsort*. The students can understand and implement the individual algorithms in a mechanical fashion. However, deep learning happens when the students try to understand and explain the fundamental differences between the two sorting algorithms such as the memory requirements and time complexity.

Learning Activity 4:

- Design criteria to distinguish between and compare two concepts: Given two approaches to solve an MIS problem, the learner is asked to develop criteria to compare the two approaches. In this case, the learner will have to think of and search for the most important aspects of the given concepts (*analytical thinking*) to be used as criteria for comparison. This Learning Activity was shown in a study by Rao that *compare-and-contrast* reveals important characteristics between two concepts and can yield deeper understanding and higher learning [16]. Further, it was one of six CT skills identified in that study [16].

  Example: In an MIS course, students were asked to develop a prototype for simple information system IS for comparing universities in the US. This activity transforms learning into another domain by asking the students to develop criteria and set of metrics to compare universities X and Y. The student will have to pursue deep thinking about what is significant (most important aspects) about universities to be used as comparison criteria; and this may lead to the following:

  > Cost of study; reputation and national ranking; location and region; sports teams; how large (number of students); activities and student life; scholarships.

  At the end, this assignment will amount to the question: *how can you compare two universities in the US?* The developed set of criteria and metrics will apply to comparing any two universities in the US. This activity is different from the third

activity as it addresses and deals with concepts whereas the third activity works with methods for solving a given problem.

More examples: Students are not required to compare two concepts, rather, students are asked to develop comparison criteria. For instance, students in a biology class are asked to compare the *prokaryotes* and *eukaryotes*. Another example, also from biology, the learners are required to compare *genes* and *proteins*. The students know *genes* and *proteins*; however, they might not be aware of the most important aspects between *genes* and *proteins* in the biological context. In this example, genes and proteins are two types of what is known as *gene products* and the set of criteria developed to compare them can be applied (to some extent) to any two gene products like *RNA* and *DNA*.

Learning Activity 5:

- Find the mistake in a given solution, or statement, for a given concept: For a given solution of a problem or statement that looks fairly good and correct, the students are asked to find and explain the mistakes (*i.e.,* to critique) or find inconsistencies in the given solution. This is a deep thinking task as the errors are usually not extracted directly from the given solution or statement.

  Example: The instructor gives a computer program that computes the PCA of a given dataset. The instructor injects a subtle error in the solution. The students are asked to locate and correct the error.

Learning Activity 6:

- Recap the most important points in a given topic: In this activity, we would like the learner to apply deep thinking in a journey to seek the most important aspects or points in a given topic. The topic can be as simple as one chapter in the textbook. For instance, summarizing the most important points in Chapter Five in one page.

  Example: In a computer networking class, the instructor asks the students, in a paper writing assignment, to write a two-page report summarizing the most important concepts about the IP protocol. Another example, a professor asks the students to summarize the three to five most important concepts in object-oriented programming.

Learning Activity 7:

- Summarize the subject or story: summarizing a topic is different than recapping or summarizing the most important concepts in a given topic as explained in the previous learning activity (L.A. 6). In this activity, a topic, narrative, or story is given to the learner to read and summarize it in one paragraph, like writing an abstract of a paper.

3.2 Practical Examples

In this section we discuss, from various disciplines, some practical examples of learning activities and problems that activate deep thinking among learners and promote critical thinking.

Example 1:

Many university disciplines require a course in computer programming including in Management Information Systems. In such *a* course, students are asked to write a program (*we use here pseudo-code to illustrate the idea*) to compute the multiplication of two numbers (e.g. *123*32*) in three different ways. Straightforwardly, students will use the direct method (method 1 below) and it will be a very simple task. The deep thinking starts when students begin to think about a second way to produce the same result:

```
Method 1:     x ← 123
              y ← 32
              z ← x * y
Method 2:     x ← 123
              y ← 32
              z ← 0
              Loop y times
                 z ← z + x  /* repeat y times: add x to z*/
              end-loop
```

Method 3: this is used only if one of the two terms in the multiplication is a power of two. In this case, the learner needs to think more deeply to realize that multiplying any number (*e.g.*, 123) by another number (e.g., 32) which is a power of two (*e.g., 32 = 2⁵*) can be done by a simple *shift left* operation available in many languages:

```
              x ← 123
              y ← 32
              z ← x << 5
```
{Note: << is the left shift bitwise operation}

This assignment enables students to exert more thinking effort in producing three different solutions to this problem (*Learning Activity 1*). Moreover, the learner in this example may be wondering which method is the best. This is again a step towards critical thinking. The learner, on comparing these three methods, may ask the questions based on what criteria can we decide the *best* solution among these three methods.

Example 2:
In low level programming course (*i.e., assembly language*), which is needed for computer science and computer engineering disciplines, the *shift* operation is important and students are asked to: write program code to do the following shift operation *without* using *shift* instructions in three different ways:
```
shl  ax,1.
```
That is, the program should shift to the left all the bits of register AX (in *Pentium* machines). This can be done using the following three solution methods:

```
Method 1:
              add  ax, ax;
Method 2:
              mov bx, ax
              add ax, bx
Method 3:
              mov cx, ax
      Lp: inc ax
              loop Lp
```

Example 3:
Perform the following addition operation without using the addition/plus (*i.e., +*) operator: $y ← x + z$. This example is for *Learning Activity 2* discussed above and can be done as follows:
```
              x ← 123
              y ← 456
              z ← x
              Loop y times
                 inc  z  /* repeat y times: increment z by 1 */
              end-loop
```

Example 4:
In software project management, one of the important concepts to learn is the requirement or what is called *Software Requirement Specifications SRS*. This concept basically includes what are the functions that a software project will do. Typically, understanding

the requirements of a project correctly is one of the most important aspects of a software project. Most importantly, the learner is asked to discuss the requirements and to highlight (and *explain*) the *most important* requirements in the project. For that, the learner will have to conduct some critical analysis and deep thinking to derive and justify the most important requirement(s).

Some of these learning activities seem like challenges, and Grabau [14] in his study about effective teaching and learning strategies showed that 'challenges to students' thinking' is one of the effective strategies for promoting critical thinking.

Example 5:
In a given course, and towards the end of the course, students are required to write down *the most fundamental and central question* in that course. That is, what is the main question that this course addresses? For instance, to answer this question in a database course, a student may propose the following question as the most fundamental: *How to design a normalized database for ABC company and write an efficient query to retrieve names and salaries of those employees of age 65 or above?*

In order to answer such a problem, the learner should deeply think about what is the most important concept that we learn in this course and so the main question will be around that concept.

3.3 Evaluation and Preliminary Results:
We evaluated these learning activities and techniques with preliminary experiments in a number of studies and the results are impressive. The main tool of results is the survey mechanism that allows students to provide feedback after applying a critical thinking activity. We administered and conducted multiple activities from activities 1 through 7 above in the form of problem solving assignments with a number of selected students. Then after each activity, the student fills a survey that includes few feedback questions that requires answer from 1 to 10 where 1: *not at all* and 10: *strongly agree*. The assignments were given limited time (*normally between 1 – 2 hours per assignment*) and open-book format to allow the learner to search for solutions.

```
- This assignment requires a deeper level of thinking than normal
  assignments:
     (not at all) 1  2  3  4  5  6  7  8  9  10 (strongly agree)
- I believe that I am now better in handling this kind of problems
  that require deep thinking:
     (not at all) 1  2  3  4  5  6  7  8  9  10 (strongly agree)
- I think I have learned a new skill for critical and deep thinking:
     (not at all) 1  2  3  4  5  6  7  8  9  10 (strongly agree)
- Doing more of this kind of problems will significantly improve
  my problem solving skills:
     (not at all) 1  2  3  4  5  6  7  8  9  10 (strongly agree)
- I do not mind working on more assignments and problems like
  these from time to time to improve my deep thinking:
     (not at all) 1  2  3  4  5  6  7  8  9  10 (strongly agree)
- Every student should practice and work on this kind of
  problems from time to time:
     (not at all) 1  2  3  4  5  6  7  8  9  10 (strongly agree)
```

The students overwhelmingly agreed that they exerted extra and extensive in-depth thinking (question 1) and reasoning about the given learning task. Moreover, they believed they attained more quality learning and they can engage in deep discussions about the concepts. All the preliminary results are very encouraging. Currently we are still in the process of conducting more extensive evaluations, analyses, and experiments.

4. DISCUSSION AND CONCLUSION

The interest of this work is how to stimulate and leverage deep and critical thinking through learning activities that can be applied in various educational settings. Some of these activities and studies have been used/applied and produced significant learning improvement results. To measure the outcomes of critical thinking activities normally students start using more advanced terms and statements that indicate critical analysis, deep thinking and higher order mental process. Students also can get engaged in more in-depth discussions about the subject concepts. Moreover, in our previous similar research, we reported few survey results which indicated that the learners were very satisfied with the level of learning due to the learning activities that involve deep and critical thinking [1]; we also observed significant improvement is students' performance in terms of academic grades. The presented learning activities, in this study, can improve students' thinking process hence promoting critical thinking. The second learning activity (*solving problem without using method m*) seems to be the hardest as it requires really deep level of thinking and some kind of extensive mental process. Overall, higher, or highest, levels of learning can be achieved upon reaching critical thinking. Therefore, education research continues to invest significantly in critical thinking and its relationship to teaching and learning. A search on Google scholar for the keyword '*Critical Thinking*' in December 2014 produced 200,000 hits, spanning books, scientific journal and conference papers and articles. A majority of these hits are from scholarly publications from 2009 onwards. We repeated the search for the words '*Critical Thinking*' to be in the title of any scholarly work using Google Scholar engine (note: Google Scholar retrieves only scientific and scholarly publications based on verified .edu email addresses of the authors) we got 9,000 scholarly publications just in the past five years. We also searched Microsoft Academic search site (http://academic.research.microsoft.com) for the same keyword '*Critical Thinking*' in the title or in the text of publication and we retrieved 12345 publications since 2008. Moreover, searching IEEE *Xplore* (http://ieeexplore.ieee.org) returned 510 articles having '*critical thinking*' in the title, just in the last five years 2009 – 2014 (with an average of more than 100 articles each year). These are scientific publication from sciences and engineering disciples (IEEE, Institute of Electrical and Electronics Engineers, is the world largest professional association of scientists and engineers). Finally, we search the ACM Digital Library with keyword '*critical thinking*' and received over 23,000 results of which over 13,000 are in the last five years 2009–2014. All these results indicate obviously that Critical Thinking has been an active area of research production in academia the last several years.

In Conclusion: We presented and discussed some applied techniques and thoughts in higher education for stimulating and leveraging critical thinking through simple class learning activities. We presented and discussed with examples seven learning activities for promoting critical thinking. Simple learning activities with higher order thinking can help learners exert more extensive mental process for a given problem thus leveraging critical thinking. The presented techniques for promoting critical thinking have been tested to a certain extent while the extensive evaluation is still in progress and the preliminary results are very encouraging. Students, after exercising these critical thinking activities, strongly believe that they exercised deeper levels of thinking and more extensive mental activity; hence more learning was attained. Students also are more confident that they can engage in focused and in-depth discussions about the concepts of the subject. We are currently in the process of designing and conducting more extensive and comprehensive evaluation with in-depth analysis of results.

It has been, and will continue to be, highly acceptable that critical thinking is of very high significance in education; and critical thinking was recognized as one of the two most essential competencies in the 21st century. Harvey et al. [15], and Razzak [23] emphasize that deep learning involves critical analysis, linking of ideas and concepts, and creative problem solving and can lead the learners for life in the 21st century. Therefore, education research continues to invest significantly in critical thinking and its relationship to creative thinking, problem solving skills, and creativity. Engineering disciplines are paying special attention to these core competencies (*critical thinking, creativity, communication, collaboration, problem-solving skills, inter-personal skills*) that engineering graduates should possess and employers are looking for such competencies.

5. REFERENCES

[1] Al-Mubaid H., "Applying and Promoting Critical Thinking in Online Education", *Proceedings of ICELW'14*, New York, NY, USA, (2014).

[2] Anderson, G. A., "Teaching creativity for professional growth and personal reward", *NACTA Journal*, 34 (4), 54-55, (1998)

[3] Baker, M.; Rudd, R. and Pomeroy, C., "Relationships between critical and creative thinking", *Journal of Southern Agricultural Education Research* 51.1 (2001): 173-188.

[4] Bloom, B. S.; Engelhart, M. D.; Furst, E. J.; Hill, W. H.; Krathwohl, D. R., "Taxonomy of educational objectives: The classification of educational goals", *Handbook I: Cognitive domain*, New York: David McKay Company, (1956).

[5] Bloom, B. S., "Reflections on the development and use of the taxonomy", in Anderson, L. W. and Sosniak, L. A. (*Eds*), *Bloom's taxonomy: A forty-year retrospective,* (1994).

[6] Boris, G.; and Hall, T., "Critical thinking and online learning: A practical inquiry perspective in higher education", *20th annual conference on distance teaching and learning*, (2005).

[7] Bruning, K., "The Role of Critical Thinking in the Online Learning Environment", *International Journal of Instructional Technology and Distance Learning*, 2(5),200, (2005)

[8] The Critical Thinking Community, official website; www.criticalThinking.org

[9] CriticalThinking.net: http://www.CriticalThinking.net

[10] Ennis, R. H., "Critical thinking: Reflection and perspective Part II", *Inquiry: Critical Thinking across the Discipline*, 26, 2 (Summer), 5-19, (2011).

[11] Finegold, D. and Notabartolo A.S., "21st-Century Competencies and Their Impact: An Interdisciplinary Literature Review", *2010, Hewlett Foundation.* http://www.hewlett.org/; retrieved December, (2014).

[12] Friston, K., "The free-energy principle: a unified brain theory?", *Nature Reviews Neuroscience*, AOP, (2010);

[13] Garrison, D.R.; Anderson, T., and Archer, W., "Critical inquiry in a text-based environment: Computer referencing in higher education", *The Internet and Higher Education,* 2(2-3), 87-105, (2000).

[14] Grabau, L.J., "Effective teaching and learning strategies for critical thinking to foster cognitive development and transformational learning", *Kentucky Journal for Excellence in College Teaching and Learning* 5:123-156, (2007).

[15] Harvey, A., and Kamvounias, P., "Bridging the implementation gap: a teacher-as-learner approach to teaching and learning policy", *Higher Education Research and Development*, 27(1), 31–41, (2008).

[16] Krishna Rao, M.R.K., "Infusing Critical Thinking Skills into Content of AI Course", *ACM ITiCSE'05*, 2005, Portugal.

[17] MacKnight, C., "Teaching Critical Thinking through Online Discussions", in *Educause Quarterly*. No. 4, (2000).

[18] Norris, S. P., "Can we test validly for critical thinking?" *Educational Researcher*, vol.18 (no.9), (1989).

[19] Parse, R. R., "A Human Becoming Teaching-Learning Model", *Nurs. Sci. Q,* 2004, vol. 17, no. 1, pp. 33-35, (2004)

[20] Paul, R.; Elder, L.; and Bartell, T., "California Teacher Preparation for Instruction in Critical Thinking: Research Findings and Policy Recommendations", *State of California, California Comm. on Teacher Credentialing,* Sacramento, CA, (1997).

[21] Paul, R., and Elder, L., "Critical Thinking Concepts and Tools. Tomales", *CA: Foundation for Critical Thinking. And - The Elements of Reasoning and the Intellectual Standards: Helping Students Assess Their Thinking,* (2009).

[22] Pohl, M., "Learning to Think, Thinking to Learn: Models and Strategies to Develop a Classroom Culture of Thinking", *Cheltenham, Vic.: Hawker Brownlow,* (2000).

[23] Razzak, N.A., "Strategies for effective faculty involvement in online activities aimed at promoting critical thinking and deep learning", in *Edu. Inf. Tech.* 25, (2014).

[24] Saade, R. G.; Morin, D.; and Thomas; J. D. E., "Critical thinking in E-learning environments", *Computer in Human Behavior*, Vol 28, No. 5, (2012).

[25] System-wide Core Competencies: "Recommendation to the General Education Council", Approved *by the GEC*, (2013), http://facultygovernance.uncc.edu/ retrieved.

[26] Yang, Y-T C.; Chuang Y-C.; Li, L-Y.; Tseng, S-S, "A blended learning environment for individualized English listening and speaking integrating critical thinking", *Computers & Education*, Vol. 63, Pages 285–305, (2013).

[27] Yeen-Ju, H.T.; Mai, N.; Kian, N.T.; Jing, K.W.; Wen, L.K. and Haw, L.C., "Authentic Learning Strategies to Engage Student's Creative and Critical Thinking", *Int'l Conf. on Informatics and Creative Multimedia ICICM'13*, (2013).

Defining Audience Awareness for Information Systems Research

Jordan Shropshire
University of Southern Alabama
Mobile, AL 36688-7274
USA
1-251-461-1597
jshropshire@southalabama.edu

Art Gowan
James Madison University
Harrisonburg, VA 22807
USA
1-540-568-8796
gowanja@jmu.edu

Chengqi Guo
James Madison University
Harrisonburg, VA 22807
USA
1-815-766-0925
guocx@jmu.edu

ABSTRACT

Above all, information systems (IS) professionals must be effective communicators. After all, a core part of the job is to translate business needs into system requirements. Conveying information in the right form is essential. Effective IS professionals have refined social cognitive abilities. They consider their audience and tailor the content of their messages accordingly. This concept is called audience awareness. It is a manifestation of social cognition and a hallmark of strong communicators. Although the concept of audience awareness has been discussed in other contexts, it has never been used within the IS field. Therefore, the purpose of this research is to develop a conceptual definition of audience awareness so that it can be used for IS personnel research. The definition is derived inductively using a content-analytical approach. The definition is further refined and validated using an expert panel. Implications and future research are also discussed.

CCS Concepts

• **Social and professional topics~Project and people management**

Keywords

personnel; technical communication; audience awareness; information systems.

1. INTRODUCTION

Information systems are essential to organizational success [1]. They ensure that the appropriate data is collected from relevant sources, is efficiently processed, and presented to employees, analysts, and managers in formats which are meaningful to their respective roles. They satisfy the needs of diverse user groups. They support planning, managerial control, operations, and transaction processing. Information systems are often considered to be the heart and lifeblood of modern enterprises. They fulfill the information needs of individuals, teams, and executives across business functions. In order for an organization to survive, its information systems must have the flexibility to adapt as operations change over time. Firms with cutting-edge information systems have a competitive advantage over their peers [2]. They are more flexible, adaptable, resilient, and make better decisions using computational intelligence [3]. These significant advantages affect the organization's bottom line: they often mean the difference between missing and beating projected earnings forecasts [4].

Developing, refining, and maintaining advanced information systems is a complex process. It takes a team of trained and knowledgeable information systems professionals to coordinate these efforts. Information systems professionals manage the process of modifying, upgrading, and redeploying systems so that they offer maximum capabilities to organizations [5]. This is no small task, given the complexities of the modern enterprise. Information systems management tasks includes expanding system edges to incorporate new business partners, vendors, downstream sales organizations, third-party cloud services, big data operations, IT solutions, and social media platforms. These projects are costly and risky to implement. Skilled information systems professionals are needed to balance the interests of different groups, blend technologies, and deliver services which provide value.

Information systems professionals are business-oriented, technology proficient individuals who ensure that companies derive maximum value from their IT investments. IS professionals build, integrate, or purchase software to create information systems. They use computing to solve problems or support digital innovation. They understand business problems and are able to match them with appropriate technological solutions. They organize disparate components into higher-order systems. To accomplish these tasks, information systems professionals work with stakeholders such as employees, managers, executives, software and hardware vendors, programmers, internal IT team members, and external end users [6]. They must determine user needs, brief decision makers, work with vendors and programmers to project system acquisition/development costs, negotiate interoperability parameters with external partners, and confer with in-house IT support staff. This requires a well-rounded skill set. Information systems professionals must excel at professional communication, problem identification, analysis, critical thinking, and teamwork.

Of all the skills which an IS professional must possess, none is more essential than communication [5, 7]. Because audiences differ with respect to their interests, knowledge, and organizational roles, effective information systems professionals must recognize these differences and tailor their messages accordingly [8]. For instance, they should know that CIOs want the bottom line, project managers' focus on budget and timeline issues, software developers need technical details, and users need simple-but-satisfactory answers. They know what is important to

SIGMIS-CPR'16, June 2–4, 2016, Alexandria, VA, USA.
© 2016 ACM. ISBN 978-1-4503-4203-2/16/06…$15.00.
DOI: http://dx.doi.org/10.1145/2890602.2890614

each group and what they least likely care about. They personalize the format, complexity, and length of messages for their various audiences. This concept is called audience awareness [9, 10]. Audience awareness is the ability to gauge the intellectual, emotional, and informational characteristics of a particular audience and adjust a message accordingly [11]. It is a manifestation of social cognition and a hallmark of strong communicators [12]. Because they must effectively communicate with different audiences, information systems professionals need an advanced sense of audience awareness. This skill helps ensure that business requirements are effectively translated into technical specifications, and that resulting systems meet or exceed user expectations.

Many firms have stressed the importance of effective use of communication styles and presentation techniques to their IS employees. In reality, as many senior level managers come to realize, people often operate under the misconception that these techniques are related to personal disposition and, therefore, difficult to be obtained through post-hoc training. Such issue has remained as a challenge not only to practitioners, but also researchers. In the industry, professionals attempt to improve the success rate of IS projects by analyzing the demographic and psychographic features of their primary audience. In academia, the IS field has not reached a consensus regarding what audience awareness entails and how the meaning of audience awareness can be accurately communicated amongst researchers. Therefore, much work is needed to bridge such conceptual gap.

Although the concept of audience awareness has been previously discussed in other fields, it lacks a formal definition for the IS field. Without a conceptual definition, it is impossible to measure and compare information system professionals' sense of audience awareness. This also hinders the development of methods for teaching audience awareness to current and future IS professionals. Therefore, the purpose of this research is define the audience awareness construct for the IS context. It uses the content analysis methodology to identify previous references to audience awareness in academic literature, interpret the context and meaning of each usage, and identify the salient characteristics of the concept. These concepts are then reconciled into a single definition. The definition is refined using feedback from an expert panel. The results provide a formal definition of the audience awareness construct as it pertains to the information systems domain

A formal definition of audience awareness will support its inclusion in personnel research and integration into expanding theoretical frameworks. This research provides significant benefit in that it lays the groundwork for future research on an important characteristic of information systems professionals. If properly measured, this concept could also be included in predictive models of employee performance. The remainder of this paper is organized as follows: Section Two provides background information on social cognition, a meta-concept from which audience awareness is derived. Section Three contains the conceptual development. Section Four contains the validity assessment. Section Five reviews the results. It also provides discussion and identifies the implications of this research. Finally, Section Six provides concluding comments.

2. BACKGROUND

People's understandings of the social environment can be studied by asking them how they make sense of others [13]. Therefore, an in-depth analysis of how people perceive themselves and others as a part of the society is an essential component of social cognition research [14]. Different than behavioral decision research, social cognition research is a descriptive field that focuses on the interpretive process as a whole. As a sub-topic of social psychology, social cognition research contributes to our knowledge with regard to how people's cognitive processes affect their social behaviors and interactions. Some researchers, however, contended that social cognition is a conceptual and empirical approach to understanding social psychological topics by investigating the cognitive underpinnings of whatever social phenomenon is being studied [15]. With this approach, social scientists analyze the process of information exchange that subsequently forms people's perceptions of the social world. A glaring feature of the social cognition approach is its reliance on personal perceptions rather than objective descriptions of the environment, as shown in Figure 1.

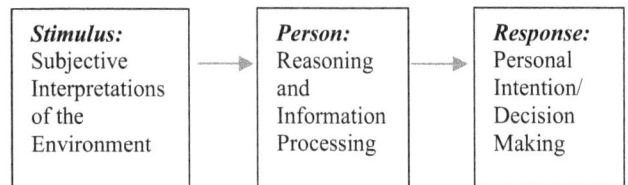

Stimulus: Subjective Interpretations of the Environment	Person: Reasoning and Information Processing	Response: Personal Intention/ Decision Making

Figure 1. A Social Cognition Approach.
Note: Adapted from "Social Cognition: from Brains to Culture," by S. Fiske and S. Taylor, 2013

An on-going debate amongst social psychologists is about which approach, social cognition versus behavioral, is superior when analyzing the influence of human cognitions in social contexts. The former is descriptive in nature while the latter is normative models oriented with some descriptive elements. Behavioral researchers have criticized social cognition approach for offering descriptions that provide little assistance toward improving the quality of people's behaviors, and social cognition researchers have criticized behavioral researchers for missing the contextual information and personal traits that contribute to the explanations of how people behave [16]. The debate has led to an integrative perspective that combines the power of both approaches. For example, researchers attempted to add social psychological variables to the classic economic models that suggest individuals act to maximize self-interest.

Central to social cognition research is the assumption that individuals develop their social perceptions differently from what normative models might predict. More and more researchers, especially in IS, try to highlight the importance of social context in behavioral studies by applying social perspectives to the issues that have been typically found in behavioral theories. For example, many researchers have studied the role of IS in organizational success using structural models (e.g., McLean's System Success Model). Audience awareness, a concept rarely discussed in IS fields, has significant potentials allowing IS professionals to achieve better accuracy in eliciting system requirements by investigating the effects of contextual variables and personal factors. Specifically, understanding how audiences perceive the roles of products, organizations, and themselves provides valuable guidance to IS professionals who execute effective communications plans that lead to successful project outcomes and high customer satisfaction.

3. CONCEPTUAL DEVELOPMENT

For this research a conceptual definition of audience awareness was developed by conducting a content analysis of selected audience awareness literature. Content analysis is a technique used within the social sciences to systematically analyze and describe the content of various forms of communication. It is employed in this research to support existing theory defining audience awareness subcomponents and extend the theory by uncovering additional elements relevant to its definition. The selected literature includes academic and practitioner-oriented articles and books from various disciplines which address audience awareness. The Google Scholar search engine was employed to identify writings which met the search criteria for inclusion: references to the phrases audience awareness or audience analysis in the keywords or in the body of the literature. In addition to searches, additional manuscripts were identified by reviewing the bibliographies of selected articles.

In the review of literature for the content analysis, all articles were processed using a previously-validated procedure [17]. The procedure consists of four steps: (1) selection of topic area, (2) identification of concepts which describe the overall construct, (3) transfer to a reusable format, and (4) use of concepts in labeling source. The articles were divided into two categories: those which describe the cognitive process of audience recognition, and those which describes the attributes by which audience should be framed. The contribution of articles related the first category are summarized in Table 1 while those related to the latter category are contained in Table 2 (both tables below).

Many of the articles which focus on procedural issues stem from the linguistics and writing fields [9, 18]. Within these works there is an implicit assumption that the communication will be conveyed in writing [19, 20]. This assumption is not maintained in the current research, as it is understood that information systems professionals may confer with others using any number of different media (e.g. in person, over the phone, video conference, virtual etc.). It cannot be assumed that the communicator will have the opportunity to refine his or her message before it is conveyed [21]. This is a departure from previous studies on audience analysis which presume there is time for reflection and message refinement [10]. It was therefore necessary to amalgamate previous descriptions in a context-neutral procedural definition: audience awareness is the process of assessing differences in interpersonal complexity and developing and implementing an audience-adapted strategy. This definition is conceptually closest to the work of Piche and Roen [12] who reconciled students' cognitive differences with the persuasiveness of their writing. However, the proposed definition does not presume that the IS professional is communicating via written message. Its global framing focuses on audience analysis rather than the message building process.

Having prescribed a procedural definition of audience awareness, it is also necessary to consider the dimensions by which audiences can be defined. These are factors that should be considered when tailoring a message for a particular audience. Several of the articles on audience-attributes stem from the persuasive writing field [18, 22]. These articles integrate non-cognitive audience dimensions, since these dimensions impact the effectiveness of an author's argument [23]. For instance, one article [10] incorporates attitude, sense of identity, emotional states, enduring traits, and general dispositions into a list of audience dimensions. Another study suggest that attributes such as beliefs, language, traditions and values should be considered [24]. While these factors stand to improve the persuasiveness of a written argument, they have less bearing within the information system context. The types of communications associated with information systems management are largely expository. IS professionals are largely

tasked with eliciting business requirements and conveying technical specifications to appropriate audiences. Their work is less concerned with persuasion than that of other business professions (e.g. sales and marketing). Therefore, the non-cognitive attributes were excluded from the current audience attributes list.

Table 1. Defining the Audience Recognition Process

Reference	Context	Procedure
Berkenkotter, 1981	The role of audience awareness in the composition processes of skilled writers	-Analyzing/constructing a hypothetical audience -Goal setting and planning for a specific audience -Evaluating content and style with regard to anticipated audience response -Reviewing, editing, and revising for a specific audience
Piche and Roen 1987	Differences in social cognition and quality of students' persuasive writing	-Assess differences in interpersonal cognitive complexity -Development of audience-adapted strategy -Implementation in variety of contexts
Rubin and Piche (1979)	Analysis of audience adaptation skills	-The writer draws from his or her knowledge base -The writer engages in social inference, representing people's knowledge, predispositions, etc. to anticipate message effects -The writer translates his or cognitive representation of the reader into task-specific knowledge of potential communication gaps and advantageous strategies. -This knowledge is transformed into tactical specifications guiding the composition of the message (e.g. matters of invention, emphasis, use of examples or figurative language). -The writer's linguistic resources are deployed to accomplish the message plan
Alamargot et al., 2011	Working memory and audience awareness during text composition	Skilled writers can transform their ideas and the manner in which they are expressed by anticipating their impact on the reader.

79

Table 2. Defining the Attributes of the Audience

Reference	Context	Attributes
Rubin 1984	Social cognition within the writing process	-Writers may represent readers' perceptual fields -Writers may represent readers' prior knowledge, values, associations, and linguistic skills -Writers may represent readers' sense of identity relative to the writers -Writers may represent readers' emotional states -Writers may represent readers' enduring traits and general predispositions
Schriver, 1997	Intuition-driven approach to audience modeling	The communicator should catalog audience demographics (age, sex, income, educational level) or psychographics (lifestyle, attitude, personality traits, work habits, etc.).
Albers, 2003	Multidimensional audience analysis	Communicators should employ dimensionality to allow for more complex views of audience: -knowledge level -detail level -cognitive abilities
Turns & Wagner (2004)	Audience analysis using 4 dimensions	Audience can be considered in relation to: -role (of user) -goals (what user wants/needs to accomplish) -knowledge (what a user brings to the table) -circumstances of use (environmental factors, including technical limitations) -culture (beliefs, language, traditions, and values)
Schriver, 2010	Key attribute audience modeling	Audience modeling tools should be limited to three attributes due to the limits of human cognition: -expertise -motivation -anxiety
Ede, 1984	Audience awareness in written communications	Audience analysis refers to methods designed to enable speakers and writers to draw inferences about the experiences, beliefs, and attitudes of an audience.
Midgette et. al., 2008	Audience awareness in persuasive communications	Writers need to anticipate the attitudes, beliefs, and arguments of the audience.
Grabe and Kaplan, 1996	Theory of writing and linguistics	Five parameters of audience influence the production of discourse: -the number of persons who are expected to read the text, -the extent of familiarity of the readers with the writer, -the status of the readers in relation to the writer, -the extent of shared background knowledge between the readers and the writer and -the extent of shared specific topical knowledge between the readers and the writer.

Several related studies provide audience dimensions lists in the form of lengthy checklists which should be considered prior to message distribution. However, these presume that the person communicating the message is doing so in writing [10, 25]. This assumption is not valid for the information systems domain. Information systems professionals communicate using a variety of mediums [26]. A long list of factors becomes impractical when the IS professional must engage in quick hallway discussions and cannot refer to a checklist [27]. Given the cognitive limitations of human memory, it is more realistic to assume a short list of audience attributes [25]. Schriver [28] tested the limits of human cognition in audience modeling and found that analysis should be limited three factors. Likewise, the proposed attributes list consists of three factors. The proposed audience dimensions are: audience role, audience objective, and audience expertise. These dimensions are closest to the work of Grabe and Kaplan [18]. After multiple reviews of the literature, it was determined that these factors are represented among the majority of the multi-attribute lists. Further, they are consistent with the role of the information system professional and meet the communication fluidity requirements.

Within the information systems context, audience role defines a person's relationship to the IS professional and/or the information system. Different groups of users may interact with a system in functionally different ways. For instance, a database administrator and a marketing professional may work with the same database in different capacities. The information systems professional must take their different roles into account in choosing which details to share [26]. Audience objective defines how the information will be used. It is presumed that the IS professional is communicating information that the audience needs in order to achieve some objective. The IS professional must anticipate the future use of the information and present it accordingly [7]. For instance, a CFO may need to know about user training costs so they can be integrated into cash flow projections while a human resources officer may need to know about training costs so they can be incorporated into hiring decisions. Hence, the same information needs to be presented in different forms to meet different goals [7]. Audience expertise is the degree of knowledge associated with a particular concept. Within the information systems domain, this is primarily an information system or technology [27]. Information systems professionals must communicate in terms which are appropriate to the knowledge level of their audience. It is therefore necessary to project the audience's familiarity with a system or tool and frame the message accordingly.

To conclude, the collective definition of audience awareness is: the process of assessing role, objective, and expertise differences and developing and implementing an audience-adapted strategy. The purpose of the next section is to refine and validate the conceptual definition using an expert panel.

4. VALIDITY ASSESSMENT
The purpose of the methodology is to validate the proposed construct definition. Because a high level of abstraction is involved and the magnitude of the inferential leap is significant, job incumbents and practitioners do not have the insights to make the required judgments [29]. Thus, the construct validity assessment is performed by researchers who can judge whether the concept of audience awareness is represented in the proposed definition [30]. These inferences are made based on their broad familiarity with the communications literature and audience awareness in particular. The construct validity panel is comprised of five scholars: two from the English and composition field, two from the technical communications field, and one from information systems. Each member of the panel was supplied with a deconstructed version of the definition. The definition was separated into its procedural and dimensional components for easier analysis. Panelists were asked via email to indicate if each component was essential to the construct and whether the construct was complete. The results were pooled and the feedback was used to refine the definition of the construct so that it more closely represents the concept of audience awareness for the information systems context.

5. RESULTS
The panelists concurrently agreed that the procedural definition of audience awareness was both essential and sufficient. However, there was disagreement among the dimensional aspects of the construct. Two of the five panelists argued that the concepts of role and objective are too conceptually similar. Role is defined as the capacity in which a person interacts with an information system. The role is a functional position such as software developer, user, or external stakeholder. Objective is defined in terms of how the audience will use the information that is conveyed to them. It is assumed the audience has an objective and needs some information in order to achieve their objectives. It was assumed that it is important for the communicator to understand the audience's objective in order to provide the right information in the right format. However, some of the panelists argued that objective is a function of position within an organization, and therefore redundant to the definition. However, three panelists countered that role is a more permanent attribute than objective. A person's objectives change as he or she completes projects and/or accomplishes less significant tasks throughout the day. An

employee with multiple assignments might have different information needs. An information systems professional might be required to communicate information in different formats as an employee's objectives change. Based on the rebuttal provided by the majority of panelists, a decision was made to not change the role and objective dimensions of the audience awareness definition. The proposed definition of audience awareness therefore remains: the process of assessing role, objective, and expertise differences and developing and implementing an audience-adapted strategy.

6. CONCLUSION
Above all, Information systems professionals must be effective communicators. After all, a core part of the job is to translate business needs into technical requirements. Conveying information in the right form is essential. The best IS professionals have refined social cognitive abilities. They personalize their messages to fit the expectations of each audience in order to communicate more effectively. The purpose of this research was to formalize this concept so that it can be used in future research. A conceptual definition of audience awareness was constructed. The definition was inductively derived using a content analysis of related work. The definition was refined and validated using feedback from an expert panel. The resulting definition provides a basis for understanding and describing audience awareness in the information systems field and throughout the social sciences. In future research, a measure should be developed so that the construct can be empirically evaluated. The measure should be developed with respect to the information systems context, so that it can be meaningfully administered to IS professionals. This will allow researchers to gauge the impact of audience awareness on various aspects of IS work performance.

7. REFERENCES
[1] B. Dehning and T. Stratopoulos, "Determinants of a sustainable competitive advantage due to an IT-enabled strategy," *The Journal of Strategic Information Systems,* vol. 12, pp. 7-28, 2003.

[2] G. Bhatt and V. Grover, "Types of Information Technology Capabilities and Their Role in Competitive Advantage: An Empirical Study," *Journal of Management Information Systems,* vol. 22, pp. 253-277, 2005.

[3] G. Piccoli and B. Ives, "Review: it-dependent strategic initiatives and sustained competitive advantage: a review and synthesis of the literature," *MIS Quarterly,* vol. 29, pp. 747-776, 2005.

[4] L. Wang and P. Alam, "Information Technology Capability: Firm Valuation, Earnings Uncertainty, and Forecast Accuracy," *Journal of Information Systems,* vol. 21, pp. 27-48, 2007.

[5] D. Graf and M. Misic, "The changing role of the systems analyst," *Information Resources Management Journal,* vol. 7, pp. 15-23, 1994.

[6] D. Tesch, J. Jiang, and G. Klein, "The Impact of Information System Personnel Skill Discrepancies on Stakeholder Satisfaction," *Decision Sciences,* vol. 34, pp. 107-129, 2003.

[7] J. Fisher, "Defining the role of a technical communicator in the development of information systems," *IEEE Transactions on Professional Communication,* vol. 41, pp. 186-199, 1998.

[8] S. Chakraborty, S. Sarker, and J. Valacich, "Understanding Analyst Effectiveness in Requirements Elicitation: A Gestalt Fit Perspective," in *European Conference on Information Systems (ECIS),* St. Gallen, CH, 2007.

[9] C. Berkenkotter, "Understanding a writer's awareness of audience," *College Composition and COmmunication 32,* vol. 4, 1981.

[10] D. Rubin, "Social cognition and written communication " *Written Communication,* vol. 1, pp. 211-245, 1984.

[11] M. Albers, "Multidimensional analysis for custom content for multiple audiences," in *SIGDOC '03,* San Fransico, CA, 2003.

[12] G. Piche and D. Roen, "Social Cognition and writing: Interpersonal cognitive complexity and abstractness and the quality of students' persuasive writing," *Written Communication,* vol. 4, pp. 68-89, 1987.

[13] F. Heider, *The psychology of Interpersonal Relations.* New York, NY: Wiley, 1958.

[14] S. Fiske and S. Taylor, *Social Cognition: from Brains to Culture.* SAGE Publications, 2013.

[15] D. Hamilton, *Social Cognition: Key Readings.* Psychology Press, 2005.

[16] M. Bazerman and A. Tenbrunsel, *Basic and Applied Social Psychology*, vol 20(1), pp. 87-91, 1998.

[17] B. Lewis, G. Templeton, and T. Byrd, "A methodology for construct development in MIS research," *European Journal of Information Systems,* vol. 14, pp. 388-400, 2005.

[18] W. Grabe and R. Kaplan, *Theory and Practice of Writing: An Applied Linguistic Perspective.* New York, NY: Routledge, 1996.

[19] L. Ede and A. Lunsford, "Audience addressed/audience invoked: The role of audience in composition theory and pedagogy," *College Composition and COmmunication 32,* vol. 35, pp. 155-171, 1984.

[20] D. Rubin and G. Piche, "Development in syntactic and strategic aspects of audience adaptation skills in written persuasive communication," *Research in the Teaching of English,* vol. 13, pp. 293-316, 1979.

[21] K. Siau and X. Tan, "Technical communication in information systems development: the use of cognitive mapping," *IEEE Transactions on Professional Communication,* vol. 48, pp. 269 - 284, 2005.

[22] E. Midgette, P. Haria, and C. MacArthur, "The effects of content and audience awareness goals for revision on the persuasive essays of fifth- and eigth-grade students," *Reading and Writing Quarterly,* vol. 21, pp. 131-151, 2007.

[23] K. Schriver, *Dynamics in Document Design: Creating Texts for Readers.* NY, NY: John Wiley, 1997.

[24] J. Turns and T. Wagner, "Characterizing audience for informational web site design," *Technical Communication,* vol. 51, pp. 68-85, 2004.

[25] D. Alamargot, G. Caporossi, D. Chesnet, and C. Ros, "What makes a skilled writer? Working memory and audience awareness during a text composition," *Learning and Individual Differences,* vol. 21, pp. 505-516, 2011.

[26] J. Fisher, "Improving the usability of information systems: the role of the technical communicator," *European Journal of Information Systems,* vol. 8, pp. 294-303, 1999.

[27] J. Hartwick and H. Barki, "Communication as a dimension of user participation," *44,* vol. 1, 2001.

[28] K. Schriver, "Document design in transition: Evolving conceptions of audiences as readers," in *Conference on College Composition and Communication*, Louisville, KY, 2010.

[29] C. Lawshe, "A quantitative approach to content validity," *Personnel Psychology,* vol. 28, pp. 563-575, 1975.

[30] D. Straub, M. Boudreau, and D. Gefen, "Validation guidelines for IS positivist research," Communications of the Association for Information Systems, vol. 13, pp. 380-427, 2004.

Black Lives Matter: The Journey of a Black IT Scholar

Curtis C. Cain
The Pennsylvania State University
307G Information Sciences and Technology Building
University Park, PA 16802
+1 814 865 8952
caincc@psu.edu

Eileen M. Trauth
The Pennsylvania State University
330C Information Sciences and Technology Building
University Park, PA 16802
+1 814 865 6457
etrauth@ist.psu.edu

ABSTRACT

In this paper, we focus on the lived experiences of a particular Black scholar in pursuit of a PhD in IT. The content of this paper was adapted from a dissertation that focused on identifying and analyzing the factors that support or undermine the achievement of Black males completing IT degrees and entering the workforce. The content of this paper centers around the factors that impacted the scholar. In light of the Black Lives Matter movement, we wanted to take a social issue and deconstruct it to apply it to academia. In order to accomplish this, we used a researcher's lived experiences as a Black male for the data for this paper. By the scholar's own admission, [blinded for review] has not reached the level of success that the scholar would like the scholar is still striving to reach those goals. These are goals that the likes of Trayvon Martin, Mike Brown, Dontre Hamilton, Eric Garner, John Crawford III, Ezell Ford and countless others no longer have, which sparked the Black Lives Matter movement.

Keywords

Black males; career choice; diversity; digital inequality; ethnicity; race; IT workforce

1. INTRODUCTION

This paper is based on a qualitative study that sought to identify and analyze the factors that support or undermine the achievement of Black males completing IT degrees and entering the workforce.

The combination of educational, environmental and personal experiences magnifies their challenging likelihood to enter a career in IT [1, 2, 3]. In the educational landscape for IT careers, Blacks are vastly underrepresented in the IT fields of study. In addition, environmentally, Blacks are underrepresented in the workforce as well as academia. Finally, preparing and adapting to careers in IT in which there are few people of color poses a challenge on a personal level.

The differences in educational, environmental and personal experiences, lend themselves to research which focuses on further understanding the ways in which these factors influence Black male IT identity development and career choice. Not all Black males are the same. There are differences among them that must be evaluated and accounted for. Their differences could provide useful insight into what attributes successful Black men in IT

SIGMIS-CPR'16, June 2–4, 2016, Alexandria, VA, USA.
© 2016 ACM. ISBN 978-1-4503-4203-2/16/06…$15.00.
DOI: http://dx.doi.org/10.1145/2890602.2890623

have. These differences among the same group are referred to as within gender variation.

This research project is concerned with the contextual investigation into the factors and influences that contribute to understanding Black male underrepresentation in IT fields. I use how I am different from many Black men as a lens and basis for understanding this topic. This study sought to identify the differences among Black men who excel in their pursuit of an IT career. It chronicles their personal triumphs, roadblocks and how they overcame them. This study analyzes both the individual as well as the group. The individual level lends itself to understanding how the Black men are different from each other and what their unique characteristics are. The group level looks across the demographic to better understand how they interact with the individual. Together, these levels of analysis provide beneficial insight into Black male qualities that are necessary for them to succeed in an IT career path.

Some have explained the low participation of women in technical fields by positing that women are either biologically limited (gender essentialism) or influenced by social messages (social construction). Trauth [5, 6] posits that these explanations are insufficient to truly address the complexities of women's technical abilities, interactions, barriers and the wide variation among women. Therefore, instead of grouping together individuals of a particular gender, the Individual Differences Theory of Gender and IT approaches underrepresentation in the IT workforce from the vantage point of adding individual agency, identity and experience in relation to life choices and societal influences [6].

The purpose of this study is to use Trauth's Individual Differences Theory of Gender and IT to identify and analyze the factors that support or undermine the achievement of Black males completing IT degrees and entering the workforce. Specifically, this research seeks to add to the growing body of knowledge about Black male participation in IT education and IT careers. Thus far, much of the research about Black male participation in IT compares Blacks and Whites, as two static groups as opposed to studying the differences within each group. This analysis can only lead to a partial explanation of Black male differences. This approach also leaves out influences, which occur at the individual level of analysis. These influences have an impact on participation. This research expands these factors to describe the ways in which societal, environmental and institutional influences impact IT career pathway for Black males. There is one overarching question: how do societal, environmental and institutional factors influence Black male IT student participation, development and degree attainment? My own story tells me that the answer to Black male underrepresentation is a combination of environmental influences and personal influences.

A successful thesis focuses on a problem situated within society or one that stems from lived experiences. This thesis is a combination of both. The statistics suggest that as a Black male in my mid-twenties, I should have spent time in prison. The media often portrays my people as simultaneously aggressive, anti-intellectual, and lazy. Therefore, it would not be much of a stretch to wonder how I got to this point in my life, where I am in the midst of writing this thesis. Even I never thought I would be in this position.

I grew up in the inner-city of Atlanta, spending the majority of my time at my Grandmother's house. My Aunt's house was located next door. The projects happened to be in our backyard. My Grandmother worked on the assembly line at General Motors and had to be to work before I woke up for school. My mother is a phlebotomist who traveled long distances for work. There would be times when I would not see my mother for days due to her hectic work life. My Dad and Mom separated shortly after my birth. He was in the Air Force and was never stationed in Atlanta. However, no matter how geographically spread out my family was, they all did the best they could. My Grandmother would make sure my breakfast was cooked before she left the house and left it wrapped in aluminum foil on the stove for me to warm once I got up. She would also give me a wakeup call, when there was a break on the assembly line, to make sure I was awake and found the lunch money she would leave me. My Mom never missed a holiday. I would see her every week and even on Valentine's Day she gave me a rose. My Auntie was a jack of all trades. Her house was like a store. If I needed anything Auntie is always there. Then there's my older brother, Rob. He's two years older than me and was the ideal student. This was not a trait of mine. He won all the awards and was a straight-A student throughout elementary and middle school. By contrast, I was a C student. This was not due to a lack of ability, but rather my refusal to put forth effort beyond what was necessary to pass. My Mother hated when I got C's. She would often ask why I could not be more like Rob. Her frustration was echoed by teachers who had taught Rob two years prior and often wondered where I had gone wrong. I do not know where I went wrong, but I do know that I get bored easily. If something did not interest me then I simply was not going to do it or at least not willingly or to my best potential.

The greatest gift my Dad ever gave to me was my first computer, which he built in the mid-1990s. The computer my Dad built for us occupied much of my time. I remember breaking it several times to the point where my Dad got tired of fixing it when he would visit. Eventually, when I was in high school my Grandmother bought us a new desktop computer. I am sure the computer cost well over $2000 at the time. It was new, which meant I could play with it and break it. I believe my Grandmother knew that's what I would do so she invested in an extended protection plan. When I broke it, a repair technician, who happened to be a Black man, Gary Vause, would come out to repair it. He had his own company, Vause Computer Systems. His company handled all the repair work orders in Atlanta from the Home Shopping Network and QVC. After coming to our house a few times he took notice that I was interested and offered me a job in his company where I could make a few bucks on the side while in high school. Thanks to his help and encouragement, I quickly became the go-to person for all things technology related at school thanks to his help.

In high school my best friend, Kim, (the same friend who would go on to tell me about graduate school), mentioned that she thought I could perform much better in class than what I was doing. She said that I did just enough to get by. I never wanted to be the type of student who stood out. I would rather blend into the crowd. There was something about that conversation that resonated with me. During the summer after 10th grade, I enrolled in the Spelman Summer Enrichment Program. This was a program where students could take a high school course over the summer and receive credit for it. Some classmates of mine all got together and took Biology. I received a B in the course. When I returned to school at the beginning of the 11th grade, I noticed my schedule still had me registered in Biology. My magnet program coordinator would hand out bus passes during our class after lunch. When I went to get my bus pass, I told her that I was enrolled in the wrong class and that I took Biology over the summer and I would like to take AP Biology. She told me in front of the entire class that I was not smart enough to take Advanced Placement (AP) classes. I went on to enroll in Microbiology and successfully passed every class that year. At the beginning of my senior year, I noticed she had enrolled me in 6 of 7 AP classes. I went to her office and had her remove me from all 6, citing her comment that I was not smart enough then so perhaps I am still not smart enough. I allowed my resentment of the magnet school coordinator to impede my own educational opportunities to take the AP courses. At the end of my 12th grade year, I raised my GPA and scored well enough on the SAT to be accepted to a few universities. After looking over my options, I elected to attend Johnson C. Smith University, a Historically Black College and University (HBCU) located in Charlotte, NC.

When I finished my Bachelor's degree in Information Systems Engineering, I had numerous job offers and initially accepted a position with Duke Energy in Charlotte, NC. The starting salary was more money than I had ever seen in my life and I thought that's what "successful" people did. In my mind they finished undergrad, if they were lucky enough to graduate from high school, and entered the workforce. Kim, who told me I could do better in high school, told me of this thing called graduate school. I had no idea what it was or what it took to get in other than taking the Graduate Record Examination (GRE). I promptly scheduled the GRE and applied for Ph.D. programs in Computer Science, as the end of the fall semester was rapidly approaching. After the initial wave of rejections, I became resigned to go into the workforce at the end of the spring semester. Then, to my surprise, I began to receive acceptance letters.

I thought to myself, "Wow, go figure, now I have options". I then scheduled visits to the schools and applied for different types of funding. I narrowed my choices down, looked a little closer at Auburn's Department of Computer Science and Software Engineering, and noticed two Black graduate faculty members, Juan Gilbert and Cheryl Seals. None of the other schools I applied to had a single Black faculty member. I thought that with two Black faculty members I would eventually find a specialty that I would be of interest. Moreover, they may understand my background more than other faculty members and be people I could identify with.

One day I was walking to the mailbox at my Grandmother's house to mail my confirmation of attendance letter, and I noticed that I received a letter from Auburn University with an offer of a National Science Foundation (NSF) Louis Stokes Alliance for Minority Participation (LSAMP) Bridge to the Doctorate Fellowship. The Bridge to the Doctorate is aimed at increasing the quality and quantity of multicultural students successfully completing science, technology, engineering and mathematics (STEM) baccalaureate degree programs, and increasing the number of students interested in, academically qualified for and matriculated into programs of graduate study. I rescinded my intent to work for Duke Energy and sent my letter of acceptance to Auburn.

I arrived to Auburn as a starry eyed kid having just finished a Bachelor's degree. However, I was met with a rude awakening of how different graduate school was from undergraduate work. Aside from the differences in coursework, I noticed a substantial difference in the ethnic makeup of this university in comparison to the one I came from and the environment I had been accustomed to. As I looked around in numerous classes the only Black people I saw were those who were advised by one of the two Black faculty members.

During my first semester as a PhD student, I had to pass the qualifying exam or take the equivalent course that corresponded to that section of the test. I went on to pass the qualifying exam. After my first year, my advisor left the university to go to Clemson University. I opted not to go with him because I had just passed all the qualifications for the qualifying exam and did not want to start over at another university. However, after my advisor left the university, most of the students of color went with him, which meant the already few became fewer.

It was around this time that I saw something that I had not seen before. I was accustomed to being around Black students as I had graduated from an Historically Black College/University (HBCU). However, when my advisor left the university and the vast majority of the Black students left with him I noticed that students were not sold on the institution or even their primary focus area but rather on the individual. I didn't realize how much one individual could mean in the eyes of students. I was also curious about why one faculty member meant so much to the underrepresented population? I was curious as to why students within a couple years of graduating with a doctorate in Computer Science would drop everything and start over fresh. This institutional and environmental change left me intrigued. A college with nearly two-dozen Black students instantly became one with a handful. As I looked around the college I noticed something about Auburn and other universities I visited, their lack of diversity.

With my advisor now gone, I turned my focus to Human Computer Interaction (HCI). My research focused on using programming languages to design culturally relevant design tools to teach minorities math and science. I changed my advisor to the only remaining Black faculty member. She took me into her already overcrowded lab for which I was greatly appreciative. When she first saw me, I wore a shirt that said "Genius by Birth, Slacker by Choice". She cautioned me that I should not wear shirts like that. I interpreted her advice as a way of saying that as a young Black male, I should mindfully shield myself from stereotyping. While I saw the usefulness of HCI and I devoted much of my time to building applications and programs, I could not help myself from thinking about the lack of diversity within the college and my curiosity to want to understand why. I would attend conferences and symposiums such as the Association for Computing Machinery's (ACM) Richard Tapia Celebration of Diversity in Computing where the topic of diversity would be the theme and I would hear the same things, "that's an interesting topic but where would you study that?" or "that's a great topic but wait until you have tenure to study it." I was led to believe that being in a Computer Science program, that this particular type of research (i.e. IT Education and Human Resource Development) was seen as community service as opposed to research. This particular research focus was ill-suited for a traditional Computer Science program, which focused primarily on Programming,

Operating Systems, Algorithms and Architecture. A focus on IT Education and Human Resource Develop with IT was regarded as intervention wand community service work rather than as legitimate research. However, I could not see myself graduating in one area when the issue that drives my curiosity goes neglected in another. I could not understand why talented researchers put such critical issues on the back burner. I also could not see myself working diligently to achieve tenure before addressing the issue of underrepresentation. Thus, two years away from finishing my doctorate in Computer Science I reached a crossroad, and questioned What should I do?

I decided to finish my Master's at Auburn and move to an institution that would be more welcoming to my ultimate research area. However, given that graduate school acceptance is anything but straightforward and guaranteed, I applied for User Experience Design positions just in case my attempt to go to another school was unsuccessful. I received a position offer at Lexmark in Lexington, KY. While the offer was very appealing but I ultimately turned it down to return to school at The Pennsylvania State University. It was here where I met my advisor, Dr. Eileen Trauth, who is a gender expert in the research field of IT. Dr. Trauth is a White woman who has researched the lack of women in the IT workforce. Our research would dovetail as she is an expert in the field and I was particularly interested in race and ethnicity. It was very difficult to leave a program where I was about two years away from graduating with a PhD to start from scratch. However, I figured this approach would be the best for my overall development. Unfortunately, it did not take long to realize that the ethnic makeup of the college at Penn State was even diverse than Auburn. Due to the location of the university, I was not surprised. At this point, I could use my own life experiences to reason why there were so few Blacks and realized just how relevant those life experienced are.

In the fall of my first year at Penn State, I applied for the NSF Graduate Research Fellowship. The title of my proposal was [blinded for review]. The fellowship helps ensure the vitality of the human resource base of science and engineering in the United States and reinforces its diversity. The program recognizes and supports outstanding graduate students in NSF-supported science, technology, engineering, and mathematics disciplines who are pursuing research-based doctoral degrees at accredited United States institutions. I received the fellowship the following spring semester.

I recently visited my undergraduate alma mater for homecoming and attended one of my undergraduate advisor's classes. I sat in the back of the classroom; similar to how I would when I was a student there. I would have on my usual clothes, which consist of jeans, t-shirt or polo and sneakers. Students in the class thought that I was just new to the class. Then my undergraduate advisor would walk in give her lecture and then introduce me. The students seemed to be shocked that I was a young, Black PhD candidate who has these NSF grants and would ask how did I become so accomplished? I never have a response to their question because I do not see myself as accomplished yet. I do not feel accomplished. I do not believe I can be accomplished until I have a thorough understanding of why there are so few Blacks who seem to navigate what they experience as convoluted academic pipeline and overcome societal obstacles that hinder success in IT higher education.

2. THEORY

One method to use to begin to understand the lack of representation of Blacks in IT is to use theory. Trauth's Individual Differences Theory of Gender and IT was developed as a means to understand the topic of underrepresentation of women in the technical workforce that essentialism and social construction could only partially explain. In Trauth and Quesenberry's critique of essentialism they argue that while some relevant differences in ability may be biologically based they are not based on gender. Further, essentialism does not add contextual factors, which may affect an individual's perspective or interaction with technology.

Social construction identifies social forces which may shape the male or female life, but minimizes individual agency or different experiences that affect responses to those factors [4, 7, 8]. Given these two differing theoretical perspectives of essentialism and social construction, they can be interpreted as describing only partial elements of the factors experienced by women in IT. As Trauth [5] points out, "current theories about gender and IT do not fully account for the variation in men's and women's relationships to information technology and the IT field" (p. 1759). It is this variation that Trauth has argued is central to different people's experiences, decisions, and relationship to technology.

The Individual Differences Theory of Gender and IT consists of three major constructs to explain gender variation in participation in the IT field: i) individual identity, ii) individual influences, and iii) environmental influences [7, 9, 10]. The individual identity construct consists of two sub-constructs: personal demographics (e.g. ethnicity, socio-economic class, family background) and career items (i.e., type of IT work). The second construct, individual influences, consists of two sub-constructs: personal characteristics (e.g., educational background, personality traits) and personal influences (e.g., mentors, role models, and significant others). Lastly, the environmental influences construct consists of four sub-constructs related to the geographic region; cultural influences, economic influences (e.g. cost of living, cost of education), policy influences, and infrastructure influences (e.g. institutional climate) [7].

3. DISCUSSION

The purpose of this paper was to reflect upon the factors that influence Black participation in IT at the individual, societal and environmental level. The narrative presented in this paper emphasized factors such as stereotype threat, significant others, race and exposure to IT in remaining in the IT field. It was found that these factors work together and often are not independent of one another. It is suggested that in order to positively encourage Black participation in IT we must take into consideration a variety of characteristics that influence that participation rather than trying to pinpoint gaps at a singular level. This supports the Individual Differences Theory of Gender and IT and dispels generalizations about Black being unable or unwilling to go into the IT field.

4. ACKNOWLEDGMENTS

This research is supported by a grant from the National Science Foundation (Grant No. DGE-0750756) and The Pennsylvania State University's Africana Research Center.

5. REFERENCES

[1] Cain, C. & Trauth, E.M. (2015). "Theorizing the Underrepresentation of Black Males in Information Technology (IT). Proceedings of the Twenty-first Americas Conference on Information Systems (Puerto Rico, August).

[2] Cain, C.C., Trauth, E.M. (2013). "Stereotype Threat: The Case of Black Males in the IT Profession," Proceedings of the 2013 ACM SIGMIS-CPR (Cincinnati, OH).

[3] Cain, C.C., Trauth, E.M. (2012). "Black Males in IT Higher Education in The USA: The Digital Divide in the Academic Pipeline Re-visited," Proceedings of the 18th Americas Conference on Information Systems (Seattle, WA).

[4] Trauth, E.M. (2002). "Odd Girl Out: An Individual Differences Perspective on Women in the IT Profession." Information Technology and People. 15, 98-118.

[5] Trauth, E.M. (2006). Theorizing Gender and Information Technology Research Using the Individual Differences Theory of Gender and IT. The Encyclopedia of Gender and Information Technology. 1154-1159.

[6] Howcroft, D. and Trauth, E.M. (2004). The Choice of Critical IS Research, in Relevant Theory and Informed Practice - Looking Forward from a 20 Year Perspective on IS Research. B. Kaplan, D.P. Truex,

[7] Trauth, E.M., Quesenberry, J.L., and Huang, H. (2009). "Retaining Women in the US IT Workforce: Theorizing the Influence of Organizational Factor." European Journal of Information Systems. Special Issue on Meeting the Renewed Demand for IT Workers(18), 476-497.

[8] Trauth, E.M. (2006). Theorizing Gender and Information Technology Research Using the Individual Differences Theory of Gender and IT. The Encyclopedia of Gender and Information Technology. 1154-1159.

[9] Morgan, A. J. 2008. "An Analysis of the Influences of Human Individual Differences on Web Searching Behavior among Black and Whites: A Case of Health Information Searching". Ph.D. dissertation, The Pennsylvania State University, 2008.

[10] Quesenberry, J.L. 2007. "Career Values and Motivations: A Study of Women in the Information Technology Workforce". Ph.D. dissertation, The Pennsylvania State University, 2007.

Putting the Consequences of IT Turnover on the Map – A Review and Call for Research

Matthäus P. Zylka
Department of Information Systems & Social Networks
University of Bamberg, Germany
+49 951 8632893
matthaeus.zylka@uni-bamberg.de

ABSTRACT

Among the many aspects of IT personnel studied by the IS research community, individual voluntary IT turnover is one of the most-examined phenomena. However, research into this phenomenon concentrates mainly on antecedents and cognitive precursors such as turnover intention. Antecedents are essential to understanding the turnover of IT personnel, but they do not represent the complete landscape of IT turnover research. The consequences of individual voluntary IT turnover, an important topic, have received too little attention from the IS community. I investigate this by conducting a multidisciplinary literature review of individual voluntary turnover consequences of IT personnel. My review reveals that only 8 of 130 IT turnover studies consider IT turnover consequences, concentrated primarily on software project management. I present a taxonomy of individual voluntary IT turnover consequences as a starting point for structured research on the consequences of individual voluntary IT turnover.

Keywords

IT turnover; individual voluntary turnover; consequences; effects; literature review

1. INTRODUCTION

Employees are as important as other resources involved in the production of goods and services. It is not surprising, therefore, that organizations seek to gain benefits by investing in employees. These benefits, though, diminish when highly skilled employees voluntarily leave an organization for, say, a better position at another organization. Hence, the competition for highly skilled personnel and their retention is critical to organizations. Such competition was dubbed the "war for talent" [10] back in 1998 and later extended to the "war for Internet talent" [17], taking into account developments after the dot-com bubble burst in 2001.

Today, IT-related firms such as Google, Facebook, Apple, and others are adding large numbers of employees with IT skills, increasingly at the expense of their competitors. This competition for the best IT talent even affects non IT-related firms and industries because of the pervasiveness of Information and Communication Technology (ICT) in other industries and so-called technological convergence, a process by which ICT sectors may be converging towards a unified market [8, 23, 64].

As a consequence, the turnover of highly skilled employees is a topic of interest for practitioners and scholars alike. It is a well-studied phenomenon in the applied psychology and management literatures (for an overview of turnover research history, see [28]). Attention to the turnover phenomenon from the information systems (IS) research community has also grown, with a focus on IT personnel. In 2007, Joseph et al. [32] showed that more than 30 IS studies of IT personnel turnover were published over the past 20 years. The most recent literature review of voluntary IT turnover by Lo [39] reveals 34 studies in IS journals and 11 in non-IS journals.

Most of these studies focus on the antecedents or cognitive precursors (e.g., turnover intention) of individual voluntary IT turnover, and use or extend common models well established in the applied psychology and management literatures [32, 39]. For instance, Niederman et al. [52] use the "unfolding model of voluntary turnover" [38] to examine the turnover process of IT personnel. Eckhardt et al. [16] propose and test a model of turnover intention across IT job types combining the "Big Five" personality traits and a basic turnover model proven reliable for western IT professionals [35], and originally rooted in management and applied psychology studies (cf. [44, 46, 50, 58, 67]). Further, Joseph et al. [32] develop a contextual model of IT turnover intention among IT professionals based on the process model of turnover by March and Simon [42], which has, by far, received the most attention from turnover researchers. Other researchers concentrate on the career paths IT employees may follow after a turnover [31, 47]. Mourmant et al. [47, 48] focus, for example, on IT entrepreneurial turnover as a specific career path after an individual voluntary turnover. Spiegel et al. [65] show that individual turnover is useful when the employees who leave use the social capital accrued with contacts at former employers to develop their start-ups' business models and ultimately make them successful.

However, despite the growing body of research on IT turnover behavior that describes voluntary leaving an IT job for a similar, alternative job across organizational boundaries [30, 31], the consequences of IT turnover remain unclear. It seems the IT turnover research community has insufficiently studied the consequences of turnover of IT personnel.

The objective of this study is to gauge whether this sense that the topic has been insufficiently studied is, in fact, true by reviewing IT turnover studies and examining if and how they considered the consequences of individual voluntary IT turnover. My research question, then, is: What is the current state of research into individual voluntary IT turnover consequences?

SIGMIS-CPR'16, June 2–4, 2016, Alexandria, VA, USA.
Copyright is held by the owner/author(s). Publication rights licensed to ACM.
ACM 978-1-4503-4203-2/16/06...$15.00
DOI: http://dx.doi.org/10.1145/2890602.2890618

I answer this question by conducting a multidisciplinary literature review of IT turnover studies with the focus on consequences. Further, I provide a taxonomic overview of individual turnover consequences that can be utilized for future research by the IT turnover research community. I identify research gaps and propose a research agenda for studying these consequences in detail.

This study contributes to research and practice in two major ways. First, it contributes to the understanding of the turnover of IT personnel. Top management aware of the antecedents and consequences of IT turnover can weigh the pros and cons of that turnover and effectively manage human resources. Second, it points out that there is still a need for research of IT turnover effects and identifies the research gaps.

The remainder of this paper is structured as follows. The next section outlines related work on the consequences of individual voluntary turnover, as well as the skills and mindsets of IT personnel. A debate about the unique skills and mindsets of IT personnel is necessary to emphasize consequences that might appear only after an IT turnover. The subsequent section describes the literature review, followed by a section that presents the research results. The paper concludes with a discussion of the results and implications for future research.

2. BACKGROUND

This section begins with an overview of the consequences of individual voluntary turnover[1] as discussed generally (i.e., independent of specific occupation) in the applied psychology and management literatures. From this overview, I derive a taxonomy that summarizes these consequences. I then provide an overview of the discussion regarding the skills and mindsets of IT personnel, important for understanding how IT personnel differ from other occupational groups and the unique consequences that may occur when an IT worker leaves an organization.

2.1 Consequences of Individual Voluntary Turnover

2.1.1 Negative Consequences
Individual turnover consequences are traditionally considered as negative [13]. They increase recruitment and training costs [15, 45], operational disruption on the organizational level, lead to demoralization on individual level [66], and may affect individuals and organizations [45, 51, 68].

Relationships with co-workers can be affected negatively by individual turnover [14, 34, 53]. Demoralization is a negative consequence in this context [66]; it can affect both the former and new co-workers. Co-workers who remain behind may question their own motivations for staying [66]. They interpret the departure of a former colleague as a rejection of the job and may begin to realize the possibility that better job opportunities exist [68]. As Steers and Mowday state: "Those who remain in the organization may have to reconcile their decision to stay in light of evidence from the behavior of another individual that the job may not be all that desirable" [68]. Remaining co-workers may re-

evaluate their present positions in the organization and ultimately develop more negative job attitudes, which in turn would initiate a search for a more attractive job [66, 68].

Finally, individual turnover has negative consequences for the individual who leaves. He or she may re-evaluate both the chosen and unchosen jobs following the choice [68]. Steers and Mowday [68] state that turnover may have important implications for attitudes toward the job the individual is leaving, as well as the employment he or she is taking. The manifestation of positive or negative feelings in the process of justifying his or her decision depends on whether the individual's behavior is consistent with his or her attitude towards the former job [68]. If a satisfied employee voluntarily leaves – meaning his or her behavior is inconsistent with that attitude – a turnover will create cognitive dissonance in his or her mind [68].[2] Another negative consequence for the individual who has left is the potential loss of social capital [62]. When he or she leaves unexpectedly and remaining co-workers have to compensate by, for example, working overtime, it may lead to bad moods and, as a consequence, remaining co-workers breaking off contact with the departed colleague. The individual who leaves may experience anxiety at his or her new job position [19]. To reduce the anxiety, attempts (e.g., through socialization) should be made to integrate the person into the informal organization. Sometimes socialization is not that easy, because arriving employees have unrealistic or unmet expectations regarding the new job or enter unfamiliar organizational settings and experience reality shocks [40]. However, arriving employees must adapt to the new organizational environment; they may experience uncertainty the first time in the new job, which leads them to engage in an "information search" by increasingly contacting colleagues and supervisors [5].

When an employee leaves an organization, it is usually the case that a new replacement employee must be recruited, selected, and hired. This process involves costs to the organization, the amount of which depends on the level and complexity of the job to be filled [45, 66]. The more demanding the job, the costlier the recruitment process [66]. Once a new employee is found, he or she must be trained to do the tasks of the former employee; the complexity of the job and the skill set of the new employee determine how the training costs [66]. Jobs with complex tasks have higher training costs than jobs with simple tasks. To minimize recruitment and training costs, organizations may promote or reassign workers to the departed employee's position [51].

Turnover may also have a negative effect on operations flows. In particular, the turnover of a key employee – especially where functional roles are closely intertwined – may result in operational disruption [45, 66]. The turnover of an employee who had an important job role in terms of coordination and communication may have a larger impact on operational disruption than that of an employee not involved in critical work tasks [45]. The individual turnover may disrupt routines and it may be more difficult to find replacements and integrate them into work groups because individuals are encouraged to stand out and bring unique skills to the job [26]. This may be more of an issue in individualistic cultures and less crucial in collective cultures (such as China, and

---

[1] I would like to emphasize that it is inappropriate to generalize individual turnover to collective turnover. Individual turnover differ from collective turnover conceptually and empirically and has different antecedents and consequences [53]. Hence, I only present consequences that occur after an individual turnover. However, several consequences presented in this section may also occur in the collective turnover context.

---

[2] Due to the lack of space, I refer to Festinger [20] on the foundations of cognitive dissonance theory, and to Steers and Mowday [68] on the discussion of the cognitive dissonance theory in employee turnover context.

Korea), where it may be simpler to find and integrate replacements into group functioning [26]. It may also be the case that individuals departing in more collective cultures may tend to be those with weaker fits to the work group or larger organization [26]. In addition, a recent study by Bermiss and Murmann [7] shows that the turnover of a top executive whose functional role focuses on internal firm processes is more harmful to the organization than losing a top executive whose functional role focuses on managing external exchange relationships.

2.1.2 Positive Consequences

Individual turnover may have also positive consequences for the individual who leaves, as well as for co-workers and organizations [45].

An individual turnover may resolve conflicts. If a conflicting supervisor or co-worker leaves an organization, it may well be a happy occasion for the remaining co-workers who have been in conflict with the departing individual. Even if well-liked and/or productive employees leave an organization, the turnover may open positions in an otherwise impenetrable hierarchy [66]. Thus, turnover may be the primary creator of promotion opportunities [13], contributing to a positive relation between the turnover and individual morale [66]. Further, the departing/arriving employee will achieve higher job satisfaction at his or her new job and a higher level of job commitment. Unlike with the early mention of cognitive dissonance, consistency in attitude and behavior that results in a turnover (i.e., a dissatisfied employee leaves voluntarily) will not generate cognitive dissonance in the departing employee's mind [68].

Further, the newly arrived employee increases his or her social capital and experiences socialization through the new employment [18]. The arrival of a new colleague may improve the organizational commitment of co-workers as well [72], because they may adopt the new employee's positive work attitude. The departure of an employee may increase the organizational commitment of co-workers at the former employer, especially in cases where the job level of the departing colleague is higher than those colleagues remaining, who may see the opportunity for job promotion [45, 66].

There is evidence that turnover increases organizational performance [66]. The argument is that voluntary turnover is good for organizational performance if the new employee possesses better job skills or brings new ideas to the unit [66]. Moreover, new employees may be more highly motivated than their longer-tenured counterparts and hence more productive [51, 66]. However, job performance depends on the job role. New employees in high-stress roles tend to have an inverted U-shaped performance curve [66]. They begin with low performance, improve as their tenure lengthens, but end their tenure with low job performance. Staw [66] argues that most jobs have an inverted U-shaped performance curve because performance is typically a joint function of skills and effort. The literature on the role of individual turnover on organizational performance further highlights the ways in which employee mobility introduces valuable human capital (and the employee's embedded know-how and skills) into target organizations [9, 21] and facilitates expansion of an organization's breadth [60]. Further, the new employee transfers social capital to the new employer (i.e., by relations to former clients [63]), and facilitates the flow of knowledge back to source firms [41] by enhancing social networks between the former and new employer [12].

Voluntary turnover of employees also resolves certain staffing problems for the former employer. An ineffective employee who

voluntarily quits is conveniently eliminated without interpersonal discomfort or increases in unemployment insurance costs [51].

Interpersonal conflicts between co-workers, which exist at every hierarchical level in organizations, may be why an employee leaves. Conflicts that cannot be resolved easily, in particular, trigger individual employee turnover. Staw [66] states that this conflict-triggered but voluntary turnover may be seen as beneficial and not as a cost to the organization, because it sometimes help to "resolve deep-seated conflicts" between the conflicting parties and contributes to organizational morale.

Turnover and the resulting inflow of a new employee may be the primary source for heterogeneity in skills and mindsets within organizations [66]. However, this consequence may be significantly more distinct with respect to collective turnover.

2.1.3 Taxonomy of Individual Turnover Consequences

Table 1 is a taxonomic overview of individual turnover consequences, derived from the discussion in subsections 2.1.1 and 2.1.2. It identifies positive and negative consequences and distinguishes between those that occur on the "former employer side" and the "new employer side." It distinguishes further between consequences for individuals (departing/arriving employees and their co-workers) and the organization as a whole.

Table 1. Taxonomy of individual turnover consequences

Consequences for		Positive	Negative
Former employer — Individual	Departing employee	• Job attitude [68]	• Social capital loss [62] • Job attitude [68]
	Co-worker	• Morale [66] • Promotion opportunity [66]	• Demoralization [66] • Job Attitude [68]
Former employer — Organization		• Morale [66] • Social capital gain [12]	• Operational disruption [66] • Human capital loss [60]
New employer — Individual	Arriving employee	• Job satisfaction [68] • Mental health [45] • Organizational commitment [68] • Job performance [51, 68] • Social capital gain [15]	• Anxiety [19] • Uncertainty [5]
	Co-worker	• Organizational commitment [72]	• Demoralization [66]
New employer — Organization		• Organizational performance [24, 27, 53, 66] • Human capital gain [9, 21] • Social capital gain [12, 15] • Skill and mindset heterogeneity [66]	• Training costs [15] • Recruitment costs [15]

2.2 Skills and Mindsets of IT personnel[3]

IT personnel differ among each other but also compared with the general population with regard to their mindsets and skills.

Lee et al. [36] considers four categories of critical IS skills all IT employees should have: (1) technical specialties skills cover a range of IS technical specialties; (2) technology management skills answer the questions of where and how to deploy information technologies effectively and profitably to meet strategic business objectives; (3) business functional skills cover both general business skills as well as knowledge of and ability to learn about business functions; and (4) interpersonal and management skills include the boundary-spanning role IT professionals must assume in organizations [6]. Further, they suggest that industry needs a diverse cadre of IT professionals with knowledge and skills in technology, business operations, management, and interpersonal relationships to lead organizational integration and process reengineering activities effectively [36].

Wynekoop and Walz [71] show that system analysts and project managers are more conservative, logical, analytical, diligent, and ambitious, with stronger leadership tendencies, higher self-confidence, and greater self-esteem than programmers.

Distinguishing between IS workers and IT professionals, Orlikowski and Baroudi [55] reveal that IS workers have a distinct occupational culture and require a different knowledge set and skills than IT professionals. Additionally, IT personnel possess some unique characteristics resulting from the rapid changes in technology that make existing skill sets obsolete [3]. They have unique business competence in conceptual development and may influence IT-business partnerships. Knowledge sharing among IT professionals is socially driven [69]; IT professionals play a potentially key role in transferring knowledge across organizational boundaries [56]. Today's IT professional should have project management knowledge, business domain knowledge, relationship skills, customer expertise, and problem solving skills in addition to technical skills [61]. These skills are critical because they enable IT departments to work effectively with other departments, internal users, and external customers and suppliers [22]. IT personnel have a strong need for growth and personal development compared to professionals in other occupations. They possess a high need for learning and they have a strong desire to be challenged [37].

To conclude, IT personnel are different from the general workforce with regard to their mindsets and skills. Based on these observations from the literature, I propose that the turnover of IT personnel may result in consequences different than those from non-IT turnover. I discuss this proposition in section 5, after presenting the current state of IT turnover consequences research in the following sections.

3. LITERATURE REVIEW

To present the state of research into IT turnover consequences, I conducted a multidisciplinary literature review, following guidelines for literature reviews by Webster and Watson [70], and Okoli and Shabram [54] to make the process as transparent as possible. I chose a broad scope for this literature review and did

---

[3] There is inconsistency in terminology and conceptualization of the IT profession in the literature, but as the present study's focus does not include resolving this and providing a universal definition of IT personnel, the exact terms used in the studies referenced are used here.

not restrict my research to a single discipline. I included the digital libraries *ScienceDirect* and *JSTOR*. Further, I included *Business Source Complete*, the American Economic Association's electronic bibliography *EconLit Database*, *SocINDEX*, and *PsycINFO*, in my search via *EBSCOhost* to cover the most important management, economics, and applied psychology journals. Leading IS journals (including the *AIS Senior Scholars' Basket of Eight*) and conference proceedings were covered by the *AIS electronic library (AISeL)*, *EBSCOhost*, *ScienceDirect* and the *IEEE digital library* (for *HICSS proceedings*). I included the proceedings of the special interest group on computer personnel research (*SIGMIS CPR*) in my search because this specific community investigates the needs, interests, and abilities of IT personnel. I limited the search population to peer-reviewed journal papers and conference proceedings, as they provide the necessary rigor and quality in scientific research. No limitations were placed on the year of publication. I set February 28, 2015 as a publication cut-off date for articles to be included in my sample.

Table 2 shows the search pattern for potentially relevant articles. It is based on synonyms and differences in terminology and for two main keywords, turnover and employee, derived from brainstorming and from articles identified initially.

Table 2. Search pattern

Title/Abstract/ Keywords (OR)		Title/Abstract/ Keywords (OR)
IT, "IT workforce," "IT worker," "IT professional," "IT labor," "IT personnel"	AND	Turnover, mobility, movement, flow

In the first step, I searched only for IT turnover studies in the aforementioned databases. The search results (without filtering) yielded 125 studies; after removing duplicates and studies that had nothing to do with IT turnover 109 IT turnover studies remained. I further scanned the reference lists of these 109 studies and conducted reverse and forward searches to identify more relevant sources. In total, 130 IT turnover studies remained for detailed manual screening of the full text (see table 3). Table 4 presents the criteria for further inclusion or exclusion of these 130 studies.

Table 3. Results of literature search

Database	Keyword search	-Duplicates -Non- IT turnover context	Applying inclusion & exclusion criteria
EBSCOhost	15	15	2
ScienceDirect	10	9	0
AISeL	28	22	2
SIGMIS CPR Proceedings	53	47	1
HICSS Proceedings	8	8	1
JSTOR	11	8	2
Forward and backward search	-	21	0
Σ	125	130	8

Table 4. Inclusion and exclusion criteria for the literature review

Inclusion Criteria	Exclusion Criteria
Quantitative IT turnover studies focused on the consequences of individual voluntary turnover	IT turnover studies focused on cognitive precursors of turnover
Qualitative IT turnover studies focused on the consequences of individual voluntary turnover	IT turnover studies focused on the antecedents of turnover
Conceptual IT turnover studies focused on consequences of individual voluntary turnover	IT turnover studies focused on collective turnover
Peer-reviewed journal papers and conference proceedings	IT turnover studies about turnover into/out of the workforce or in entrepreneurship
	IT turnover studies that mention consequences of individual voluntary turnover in an anecdotal way
	Literature emphasizing retention strategies for IT personnel
	Job mobility studies that focus more on turnaway-within and turnaway-between mobility than on turnover mobility

In total, eight articles were retained as source material for the review. Only eight out of 130[4] IT turnover studies focus on individual voluntary IT personnel consequences.

I scanned and coded the eight publications identified and then verified their inclusion in terms of quality. The quality assessment was performed to evaluate the rigor of the presented research in each publication. I assessed the eight relevant studies using seven quality criteria presented in table 5. All questions had three possible answers: *Yes*, *Partially*, and *No*. These answers were scored as follows: (1), (0.5), and (0) respectively.

Table 5. Criteria for quality assessment

Problem statement Q1. Is the research objective sufficiently explained and well-motivated?
Research design Q2. Is the context of study clearly stated? Q3. Is the research design prepared sufficiently?
Data Q4. Are the data collection & measures adequately described? Q5. Is the data analysis used in the study adequately described?
Discussion & conclusion Q6. Are the findings of study clearly stated and supported by the results? Q7. Does the paper discuss limitations?

---

[4] A complete list of the reviewed IT turnover literature can be found under: http://www.zylka.it/research/it-turnover/cpr25fp-zylka-appendix.pdf

Even though the quality assessment criteria and their evaluation scales may be subjective, they do provide a common framework for comparing the selected papers. In order to ensure the validity of the eight studies and the reliability of my findings, a study was included if its quality score exceeded 3.5 points (50% of the maximum quality score of an article: 7 points). The quality scores of the eight selected articles are presented in table 6. All eight studies had acceptable quality scores and were included in this review.

Table 6. Quality assessment results

Reference	Q1	Q2	Q3	Q4	Q5	Q6	Q7	Score
[1]	1	1	1	1	1	1	0	6
[2]	1	1	1	1	1	1	1	7
[11]	1	1	1	1	1	0.5	1	6.5
[25]	1	1	1	1	1	0.5	0	5.5
[29]	1	1	1	1	1	1	1	7
[30]	1	1	1	1	1	1	1	7
[43]	1	1	1	1	1	1	1	7
[57]	1	1	1	1	1	1	1	7

4. RESEARCH RESULTS

This section presents and discusses the eight studies focused on IT turnover consequences that resulted from my literature review: five that focus on the consequences of IT personnel turnover in software projects, one that addresses the consequences of CIO turnover with respect to IT alignment, and two that address positive consequences for IT professionals in terms of salary growth.

Abdel-Hamid [1] investigates how staff turnover, acquisition, and assimilation rates affect software development costs and schedules. The study's results indicate that staff turnover, acquisition, and assimilation rates can increase a project's costs and duration up to 60 percent in worst-case scenarios. This suggests that turnover is critical for the successful development of software systems, as well as for the accurate estimation of software development costs and schedules.

In a further study, Abdel-Hamid [2] examines the impacts of managerial turnover/succession on software project performance. In particular, the study examines the staffing and cost/schedule tradeoff choices of successor project managers, and compares them with the choices made by managers who run their projects from start to finish without interruption. The results indicate that managerial turnover can lead to a visible shift in cost/schedule tradeoff choices, affecting staff allocations and ultimately project performance in terms of both cost and duration.

Pee et al. [57] study 151 development teams and claim that turnover can result in losing knowledge and weakens project performance when new members with different experiences join teams. The use of succession planning, knowledge repositories, and employee orientation programs to manage different types of organizational knowledge loss can effectively mitigate the detrimental effects of turnover.

Izquiredo-Cortazar et al. [29] state that a turnover of senior developers leaves a knowledge gap that must be managed. Junior developers who replace a departed senior developer require some time to achieve the desired level of productivity. The time to learn how the project works results in significant productivity losses that are unavoidable when senior developers leave a project and are substituted for by others new to the project or to parts of the code they have to maintain.

The results of the Hall et al. [25] study on the impact of staff turnover on software projects show that there may be a relationship between staff turnover and project success. However, the authors note that this relationship is not distinct and may vary across projects. Additionally the results suggest that project success is likely to be improved if staff turnover is controlled [25].

The study by Chowa, examines the organizational impact of CIO turnover and its effects on IT alignment [11]. Results show that, on average, CIO turnover does not lead to fundamental change in the firm and has little impact on IT alignment [11].

Mithas and Krishnan [43] study the influence of supply- and demand-side factors on the compensation of IT professionals. Their study reveals that individual voluntary IT turnover leads to higher wages for the leaving employee. The former employer has to pay higher compensation for a new IT professional with the same skill and experience. The Mithas and Krishnan results confirm the widely prevalent notion that "job hopping is necessary for salary growth in the IT profession" [43]. The study of Joseph et al. [30] reveals quite similar findings: IT professionals are able to increase job status and pay levels when moving to jobs within the IT profession.

5. DISCUSSION AND CONCLUSION

In this study, I conducted a literature review of IT turnover literature focused on the consequences. The results reveal several things.

First, there is not a lot of research on the consequences of voluntary individual IT turnover to date. While there is a growing body of literature on the turnover intentions of IT personnel and other direct and indirect antecedents of the actual turnover behavior, studies focused on the consequences are rare.

I identified eight studies that discuss consequences of IT turnover. Most discuss potential negative consequences such as operational disruption, costs, low project performance, and productivity and knowledge loss (see table 7). The majority of these studies (five) are in the context of software development projects. Two studies mention the positive consequences (salary growth and job status) that turnover might imply. Further, all negative consequences focus only on the consequences for the former employer (see table 7).

Second, the review in section 2 shows that related disciplines consider consequences of individual turnover that have not been considered in the context of IT turnover. This is quite astounding, because research on employee turnover consequences traces its beginning to work in 1977 by Price [59], that is, many decades ago.

What implications can we derive from the literature presented in section 2 and what consequences are valid for IT personnel?

I suspect that training costs due to the heterogeneous skillset and the high need for growth and personal development and learning of IT professionals [37] may be rather low compared to other occupations.

IT professionals play a key role in transferring knowledge across organizational boundaries, and hence knowledge loss may be a critical negative consequence [56]. Two IT turnover studies from my literature review show that knowledge loss is a negative consequence of individual voluntary IT turnover [29, 57].

I reviewed the literature from disciplines such applied psychology and organizational management to identify consequences that

have not been researched in regard of IT personnel before. One example is demoralization [66], a consequence that has not been researched in the IT turnover context. The consequences of individual IT turnover on socialization should also be studied, because they have significant influence on the socialization tactics utilized by the employer [33]. I posit that IT professionals who changed their employer are more willing to learn to deal with their new environment. This would match with their high need for learning and their strong desire to be challenged [37]. However, this may not be valid for all IT-related occupations. "IT road warriors" [4] may experience socialization in a different way, because they are socialized mostly by their clients and not by their employer organizations. By examining the relevance of these consequences, I propose that researchers can reveal new insights into IT personnel, especially about their mindsets.

Table 7. Consequences of individual voluntary IT turnover

Consequences for			Positive	Negative
Former employer	Individual	Departing employee	-	-
		Co-worker	-	• Staff allocation [2]
	Organization		-	• Project performance [2, 25, 57] • Project costs [1, 2, 25, 57] • Project schedule [1, 2] • Knowledge loss [29], [57] • IT alignment [11] • Higher compensation costs [43]
New employer	Individual	Arriving employee	• Salary growth [30, 43] • Job status [30]	-
		Co-worker	-	-
	Organization		-	-

As with every study, there are some limitations that need to be taken into account. My analysis and the taxonomy are limited to what is reported in the studies discussed. Several consequences presented in this study are conceptual and have yet to be tested empirically. Further, one has to consider that consequences have moderating variables. Staw [66] presents an overview of potential moderating variables that affect the significance of several consequences I present in section 2. Moreover, it is not trivial to separate between consequences for individuals and for organizations. Also, future IT turnover research concerning the consequences of individual voluntary turnover should be aware of the distinct forms of job mobility. We need to distinguish between employees who take similar jobs in the same occupation and those who take different jobs in different occupations [30, 49]. Joseph et al. propose a differentiation between turnover, turnaway-within, and turnaway-between job mobility forms [30]. Turnover may result in different consequences than a turnaway-between job mobility. Hence, context is very important. Studying turnover consequences implies that one has a clear understanding of the unit of analysis. Further, a researcher who builds a causal model of turnover and its consequences cannot take everything into account at the same time, and so exclusions of the individual or organizational effects are reasonable and make the task of model construction more manageable.

I believe this study contributes to research and practice in several ways. Only after weighing the pros and cons of turnover and the consequences can managers effectively manage their human resources. Turnover makes it crucially important that top management understand the impacts, both direct and indirect, of turnover so they can plan it, or at least plan for it. Further, this study contributes to a better understanding of IT turnover in general and the consequences of IT turnover in particular.

In summary, more focused research is needed on the consequences of individual voluntary IT turnover. We really have only a sketchy understanding of what consequences IT turnover has on organizations and individuals. I hope that my brief overview provides a starting point for further IT turnover research not only about the antecedents but the consequences as well.

6. REFERENCES

[1]   Abdel-Hamid, T. K. 1989. A study of staff turnover, acquisition, and assimilation and their impact on software development cost and schedule. *Journal of Management Information Systems* 6, 1, 21–40.

[2]   Abdel-Hamid, T. K. 1992. Investigating the impacts of managerial turnover/succession on software project performance. *Journal of Management Information Systems* 9, 2, 127–144.

[3]   Agarwal, R. and Ferratt, T. W. 2002. Enduring practices for managing IT professionals. *Communications of the ACM* 45, 9, 73–79.

[4]   Ahuja, M. K., Chudoba, K. M., Kacmar, C. J., McKnight, D. H., and George, J. F. 2007. IT road warriors: Balancing work-family conflict, job autonomy, and work overload to mitigate turnover intentions. *MIS Quarterly* 31, 1, 1–17.

[5]   Ashford, S. J. and Cummings, L. L. 1983. Feedback as an individual resource: Personal strategies of creating information. *Organizational Behavior & Human Performance* 32, 370–398.

[6]   Baroudi, J. J. 1985. The impact of role variables on IS personnel work attitudes and intentions. *MIS Quarterly* 9, 4.

[7]   Bermiss, Y. S. and Murmann, J. P. 2015. Who matters more? The impact of functional background and top executive mobility on firm survival. *Strategic Management Journal* 36, 11, 1697–1716.

[8]   Borés, C., Saurina, C., and Torres, R. 2003. Technological convergence: A strategic perspective. *Technovation* 23, 1, 1–13.

[9]   Carnahan, S., Agarwal, R., and Campbell, B. A. 2012. Heterogeneity in turnover: The effect of relative compensation dispersion of firms on the mobility and entrepreneurship of extreme performers. *Strategic Management Journal* 33, 12, 1411–1430.

[10]   Chambers, E. G., Foulon, M., Handfield-Jones, H., Hankin, S. M., Michaels, III, and Edward G. 1998. War for talent. *McKinsey Quarterly,* 3, 44–57.

[11]   Chowa, C. K. 2010. CIO turnover, IS alignment and revolutionary change. In *AMCIS 2010 Proceedings*.

[12]   Corredoira, R. A. and Rosenkopf, L. 2010. Should auld acquaintance be forgot? The reverse transfer of knowledge through mobility ties. *Strategic Management Journal* 31, 2, 159–181.

[13]   Dalton, D. R. and Todor, W. D. 1979. Turnover turned over: An expanded and positive perspective. *Academy of Management Review* 4, 2, 225–235.

[14]   Dalton, D. R., Todor, W. D., and Krackhardt, D. M. 1982. Turnover overstated: The functional taxonomy. *Academy of Management Review* 7, 1, 117–123.

[15]   Dess, G. G. and Shaw, J. D. 2001. Voluntary turnover, social capital, and organizational performance. *Academy of Management Review* 26, 3, 446–456.

[16]   Eckhardt, A., Laumer, S., Maier, C., and Weitzel, T. 2014. The effect of personality on IT personnel's job-related attitudes: Establishing a dispositional model of turnover intention across IT job types. *Journal of Information Technology*.

[17]   Efrati, A. and Tam, P.-W. 2010. *Google battles to keep talent*. http://www.wsj.com/articles/ SB10001424052748704804504575606871487743724. Accessed 13 January 2015.

[18]   Feldman, D. C. 1976. A Contingency Theory of Socialization. *Administrative Science Quarterly* 21, 3, 433–452.

[19]   Feldman, D. C. and Brett, J. M. 1983. Coping with new jobs: A comparative study of new hires and job changers. *Academy of Management Journal* 26, 2, 258–272.

[20]   Festinger, L. 1962. *A theory of cognitive dissonance*. Stanford Univ. Press, Stanford.

[21]   Franco, A. M. and Filson, D. 2006. Spin-outs: Knowledge diffusion through employee mobility. *RAND Journal of Economics* 37, 4, 841–860.

[22]   Gallagher, K. P., Kaiser, K. M., Simon, J. C., Beath, C. M., and Goles, T. 2010. The requisite variety of skills for IT professionals. *Communications of the ACM* 53, 6, 144–148.

[23]   García-Murillo, M. and MacInnes, I. 2003. The impact of technological convergence on the regulation of ICT industries. *Journal of Media Management* 5, 5, 57–67.

[24]   Grusky, O. 1960. Administrative succession in formal organizations. *Social Forces* 39, 105–115.

[25]   Hall, T., Beecham, S., Verner, J., and Wilson, D. 2008. The impact of staff turnover on software projects. In *Proceedings of the 2008 ACM SIGMIS CPR Conference*, 30–39. DOI=10.1145/1355238.1355245.

[26]   Hancock, J. I., Allen, D. G., Bosco, F. A., McDaniel, K. R., and Pierce, C. A. 2013. Meta-analytic review of employee turnover as a predictor of firm performance. *Journal of Management* 39, 3, 573–603.

[27]   Hausknecht, J. P. and Trevor, C. O. 2011. Collective turnover at the group, unit, and organizational levels: Evidence, issues, and implications. *Journal of Management* 37, 1, 352–388.

[28]   Holtom, B. C., Mitchell, T. R., Lee, T. W., and Eberly, M. B. 2008. Chapter 5: Turnover and retention research: A glance at the past, a closer review of the present, and a venture into the future. *Academy of Management Annals* 2, 1, 231–274.

[29]   Izquierdo-Cortazar, D., Robles, G., Ortega, F., and Gonzalez-Barahona, J. M. 2009. Using software archaeology to measure knowledge loss in software projects due to developer turnover. In *Proceedings of the 42nd Hawaii International Conference on System Sciences (HICSS)*. DOI=10.1109/HICSS.2009.498.

[30]   Joseph, D., Ang, S., and Slaughter, S. A. 2015. Turnover or turnaway? Competing risks analysis of male and female IT

professionals' job mobility and relative pay gap. *Information Systems Research* 26, 1.

[31] Joseph, D., Fong Boh, W., Ang, S., and Slaughter, S. A. 2012. The career paths less (or more) traveled: A sequence analysis of IT career histories, mobility patterns, and career success. *MIS Quarterly* 36, 2, 427–A4.

[32] Joseph, D., Kok-Yee Ng, Koh, C., and Soon Ang. 2007. Turnover of information technology professionals: A narrative review, meta-analytic structural equation modeling, and model development. *MIS Quarterly* 31, 3, 547–577.

[33] King, R. C. and Xia, W. 2001. Retaining IS talent in the new millennium: Effects of socialization on IS professionals' role adjustment and organizational attachment. In *Proceedings of the 2001 Special Interest Group Computer Personnel Research Annual Conference*.

[34] Krackhardt, D. M. and Porter, L. W. 1985. When friends leave: A structural analysis of the relationship between turnover and stayers' attitudes. *Administrative Science Quarterly* 30, 2, 242–261.

[35] Lacity, M. C., Iyer, V. V., and Rudramuniyaiah, P. S. 2008. Turnover intentions of Indian IS professionals. *Information Systems Frontiers* 10, 2, 225–241.

[36] Lee, D. M., Trauth, E. M., and Farwell, D. 1995. Critical skills and knowledge requirements of IS professionals: A joint academic/industry investigation. *MIS Quarterly* 19, 3, 313–340.

[37] Lee, P. C. 2000. Turnover of information technology professionals: A contextual model. *Accounting, Management and Information Technologies* 10, 2, 101–124.

[38] Lee, T. W. and Mitchell, T. R. 1994. An alternative approach: The unfolding model of employee turnover. *Academy of Management Review* 19, 1, 51–89.

[39] Lo, J. 2015. The information technology workforce: A review and assessment of voluntary turnover research. *Information Systems Frontiers* 17, 2, 387–411.

[40] Louis, M. R. 1980. What newcomers experience in entering unfamiliar organizational settings. *Administrative Science Quarterly* 25, 226–251.

[41] Madsen, T. L., Mosakowski, E., and Zaheer, S. 2003. Knowledge retention and personnel mobility: The nondisruptive effects of inflows of experience. *Organization Science* 14, 2, 173–191.

[42] March, J. G. and Simon, H. A. 1958. *Organizations*. Wiley, New York, NY, USA.

[43] Mithas, S. and Krishnan, M. S. 2008. Human capital and institutional effects in the compensation of information technology professionals in the United States. *Management Science* 54, 3, 415–428.

[44] Mobley, W. H. 1977. Intermediate linkages in the relationship between job satisfaction and employee turnover. *Journal of Applied Psychology* 62, 2, 237–240.

[45] Mobley, W. H. 1982. *Employee Turnover: Causes, Consequences, and Control*. Addison-Wesley Series on Managing Human Resources. Addison Wesley.

[46] Mobley, W. H., Griffeth, R. W., Hand, H. H., and Meglino, B. M. 1979. Review and conceptual analysis of the employee turnover process. *Psychological Bulletin* 86, 3, 493–522.

[47] Mourmant, G., Gallivan, M. J., and Kalika, M. 2009. Another road to IT turnover: The entrepreneurial path. *European Journal of Information Systems* 18, 5, 498–521.

[48] Mourmant, G. and Voutsina, K. 2010. From IT employee to IT entrepreneur: The concept of IT entrepreneurial epiphany. In *ICIS 2010 Proceedings*.

[49] Mowday, R. T., Koberg, C. S., and McArthur, A. W. 1984. The psychology of the withdrawal process: A cross-validational test of Mobley's intermediate linkages model of turnover in two samples. *Academy of Management Journal* 27, 1, 79–94.

[50] Mowday, R. T., Porter, L. W., and Steers, R. M. 1982. *Employee-organization linkages. The psychology of commitment, absenteeism, and turnover*. Organizational and Occupational Psychology. Academic Press, New York.

[51] Muchinsky, P. M. and Morrow, P. C. 1980. A multidisciplinary model of voluntary employee turnover. *Career Adaptability* 17, 3, 263–290.

[52] Niederman, F., Sumner, M., and Maertz Jr., Carl P. 2007. Testing and extending the unfolding model of voluntary turnover to IT professionals. *Human Resource Management* 46, 3, 331–347.

[53] Nyberg, A. J. and Ployhart, R. E. 2013. Context-emergent turnover (CET) theory: A theory of collective turnover. *Academy of Management Review* 38, 1, 109–131.

[54] Okoli, C. and Schabram, K. 2010. A guide to conducting a systematic literature review of information systems research. *Sprouts: Working Papers* 10, 10–26.

[55] Orlikowski, W. J. and Baroudi, J. J. 1988. The information systems profession: Myth or reality? *Office Technology and People* 4, 1, 13–30.

[56] Pawlowski, S. D. and Robey, D. 2004. Bridging user organizations: Knowledge brokering and the work of information technology professionals. *MIS Quarterly* 28, 4, 645–672.

[57] Pee, L. G., Tham, Z.-C., Kankanhalli, A., and Tan, G. W. 2008. Turnover in information systems development projects - Managing forgetting. In *PACIS 2008 Proceedings*.

[58] Porter, L. W., Crampon, W. J., and Smith, F. J. 1976. Organizational commitment and managerial turnover: A longitudinal study. *Organizational Behavior & Human Performance* 15, 1, 87–98.

[59] Price, J. L. 1977. *The study of turnover*. Iowa State Univ. Press, Ames, Iowa.

[60] Rosenkopf, L. and Almeida, P. 2003. Overcoming local search through alliances and mobility. *Management Science* 49, 6, 751–766.

[61] Rutner, P. S., Hardgrave, B. C., and McKnight, D. H. 2008. Emotional dissonance and the information technology professional. *MIS Quarterly* 32, 3, 635–652.

[62] Shaw, J. D., Duffy, M. K., Johnson, J. L., and Lockhart, D. E. 2005. Turnover, social capital losses, and performance. *Academy of Management Journal* 48, 4, 594–606.

[63] Somaya, D., Williamson, I. O., and Lorinkova, N. 2008. Gone but not lost: The different performance impacts of employee mobility between cooperators versus competitors. *Academy of Management Journal* 51, 5, 936–953.

[64] Spiegel, O., Abbassi, P., Zylka, M. P., Posegga, O., Fischbach, K., Schlagwein, D., and Schoder, D. 2014. Getting boundary conditions right: Towards a classification of the Information Economy sectors. In *Academy of Management Proceedings*. *DOI*=10.5465/AMBPP.2014.15984abstract.

[65] Spiegel, O., Abbassi, P., Zylka, M. P., Schlagwein, D., Fischbach, K., and Schoder, D. 2015. Business model development, founders' social capital and the success of

early stage internet start-ups - A mixed-method study. *Information Systems Journal*.

[66] Staw, B. M. 1980. The consequences of turnover. *Journal of Occupational Behavior* 1, 4, 253–273.

[67] Steers, R. M. 1977. Antecedents and outcomes of organizational commitment. *Administrative Science Quarterly* 22, 1, 46–56.

[68] Steers, R. M. and Mowday, R. T. 1981. Employee turnover and post-decision accommodation processes. In *Research in Organizational Behavior*, L. L. Cummings and B. M. Staw, Eds. JAI Press, Greenwich, CT, USA.

[69] Tsai, M.-T. and Cheng, N.-C. 2012. Understanding knowledge sharing between IT professionals – An integration of social cognitive and social exchange theory. *Behaviour & Information Technology* 31, 11, 1069–1080.

[70] Webster, J. and Watson, R. T. 2002. Analyzing the past to prepare for the future: Writing a literature review. *MIS Quarterly* 26, 2, xiii–xxiii.

[71] Wynekoop, J. L. and Walz, D. B. 1998. Revisiting the perennial question: Are IS people different? *SIGMIS Database* 29, 2, 62–72.

[72] Yang, J.-T. 2008. Effect of newcomer socialisation on organisational commitment, job satisfaction, and turnover intention in the hotel industry. *Service Industries Journal* 28, 4, 429–443.

Experienced Meaningfulness and Calling: Effects on IT Professionals' Retention Intention

Christine Koh
Nanyang Technological University
50 Nanyang Avenue S3-01C-101
Singapore 639798
askkoh@ntu.edu.sg

Damien Joseph
Nanyang Technological University
50 Nanyang Avenue S3-B2C-99
Singapore 639798
adjoseph@ntu.edu.sg

ABSTRACT

Research in the broader management and related fields have consistently highlighted the importance of calling and experienced meaningfulness of work on work outcomes. Interestingly, these concepts have made little in-roads into the field of IT research. In this paper, we propose that experienced meaningfulness and calling offer a new perspective to understand IT professionals' turnover and turnaway intentions. Drawing on extant theory, we hypothesize that experienced meaningfulness has a negative direct effect on both turnover and turnaway intentions. Calling, on the other hand, has a negative direct effect on turnaway intentions, but moderates the effect of experienced meaningfulness on turnover intentions. Results from our large-scale study showed support for the hypothesized relationships.

Keywords

Information Technology; Meaning; Meaningfulness; Calling; Turnover; Turn-away; IT Professionals

1. INTRODUCTION

Retaining IT personnel has long been recognized as a perennial challenge, where a high turnover culture [26] seems to be a widely accepted norm in the profession. Despite numerous studies examining this issue, the general turnover and turnaway trend remains high, and continues to be a major issue for the field [22] [13].

In an effort to understand how best to retain IT talent, IT research has examined a broad range of factors relating to turnover and turnaway of IT professionals (see recent review of IT turnover [20] and study on IT turnover and turnaway [19]). Interestingly, an area that remains unexplored is how meaningful IT professionals find their current work, and the implications thereof on retention cognitions.

The topic of meaning of work has, however, attracted much interest across many other disciplines, especially among organizational behavior and psychology (for example, see reviews by [18], [29], [1]). The term "meaning of work" refers to *what* work signifies within the context of the individual's life [28] [29]. The meaning of work is inherently subjective, and often signifies

SIGMIS-CPR'16, June 2–4, 2016, Alexandria, VA, USA.
© 2016 ACM. ISBN 978-1-4503-4203-2/16/06...$15.00.
DOI: http://dx.doi.org/10.1145/2890602.2890615

different things to different individuals, being "rooted in individuals' subjective interpretations of work experiences and interactions" ([29], p.94). Understanding the meaning of work is important, because it is fundamental to how employees approach, enact, and experience their work and workplaces [27].

The meaning one ascribes to work is an important source of work values, attitudes and motivation [14]. In particular, "meaningful work" or experienced meaningfulness refers to the amount of significance work holds for an employee [28]. The thesis is that employees are motivated by meaningful work and are seeking a greater sense of meaning in their work [3]. The extent to which employees experience their work as meaningful has been demonstrated to have substantial impacts on important outcomes such as work engagement, job satisfaction, organizational commitment and turnover cognitions (see for example, [12]). As succinctly stated, "talented people demand meaningful work ... deny it, they leave" ([20], p.2).

A closely related concept to experienced meaningfulness is calling, defined as a "consuming, meaningful passion for a particular career domain" ([17], p.479). When viewed as a calling, work provides individuals with a sense of meaning and purpose [28] [29]. This is particularly relevant for the IT profession, which is often viewed as attracting those who have a deep passion / calling for the technical work [11].

While calling has often been associated with experienced meaningfulness of work (e.g. [8] [17]), the two are distinct. Work can be perceived as meaningful due to certain job characteristics that are independent of whether the work is perceived as one's calling [18]. The work context plays a major role in how employees experience their work as meaningful or not [18]. The experienced meaningfulness of work is not only derived from the formal requirements and objective conditions of the work itself, but also from subjective assessments of the work context. This is consistent with the job crafting literature, which argues that people actively make sense of their work, define and enact their job in a way that provides a sense of meaning [34].

Accordingly, this paper sets out to assess the impact of (1) experienced meaningfulness and (2) calling, of IT professionals on two important withdrawal cognitions – turnover and turnaway intentions. For our purposes, we define turnover as leaving one's existing job for another IT job in a different firm, while turnaway refers to leaving one's existing job for a non-IT job, either within the same firm or to a different firm [20].

In the sections below, we review the related literature to develop our theoretical model, and describe results from our large-scale field study of IT professionals.

2. THEORETICAL MODEL
2.1 Experienced Meaningfulness
We define experienced meaningfulness as "the degree to which an employee experiences the job as one which is generally meaningful, valuable, and worthwhile" [1]. Experienced meaningfulness is thus work *experienced* as significant and holding positive meaning for IT professionals.

Experienced meaningfulness is to be distinguished from the term "meaning of work" [28] [29]. The meaning of work is inherently subjective and often signifies different things to different individuals. A recent review [29] of the meaning of work derived three types of meanings of work - self, others and the context. Meanings related to the "self" describe the meaning of work in terms of personal values, personal beliefs and intrinsic work motivations. Meanings related to "others" describe meaning of work in terms of interactions and relationships with other individuals within and outside the workplace. Meanings related to "context" describe meaning of work in terms of interactions with workplace and non-workplace environments.

While there are commonalities in the meanings of work across occupations, there also exist subtle differences in the descriptors or themes of meanings [15]. Specific to the IT context, recent research [22] has identified a list of 15 themes representing what IT professionals look for in their work, consistent with the three categories of self, others, and context.

While IT professionals look for meaning in the form of these self, others and context-related themes, the degree to which they experience their current work as meaningful will vary among individuals. "The fact that work has a particular meaning does not necessarily determine that it is [experienced as] meaningful" ([29], p.95). The actual work context and experience of IT professionals are likely to differ across organizations and job roles. Even for the same job role in the same organization, IT professionals are likely to experience their work differently.

Research has demonstrated that experienced meaningfulness is related to a wide range of positive work outcomes, such as work motivation, absenteeism, work behavior, engagement, job satisfaction, empowerment, stress, organizational identification, career development, individual performance and personal fulfillment [29]. Employees who experience their work as meaningful are more engaged with and committed to their organizations [21] [31], hold higher job satisfaction [8] [23], and are more motivated to work, leading to better performance [25] [1].

A logical extension of the preceding arguments is that employees who experience meaningfulness at work will be less motivated to leave their current job. Meaningful work is intrinsically motivating [18], and the quest for meaningful work is considered "one of the most important factors prompting career change" ([3], p.204). In the same vein, we argue that employees who experience meaningfulness at work will have lower withdrawal cognitions, i.e. are less likely to leave their current job for either another IT job (turnover intention) or a non-IT job either within or outside their current organization (turnaway intention).

When employees experience low meaningfulness at work, there is a constant need to consciously motivate oneself to perform. This conscious effort depletes employees' energy and leave them feeling emotionally drained, frustrated, and worn out" ([1], p.140). Thus, such employees are more likely to withdraw from such an unpleasant job context by leaving their current job.

Employees who attribute their low experienced meaningfulness to the nature of the IT work itself, are likely to withdraw by leaving their current job for a non-IT job (i.e. turnaway). On the other hand, employees who attribute their low experienced meaningfulness to the context of the organization rather than the IT work itself, are likely to leave their current job for another IT job (i.e. turnover).

Thus, we hypothesize that:

H1: Experienced meaningfulness is negatively related to (a) turnover intent and (b) turnaway intent.

2.2 Calling
Research has shown that people tend to see their work as either a job (focus on financial rewards and necessity), a career (focus on advancement and achievement) or a calling (focus on enjoyment of fulfilling, socially useful work) ([12], p.21). The concept of calling has attracted much interest in recent years, with many studies examining how a sense of calling links to various work-related and well-being outcomes such as greater career maturity, career commitment, work meaning, life meaning, job satisfaction, and life satisfaction (see recent review - [9]).

There exist different definitions of "calling." For our purposes, we adopt the recent conceptualization of calling as a "consuming, meaningful passion for a particular career domain ... or work that a person perceives as her or his purpose in life" ([17], p.479). This is consistent with how the construct is viewed in the current literature, as 'working in the career that aligns with [one's] strongest internal passions" ([10], p.429). While the term calling is often associated with certain symbolically significant professions, calling could be found in any work setting [2]. In fact, studies have shown that "between one third and one half of employees in a wide range of occupations endorse having a calling in their careers" ([7], p.626). Even within the same occupation, individuals often hold differing views of work as job, career or calling [34]. Accordingly, IT professionals can similarly vary in the extent to which they view their IT work as a calling.

Research has consistently shown the importance of calling on work outcomes (see for example, [9] [17]). When viewed as a calling, work assumes both personal and social significance, and accordingly, provides individuals with a sense of meaning and purpose [28] [29]. Individuals who view their work as a calling would work for the fulfillment that comes from doing the work. Not surprisingly, most literature has looked at experienced meaningfulness as mediating the effect of calling on work outcomes.

While we agree that experienced meaningfulness can mediate the effect of calling on work outcomes, we argue that this need not always be the case. A mediation effect implies causality – suggesting that X (e.g. calling) leads to Y (e.g. experienced meaningfulness) which in turn leads to Z (e.g. work outcomes). As succinctly explained by ([2], p.52), "calling is not always an exogenous driver ... it could be that people select an occupation for more mundane purposes ... and are then motivated to make sense of their occupational choice to make it meaningful and justify whatever sacrifices it entails." In other words, employees can still experience meaningfulness even when they do not feel a calling to their work. Accordingly, rather than looking at the effect of calling as mediated through experienced meaningfulness, in this paper, we adopt an alternative perspective by examining the differential effects of calling on turnover and turnaway intent.

Consistent with the conceptualization of calling as a "consuming, meaningful passion for a particular career domain" [17], the focus of one's calling is one's profession. Accordingly, the higher one's calling, the more committed the person will be to living out that calling in the profession, and therefore, is less likely to leave that profession (turnaway). Thus, we hypothesize that

H2: Calling has a direct negative relationship with turnaway intent.

In contrast, given that the focus of calling is the work/profession, rather than the specific context of one's current employer, we do not expect calling to have any direct effect on turnover intent. When an employee with a strong calling to the profession experiences low meaningfulness in the current job, he/she is likely to attribute the low experienced meaningfulness to the context of the current workplace, rather than the nature of the work. As such, the person will endeavor to continue his/her calling in the same profession, by seeking out another IT job in a different organization, i.e. turnover.

In other words, when one with a high calling experiences low meaningfulness at work, he/she is likely to exhibit continued commitment to the profession but may withdraw from the employer to live out his/her calling by looking for an alternative IT job (whether in the same or different organization), in the attempt to find meaning in the work in a different context. Thus, we hypothesize that:

H3: Calling moderates the relationship between experienced meaningfulness and turnover intent, so that where calling is high, the effect of experienced meaningfulness is more negative.

In sum, we expect calling to have a direct negative effect on turnaway intent, but a moderated effect on the relationship between experienced meaningfulness and turnover intent. Figure 1 shows our research model.

3. METHOD
The key objective of this paper is to test the relationships between experienced meaningfulness and calling on turnover and turnaway intention. Accordingly, we conducted a large-scale field study of IT professionals.

3.1 Data Collection
Data study was gathered via an online web survey, as part of a broader study conducted in collaboration with the local computer society, to understand the needs and issues of local infocomm professionals. Email invitations were sent to members of this society, as well as members of other IT related associations (e.g. associations of IT managers, IT vendors and IT users), inviting them to participate in the study.

3.2 Sample
A total of 824 responses were obtained. The profile of respondents is representative of the local infocomm industry, indicating that response bias is not an issue.

Respondents in the sample are predominantly male (76%), and 40 years old and younger (61%). Majority of respondents have attained a bachelor's degree or higher (94%), with the remaining (6%) attaining either a diploma or high school education. Respondents held a wide variety of job roles, including IT project management (27%), IT management (17%), IT services (15%), and systems development (13%). The sample comprised almost equal numbers of IT professionals working as in-house IT expertise (53%) versus as IT vendors (47%).

3.3 Measures
The questionnaire contained multiple measurement items relating to each of the constructs in the research model. Where possible, validated scales from prior studies were used. The final set of items was reviewed by the committee of senior IT professionals from the society. All items were measured using a seven-point Likert-type scale (1=strongly disagree; 7=strongly agree).

Experienced meaningfulness. We operationalized meaning of IT work using the fifteen (15) themes identified by [22]. Respondents were presented with the list of themes, and asked to select the five (5) "that best describes what meaningful IT work is to you". For the five themes selected, respondents were then asked to rate the extent these statements described their current work.

Calling. This was measured with four items adapted from [2] (Cronbach's alpha = 0.87). A sample item is "Working in the IT profession feels like my calling / niche in life."

Turnover intent. This was measured with three items (Cronbach's alpha = 0.91) adapted from [30]. A sample item is "I am thinking about quitting my current job for an alternative IT job."

Turnaway intent. This was measured with three items (Cronbach's alpha = 0.94) adapted from [30]. A sample item is "I am thinking about quitting my current job for an alternative non-IT job."

Controls. We controlled for gender (1=male, 2=female), and IT work experience (years).

3.4 Data Analysis
Before testing our hypothesized model, we first assessed the psychometric properties of the measures using exploratory factor analysis and reliability analysis. The results from principal component factor analysis show that all items loaded onto their expected factors (turnover intent, turnaway intent, calling), with primary loadings all above 0.78 (range 0.79 – 0.94), with cross-loadings all lower than 0.34. Reliability analysis reports Cronbach's alphas above recommended guidelines for all constructs (range 0.87 – 0.94). Overall, results indicate the convergent and discriminant validity of the measures. Table 1 shows the reliabilities and inter-correlations of the constructs.

We tested our hypotheses with hierarchical regressions. Consistent with recommended guidelines [6], we used standardized variables (i.e. all values are centered around zero and scaled to a standard deviation of one), as it makes the interpretation of coefficients simpler. Specifically, we standardized both the independent variable (experienced meaningfulness) and moderator (calling) before calculating the product term (experienced meaningfulness x calling). In our regression, we entered controls (gender, IT experience) in step one (Model 1); added experienced meaningfulness (model 2A) and calling (model 2B) respectively in step two, and the product term (experienced meaningfulness x calling) in step three. We interpreted results with changes in F (ΔF) and individual parameter t-values. Table 2 shows the regression results.

4. RESULTS AND DISCUSSION
4.1 Experienced meaningfulness
For the five themes selected by respondents as representing the meaning of IT work, respondents rated the extent these statements described their current work. Overall, the results show a promising picture. IT professionals generally find their current

work meaningful, with 12 out of the 15 statements achieving an average rating above 5 (on a 7-point scale).

The ratings reveal an interesting pattern across themes. IT professionals reported that their current work is most meaningful in terms of Others-related themes, followed by Self-related themes, and least meaningful for Context-related themes.

4.2 Hypotheses testing

Hierarchical regression results showed support for Hypothesis 1. Even after controlling for gender and IT experience, experienced meaningfulness significantly predicted both turnover (β = -0.27, $p<.01$) and turnaway (β = -0.36, $p<.01$) intent. The addition of experienced meaningfulness explained significant variance in both turnover (R^2 change = 0.07, F-change = 63.05, $p<.01$; overall adjusted R^2=0.10) and turnaway (R^2 change = 0.12, F-change = 110.66, $p<.01$; overall adjusted R^2=0.12) intent.

Hypothesis 2 stated that calling has a direct negative effect on turnaway intent. Results showed that, when entered on its own (Model 2B), calling was significantly related to turnaway intent (β = -0.28, $p<.01$). With all the variables entered together (model 3), calling remained significant (β = -0.17, $p<.01$) but the interaction term between calling and experienced meaningfulness was not significant (β = 0.02, ns). In other words, calling is still associated with lower (albeit of smaller magnitude) turnaway intent, once the person's level of experienced meaningfulness is taken into account. In sum, the results showed support for H2, that calling has a direct negative effect on turnaway intent, and did not moderate the effect of experienced meaningfulness on turnaway intent.

Hypothesis 3 stated that calling moderates the relationship between experienced meaningfulness and turnover intent, such that where calling is high, the effect of experienced meaningfulness on turnover intent is more negative. Results (Model 3) showed that the interaction of experienced meaningfulness and calling was a significant predictor (β = -0.13, $p<.01$) of turnover intent, even after accounting for the variance contributed by experienced meaningfulness and calling.

For ease of interpretation, we created interaction plots (see Figure 2). The plots showed that the effect of experienced meaningfulness on turnover intent is stronger when calling is high; but the effect of experienced meaningfulness on turnaway intent remains the same for both high and low calling.

Though not hypothesized, the results show an interesting pattern. For turnover intention, when entered alone (Model 2B), calling did not have a significant effect on turnover intent (β = -0.01, ns). But in the presence of experienced meaningfulness (Model 3), calling showed a positive direct relationship (β = 0.14, $p<.01$) with turnover intent. This suggests the presence of a suppressor effect, indicating that in the presence of experienced meaningfulness, calling has a direct positive effect on turnover intent. In other words, calling is associated with greater turnover intentions once the person's level of experienced meaningfulness is taken into account. This is consistent with some evidence that career commitment acted as a suppressor effect in the link between calling and withdrawal intentions; that is, individuals with a calling who were not committed to their career were more likely to have intentions of withdrawing from their current job [9]. Drawing the same parallel, our results suggest that experienced meaningfulness has a suppressor effect in the link between calling and turnover intent.

5. CONCLUSION

The objective of this paper is to assess the extent to which IT professionals find their current work meaningful, and to test the relationships between experienced meaningfulness and calling on turnover and turnaway intent.

Results from the large-scale field survey showed that IT professionals generally experienced their current work as meaningful across all the three themes – Others, Self, and Context.

Overall, the analyses supported our hypotheses. Experienced meaningfulness was negatively related to both turnover and turnaway intentions. Consistent with our hypotheses, calling showed differential effects on turnover versus turnaway intentions. While calling has a direct effect on turnaway intentions, calling moderated the effect of experienced meaningfulness on turnover intentions. The results show that IT professionals who see their work as a calling are highly committed to the profession and thus less likely to leave the IT profession. As such, even when they experience little meaning in their current job context, IT professionals who see their work as a calling will still choose to remain in the IT profession. Instead, they are likely to leave their current job for another IT job in another organization, in an endeavor to continue their calling in another context.

This study highlighted several theoretical and practice implications. First, the introduction of a new theoretical perspective – experienced meaningfulness of work – helps understand what motivates IT professionals. The meaning one ascribes to work is an important source of work values, attitudes and motivation. Our results on the effect of experienced meaningfulness on turnover and turnaway intent highlight the importance of organizations ensuring that their IT professionals experience meaningfulness at their workplace. The list of fifteen themes of meaning of work provide a useful starting point, that organizations can look into to ensure that these areas are fulfilled in the workplace.

Second, as far as we are aware, our study is the first to demonstrate the effect of experienced meaningfulness and calling on turnover and turnaway intent, beyond the more commonly studied mediated model. Our results on the differential effect of calling on turnover (moderated effect) and turnaway intent (direct effect) highlight the importance of creating a stronger sense of calling among IT professionals.

Future research should closely examine the role of calling in motivating IT professionals' work. We encourage the replication of this study in other work settings and in other cultures. This would help establishing the generalizability of the themes of meanings pertaining to IT work, as well as surface differences.

Our results also have implications for practice. Organizations need to play a bigger role in developing meaning in the workplace for IT professionals. Specifically, human resource practitioners and IT managers should consider providing ample opportunities for continual self-development and tasks for which IT professionals are able to leverage their knowledge and skills. Further, recognition systems may emphasize achievements and value creation. These recommendations are made because specific job characteristics are known to influence individuals' sense-making of what work means and what it signifies. Further, given the importance of calling, educational institutions and professional associations should look into ways to foster IT as a calling, and attracting IT professionals who see IT work as their calling.

6. REFERENCES

[1] Barrick, M.R., Mount, M.K., and Li, N. 2013. The theory of purposeful work behavior: The role of personality, higher-order goals, and job characters. *Academy of Management Review*, 38(1): 132-153.

[2] Bunderson, J.S. and Thompson, J.A. 2009. The call of the wild: Zookeepers, callings, and the double-edged sword of deeply meaningful work. *Administrative Science Quarterly*, 54(1): 32-57.

[3] Cartwright, S. and Holmes, N. 2006. The meaning of work: The challenge of regaining employee engagement and reducing cynicism. *Human Resource Management Review*, 16(2): 199-208.

[4] Chen, G.A., 2007. *The Meaning of Meaningful Work: The Subjective-Objective Meaningfulness in Knowledge Work*, in Stephen A. Ross Business School. University of Michigan: Ann Arbor, MI.

[5] Cohen, J., Cohen, P., West, S.G., and Aiken, L.S. 2003. *Applied Multiple Regression/Correlation Analysis for the Behavioral Sciences*. Mahwah, NJ: Lawrence Erlbaum.

[6] Dawson, J.F. 2014. Moderation in management research: What, why, when and how. *Journal of Business Psychology*, 29: p. 1-19.

[7] Dik, B.J., Duffy, R.D., and Eldridge, B.M. 2009. Calling and vocation in career counseling: Recommendations for promoting meaningful work. *Professional Psychology: Research and Practice*, 40(6): 625-632.

[8] Duffy, R.D., Bott, E.M., Allan, B.A., Torrey, C.L., and Dik, B.J. 2012. Perceiving a calling, living a calling, and job satisfaction: Testing a moderated, multiple mediator model. *Journal of Counseling Psychology*, 59(1): 50-59.

[9] Duffy, R.D., and Dik, B.J. 2013. Research on calling: What have we learned and where are we going? *Journal of Vocational Behavior*, 83: 428-436.

[10] Elangovan, A.R., Pinder, C.C., and McLean, M. 2010. Callings and organizational behavior, *Journal of Vocational Behavior*, 76: 428-440.

[11] Eris, H.G., Ferratt, T.W., Prasad, J. 2006. Beyond stereotypes of IT professionals: Implications for IT HR practices. *Communications of the ACM*, 49(4):105-109.

[12] Farlie, P. 2011. Meaningful work, employee engagement, and other key employee outcomes: Implications for Human Resource Development. *Advances in Developing Human Resources*, 13(4): 508-525

[13] Ford, V.F., Swayze, S., and Burley, D.L. 2013. An exploratory investigation of the relationship between disengagement, exhaustion and turnover intention among IT professionals employed at a university, *Information Resources Management Journal*, 26(3): 55-68.

[14] Guion, R.M. and Landy, F.J. 1972. Meaning of work and motivation to work. *Organizational Behavior and Human Performance*, 7(2): 308-339.

[15] Harpaz, I. 1985. Meaning of working profiles of various occupational groups. *Journal of Vocational Behavior*, 26(1): 25-40.

[16] Havener, C. 1999. *Meaning: The Secret of Being Alive*. Beaver's Pond Press.

[17] Hirschi, A., 2012. Callings and work engagement: Moderated mediation model of work meaningfulness, occupational identity, and occupational self-efficacy. *Journal of Counseling Psychology*, 59(3): 479-485.

[18] Humphrey, S.E., Nahrgang, J.D., and Morgeson, F.P. 2007. Integrating motivational, social, and contextual work design features: A meta-analytic summary and theoretical extension of the work design literature, *Journal of Applied Psychology*, 92(5): 1332-1356.

[19] Joseph, D., Ang, S., and Slaughter, S.A. 2015. Turnover or turnaway? Competing risks analysis of male and femal IT professionals' job mobility and relative pay gap. *Information Systems Research*, 26(1): 145-164.

[20] Joseph, D., Ng, K.Y., Koh, C., and Ang, S. 2007. Turnover of information technology professionals: A narrative review, meta-analytic structural equation modeling, and model development. *MIS Quarterly*, 31(3): 547-577.

[21] Kahn, W.A. 1990. Psychological conditions of personal engagement and disengagement at work, *Academy of Management Journal*, 33(4): 692-724.

[22] Lim, G., Yeh, S.H., Koh, C., and Joseph, D. 2013. The meaning of IT work, *Proceedings of the ACM SIGMIS CPR.*.

[23] Littman-Ovadia, H., and Steger, M. 2010. Character strengths and well-being among volunteers and employees: Toward an integrated model. *The Journal of Positive Psychology*, 5: 419-430.

[24] Lo, J. 2015. The information technology workforce: A review and assessment of voluntary turnover research. *Information Systems Frontier*, 17: 387-411.

[25] May, D.R., Gilson, R.L., and Harter, L.M. 2004. The psychological conditions of meaningfulness, safety and availability and the engagement of the human spirit at work. *Journal of Occupational and Organizational Psychology*, 77(1): 11.37.

[26] Moore, J.E. and Burke, L.A. 2002. How to turn around 'turnover culture' in IT. *Communications of the ACM*, 45(2): 73-78.

[27] Morse, N.C. and Weiss, R.S. 1955. The function and meaning of work and the job. *American Sociological Review*, 20(2): 191.

[28] Pratt, M.G. and Ashforth, B.E. 2003. Fostering meaningfulness in working and at work, in *Positive Organizational Scholarship*, K.S. Cameron, J.E. Dutton, and R.E. Quinn, Editors. Berrett-Koehler Publishers, Inc.: San Francisco. p. 309–327.

[29] Rosso, B.D., Dekas, K.H., and Wrzesniewski, A. 2010. On the meaning of work: A theoretical integration and review, in *Research in Organizational Behavior: An Annual Series of Analytical Essays and Critical Reviews*, Vol 30, A.P. Brief and B.M. Staw, Editors. p. 91-127.

[30] Rusbult, C.E., Farrell, D., Rogers, G., and Mainous III, A.G. 1988. Impact of exchange variables on exit, voice, loyalty and neglect: An integrative model of responses to declining job satisfaction. *Academy of Management Journal*, 31(3): 589-599.

[31] Tyler, T.R., and Blader, S.L. 2003. The group engagement: Procedural justice, social identity, and cooperative behavior. *Personality and Social Psychology Review*, 7(4): 349-361.

[32] Wrzesniewski, A.C., Dutton, J.E., and Debebe, G. 2003. Interpersonal sensemaking and the meaning of work. *Research in Organizational Behavior*, 25: 93-135.

[33] Wrzesniewski, A., and Dutton, J.E. 2001. Crafting a job: Revisioning employees as active crafters of their work, *The Academy of Management Review*, 26(2): 179-201.

[34] Wrzesniewski, A., McCauley, C., Rozin, P., and Schwartz, B. 1997. Jobs, careers, and callings: People's relations to their work, *Journal of Research in Personality*, 31: 21-33.

Table 1. Descriptives, Reliabilities, and Inter-correlations [a]

	M	*SD*	*1*	*2*	*3*	*4*	*5*	*6*
(1) Turnover intent	3.62	1.71	(.91)					
(2) Turnaway intent	3.26	1.77	0.36**	(.94)				
(3) Experienced meaningfulness	5.21	1.06	-0.27**	-0.35**	-			
(4) Calling	4.53	1.26	0.02	-0.28**	0.41**	(.87)		
(5) Gender [b]	1.24	0.43	-0.14**	0.04	-0.05	-0.19**	-	
(6) IT experience (years)	13.13	8.37	-0.11**	-0.01	0.16**	-0.02	0.11**	-

Values on the diagonal are Cronbach's alpha
[a] N=824
[b] Gender = 1 (male) / 2 (female)
* $p < 0.5$; ** $p<0.01$; *** $p< 0.01$

Table 2. Regression Results

	Turnover Intent				Turnaway Intent			
	Model1	*Model2A*	*Model2B*	*Model3*	*Model1*	*Model2A*	*Model2B*	*Model3*
Gender	-0.13**	-0.15**	-0.13**	-0.13**	0.04	0.02	-0.01	-0.01
IT experience	-0.10**	-0.05	-0.10**	-0.05	-0.01	0.05	-0.01	0.04
Experienced meaningfulness		-0.27**		-0.35**		-0.36**		-0.29**
Calling			-0.01	0.14**			-0.28**	-0.17**
Experienced meaningfulness X Calling				-0.13**				0.02
R^2	0.03	0.10	0.03	0.13	0.00	0.12	0.08	0.15
R^2 change		0.07	0.00	0.03		0.12	0.08	0.03
Adjusted R^2	0.03	0.10	0.03	0.12	0.00	0.12	0.08	0.14
F-change		63.05**	0.02	13.08**		110.66**	66.05**	10.16**
Overall F	11.66**	29.40**	7.77**	23.41**	0.75	37.45**	22.56**	27.06**

* $p < 0.5$; ** $p<0.01$

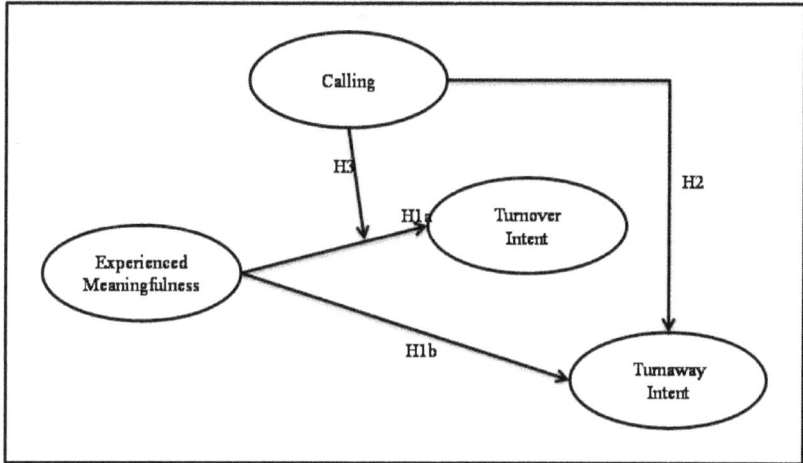

Figure 1. Research Model

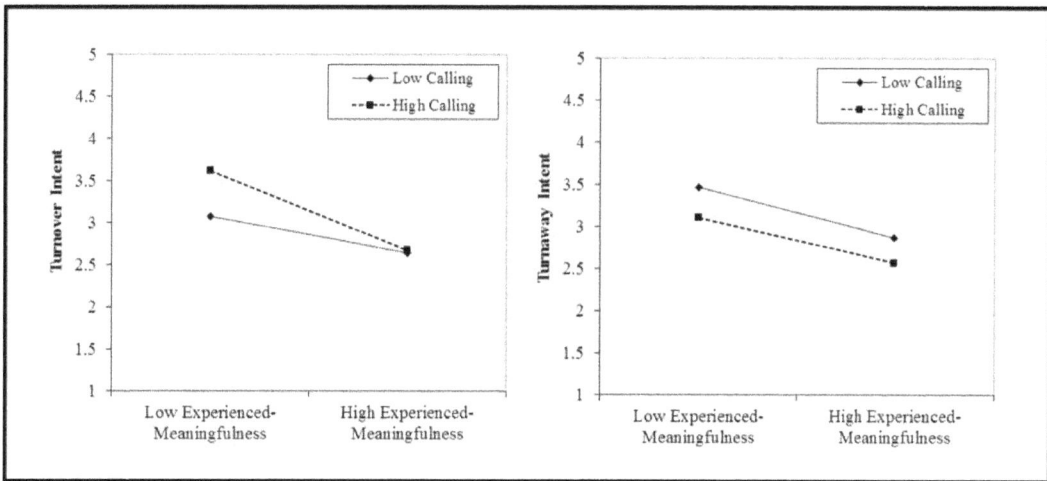

Figure 2. Interaction Charts

How Temporal Work Styles and Product Modularity Influence Software Quality and Job Satisfaction

Jens Foerderer
Business School
University of Mannheim
foerderer@uni-mannheim.de

Thomas Kude
Business School
University of Mannheim
kude@uni-mannheim.de

Sunil Mithas
Robert H. Smith School of
Business, University of Maryland
smithas@rhsmith.umd.edu

Armin Heinzl
Business School
University of Mannheim
heinzl@uni-mannheim.de

ABSTRACT

This paper investigates how two key outcomes in software development—software quality and job satisfaction of software developers—are influenced by product modularity and developers' temporal work style, i.e., the preferences for completing the bulk of work closer to the deadlines. We argue that high deadline orientation positively interacts with product modularity to influence software quality and job satisfaction of developers. An empirical test using a unique data set on more than 140 software developers working at a large global software vendor confirms our hypotheses. We contribute to the literature on software development by showing that software quality and job satisfaction can be increased by matching the fit between technological characteristics of the software product and people factors (i.e., the preferred temporal work style of developers). Our study has wider implications for literature on temporal work styles and product modularity and can be informative for practitioners who are tasked with hiring or allocating software developers for software products with varying modularity.

Keywords

Software development; software quality; job satisfaction; deadline orientation; modularity

1. INTRODUCTION

Two outcomes are central to many efforts of software product managers: software quality and job satisfaction. First, software quality is important because the increasing ubiquity of software has made competition fierce and the development of high-quality software vital to firm survival. For example, a premium car today may run on 100 million lines of software code [1] and severe security issues are increasingly caused by software quality problems (e.g., plane accidents or large-scale data breaches, see [2], [3]). Second, ensuring high levels of job satisfaction among their developers is important for managers

SIGMIS-CPR'16, June 2-4, 2016, Alexandria, VA, USA.
© 2016 ACM. ISBN 978-1-4503-4203-2/16/06…$15.00
DOI: http://dx.doi.org/10.1145/2890602.2890608

because lower job satisfaction will likely reduce the well-being of software developers and increase turnover intentions [4], which is particularly problematic given the shortage of software developers in many countries. Although jobs related to software development (compared to other jobs) are consistently ranked high regarding job satisfaction (e.g., [5]), the increasing pressure to deliver software may negatively affect the job satisfaction of some software developers. Thus, increasing the quality of software and the job satisfaction of software developers are essential challenges for software managers [6].

Prior work on software quality and job satisfaction has mostly focused on organizational levers to increase quality and satisfaction. For example, the Capability Maturity Model (CMM) aims to increase software quality through prescribing and assessing process maturity in the context of software development [7], [8]. More recently, agile software development has been suggested as an approach to re-organize software development under the objective of increasing software quality and developers' self-determination [9]. Empirical studies have shown that agile software development has a positive effect on code quality [10] and on the satisfaction of software developers [11]. As another example, Ahuja et al. [12] studied the work-life balance of information technology workers and found job autonomy to decrease work exhaustion and turnover intentions. Thus, organizational factors appear critical to ensure code quality and increase job satisfaction.

Although organizational approaches—including CMM and agile development processes—are important for ensuring software quality and job satisfaction, there is also a need to consider individual characteristics of software developers, such as differing temporal work styles of software developers, and product modularity. Prior literature points to the importance of individual characteristics in influencing work-related outcomes in software development [13]. Understanding the effect of individual characteristics on software quality and job satisfaction is important for managers who hire software developers and deploy human resources to software products that vary in their degree of modularity. Against this backdrop, we aim to better understand the effect of software developers' temporal work style and product modularity on software quality and job satisfaction.

We model developers' temporal work style in terms of individuals' preferences for distributing activities toward deadlines [14]. Individuals' deadline orientation is particularly relevant in software development because software is increasingly developed in an iterative and collaborative way [9]. For example, agile development methods, such as Scrum [15], prescribe developing and delivering software in short iterations, thus increasing the frequency with which developers face deadlines. Generally, deadlines play an increasingly important role for software developers due to the higher clockspeed of industries or firms [16]–[19], involving hypercompetition and rapidly changing technologies and customer needs [9].

Deadline orientation of software developers will likely vary. Whereas some developers may prefer spreading their work evenly over the available time (low deadline orientation), others may prefer engaging in other activities until the deadline is imminent and then work until time runs out (high deadline orientation). We argue that given the socio-technical nature of software development, individual characteristics will likely interact with technological factors in influencing quality and job satisfaction [20]. In addition, software products are often developed by several individuals and products of varying modularity are assigned to individuals [10]. Thus, software developers have to collaborate with others when developing products, which raises questions about the implications of varying deadline orientation and product modularity on the quality of software and job satisfaction.

To the best of our knowledge, no prior work has studied the effect of software developers' preferred deadline orientation on software quality and job satisfaction under different technological conditions, e.g., varying product modularity. Based on existing literature on temporal work style and product modularity, we hypothesize that deadline orientation—in terms of preferring to work in a deadline-driven way—positively interacts with product modularity in influencing software quality and job satisfaction. We empirically test our model using a unique data set on more than 140 software developers of one of the largest software-producing firms worldwide. Our empirical results support the hypothesized relationships.

Our study complements prior work on software development that has so far mostly focused on organizational factors to influence software quality and job satisfaction [7], [10], [12]. Specifically, we show that managers can increase software quality and job satisfaction by assigning developers to software products that fit their temporal preferences. Our study also has wider implications for the literature on temporal work styles that has so far mostly focused on time pressure, temporal leadership, or the interaction of the deadline orientation of collaborating individuals [10], [21]. We add to this by considering product modularity as a context factor that determines the need to interact with individuals. This paper also contributes to literature on product modularity [20], [22] which has long been seen as an important way to coordinate activities by reducing the need for mutual adjustment [22]. Our study substantiates this view in the context of software development and shows that reducing the need for mutual adjustment is particularly beneficial—in terms of increasing quality and job satisfaction—if individuals prefer working in a deadline-driven way. The results of our study provide important insights for practitioners who have to hire software developers or deploy developers to particular products.

2. BACKGROUND

A key work outcome of software developers is the degree to which software developers deliver software with high quality, i.e., software code with few bugs and low complexity [10]. Understanding variation in the quality delivered by software developers has been a mainstay of prior research. In particular, a number of studies have shown that through establishing organizational structures and processes, including CMM and agile software development, software quality can be significantly increased [7], [9], [10].

Besides software quality as a work outcome, a second, increasingly important aspect for managers is ensuring a high job satisfaction of the developers working on a product. More specifically, job satisfaction refers to the positive emotional response to the job resulting from an employee's appraisal of the job as fulfilling or congruent with an individual's values (see [23]). Clearly, job satisfaction is an important outcome in its own right and has been linked to a number of consequences, including organizational commitment, turnover intentions, and job performance (e.g., [4]). Dissatisfied employees are costly and more likely to quit their jobs [24]. Importantly, prior studies suggest that job satisfaction has a stronger effect on turnover intention than financial reward [4]. Understanding the determinants of these outcomes is critical because software products may meet software quality requirements but may fail to create a sustainable atmosphere for developers to work—or vice versa.

A factor that has been recognized as an important determinant of work effectiveness and satisfaction is how employees manage their temporal resources [14], [21]. Managing temporal resources represents a challenging part of software developers' work that is not well understood in research today. One important aspect of managing temporal resources is the extent to which individuals follow their deadline orientation, i.e., their preferences for the allocation of time in task execution under deadline conditions [14]. The concept of deadline orientation originates from the assumption that individuals have explicit expectations and preferences regarding the progression of events and activities over time [14]. An individual's deadline orientation comprises two elements: (1) the amount of time perceived as available to complete a task and (2) how an activity is paced out over that time [14]. Whereas some individuals prefer putting less effort into a task until shortly before the deadline and then work until time runs out, others prefer spreading their effort evenly to the available time. We refer to the first—preferring to complete the bulk of the work in a relatively short period before the deadline—as high deadline orientation. We refer to the other extreme—preferring to engage in constant work pace and spreading out task activities evenly over time—as low deadline orientation. Deadline orientation has been conceptualized as a relatively stable part of an individual's personality [14]. Thus, adopting a deadline-oriented work style may prove unpleasant or difficult for individuals preferring a steady work style and vice versa.

Prior research has mainly paid attention to time urgency and procrastination as conceptualizations of how individuals use their temporal resources [25]. Time-urgent individuals are concerned with the scarcity of temporal resources that must be conserved. In contrast to time urgency, which emphasizes when work is due, deadline orientation captures how time is allocated toward task completion. Whereas time is viewed as hostile and a source of constant pressure for time-urgent individuals, deadline-oriented individuals are most energized as the deadline approaches [21]. To voluntarily delay an intended course of action despite being aware of negative consequences is referred to as procrastination [26]. In contrast to procrastination, deadline orientation is based on the argumentation that positive and negative outcomes may result from the behavior, depending on person-task or person-environment fit [14]. Whereas procrastination is viewed as an irrational behavior because individuals expect negative outcomes [26], deadline-oriented individuals may rationally and intentionally delay starting tasks until the deadline because they expect favorable outcomes.

Prior empirical work has mostly studied temporal work styles in the context of work teams and found that diversity in deadline orientation among team members can increase team performance under conditions of adequate temporal leadership [21]. Existing work also suggests that if most team members tend to work in a deadline-oriented way, then the team is less likely to meet deadlines [27]. However, few, if any, studies have examined how the deadline orientation of software developers affect software quality and job satisfaction, and how this effect is moderated by technological characteristics of software products.

Inconsistent work outcomes may be particularly evident if software developers have to interact with others to exchange task-related information because of dependencies among the software modules. Given that software development is a socio-technical activity, the extent to which software developers have to coordinate their work with others is influenced by technological characteristics of the software product, including the product's degree of modularity [20].

Modularity is a general property of complex systems and grounded in the premise that complex systems are composed of subsystems that are both interdependent and independent [22], [28]. Modular systems encapsulate portions of functionality into distinct, loosely-coupled components that interact through well-defined interfaces [22]. Coupling refers to the degree to which changes in one component affect the behavior of others—systems are loosely-coupled if changes in one component have only small or no effects on other components [29]. Standardization refers to the degree to which policies specify how components interact and communicate with each other [29].

3. HYPOTHESES

We argue that product modularity and individuals' deadline orientation will jointly influence the quality of a software product. Whereas products with a high degree of modularity represent a manageable set of distinct components for developers, products with a low degree of modularity are more complex because they comprise tightly integrated functionality with reciprocal interdependencies regarding technical and social dimensions [30]. Resolving these interdependencies requires developers to continuously coordinate their efforts [20], [31]. For developers, continuous coordination on technical and social dimensions will likely require working in a continuous and synchronized way. Whereas software developers who prefer a low deadline orientation are likely to strive in such environments, software developers preferring deadline orientation may be less motivated or underperform when forced to work in a continuous and steady way [32]. Thus, following prior literature on the congruence of work environments and preferred work styles e.g., [33], a misfit between deadline orientation and the actual work style required to perform a certain product will likely reduce the quality of the software they deliver.

By contrast, with an increasing degree of modularity, products are composed of distinct subsystems that decrease developers' needs for coordination by limiting technical and social

interdependencies [20]. With decreasing interdependencies, developers who prefer deadlines will be able to work in accordance with their preferences. Setting and fulfilling personal preferences, such as regarding deadlines, is easier when less coordination regarding social and technical dimensions is required [31]. Because software quality will likely be higher when software developers work in accordance with their deadline orientation [34], we expect deadline-oriented software developers to deliver higher quality when working on high-modularity products. Thus, we posit the following hypothesis:

Hypothesis 1: Product modularity moderates the effect of deadline orientation on software quality such that developers with high deadline orientation will deliver higher software quality when working on products with high modularity compared to when working on products with low modularity.

Deadline orientation will also have implications for job satisfaction because developers have to work with a pace that is different from their preferences, which may result in less enjoyable work, or because their deadline orientation may cause conflicts with others. These factors will likely interact with technological characteristics of the software product. This is because technological characteristics, including the degree of product modularity, may affect the level of self-determination of software developers and the degree to which developers have to interact with others in fulfilling their tasks [31].

Prior research argues that loose coupling fosters self-determination [35]. Modular product designs represent a certain degree of autonomy that frees developers from being forced into working in a steady and continuous way. Thus, deadline-oriented software developers will particularly enjoy the freedom to work in accordance with their preference. Moreover, a number of studies argue that modularity reduces conflict by eliminating the necessity to agree, interact with, or adapt to other developers or entities involved in product development [31]. Whereas distributing work evenly over the available time can be assumed to be less conflict-prone, deadline orientation may accentuate conflict situations if products require significant coordination. Thus, the reduction of conflict associated with modular products can be assumed to be particularly salient for software developers with a high deadline orientation. Taken together, the independence engendered by modularity and the reduced need for interaction provide developers greater autonomy to utilize deadline orientation to accomplish tasks without causing conflicts. This will likely enhance job satisfaction.

By contrast, we expect deadline-oriented developers to be less satisfied with their job when working on less modular products because the integrated structure of the product does not allow self-determination to the extent necessary. Specifically, when working on low-modularity products, software developers face a continuous need for coordination in order to fulfill their task. In such a context, deadline-oriented developers may not be able to align the required work style with their preferences because moving workload toward the end of a deadline is not compatible with the coordination requirements caused by the technological properties of the developed product. Thus, software developers with a preference for completing most of their work when deadlines are close may be forced into a low deadline orientation. As a result, deadline-oriented software developers may find less enjoyment in their work and be less satisfied with their job when working on low-modularity products [36]. In addition, given their tendency to move activities toward the deadline, deadline-oriented software developers will likely face conflicts with others. This will be particularly the case when working on low-modularity products because such products require more interaction and coordination among developers. It follows:

Hypothesis 2: Product modularity moderates the effect of deadline orientation on job satisfaction such that developers with high deadline orientation have higher job satisfaction when working on products with high modularity compared to when working on products with low modularity.

Figure 1 shows our research model.

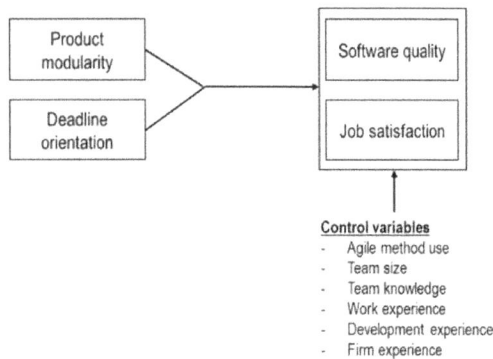

Figure 1. Research model

4. METHOD
4.1 Data Collection
We collected data for testing the hypotheses at a large global software vendor. The company employs several thousand software developers worldwide. We tested our model by surveying software developers and product managers. Respondents' participation in the study was voluntary and incentivized with comprehensive reports regarding the study's results. We gathered data on site using paper-based questionnaires.

We used role-specific questionnaires to collect insights from different perspectives, thus effectively mitigating common method variance [37]. We collected data on deadline orientation and job satisfaction from individual developers, and data on product modularity and software quality from product stakeholders. Product stakeholders act as internal customers and can judge software quality. Moreover, product owners pass on requirements to teams of software developers and have a comprehensive view on the software product's architectures. To account for potential alternative explanations of the hypothesized relationships, we controlled for several other factors, including developers' work experience, experience as a software developer, firm experience, and the use of agile software development methods, team size, and team knowledge.

4.2 Measures, Model, and Data Analysis
We measured the constructs of our model based on items validated in prior work that were adapted to the context of our study. The items we used for measuring job satisfaction were based on Judge et al. [38]. We used a 7-point Likert scale for measuring job satisfaction of software developers and one exemplary item was "I feel very satisfied with my present job." We measured software quality by adapting items from Lee and

Xia [9], using a 10-point scale. For example, we asked product stakeholders regarding their agreement with the statement "The capabilities of the software meet the needs of the team's requirements." Software developers' deadline orientation was measured by relying on the instrument suggest by Gevers et al. [14]. We used a 7-point Likert scale and asked developers to rate their agreement with items including "I prefer to do most of the work for a project when the due date is close." For measuring product modularity, we adapted items from Worren et al. [39], using a 7-point Likert scale. One exemplary item was "The team's software can be decomposed into separate, independent functional sub-units."

We assessed agile methods use by asking software developers about the extent to which they applied agile practices. We used a 10-point Likert scale and one exemplary item was "How much of your code do you develop with a programming partner?" We assessed work experience, developer experience, and firm experience by directly asking software developers about the respective number of years. We measured team knowledge by asking team managers, for instance, about the "Current level of application domain knowledge in the team that is necessary to accomplish the team tasks" (adapted from [40]), using a 10-point Likert scale. Among other factors we controlled for developers' work experience (What is your total work experience?), development experience (How many years have you been working as professional software developer?), and firm experience (How long have you been working for [vendor]?).

Table 1 describes the constructs and their correlations[1]. All Cronbach alphas were consistently larger than .6 for all scales [41]. To test our models, we followed prior work on the antecedents of software quality that used a seemingly unrelated regression equations approach [10], [42].[2] Given that product stakeholders are responsible for a number of software development teams, we used clustered regression analysis [43].

5. RESULTS
Hypothesis 1 predicted that software developer's deadline orientation positively interacts with product modularity in influencing software quality, such that the positive effect of deadline orientation on software quality is particularly strong when working on high-modularity products compared to when working on low-modularity products. As Model 1 in Table 2 shows, the interaction effect between deadline orientation and modularity on software quality was significant and positive (beta=.3, p<.01), thus providing support for hypothesis 1.

---

[1] Deadline orientation takes negative values because it is mean-centered.

[2] We obtained similar results when estimating both models separately using OLS, which is not surprising because the equations use the same predictors.

Table 1. Descriptive statistics and correlation

		Alpha	Mean	S.D.	Min	Max	1	2	3	4	5	6	7	8	9
1	Software quality	.83	7.62	1.24	4.5	9.25									
2	Job satisfaction	.89	5.39	1.10	1.5	7	.13								
3	Deadline orientation	.61	.85	.92	-1.83	2.83	-.02	-.17*							
4	Product modularity	.88	5.08	1.11	1.33	6.33	.29***	.14	-.10						
5	Agile method use	.73	.41	.17	.00	.75	.11	.15	.01	-.11					
6	Team size	N.A.	8.93	2.34	2.00	13.00	.19*	-.06	.07	.24**	-.25**				
7	Team knowledge	.79	6.66	1.49	3.33	9.00	.01	-.04	-.06	-.37***	.24**	-.38***			
8	Work experience	N.A.	5.63	3.13	.00	15.00	-.04	-.03	-.18*	.05	-.19	.12	-.09		
9	Development experience	N.A.	4.29	2.61	.00	15.00	-.12	-.04	-.15	-.07	-.09	.14	-.07	.8***	
10	Firm experience	N.A.	5.21	3.02	.00	13.00	-.05	-.06	-.16	.04	-.19*	.16*	-.09	.93***	.73***

Table 2. Regression results

VARIABLES	(1) Software quality	(2) Job satisfaction
Main effects:		
Deadline orientation	-0.04	-0.23**
	(0.07)	(0.08)
Product modularity	0.18*	0.05
	(0.09)	(0.10)
Interaction effects:		
Deadline orientation X Product modularity	**0.30****	**0.34*****
	(0.09)	**(0.10)**
Controls:		
Agile method use	0.16*	0.06
	(0.08)	(0.08)
Team size	0.20*	-0.04
	(0.08)	(0.08)
Team knowledge	0.18*	0.01
	(0.08)	(0.09)
Work experience	0.22	-0.01
	(0.22)	(0.23)
Developer experience	-0.12	0.03
	(0.12)	(0.12)
Firm experience	-0.11	-0.07
	(0.20)	(0.21)
Constant	0.10	0.01
	(0.07)	(0.07)
R-squared	0.22	0.16
Chi2 test	40.51***	28.28***

N=144 Standard errors in parentheses, clustered analysis.
* p < 0.05, ** p < 0.01, *** p < 0.001

Hypothesis 2 predicted that developers with a preference for deadline-oriented work show higher job satisfaction when working on high-modularity products compared to when working on low-modularity products. As Model 2 in Table 2 shows, the interaction effect between deadline orientation and modularity on job satisfaction was significant and positive (beta=.34, p<.001), thus providing support for hypothesis 2.

Figure 2 shows the interaction of deadline orientation and modularity on software quality (low indicates -1 standard deviation, high indicates +1 standard deviation). The graph shows that the software quality associated with deadline-oriented developers is substantially higher on high-modularity products compared to low-modularity products. Similarly, Figure 2 shows the interaction effects of deadline orientation on job satisfaction at different levels of modularity (low indicates -1 standard deviation, high indicates +1 standard deviation). The graph shows that the job satisfaction of deadline-oriented developers is substantially higher on products with high modularity compared to products with low modularity.

Among other findings, in line with prior empirical studies, we found a significant effect of agile method use on software quality (see Table 2) [9], [10]. We did not observe a significant effect of agile method use on job satisfaction. In addition, software quality was significantly higher if software developers work in larger teams and in teams that have the requisite team knowledge. In this context, we did not find evidence for the effect of work experience, developer experience and tenure on software quality and job satisfaction.

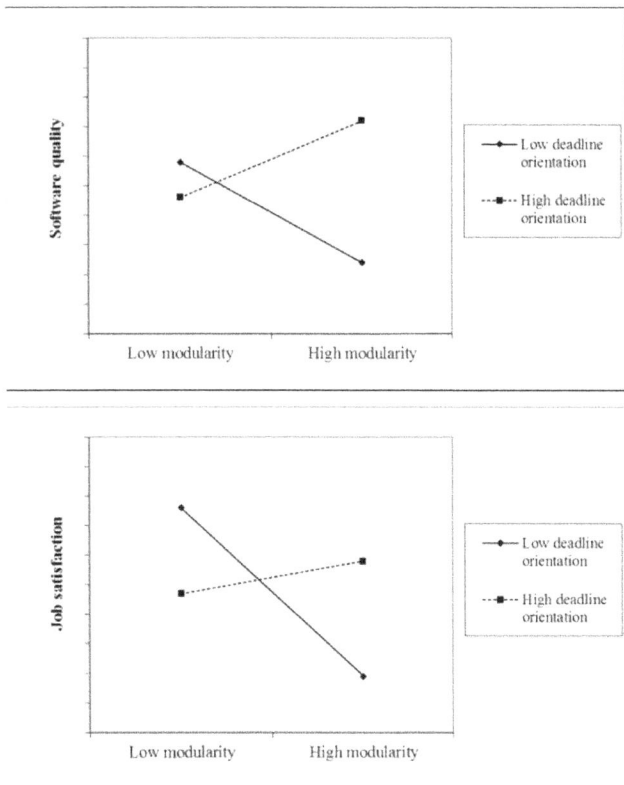

Figure 2. Interaction effect of deadline orientation and modularity on software quality and job satisfaction

6. DISCUSSION

The goal of this study was to examine the role of product modularity and software developers' temporal work style—in terms of their deadline orientation—in explaining variance in software developers' key work outcomes, namely software quality and job satisfaction. Our research was motivated by the concern that increasing pressure faced by software developers—in terms of delivering high quality products within a short time—may require "fit" between their temporal work style (how individual developers manage their temporal resources when approaching deadlines) and the types of products they are assigned to. Based on existing literature on temporal work style and product modularity, we hypothesized that deadline orientation—i.e., preferring to work in a deadline-driven way—positively interacts with product modularity in influencing software quality and job satisfaction. Our empirical results support the hypothesized relationships by showing that software quality and job satisfaction of software developers with a deadline-oriented preference increase with increasing modularity in product design.

Our findings provide four main contributions. First, our study complements prior work on software development that has so far mostly focused on organizational factors to influence software quality and job satisfaction [7], [10], [12]. Specifically, we show that managers can increase software quality and job satisfaction if the temporal work style of developers fits with the technological characteristics of the software development product. Interestingly, the literature on software development has largely focused on explaining software quality by variation in team processes rather than individual-level differences (e.g., [9], [10]). Our findings emphasize the importance of considering individual preferences of software developers and appropriately matching those with software product characteristics for enhancing quality and job satisfaction. More generally, our findings underscore the importance of considering individual differences of software developers when explaining software quality and job satisfaction. Finally, we contribute to the larger array of work on software development [44], [45].

Second, our study has wider implications for research on temporal work styles that has so far mostly focused on time pressure, temporal leadership, or the interaction of collaborating individuals' deadline orientation [21], [25]. We add to this body of work by considering product modularity as a context factor that determines the need to interact with individuals. Empirical evidence on the influence of deadline orientation is scarce and directed toward actual work behavior rather than preferences [21]. We also complement the understanding of temporal cognitions by providing an empirical examination of how deadline orientation influences two key work outcomes, namely software quality and job satisfaction.

Third, our study also contributes to the broader modularity literature [20], [22] and to prior work that uses modularity ideas in IT outsourcing and offshoring contexts [46]–[48]. Modularity has long been seen as an important way to coordinate activities among organizations and team members by reducing the need for mutual adjustment in manufacturing and related settings. Our findings suggest that people-intensive processes, such as software development, require that modularity decisions are accompanied with appropriate allocations of developers with specific temporal work styles to achieve desirable outcomes such as enhanced quality and job satisfaction.

Finally, our findings provide useful insights for managers of software development products. The finding that deadline-oriented developers produce higher software quality and are more satisfied when assigned to high-modularity products implies that managers should be mindful when hiring and staffing developers for different types of projects. In particular, managers should pay attention to deadline preferences of developers and assign them accordingly to products that "fit" better in terms of their modularity properties.

7. REFERENCES

[1] Financial Times, "Software is Steering Auto Industry," 2015. [Online]. Available: http://www.ft.com/intl/cms/s/0/dce10162-b5f1-11e4-a577-00144feab7de.html#axzz3daxRmc5e. [Accessed: 21-Jun-2015].

[2] Business Insider, "A Software Problem Caused a Brand-New Airbus Military Plane to Crash," 2015. [Online]. Available: http://uk.businessinsider.com/a-software-problem-caused-an-airbus-a400m-to-crash-2015-6?r=US. [Accessed: 21-Jun-2015].

[3] Techradar, "The Top 10 Data Breaches of the Past 12 Months," 2014. [Online]. Available: http://www.techradar.com/news/software/security-software/the-top-10-data-breaches-of-the-past-12-months-1248890/2. [Accessed: 21-Jun-2015].

[4] R. P. Tett and J. P. Meyer, "Job Satisfaction, Organizational Commitment, Turnover Intention, and Turnover: Path Analyses Based on Meta-Analytic Findings," *Personnel Psychology*, vol. 46, no. 2, pp. 259–293, 1993.

[5] CNN Money, "Best Jobs in America," 2013. [Online]. Available: http://money.cnn.com/pf/best-jobs/2013/snapshots/1.html. [Accessed: 21-Jun-2015].

[6] The Economist, "How to Bag a Geek," *The Economist*, 21-Feb-2015. [Online]. Available: http://www.economist.com/news/business/21644150-battle-software-talent-other-industries-can-learn-silicon-valley-how-bag. [Accessed: 21-Jun-2015].

[7] D. E. Harter, M. S. Krishnan, and S. A. Slaughter, "Effects of Process Maturity on Quality, Cycle Time, and Effort in Software Product Development," *Management Science*, vol. 46, no. 4, pp. 451–466, 2000.

[8] N. Ramasubbu, S. Mithas, M. S. Krishnan, and C. F. Kemerer, "Work Dispersion, Process-Based Learning, and Offshore Software Development Performance," *MIS Quarterly*, vol. 32, no. 2, pp. 437–458, 2008.

[9] G. Lee and W. Xia, "Toward Agile: An Integrated Analysis of Quantitative and Qualitative Field Data," *MIS Quarterly*, vol. 34, no. 1, pp. 87–114, 2010.

[10] L. M. Maruping, V. Venkatesh, and R. Agarwal, "A Control Theory Perspective on Agile Methodology Use and Changing User Requirements," *Information Systems Research*, vol. 20, no. 3, pp. 377–399, 2009.

[11] K. Mannaro, M. Melis, and M. Marchesi, "Empirical Analysis on the Satisfaction of IT Employees Comparing XP Practices with Other Software Development Methodologies," in *Extreme Programming and Agile Processes in Software Engineering*, vol. 3092, J. Eckstein and H. Baumeister, Eds. Springer Berlin Heidelberg, 2004, pp. 166–174.

[12] M. K. Ahuja, K. M. Chudoba, C. J. Kacmar, D. H. McKnight, and J. F. George, "IT Road Warriors: Balancing Work-Family Conflict, Job Autonomy, and Work Overload to Mitigate Turnover Intentions," *MIS Quarterly*, vol. 31, no. 1, pp. pp. 1–17, 2007.

[13] S. T. Acuña, M. Gómez, and N. Juristo, "How Do Personality, Team Processes and Task Characteristics Relate to Job Satisfaction and Software Quality?," *Information and Software Technology*, vol. 51, no. 3, pp. 627–639, 2009.

[14] J. Gevers, S. Mohammed, and N. Baytalskaya, "The Conceptualisation and Measurement of Pacing Styles," *Applied Psychology*, pp. 1464–1597, 2013.

[15] K. Schwaber and M. Beedle, *Agile Software Development with Scrum*, 1st ed. Upper Saddle River, NJ, USA: Prentice Hall PTR, 2001.

[16] H. Mendelson, "Organizational Architecture and Success in the Information Technology Industry," *Management Science*, vol. 46, no. 4, pp. 513–529, 2000.

[17] H. Mendelson and R. R. Pillai, "Clockspeed and Informational Response: Evidence from the Information Technology Industry," *Information Systems Research*, vol. 9, no. 4, pp. 415–433, 1998.

[18] H. Mendelson and R. R. Pillai, "Industry Clockspeed: Measurement and Operational Implications," *Manufacturing & Service Operations Management*, vol. 1, no. 1, pp. 1–20, 1999.

[19] H. Mendelson and R. R. Pillai, "Information Age Organizations, Dynamics and Performance," *Journal of Economic Behavior & Organization*, vol. 38, no. 3, pp. 253–281, 1999.

[20] R. Sanchez and J. T. Mahoney, "Modularity, Flexibility, and Knowledge Management in Product and Organization Design," *Strategic Management Journal*, vol. 17, no. 1, pp. 63–76, 1996.

[21] S. Mohammed and S. Nadkarni, "Temporal Diversity and Team Performance: The Moderating Role of Team Temporal Leadership," *Academy of Management Journal*, vol. 54, no. 3, pp. 489–508, 2011.

[22] M. A. Schilling, "Toward a General Modular Systems Theory and Its Application to Interfirm Product Modularity," *Academy of Management Review*, vol. 25, no. 2, pp. 312–334, 2000.

[23] O. Janssen, "Fairness Perceptions as a Moderator in the Curvilinear Relationships Between Job Demands, and Job Performance and Job Satisfaction," *Academy of Management Journal*, vol. 44, no. 5, pp. 1039–1050, 2001.

[24] L. Dong, T. R. Mitchell, T. W. Lee, B. C. Holtom, and T. R. Hinkin, "When Employees Are Out of Step with Coworkers: How Job Satisfaction Trajectory and Dispersion Influence Individual- and Unit-Level Voluntary Turnover.," *Academy of Management Journal*, vol. 55, no. 6, pp. 1360–1380, 2012.

[25] L. Maruping, V. Venkatesh, S. Thatcher, and P. Patel, "Folding Under Pressure or Rising to the Occasion? Perceived Time Pressure and the Moderating Role of Team Temporal Leadership," *Academy of Management Journal*, vol. 58, no. 5, 2015.

[26] P. Steel, "The Nature of Procrastination: A Meta-Analytic and Theoretical Review of Quintessential Self-Regulatory Failure," *Psychological bulletin*, vol. 133, no. 1, pp. 65–94, 2007.

[27] J. M. Gevers, C. G. Rutte, and W. Van Eerde, "Meeting Deadlines in Work Groups: Implicit and Explicit Mechanisms," *Applied Psychology*, vol. 55, no. 1, pp. 52–72, 2006.

[28] H. A. Simon, "The Architecture of Complexity," *Proceedings of the American Philosophical Society*, vol. 106, no. 6, pp. 467–482, 1962.

[29] K. Ulrich, "The Role of Product Architecture in the Manufacturing Firm," *Research Policy*, vol. 24, no. 3, pp. 419–440, 1995.

[30] J. D. Thompson, *Organizations in Action: Social Science Bases of Administrative Theory*. Transaction Publishers, 1967.

[31] J. D. Orton and K. E. Weick, "Loosely Coupled Systems: A Reconceptualization," *Academy of Management Review*, vol. 15, no. 2, pp. 203–223, 1990.

[32] M. Gagné and E. L. Deci, "Self-Determination Theory and Work Motivation," *Journal of Organizational Behavior*, vol. 26, no. 4, pp. 331–362, 2005.

[33] A. Tziner, E. I. Meir, and H. Segal, "Occupational Congruence and Personal Task-Related Attributes: How Do They Relate to Work Performance?," *Journal of Career Assessment*, vol. 10, no. 4, pp. 401–412, 2002.

[34] A. Cockburn and J. Highsmith, "Agile Software Development: The People Factor," *Computer*, vol. 34, no. 11, pp. 131–133, 2001.

[35] K. E. Weick, "Educational Organizations as Loosely Coupled Systems," *Administrative Science Quarterly*, vol. 21, no. 1, pp. 1–19, 1976.

[36] B. M. Meglino, E. C. Ravlin, and C. L. Adkins, "A Work Values Approach to Corporate Culture: A Field Test of the Value Congruence Process and Its Relationship to Individual Outcomes.," *Journal of Applied Psychology*, vol. 74, no. 3, pp. 424–432, 1989.

[37] P. M. Podsakoff, S. B. MacKenzie, J. Y. Lee, and N. P. Podsakoff, "Common method biases in behavioral research: a critical review of the literature and recommended remedies," *Journal of Applied Psychology*, vol. 88, no. 5, pp. 879–903, Oct. 2003.

[38] T. A. Judge, C. J. Thoresen, J. E. Bono, and G. K. Patton, "The Job Satisfaction–Job Performance Relationship: A Qualitative and Quantitative Review," *Psychological Bulletin*, vol. 127, no. 3, p. 376, 2001.

[39] N. Worren, K. Moore, and P. Cardona, "Modularity, Strategic Flexibility, and Firm Performance: A Study of the Home Appliance Industry," *Strategic Management Journal*, vol. 23, no. 12, pp. 1123–1140, 2002.

[40] S. Faraj and L. Sproull, "Coordinating Expertise in Software Development Teams," *Management Science*, vol. 46, no. 12, pp. 1554–1568, 2000.

[41] J. C. Nunnally and I. Bernstein, *The Assessment of Reliability*. New York: McGraw-Hill, 1994.

[42] C. F. Baum, *An Introduction to Modern Econometrics Using STATA*. College Station, USA: STATA press, 2006.

[43] I. D. Gow, G. Ormazabal, and D. J. Taylor, "Correcting for Cross-Sectional and Time-Series Dependence in Accounting Research," *The Accounting Review*, vol. 85, no. 2, pp. 483–512, 2010.

[44] T. Kude, C. Schmidt, S. Mithas, and A. Heinzl, "Disciplined Autonomy and Innovation Effectiveness: The Role of Team Efficacy and Task Volatility," in *Academy of Management Proceedings*, Vancouver, CA, 2015, vol. 2015.

[45] C. Schmidt, T. Kude, A. Heinzl, and S. Mithas, "How Agile Practices Influence the Performance of Software Development Teams: The Role of Shared Mental Models and Backup," in *Proceedings of the 34th International Conference on Information Systems*, Auckland, New Zealand, 2014.

[46] U. M. Apte and R. O. Mason, "Global Disaggregation of Information-Intensive Services," *Management Science*, vol. 41, no. 7, pp. 1250–1262, 1995.

[47] S. Mithas and J. Whitaker, "Is the World Flat or Spiky? Information Intensity, Skills, and Global Service Disaggregation," *Information Systems Research*, vol. 18, no. 3, pp. 237–259, 2007.

[48] P. B. Tambe and L. M. Hitt, "How Offshoring Affects IT Workers," *Communications of the ACM*, vol. 53, no. 10, pp. 62–70, 2010.

A Literature Review on Enterprise Social Media Collaboration in Virtual Teams: Challenges, Determinants, Implications and Impacts

Sebastian Dürr
University of Bamberg
An der Weberei 5
96047 Bamberg
+49 951 863-2877
Sebastian.duerr@uni-bamberg.de

Caroline Oehlhorn
University of Bamberg
An der Weberei 5
96047 Bamberg
+49 951 863-2879
Caroline.oehlhorn@uni-bamberg.de

Christian Maier
University of Bamberg
An der Weberei 5
96047 Bamberg
+49 951 863-3919
Christian.maier@uni-bamberg.de

Sven Laumer
University of Bamberg
An der Weberei 5
96047 Bamberg
+49 951 863-2873
Sven.laumer@uni-bamberg.de

ABSTRACT

This literature review focusses research on Enterprise Social Media (ESM) and its use within virtual teams. The paper includes results from 38 articles outlining the existing body of knowledge and showing the steady progress in this research field. Previous literature often thematizes the external use of social media and technological aspects, but this research concentrates on the internal collaborative use, its challenges, related determinants, managerial implications and its impact on business. Existing research illustrates key factors in each of the previously mentioned subjects. However, as research should consider the entire field, a research agenda for further studies in this ESM topic is developed.

General Terms

Management; Performance; Human Factors; Theory

Keywords

Enterprise Social Media; Virtual Collaborating Teams; Challenges; Determinants; Implications; Impact

1. INTRODUCTION

In 2004, Mark Zuckerberg's social media platform Facebook revolutionized the way people communicate and interact. Step by step, a broad variety of different social media tools emerged and started to influence our daily life [37]. Such trends often start with consumers, but the implementation also increased sharply in enterprises [1]. According to a report by McKinsey & Company, a great potential, e.g. pre-perceived improvement of communications and collaboration within and between organizations and their external partners, can be unlocked using social media strategically with an estimated annual value between $900bn and $1.3tn. The report further estimates that the use of social media platforms potentially improves industries workforces' productivity by 20 to 25 percent due to reduced emailing, providing faster access to information and increased collaboration which leads to higher business revenue [6, 27]. Yet, complexity evolves from these people-oriented systems, because they are less intuitive as they are innovative and it is complicated to integrate them into daily work routines – unlike task- or document-oriented systems that are very straightforward and more convenient to use [31, 47]. Other difficulties, such as interactions between globally distributed teams, several members who are geographical dispersed, facing time zone differences and cultural diversity complicate the situation even more [28]. Due to these unique barriers which are generated by this spatial, temporal, and configurational dispersion, a lot of resistance against the use of collaboration through Enterprise Social Media (ESM) may emerge [30, 37]. ESM is referred to that kind of platform which companies or teams use in order to collaborate, when they are geographically distributed, e.g. blogs, wikis or social networks. However, a more precise definition is given by Leonardi et al. [34]: "[ESM are] web-based platforms that allow workers to (a) communicate with specific coworkers or broadcast messages to everyone in the organization; explicitly indicate or implicitly reveal coworkers as communication partners; post, edit, and sort text and files linked to themselves or others; (b) and view the messages, connections, text, and files communicated, posted, edited, and sorted by anyone else in the organization at any time of their choosing."

Although earlier technologies, e.g. email and video conferencing, enable team members to deal with (a). In that way, collaboration in ESM is unique and supports these activities. Additionally, it offers functionalities to disclose interactions between coworkers allowing information to be accessible in the future (b) [55]. For instance, proprietary software that enables these features is IBM's Connections, Yammer, Oracle's Social Network, Jive from Jive

SIGMIS-CPR'16, June 2–4, 2016, Alexandria, VA, USA.
© 2016 ACM. ISBN 978-1-4503-4203-2/16/06...$15.00.
DOI: http://dx.doi.org/10.1145/2890602.2890611

Software, Salesforce Buddy Media or Microsoft Sharepoint. As this type of collaboration may be of importance for geographically dispersed IT staff within an organization e.g. for the coordination of developers and IT professionals [45], we propose the following research question: *"What is the status quo of research focusing on ESM use in virtual teams?"*

In this respect, a representative amount of research articles examined the application of ESM collaboration as well as emerging challenges, beneficial determinants, managerial implications and its possible impact on business. These aspects were classified and structured to model a comprehensive framework for an overall understanding of ESM collaboration. Furthermore, we chose a literature review for our paper, because these are usually utilized to indicate research gaps and represent an important part of larger research endeavors [5]. In this vein, we perceived that the formerly unconnected aspects need to be related as in our proposed comprehensive framework, which conveys an overall comprehension of the given topic (cf. Section 4). For that, the analysis of 38 articles (29 journal papers, 2 conference papers, and 7 magazine articles) serves as a foundation for our literature analysis and offers an overview about existing research, previous results and an agenda for future research. Our analysis is used to formulate our three research proposals, from which we develope a research agenda for future ESM collaboration studies.

In the following section, the applied methodology (i.e., literature review) and the process to identify relevant literature as well as existing related research will be explained in detail. Section three contains our results after having analyzed the identified literature that addresses ESM collaboration with a focus on challenges, determinants, managerial implications and business impact. In the fourth section the results will be discussed and a research agenda for future ESM collaboration research will be presented. Our paper concludes with a summary including limitations and possibilities for future research within ESM collaboration.

2. METHODOLOGY AND OVERVIEW

This paper's methodology follows a framework proposed by vom Brocke et al. [5] which is based on a screening of the review literature itself and especially highlights the need for comprehensibly documenting the process of literature search in such an article. The framework is structured into the following five phases: (1) definition of review scope, (2) conceptualization of topic, (3) literature search, (4) literature analysis and synthesis, (5) research agenda. Each of the steps will be briefly explained, when it will be addressed in the course of this work.

Characteristic	Categories			
focus	research outcome	research methods	theories	applications
goal	integration	criticism		central issues
organization	historical	conceptual		methodological
perspective	neutral representation		espousal of position	
audience	specialized audience	general scholars	practicioniers/politicians	general public
coverage	exhaustive	exhaustive and selective	representative	central/pivotal

Figure 1. Taxonomy of this literature review on the collaborative use of ESM (following vom Brocke et al. [5])

(1) The *definition of the review scope* of this literature review is summarized in Figure 1 (categories applicable to this review on ESM research are highlighted) which is based on the taxonomy adapted by vom Brocke et al. [5].

This literature review *focuses* on outcomes of applied research, but also theories in the domain of ESM. The *goal* is to integrate findings with respect to four areas of ESM research, i.e., challenges, determinants, managerial implications and business impact. These four areas of our research were chosen as we address the internal and non-technical perspective of virtual teams and its conflation with ESM. We selected this field, because the external perspective is already more commonly studied i.e. communication with external stakeholders which includes customers, suppliers and the public at large [32, 41]. Numerous studies emphasize problems that may arise from the integration of private and professional information as well as the risk of carelessly released information [29, 50]. We also realized that the main attention in previous research on globally distributed teams centered technical aspects. Thus, previous research claims that the proper application of technical and operational mechanisms, such as collaborative technologies, tools, and coordination mechanisms is a key to team success [21]. Minding the various dimensions 'internal' vs. 'external' and 'technical' vs. 'functional/collaborative', we faced a lack of investigation in the 'internal' and 'collaborative' perspective and therefore scrutinized it. Thus, this paper is organized along a *conceptual* structure. We did not take a particular *perspective* as we want to provide a neutral representation of the review results. As an *audience* of this review we chose specialized scholars having an interest in the field of ESM. For *coverage* our literature review can be categorized as representative as our research has been limited to certain journals, but does not consider the totality of the literature.

The second step is (2) *conceptualization of the topic*. It addresses the point that the author of a review article must begin with a topic in need of review and a broad conception of what is known about the topic and potential areas where new knowledge may be needed [54]. As indicated before, this review draws on the framework for analyzing ESM research, and classifies ESM research with respect to the following areas: challenges, determinants, managerial implications, and business impact.

(3) The literature search considered the sources presented in Table 1 (see Appendix). These sources are selected based on 27 journals (e.g. [36]) published in the last 20 years. Table 1 lists investigated journals, the name of the database used for searching, the respective fields which were searched (if possible: title, abstract and keywords) and the coverage (1996 to 2015). Further, seven apparently relevant search terms (Enterprise, Organization, Social Media, Social Networks, Collaboration, Virtual Teams, and Distributed Teams) evolved from readings related to our topic, which in combination only resulted in a few journals. Therefore, we refined our search using several further tests leading to the hits resulting from our final query using the keywords "Enterprise" or "Organization" being concatenated with the terms "Social media" respectively "Social networks" for the particular outcome. The choice whether a retrieved article will be studied in detail in this literature review is based on the abstract. After reading the identified articles and verifying their thematic consistency with the objective, the citations used in each article are analyzed to search for articles that have not been identified in the initial search process (Table 1).

Finally, Web of Science and Google Scholar are used to deploy forward and backward search [57] for articles citing the identified article, and again it is analyzed whether these are consistent with the objective and have not been identified in the initial process. This process served for enlarging the quantity of the main sources and unveiled another 28 relevant articles from journals, conferences and magazines. The two last steps of the framework for literature reviewing [5] are (4) literature analysis and synthesis for classifying the identified articles as well as developing a (5) research agenda are explained thoroughly in the following sections, as these are the main outcomes of our work.

3. RESULTS OF THE LITERATURE REVIEW

The following paragraph shows the results of previous research (literature analysis and synthesis). Here, we focus the four fields of ESM research (challenges, determinants, managerial implications, and business impact) that we chose for addressing our research question: *'What is the status quo of research focusing on ESM use in virtual teams?'*

3.1 Challenges of ESM Collaboration

Besides advantages of virtual teams that collaborate on ESM, e.g. decreased expense, greater team variety, improved decision-making, faster innovation, increased communication [4, 8, 11], the awareness of negative aspects resides, too. These challenges are distinguished in different dimensions of challenges, depending whether they affect one team only or an entire organization (Appendix - Table 2). This distinction was chosen as some challenges are more attributable to a small group of people (likely to occur in a team), whereas others just emerge when collaborating in a larger endeavor (e.g. all employees of different teams on different continents from one company) is given. Identified challenges (column 2) where then ordered alphabetically within their dimension. In total 15 of 38 identified articles handled challenges of ESM collaboration, which are further explained in the third column - peculiarities. Here, an exemplary definition of each identified challenge is provided. Finally, the forth column names the source in which the challenge was identified.

3.2 Determinants for ESM Collaboration

Retrieved articles with required determinants for ESM collaboration are represented in 11 of the 38 identified articles on ESM collaboration. Prior research [47] recognizes certain key skills for successful collaboration in virtual teams, distinguishing them into different capability classes, which we elaborated and extended by recommendations of further authors that result in Table 3 (see Appendix). In the first column of this table, these determinants are summarized into three groups namely relationship, communication, and participation. The relationship group emphasizes on the main barriers of collaboration in a virtual team, e.g. confusion and inaccessibility and presents identified determinants in alphabetical order. Then, communication highlights the abilities required to improve mutual understanding amongst team members in ESM projects and participation contains the proficiencies that are required by a person working on an ESM, such as the aptitude to work autonomously.

Table 3 presents determinants that need to be considered while operating a distributed team on ESM. The next section then identifies approaches to improve these processes.

3.3 Managerial Implications for ESM Collaboration

Facing challenges can not only be accomplished through a sheer presence of those determinants. It rather depends on how those determinants are applied and established in the daily routine of a virtual diverse team. This can be created and supported by deploying managerial implications that aim to foster interactions in virtual teams. In total, 13 of 38 identified articles contained several implications from a managerial point of view for effective collaboration. As Table 4 (Appendix) shows, these managerial implications address three different recipients in the organization: team leaders, team members and the network. We unveiled these implications that will impact business performance according to authors presented in resources and ordered them alphabetically within their recipient group.

The awareness of challenges, related skills and managerial implications for ESM will lead to certain business impact presented in the following.

3.4 ESM's Business Impact

ESM's impact on business could be identified in 7 of 38 chosen articles that provide information about how the use of ESM may increase a team's performance and, thereby, creates business value. Withal, business value will not be directly generated, but implicit through the employees' interaction within the network and the information and knowledge that is supplied by ESM (see Appendix – Table 5).

Based on our findings in this chapter, we considered a framework along with certain research proposals which may serve further researchers as an agenda on the topic of internal ESM collaboration. Hereafter, we firstly present our work, but also critically review it in the remainder of our review.

4. DISCUSSION

This section displays the last step of the framework for literature reviewing [5]: developing a (5) research agenda. As our proposed agenda for future collaboration-oriented research in the field of ESM shows (Figure 2), an unambiguous and concise comprehension of how managerial implications influence the determinants to overcome challenges is crucial in order to investigate the business impact which depends on the concept of internal ESM usage.

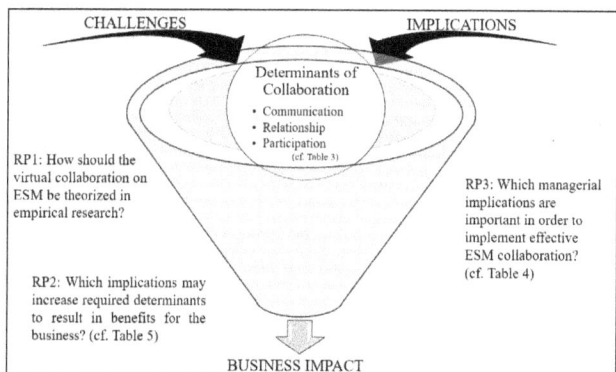

Figure 2. Proposed research agenda for future collaboration-oriented research on ESM

The identified challenges (see Appendix - Table 2) add a certain degree of complexity to the success of collaboration in a virtual team. However, their awareness sensitizes for the actions that might be taken into consideration for practitioners who form or operate such teams. They can be evaluated in terms of our determinants and thus may lead to certain business impact. Understanding the determinants is crucial in order to trigger benefits which depend on minding the challenges and an appropriate realization of managerial implications. Accordingly, our framework encompasses four identified aspects of ESM (challenges, determinants, managerial implications, and business impact) that have not been comprehensively considered in articles published in the journals considered for this review before. For evaluating our approach, the research proposal (RP1) *'How should the virtual collaboration on ESM be theorized in research?'* has to be answered first in order to use this instrument as a remainder of the identified research proposals. Consequently, this framework can be used to investigate different approaches to exploit the benefits of collaboration through ESM. For example, whether team managers concentrate more on collaborative or communicational deeds, or balance between given determinants they apply when dealing with a virtual distributed team in their organization. Second, the collaborative ESM concept with its three main determinants (Appendix - Table 4) is the main dependent variable in research investigating determinants influencing the outcome of managerial implications (Appendix - Table 3) which leads to research answering RP2: *'Which implications may increase required determinants to result in benefits for the business?'* Thereby, especially management fad and fashion as largely neglected should be investigated. Future research should further investigate the holistic picture of realizable ESM impacts based on collaboration. Investigating managerial mechanisms (cf. Table 4) realized through presented implications could provide further insights regarding RP3: *'Which managerial implications are important in order to implement effective internal ESM collaboration?'*

Overall, the results show that empirical research methods enhanced the knowledge regarding what adoption determinants and governance mechanisms should be further investigated in order to understand the concept of ESM for collaboration in virtual teams and its achievable business impact. Nonetheless, while in each of the four research fields only a very few case studies exist that aim to cover the field completely, most of previous research is fragmented. Thus, applying case studies and quantitative methods to each of the internal ESM research fundaments allow to compare the relative position of each of the characteristics taken out from various articles. As the technology of Social Media offers great possibilities to overcome difficulties e.g. asynchrony or geographical distance, team members need to build up trust and familiarity that leads to cohesion and fosters creativity and innovation. In addition, we face not only technological aspects that 'make things work', but multiple aspects, such as different cultures and mutual respect that cannot simply be extinguished through employing a social media platform. In the end, it is the team leader who has the responsibility to form a team, to delegate tasks and to keep the conversation going in order to maintain what this great environment of diversity in a virtual team can offer. Multiple approaches combined with a melting pot of cultures may have true impact on and for an organization. The key determinants presented in Section 3.2 attempt to convey aspects to address the managerial implications of Section 3.3 forming a framework and starting point for the team manager to create and maintain a collaborative atmosphere with people that are geographically dispersed.

5. CONCLUSION

This literature review synthesizes the existing research on internal ESM used for collaboration in virtual teams by considering 38 sources and integrating their results in order to provide an overview about the existing body of knowledge as well as proposing a research agenda which unites and encompasses previous efforts. Previous research regarding internal ESM has moved on from a pure focus on technical to collaborative aspects surrounding ESM which in particular leads to our framework. Identified articles were consistent, but apparently lack sophisticated integration. Therefore, we consider them in a rather early and fragmented stage.

This literature review regarding ESM research faces some limitations itself. First, this literature review mainly covers the years 1996-2015. Undeniably, additional articles were published in the meantime which should be included in a future version. Firstly, this review concentrated only on a selection of top journals, but as we were not fully satisfied with our results, we use backward and forward search [57] which may lead to less sophisticated sources. Moreover, it cannot be guaranteed that the framework is complete or will succeed. The presented approach addresses most pressing issues and should be used as a starting point for actions and further research. Therefore, it needs to be emphasized that no skill solely, but multiple interactions, such as an environment of trust and strong relations, will ensure successful project teams. Unfortunately, some variables that influence team effectiveness cannot be controlled (e.g. demographics, culture, familiarity of employees with social tools, technical aptitude), but should be considered twice [12, 37]. In general, we do not see a 'one size fits all' approach. Some managerial implications may work better than others in certain settings, but different in others. Pulse checks and reiterating the team strategy need to be derived continuously, as behaviors, attitudes, circumstances and usage will change. However, the identified articles, the rigorous and transparent documentation of the literature search process, the proposed categorization of the aspects in each of the research fields, and the proposed research agenda that was initiated by our research question: *'What is the status quo of research focusing on ESM use in virtual teams?'*. This may serve as a good starting point for further literature reviews and future research in the internal collaborative ESM research field.

To conclude, this paper has acknowledged skills that should be present when collaborating in a virtual environment including relationship building, communication and co-working. Despite many advantages presented through the use of virtual collaborating teams, resistance against their deployment is still existing, because of their unique challenges, and the users' restrictions as many people still prefer face-to-face collaboration [13, 38]. Ultimately, success depends also on good management of the presented implications and a great knowledge of human nature that will improve the collaboration of team members in ESM which may trigger great potential. Our research agenda minding challenges, managerial implications, business impact and ultimately business value of ESM collaboration proposes a direction to release this potential.

6. REFERENCES

[1] Aral, S. et al. 2013. Social Media and Business Transformation: A Framework for Research. *Information Systems Research.* 24, 1 (Mar. 2013), 3–13.

[2] Baumard, P. 2002. Tacit knowledge in professional firms: the teachings of firms in very puzzling situations. *Journal of Knowledge Management.* 6, 2 (2002), 135–151.

[3] Beinhauer, M. 2010. Revolution 2.0 - Organizational Impact of Social Media on Society and Enterprises. *International Scientific Conference XI.* 7 (Mar. 2010), 10–14.

[4] Brake, T. 2006. Leading Global Virtual Teams. *Industrial and Commercial Training.* 38, 3 (2006), 116–121.

[5] Vom Brocke, J. et al. 2009. Reconstructing the Giant: On the Importance of Rigour in Documenting the Literature Search Process. *17th European Conference on Information Systems.* (2009), 2206–2217.

[6] Chui, M. et al. 2012. The Social Economy: Unlocking Value And Productivity Through Social Technologies. *McKinsey Global Institute.* July (2012), 1–18.

[7] Conklin, J. and Jeff Conklin 2005. Dialogue mapping: building shared undestading of wicked problems. *Dialogue Mapping: Building Shared Understanding of Wicked Problems.* John Wiley & Sons. 1–25.

[8] Cottone, P. et al. 2007. "Solving" ambiguity in the virtual space: communication strategies in a collaborative virtual environment. *Cognition, Technology & Work.* 11, 2 (2007), 151–163.

[9] Cottone, P. et al. 2009. "Solving" ambiguity in the virtual space: communication strategies in a collaborative virtual environment. *Cognition, Technology & Work.* 11, 2 (2009), 151–163.

[10] Cross, R. et al. 2010. How Organizational Network Analysis Facilitated Transition From Regional To A Global IT Function. *MIS Quarterly Executive.* 9, 3 (Sep. 2010), 133–145.

[11] David, G.C. et al. 2008. Integrated collaboration across distributed sites: the perils of process and the promise of practice. *Journal of Information Technology.* 23, 1 (2008), 44–54.

[13] Eckhardt, A. et al. 2015. The effect of personality on IT personnel's job-related attitudes: Establishing a dispositional model of turnover intention across IT job types. *Journal of Information Technology.* 31, 1 (2015), 48–66.

[14] Eom, M. 2009. Cross-cultural virtual team and its key antecedents to success. *The Journal of Applied Business and Economics.* 10, 1 (2009), 1–14.

[15] Fedorowicz, J. et al. 2008. Creativity, Innovation and E-Collaboration. *International Journal of e-Collaboration.* 4, 4 (2008), 1–11.

[16] Fruchter, R. et al. 2010. Tension between perceived collocation and actual geographic distribution in project teams. *Ai & Society.* 25, 2 (2010), 183–192.

[17] Garmestani, A.S. and Benson, M.H. 2013. A Framework for Resilience-based Governance of Social-Ecological. *Ecology and Society.* 18, 1 (2013).

[18] Gibson, C.B. et al. 2014. Where Global and Virtual Meet: The Value of Examining the Intersection of These Elements in Twenty-First-Century Teams. *Annual Review of Organizational Psychology and Organizational Behavior.* 1, 1 (2014), 217–244.

[19] Gibson, C.B. and Gibbs, J.L. 2006. Unpacking the Concept of Virtuality : on Team Innovation. *Administrative Science Quarterly.* 51, (2006), 451–495.

[20] Harper, F.M. et al. 2007. Social Comparisons to Motivate Contributions to an Online Community. *Persuasive Technology.* 4744, (2007), 148–159.

[21] Herbsleb, J.D. et al. 2002. Introducing Instant Messaging and Chat in the Workplace. *Proceedings of the Conference on Human Factors in Computing Systems (CHI'02).* (2002), 171–178.

[22] Ibarra, H. and Hansen, M.T. 2011. Are you a collaborative leader? *Harvard business review.* 89, 7-8 (2011).

[23] Kane, G.C. 2015. Enterprise Social Media: Current Capabilities and Future Possibilities. *MIS Quarterly Executive.* 14, 1 (Mar. 2015), 1–16.

[24] Kim, G. et al. 2011. IT Capabilities, Process-Oriented Dynamic Capabilities, and Firm Financial Performance. *Journal of the Association for Information Systems.* 12, 7 (Jul. 2011), 487–517.

[25] Kim, S. and Lee, H. 2006. The Impact of Organizational Context and Information Technology on Employee Knowledge-Sharing Capabilities. *Public Administration Review.* 66, 3 (May 2006), 370–385.

[26] Kirkman, B.L. et al. 2004. The Impact of Team Empowerment on Virtual Team Performance: The Moderating Role of Face-To-Face Interaction. *Academy of Management Journal.* 47, 2 (2004), 175–192.

[27] Kiron, D. et al. 2013. Social Business: Shifting Out of First Gear. *MIT Sloan Management Review.* (2013).

[28] Kotlarsky, J. and Oshri, I. 2005. Social ties, knowledge sharing and successful collaboration in globally distributed system development projects. *European Journal of Information Systems.* December 2004 (2005), 37–48.

[29] von Krogh, G. 2012. How does social software change knowledge management? Toward a strategic research agenda. *The Journal of Strategic Information Systems.* 21, 2 (2012), 154–164.

[30] Laumer, S. et al. 2015. User personality and resistance to mandatory information systems in organizations: a theoretical model and empirical test of dispositional resistance to change. *Journal of Information Technology.* (2015), 1–16.

[31] Laumer, S. et al. 2016. Work routines as an object of resistance during information systems implementations: Theoretical foundation and empirical evidence. *European Journal of Information Systems.* Forthcomin, (2016).

[32] Leonardi, P.M. et al. 2013. Enterprise Social Media: Definition, History, and Prospects for the Study of Social Technologies in Organizations. *Journal of Computer-Mediated Communication.* 19, 1 (2013), 1–19.

[33] Leonardi, P.M. 2014. Social Media, Knowledge Sharing, and Innovation: Toward a Theory of Communication Visibility. *Information Systems Research.* 25, 4 (Dec. 2014), 796–816.

[34] Leonardi, P.M. 2013. When does technology use enable network change in organizations? A comparative study of feature use and shared affordances. *MIS Quarterly*. 37, 3 (Sep. 2013), 749–775.

[35] Lombard, M. and Ditton, T. 1997. At the Heart of It All: The Concept of Presence. *Journal of Computer-Mediated Communication*. 3, 2 (1997), 0.

[36] Lowry, P.B. et al. 2013. Evaluating Journal Quality and the Association for Information Systems Senior Scholars' Journal Basket Via Bibliometric Measures: Do Expert Journal Assessments Add Value? *MIS Quarterly*. 37, 4 (2013), 993–1012.

[37] Maier, C. et al. 2015. The Effects of Technostress and Switching-Stress on Discontinued Use of Social Networking Services: A Study of Facebook Use. *Information Systems Journal*. 25, 3 (2015), 275–308.

[38] Maier, C. et al. 2015. Who really quits? A longitudinal analysis of voluntary turnover among IT personnel. *ACM SIGMIS Database*. 46, 4 (2015), 26–47.

[39] Nuyens, G. 2009. Advanced Collaboration Techniques for More Effective Management. *Public Manager*. 38, 3 (2009), 14–18.

[40] Osch, W. Van et al. 2015. Enterprise Social Media: Challenges and Opportunities for Organizational Communication and Collaboration. *48th Hawaii International Conference on System Sciences Enterprise* (2015), 763–772.

[41] Osch, W. Van 2012. The Duality of Social Media : Structuration and Socialization through Organizational Communication The Duality of Social Media : Structuration and Socialization through Organizational Communication. *Special Interest Group on Human-Computer Interaction* (2012), 1–6.

[42] Pyöriä, P. 2009. Virtual collaboration in knowledge work: from vision to reality. *Team Performance Management: An International Journal*. 15, 7/8 (2009), 366–381.

[43] Rashid, A.M. et al. 2006. Motivating participation by displaying the value of contribution. *ACM Conference on Human Factors in Computing Systems*. (2006), 955 – 958.

[44] Ray, D. 2014. Overcoming cross-cultural barriers to knowledge management using social media. *Journal of Enterprise Information Management*. 27, 1 (Feb. 2014), 45–55.

[45] Richter, D. et al. 2011. Internet Social Networking. *Business & Information Systems Engineering*. 3, 2 (2011), 89–101.

[46] Robert Lionel P., J. et al. 2008. Social Capital and Knowledge Integration in Digitally Enabled Teams. *Information Systems Research*. 19, 3 (Sep. 2008), 314–334.

[47] Roy, S. 2012. Virtual Collaboration: The Skills Needed to Collaborate in a Virtual Environment. *Journal of Internet Social Networking & Virtual Communities*. 2012, (2012), 1–8.

[48] Sarker, S. and Sahay, S. 2004. Implications of space and time for distributed work: an interpretive study of US–Norwegian systems development teams. *European Journal of Information Systems*. 13, 1 (2004), 3–20.

[49] Shachaf, P. 2005. Bridging cultural diversity through e-mail. *Journal of Global Information Technology Management*. 8, (2005), 46–60.

[50] Skeels, M.M. and Grudin, J. 2009. When Social Networks Cross Boundaries : A Case Study of Workplace Use of Facebook and LinkedIn. *Group*. 10, 3 (2009), 95–103.

[51] Smith, P.G. and Blanck, E.L. 2002. From experience: Leading dispersed teams. *Journal of Product Innovation Management*. 19, 4 (2002), 294–304.

[52] Subramaniam, N. et al. 2013. Exploring social network interactions in enterprise systems: the role of virtual co-presence. *Information Systems Journal*. 23, 6 (Nov. 2013), 475–499.

[53] Suduc, A.-M. et al. 2009. Exploring Multimedia Web Conferencing. *Informatica Economica*. 13, 3 (2009), 5–17.

[54] Torraco, R.J. 2005. Writing Integrative Literature Reviews: Guidelines and Examples. *Human Resource Development Review*. 4, 3 (2005), 356–367.

[55] Treem, J.W. and Leonardi, P.M. 2012. Communication Yearbook, 36 (2012). (2012).

[56] Volpe, C.E. et al. 1996. The impact of cross-training on team functioning: an empirical investigation. *Human factors*. 38, 1 (1996), 87–100.

[57] Webster, J. and Watsons, R.T. 2002. Analyzing the Past to Prepare for the Future: Writing a Literature Review. *MIS Quarterly*.

[58] Wenger, E.C. and Snyder, W.M. 2000. Communities of practice: The organizational frontier. *Harvard Business Review*. 78, (2000), 139–145.

[59] Yamauchi, Y. and Swanson, E.B. 2010. Local assimilation of an enterprise system: Situated learning by means of familiarity pockets. *Information and Organization*. 20, 3-4 (Jul. 2010), 187–206.

7. APPENDIX

Table 1. Considered Sources

Journal	Database	Search fields	Coverage	Hits	Analyzed
MIS Quarterly	Ebsco Host Premier	Abstract	1996 - 2015	9	0
Information Systems Research	Ebsco Host Premier	Abstract	1996 - 2015	12	1
Journal of Management Information Systems	Ebsco Host Premier	Abstract	1996 - 2015	5	0
Management Science	Ebsco Host Premier	Abstract	1996 - 2015	5	0
Communications of the ACM	Ebsco Host Premier	Abstract	1996 - 2015	19	1
Decision Sciences	Ebsco Host Premier	Abstract	1996 - 2015	2	0
Decision Support Systems	Ebsco Host Premier	Abstract	1996 - 2015	11	0
IEEE Transactions	Ebsco Host Premier	Abstract	1996 - 2015	0	0
Information and Management	Ebsco Host Premier	Abstract	1996 - 2015	0	0
ACM Transactions	Ebsco Host Premier	Abstract	1996 - 2015	0	0
European Journal of Information Systems	Ebsco Host Premier	Abstract	1996 - 2015	0	1
Journal of the Association Information Systems	Ebsco Host Premier	Abstract	1996 - 2015	5	0
Information Systems Journal	Ebsco Host Premier	Abstract	1996 - 2015	9	1
Organization Science	Ebsco Host Premier	Abstract	1996 - 2015	33	0
Harvard Business Review	Ebsco Host Premier	Abstract	1996 - 2015	3	2
Journal on Computing	Ebsco Host Premier	Abstract	1996 - 2015	0	0
Operations Research	Ebsco Host Premier	Abstract	1996 - 2015	0	0
Journal of Strategic Information Systems	Ebsco Host Premier	Abstract	1996 - 2015	0	0
Journal of Information Systems	Ebsco Host Premier	Abstract	1996 - 2015	3	0
Info and Organization	Ebsco Host Premier	Abstract	1996 - 2015	0	1
Information Systems	Ebsco Host Premier	Abstract	1996 - 2015	0	0
IEEE Transactions on Software Engineering	Ebsco Host Premier	Abstract	1996 - 2015	0	0
Journal of Computer Information Systems	Ebsco Host Premier	Abstract	1996 - 2015	6	0
Business & Information Systems Engineering	Ebsco Host Premier	Abstract	1996 - 2015	0	0
IEEE Computer	Ebsco Host Premier	Abstract	1996 - 2015	0	0
Journal of Information Technology	Ebsco Host Premier	Abstract	1996 - 2015	5	1
MIS Quarterly Executive	Ebsco Host Premier	Abstract	1996 - 2015	11	2

Table 2. Challenges of ESM collaboration

Dimensions of Challenges	Challenge	Peculiarities	Source
Team	Complexity	The probability of misinterpreting e-mail messages might increase, since there is a lack of supportive information represented through language, cultural, contextual and time-zone barriers.	[8]
		Diverted attention and personality differences of the team members jeopardizes concentration amongst the team members.	[16]
		Virtual communication increases the cognitive load on a teams' members, because they need to process the information they receive, and then type their replies when using Social Media. In addition to this, the use of chats intensifies the likelihood of conversations on different topics concurrently.	[46]
	Cultural Diversity	It is claimed that homogeneous teams interact more effectively than heterogeneous, because of sharing a common language, already established relations, and a common background.	[7]
	Distance	Cultural differences (e.g. languages, morals, working and communication styles that are included in collective knowledge of a culture) increase the further a distance grows, and consequently may gain misunderstandings and conflicts.	[2]
		Different time zones complicate simultaneous collaboration, as response time increases significantly when office hours at distant locations do not or only partially overlap.	[48]
		Distance reduces the depth of communications the further it increases, especially if team members are exposed to issues, such as misunderstandings in Social Media, which cannot comprehensively replace face-to-face communication.	[51]
	Face-to-Face Meetings	Collaborative technologies cannot fully replace face-to-face communications.	[4]
		Technological issues, i.e. the amount of time it takes members to type messages in instant messaging, may be neglected in face-to-face.	[9]
		The success of VCTs is subject to the capability of crossing physical and cultural differences which implies more conflict potential in VCTs than in face-to-face teams as it is harder to establish common ground within the team.	[15]
		Different access to technologies/infrastructure or the need for the same technological platform can result in ceasing participating in the collaborative process, because of lacking motivation.	[16]
		The likely incapability of some team members becoming uncomfortable working on Social Media Platforms, the intricacy of knowledge sharing, and the lack of non-verbalism results in barriers that may not occur in face-to-face meetings.	[46]
Organizational	Inefficiencies	Social Media appears to be the undermining of efficient coordination and collaboration. The structure of interpersonal connections and a relatively chaotic environment in which information is stored and retrieved may be accountable for that.	[40]
	Introversion	There is a clear necessity to explore strategies for encouraging introverted employees in participating strongly in ESM.	[20, 43]
	IT Governance	External Social Media activities direct to risk management and managing public channels which are crucial for brand identity and preventing public relations crises. Whereas internal governance of ESM needs to be more supportive and nurturing rather than controlling and managing.	[17]
	Natural growth	Although firms are organized around project teams, ESM tends to form itself around communities. These communities seem to be naturally evolving as dynamic units with variable levels of professionalism and privacy. Such communities are organized internally and grow naturally rather than being controlled and managed externally. This is due to common interests or activities, rather than simply being project-oriented.	[58]
	Neglecting	Another challenge of ESM for individuals within the organization might be that their perceived information represents the entire organization. In that manner, certain people, sites, or cultures might be less perceptible as they are more reserved in ESM participation. Which may lead to isolated entities, whereas central locations may be focused stronger by the whole organization's work-force.	[24]

Table 3. Determinants of ESM collaboration

Determinant Group	Determinant	Findings and recommendations	References
Relationship	Context	The VCT must institute a shared context that coalesces the diverse members and increases their willingness to accept feedback, constructive criticism, and to share information which can be achieved through the creation of a set of team morals.	[22]
	Diversity	More diversity helps leads to better decisions by preying the knowledge, skills, abilities, mindsets, and cultural perspectives of each individual.	[4]
		Virtual teams are mostly independent from temporal and geographic dimension, thus they allow greater diversity than face-to-face teams, at least on a cheaper budget.	[4, 42]
		It requires less efforts to collate qualified team potentials using Social Media than creating a similar diverse team in a face-to-face environment.	[11, 42]
	Environment	To further foster the relationship building process, a team must implement an environment that promotes open communication and motivates its members to take part in active discussion.	[4]
	Familiarity	A team must begin with the process of familiarization by getting to know the cultural matrix.	[14]
		Familiarity helps to diminish the potential cultural conflicts which might otherwise impede the success of the team. Through familiarity an all-encompassing objective that unites the members of a VCT can be created.	[14]
		Also geographic situations, knowledge, skills, and abilities of each member must be familiar.	[46]
	Trust	Trust is the key characteristic in the collaborative efforts of a team. It serves as the fundamental basis for strong team cohesion and qualifies a team to mutually pay respect, endorse diversity, exchange information, and to communicate openly with each other.	[4, 14]
Communication	Ambiguity	Ambiguity will always remain, because of the lack of non-verbal communication. To approach this ambiguity, teams can replace their Social Media platform.	[46]
	Knowledge Sharing	A trustful, conflict-free and cohesive environment will facilitate information exchange between team members which can even be supplemented by the values of understanding, being openly communicative, and being supportive of ideas.	[4, 14]
		The sharing of knowledge qualifies teams that collaborate on ESM to critically debate issues, brainstorm, transform; plus to share ideas, experiences and opinions.	[15, 42]
	Simple Language	A team needs to establish a simple language which implies that the whole team uses the same definitions for the same terms to prevent potential misunderstandings or misinterpretations.	[11]
		Social Media that works with asynchronous communication, like wikis or forums, might result in more sophisticated messages than those being formulated by synchronous communication as employees have more time to consider what to express.	[53]
Participation	Adaptability	Virtual teams need to remain focused towards altering goals and deliverables.	[4]
		As the average product life cycle in the IT industry is six months, the fast-pace of global business processes and strong competition requires virtual teams to adapt their focus rapidly.	[4]
		Members need to adapt regularly to varying collaborative technologies.	[46]
	Autonomy & Delegation	The virtual team needs to determine the level of autonomy for each member, but also guidelines for reasonable delegation.	[4, 14]
		Due to its diversity, each team member requires a different level of autonomy and the team leader needs to take responsibility for delegating tasks equally, while paying mind to the skills of each team member.	[16]
	Innovation	Virtual teams need to develop a culture that is beneficial to collaboration and extracts the knowledge, skills, abilities, and cultural perspectives of their members to increase innovation.	[4]
		Due to their diversity, virtual teams form a supportive environment for innovation which can lead to a competitive advantage for organizations.	[22]
		For the purpose of debating multiple approaches to an issue a common language must be found. The team must be on the same level cognitively and mentally and the communication lines must stay open.	[46]
	Motivation	Maintaining motivation is essential for virtual teams, because of the high probability for team members to become frustrated. Thus, it is the obligation of the team leader to endorse each member and to understand the impact that each individual can have to the team.	[4, 39]

Table 4. Managerial Implications for ESM collaboration

Recipient	Implication	Findings	Resources
Team leader	Choice of Communication Channel	Negative aspects of cultural diversity can be mitigated when team leaders choose the right communication channels for certain issues. Some patterns of cultural exchange are more accentuated when using certain platforms (e.g. distortion of pronunciations in video conferences), while others might be neglected (e.g. non-verbalism in email)	[18, 23, 49]
	Communication Environment	Team leaders should create a comfortable communication environment by regularly asking members for their input, being permanently amenable and discussing a member's issues in a constructive atmosphere.	[19]
	Face-to-Face Activities	Face-to-face meetings or team-building events besides the virtual collaboration are recommended for diverse teams at the beginning of the collaboration and periodically during teamwork. Face-to-face activities support team empowerment by cementing relationships, improving processes and building awareness among themselves.	[4, 10, 26, 35]
	Management Practices, Promotion and Commitment	Team leaders cannnot assume that all team members participate in the network right from the beginning. They have to actively encourage the members and promote the network for their commitment.	[25, 52]
	Seizure of Recognition	Especially in diverse teams, leaders need to ensure that all members recognize the background, objectives, responsibilities, and challenges of their partners. Hence, leaders should use multiple approaches to ascertain diversity, and they should be aware of potential problems by evaluating members' morals and high-lighting likely areas of tension.	[56]
	Team Identity	Team leaders need to emphasize the development of a team identity which fosters trust, mutual respect and allegiance within the group. This can be enhanced by providing the possibility for employees to use various communication platforms in their virtual teams	[4]
Team members	Information Sharing	Team members should also publish some personal information (e.g. biographical information or pictures) on the platform to show "the human being" behind the virtual representation.	[14]
Network	Transparency and Visualization	Network transparency – the ability to visualize the entire social network and one's place in it - is a key capability provided by social media platforms. To ensure this, networks need to offer a variety of features, e.g. connections with other users or illustration of relationships.	[23]

Table 5. ESM's Business Impact

Dimension	Impact	Peculiarities	Resources
Information / Knowledge	Knowledge Provision, Exchange and Combination	ESM networks collect information provided by employees, connect them and transform it into organizational knowledge that can be used by everyone in the system.	[3, 23, 44, 52]
	Knowledge Visibility and Transparency	Employees may benefit from the connected knowledge. Furthermore, everyone knows "who knows what" meaning the network shows who is a contact person for a special issue. This also helps to reduce silo effects.	[3, 10, 33]
Interaction	Loss of Hierarchies	Hierarchal boundaries (horizontal and vertical) blur in social networks within the organization. It is less important which job position an employee has or how much power for directions someone has. Everyone can interact with everyone, even the CEO and a shift worker.	[3]
	New Routines	Employees learn new ways to interact with each other in their daily routine	[52, 59]

Making Black Lives Matter in the Information Technology Profession

Eileen Trauth
Pennsylvania State University
330C IST Building
University Park, PA 16802
1.814.865.6457
etrauth@ist.psu.edu

K.D. Joshi
Washington State University
Todd 437J
Pullman, WA 99164
1.509.335.5722
joshi@wsu.edu

Lynette Kvasny
Pennsylvania State University
329C IST Building
University Park, PA 16802
1.814.865.6458
lyarger@ist.psu.edu

Allison J. Morgan
Howard University
2600 Sixth St., N.W., Rm. 448
Washington D.C. 20059
1.202-806-1605
aj_morgan@howard.edu

Fay Cobb Payton
North Carolina State University
Campus Box 7229
Raleigh, NC 27695
1.919.513.2744
fay_payton@ncsu.edu

ABSTRACT

The phrase "social change is a beautiful thing," appeared in a tweet from a student during demonstrations at the University of Missouri in November 2015. The events that motivated this tweet point to the work that still needs to occur to bring greater racial equality to American society. In this regard, a question for IT professionals, both academics and practitioners, is: "What can the SIGMIS CPR community do to foster greater inclusion of underrepresented racial and ethnic groups into our profession?" These panelists provide some answers to this question by discussing their research and interventions to diversify the IT field and promote greater racial and ethnic representation within it.

Keywords

African American men; Career choice; Digital Divide; Diversity; Ethnicity; Inequality; IT workforce; Race

1. PANEL DESCRIPTION

Eileen Trauth moderates the panel and discusses the results of an empirical study of the influence of gender-ethnic intersectionality on gender stereotypes about the IT profession. Analysis of survey responses from over 4000 contemporary American university students reveals significant within-gender differences, based on race and ethnicity, in gender stereotypes of the IT field. These findings suggest promising avenues for interventions to address not only the masculine gender stereotyping of skills in the IT profession, but also differential gender stereotyping of technical vs. nontechnical skills and variation in gender stereotyping by the intersectionality of gender-ethnic groups. She also discusses two other studies which address underrepresentation in the IT field: military service members with disabilities and theatre as an intervention to address stereotypes about the IT field.

SIGMIS-CPR '16, June 2-4, 2016, Alexandria, VA, USA.
ACM 978-1-4503-4203-2/16/06.
http://dx.doi.org/10.1145/2890602.2890617

K.D. Joshi describes the use of Bourdieu's framework to investigate how Black men succeed in IT careers by accumulating the following five forms of capital— Cultural, Social, Symbolic, Technical, and Economic. The accumulated capital affects Black men's IT career choices both positively and negatively. In addition, she talks about the effects of "Being a Black Man" in IT, i.e., the negative experiences (such as frequent encounters with police, pressures of belonging to a gang, and dealing with the expectations of hegemonic Black masculinity), as well as positive experiences (such as more opportunities because of their underrepresentation in IT, and being viewed as competent because of low academic expectations), which have much broader implications (beyond IT careers).

Lynette Kvasny and Fay Cobb Payton use the intersectionality framework proposed by Crenshaw and social media content to inform a talk on how Black faculty and college students cope with their intersectional experiences of race/ethnicity and gender inequality. Current events discussed in both mass and social media indicate that Black students and faculty continuously experience racial tensions on college campuses. The emerging social movements around the hashtag #BlacksLivesMatter and the tweet "social change is a beautiful thing" clearly articulate the need for social and structural changes at predominantly white institutions. They discuss the impacts of these movements relative to faculty and students in IT disciplines because the stress of "racial battle fatigue" can be compounded for Black students in majors where they are woefully underrepresented and where there are few Black faculty mentors present.

Allison Morgan discusses the role of historically Black colleges and universities (HBCU's) in addressing the underrepresentation of minorities in STEM and producing top talent in multiple technical areas. HBCU's are valuable in not only educating technical professionals, they are also a vehicle to bring awareness to the importance of Black issues in relation to technology and key to spearheading discussion about 'Black Lives Matter' in all areas of the educational process. Lastly, she talks about the need and the value for a diversity of people in the development of IT processes (such a search).

2. PANELISTS

Dr. Eileen Trauth is Professor of Information Sciences & Technology, and Women's, Gender & Sexuality Studies at The Pennsylvania State University. Her research is concerned with societal, cultural and organizational influences on the information technology professions with a special focus on gender and social inclusion. Dr. Trauth has lectured about and investigated issues of gender underrepresentation in the information technology professions in Europe, Africa and the Asia Pacific, and throughout the United States. She is currently studying the intersectionality of gender and identity characteristics such as ethnicity, socio-economic class, sexuality, nationality and disability status. Dr. Trauth is editor of *Information Systems Journal,* the *Encyclopedia of Gender and Information Technology,* and two conference proceedings on diversity and social inclusion. She is the recipient of the 2008 Universität Klagenfurt (Austria) – Fulbright Distinguished Chair in Gender Studies, and serves on the advisory board for the European Union project, *Female Empowerment in Science & Technology Academia (FESTA).* With funding from the National Science Foundation, she has written a play, *iDream* (iDreamThePlay.com), based on her interviews with women in the information technology field, as a way to increase awareness about gender barriers in the scientific and technological professions.

Dr. K. D. Joshi is the Philip L. Kays Distinguished Professor of Information Systems at Washington State University. She received her Master of Science in Engineering from the University of Michigan and received her Doctor of Philosophy in Business Administration from the University of Kentucky. Dr. Joshi's research interests focus on IT Workforce, Knowledge Management, Crowdsourcing, IT-Enabled Innovation, Value Sensitive Designs, and Health IT. Her published research is cited over 3,500 times (h-index: 22; i10-index: 35). She has received multiple research grants worth $1.93M from the National Science Foundation that focus on social inclusion by broadening the participation and representation of women and minorities in STEM disciplines. She was also a Co-Principle Investigator on the Institutional Transformation Grant worth $3.75M which Washington State University received from NSF to advance women in STEM disciplines. Her research has appeared in journals such as *Information Systems Research, MIS Quarterly, Decision Support Systems, IEEE TEM, and Communications of the ACM.* Dr. Joshi is currently a Senior Editor of the *Information Systems Journal* and *Information Systems Management* journal. She is a Special Section Editor for Social Inclusion and IS at the *DATABASE* Journal. She is an Associate Editor of the *Communications of the AIS* and *Journal of Organizational Computing and Electronic Commerce.*

Dr. Lynette Kvasny is an Associate Professor in the College of Information Sciences and Technology. She earned her Ph.D. in Computer Information Systems from the Robinson College of Business at Georgia State University. Her research focuses on how and why historically underserved groups use information and communication technologies. She has designed, implemented and assessed community computing projects in economically challenged neighborhoods in Atlanta, West Philadelphia, and Harrisburg. She is also a co-founder of the social network experience that focuses on health and social media interventions for African American collegians: MyHealthImpactNetwork. Her current research examines the performance of racial and gender identities in the construction of social media content by African American teens and young adults, and the IT career pathways of African American males. Dr. Kvasny's research has been supported by the National Science Foundation (including the prestigious Career Award), the Oracle Help Us Help Foundation, AmeriCorps VISTA, the Penn State Children, Youth and Family Consortium, and the Penn State Africana Research Center.

Dr. Allison J. Morgan is an Associate Professor of Information Systems and Supply Chain Management and the Director of Special Programs at the Howard University School of Business. She received her Ph.D. in Information Sciences and Technology from The Pennsylvania State University and a B.B.A. in Computer Based Information Systems from Howard University. She is one of only 50 African American Female Information Systems Business School Professors in the United States. Her research focuses on online health information, human information searching behavior, diversity of the information technology workforce, and the socio-cultural impact of technology. She has published articles on the impact of individual differences on user behavior, diversity in the global workplace, information searching behavior, and gender and information technology with specific focus on social networks and work-life balance among women. She has received grants from Facebook, The National Science Foundation, and the GM Foundation. She has a true passion for teaching and for students, and loves nothing more than to be in the classroom. She was formerly employed as a consultant at Accenture and as a Usability Engineer at the United States Census Bureau. She is a member of the Ph.D. Project, Association for Information Systems (AIS), and the Golden Key National Honor Society.

Dr. Fay Cobb Payton is Professor of Information Systems/Technology in the Poole College of Management at North Carolina State University. With support from the National Science Foundation, she founded and directs MyHealthImpactNetwork, a social network focusing on health and social media interventions. @MyHealthImpact gives "voice" to millennials about sexual and mental health, culture, and technology. She authored *Leveraging Intersectionality: Seeing and Not Seeing,* an anthology of research on STEM education in academe and corporate environments. Dr. Payton is an editor of *Health Systems,* and Associate Editor of *Decision Sciences* and *Information Technology & People.* She is a member of the NC State University Women in Science and Engineering Advisory Board. She received the National Coalition of Women in Information Technology Undergraduate Mentoring Award. As an American Council on Education (ACE) Fellow, she shadowed over 30 national and international academic leaders to understand the educational models of research, outreach and technology innovation, and worked on issues of academic review, interdisciplinary graduate research and education, and institutional economic and community impact. She worked in engineering, consulting and corporate IT at International Business Machines, Ernst & Young/CAP Gemini and Time Inc. before joining the academy. Her research has been supported by the National Science Foundation, National Institutes of Health, KPMG Foundation, NC State University, NC State University Foundation and AT&T.

Evaluating Effective Use of Social Networks for Recruitment

Malmi Amadoru
Department of Computer Science & Engineering
University of Moratuwa
Sri Lanka
amadoru.ms@gmail.com

Chandana Gamage
Department of Computer Science & Engineering
University of Moratuwa
Sri Lanka
chandag@cse.mrt.ac.lk

ABSTRACT

Social media applications and services have become popular over the years and organizations are increasingly exploiting social media related services in business functions. Human resource recruiting is one such function, which has stepped into a new era of social recruitments. Talent sourcing plays a major role in any organization as recruiting competent people with right skills for right positions leads organizations to achieve their vision, mission, and objectives. Therefore, it is important for organizations to adopt innovative recruitment techniques. As organizations are increasingly exploiting social networks for recruitment, it is important to research and evaluate how useful social networks are as a recruitment tool and how it can be used effectively. The main objective of this study was to evaluate social networks as a recruitment tool for HR professionals and identify effective uses of social networks for recruitments. The research shows that process efficiency, reachability and passive talent attraction can be identified as effective uses of social networks for recruitment.

Keywords

Social networks, recruitment, HR professionals, LinkedIn, IT industry

1. INTRODUCTION

Human resources recruiting have been evolving over the years shifting from traditional methods to online schemes to social recruiting. The traditional methods mostly involved recruiting via succession planning, existing contacts, external contacts and print media advertising. With the proliferation of online activities, online recruiting methods such as company websites, job listing sites, digital media advertising have become popular. As web based applications proliferated, online recruiting also changed and human resource recruiting stepped into a new era of social recruiting. In contrast to traditional methods, social media assisted methods enable recruiters to observe candidate's online activities

SIGMIS-CPR '16, June 02-04, 2016, Alexandria, VA, USA

© 2016 ACM. ISBN 978-1-4503-4203-2/16/06. . . $15.00

DOI: http://dx.doi.org/10.1145/2890602.2890604

openly and repeatedly. As organizations acquire a greater online competency, it results in a reputation as a special place to work and enables the company to build new relationships with potential future candidates [15, 16]. The social media sites that provide this capability to companies cover a wide spectrum of users ranging from a general audience (Facebook) to largely unclassified professionals (LinkedIn) to IT experts (Stack Overflow).

Research has shown that finding talent is becoming more difficult even in larger markets, as the overall demand tends to remain high [10, 14]. An example is the SF Bay Area that has the largest talent population of approximately 480,000 software engineers in United States but with a significant difficulty in sourcing top talent as per the 2012 LinkedIn Talent Pool report [14]. Ability to acquire talent can be categorized into three broad categories: *Saturated, Hidden Gems* and *High-Demand*. Hidden Gems are mid-sized markets with lower demand whereas Saturated are small to mid-sized markets with very high demand. High-Demand markets are the largest markets with very high demand. It was reported that hiring is difficult in both Saturated and High-Demand markets. Thus, mastering innovative methods of recruitment remain a priority for HR professionals.

Due to the difficulty in acquiring right talent in an era where hiring volumes tend to surpass hiring budget, companies need to revisit their recruitment strategy by adopting more innovative and advanced recruitment techniques [7]. Increasingly, recruiters are relying on social media for talent acquisition. As per the findings from Jobvite, 73% of recruiters have hired a candidate through social media in 2014 [10]. Among various social networks, LinkedIn is the leading professional network for hiring talent.

Although HR professionals use social networks in recruitment activities, they lack mechanism to evaluate how effectively they use social networks in the recruitment process [4]. It is important for HR professionals to know how they can utilize social recruiting methods, because vast majority of HR professionals do not feel that they are using it effectively. This is evident in industry studies such as the survey done by Jobvite, which shows that only 18% of recruiters consider themselves experts at social recruiting [10]. Therefore, present study was conducted with the stated research objectives of identifying effective uses of social networking tools for HR professionals for talent attraction and selection activities of recruitment process and building a framework to evaluate social networking tools as a recruitment tool. To address the stated research objectives, following research question was formed.

How effective is the use of social networks in attraction and selection activities of recruitment process for HR Professionals?

LinkedIn is a widely used social network having hundreds of million members among various social recruiting sources [10, 13]. It is a tool to help HR professionals to find, engage, and hire highly competent candidates [13]. It also acts as a channel for marketers to engage and interact with world's best professionals. Therefore, LinkedIn was chosen as the social networking tool for the present study and research framework was validated using a case study done on recruitment of Sri Lankan IT professionals.

2. RELATED WORK

Recruiting is considered a complex process as both recruiters and candidates are highly complex individuals who act in numerous different patterns [19]. The virtual presence of professionals and networking among professionals has created the foundation for organizations to leverage social media based recruitment over traditional methods. Therefore, with wider usability and accessibility of major social media sites such as Facebook, Twitter, LinkedIn and YouTube, social networking has become more powerful and more attractive and it has lead social networking into new levels of applications. Thus, it has become the norm for organizations to seek information from social media sites to study candidate profiles.

Social recruiting is defined by Meister and Willyerd [16] as a practice that leverages social and professional networks, both online and offline, from both a candidate's perspective and the hiring side to connect, communicate with, engage, inform, and attract future talent. Professional networking sites enable individuals to track and publish their career paths, skills and experiences in a more accessible way. Unlike traditional resumes, a profile listed in a professional social networking site can be verified effectively and easily. Social media sites enable the traditional referencing mechanism into digital means and it has become an easier approach to appraise individuals. However, candidates and recruiters should also be aware of the leniency bias of online recommendations [4].

Online recruiting methods offer various benefits to HR professionals over traditional methods. It is generally accepted that traditional recruiting methods consume longer processing time and higher hiring costs compared to newer online methods. Studies done by Chapman and Webster [5], Doherty [6], Galanaki [8], Gale [9], Iee [12], Miller [17], Munger [18], Reger [20] and Tomlinson [22] have shown online methods provide cost effectiveness, process efficiency, access to wider audience, quicker response time, ease of use, access to specialized skills, company reputation enhancement, and attraction of passive candidates compared to traditional methods as stated in Table 1. Cost saving is achieved mainly due to lesser manual intervention and paper based advertising. Shorter recruiting cycles, frequent cycles, lesser human intervention, and better control lead to process efficiency when using online methods. In spite of the advantages offered by online methods, it also offers set of disadvantages such as potential for greater amount of low quality information [5, 8, 20], overload of resumes etc. Digital identity is another challenge in using online recruiting methods. It is harder to build a level of trust with a candidate only by interacting with that person online. Therefore, level of

personal touch is another concern that creates a challenge in getting candidates of person-fit-organization. Thus, the decision for an organization to adopt e-recruiting is primarily evaluated based on these factors.

The major metrics used for measuring e-recruiting performance by leading companies in terms of efficiency and effectiveness are categorized by Munger [18] into three levels; strategic, operational and functional. Strategic level metrics include number of online applicants, ratio of qualified applicants, aggregate profile of online applicants, time to hire, quality of online job information, satisfaction level of job applicants and recruiters with the e-recruiting system, and number of passive job seekers. Operational metrics include efficiency of various phases of e-recruiting process, tool utilization rate, number of page views, click-through rate, time-to-access a company career website, time-to-search jobs, and quantity of online job information. Cost per hire, system acquisition cost, website operating expense, and cost savings in recruiting are considered as functional level metrics.

As this research used a case study on IT professionals for validating research results, prior work specific to IT profession was also reviewed. Setting itself apart from other professions, IT profession possesses some unique characteristics such as rapid changes in technology that makes skill sets to be obsolete in short cycles, periodic labour market fluctuations and increase in outsourcing opportunities [2]. As per a study done by Agarwal and Ferratt [2], successful recruitment methods for sourcing IT professionals include college relationships, recruitment firms, contractors, Internet, employee referrals, job fairs, co-ops, interns, social minority, women sourcing and networking at professional events. These issues need to be considered in the development of an evaluation framework for using social media for recruitment.

LinkedIn, which is a widely used social networking tool, was chosen as the recruitment tool for the case study of this research. As provided in its main site, the value proposition of LinkedIn includes: *Identity, Insights* and *Everywhere*. Some of the benefits HR professionals can gain using LinkedIn business solution are attracting both passive and active talent, advertising job positions, locating specialized skill, enhancing company brand and acquiring deeper information about candidates. However, some of the inherent limitations of an open platform like LinkedIn are its inability to validate information, privacy risks due to disclosure of personal data and partial control over connections [11, 20].

3. HYPOTHESIS DEVELOPMENT

Although HR professionals use various social networking tools in recruitment process to acquire talent, there is no standard mechanism to evaluate whether they are exploiting it in the best suitable way [4]. Thus, this research was conducted to answer the question of how effective is the use of social networks in attraction and selection activities of recruitment process for HR professionals.

The key factors relating to HR professionals' expectations in the overall recruitment process to obtain an advantage over rivals in acquiring talent were identified through a study of literature presented in the previous section. Thereafter, the identified factors were used to evaluate the effective uses of social networks in recruitment process. The set of factors identified includes level of passive talent attraction, level of active talent attraction, level of reachability, level of company image enhancement, level of niche market targeting,

Table 1: Factors for adopting online recruiting methods over traditional methods

Process Efficiency	Chapman and Webster [5], Doherty [6], Galanaki [8], Gale [9], Iee [12], Miller [17], Reger [20], Tomlinson [22]
Reachability	Chapman and Webster [5], Galanaki [8], Iee [12], Munger [18], Reger [20]
Company Image Enhancement	Chapman and Webster [5], Galanaki [8]
Passive Talent Attraction	Galanaki [8], Reger [20]
Niche Market Target	Galanaki [8], Iee [12], Reger [20]
Quality of Information	Chapman and Webster [5], Galanaki [8], Reger [20]

level of recruitment efficiency and level of quality of information. Six hypotheses were developed based on identified factors to evaluate effective uses of social networks.

Previous studies have shown that improving the efficiency of recruitment process is very crucial, because the delays in hiring result in early applicant withdrawal from the selection process [5, 12] amid the high competition for talent. One of the potential benefits of increased efficiency is to shorten hiring cycles, and being more responsive to applicants while competing with other organizations for the best applicant to hire as early as possible [5, 8, 9, 17]. Other benefits include the ability to increase frequency of recruitment cycles and a higher level of control over the recruitment process [5, 6, 8, 9, 17, 20, 22]. Hence, based on a careful review of previous literature, following hypothesis was developed.

H_A denotes the alternate hypothesis.

$H1_A$: The use of social networks in recruitment process and the level of process efficiency improvement are strongly positively correlated.

Regardless of geographical setting, organizations are looking for the best talent to be successful in a competitive global marketplace [5, 12]. Thus, it is important to reach a large pool of potential job seekers. As reachability is considered a main factor when choosing a particular method for attracting candidates during the recruitment process, following hypothesis was developed.

$H2_A$: The use of social networks in recruitment process and the level of reachability achieved are strongly positively correlated.

Previous studies have shown that one of the objectives of adopting online recruiting is to promote organizational image [5, 8] and earn improved reputation in the industry. While locating desired candidates, it enables expanding the company image and making it up-to-date. Hence, following hypothesis was formed.

$H3_A$: The use of social networks in recruitment process and the level of company image enhancement are strongly positively correlated.

It is required to attract and locate specialized skills for some professions such as engineering, programming etc [12]. HR professionals seek for opportunities to address specific labor market niches, because such skilled resources are not common and such talent is not readily available. Online recruiting methods allow locating community of professionals and gatherings of passive job seekers [8, 20]. Targeting niche skills and attracting passive job seekers are important in in-

dustries such as IT due to the vast number of expertise areas. Hence, following two hypotheses were developed based on the two factors, accessing specific niche and attracting passive talent.

$H4_A$: The use of social networks in recruitment process and the capability of targeting niche markets are strongly positively correlated.

$H5_A$: The use of social networks in recruitment process and the level of passive talent attraction achieved are strongly positively correlated.

Through the previous literature, it was found that HR professionals are concerned on quality of information due to the increase in quantity of applications via online recruitment methods [5, 8]. Furthermore, accuracy and validity of information affects the trustworthiness of recruiting mechanism. Thus, based on previous work, following hypothesis was developed.

$H6_A$: The use of social networks in recruitment process and the quality of information achieved are strongly positively correlated.

4. METHODOLOGY

The conceptual framework developed for this study based on factors extracted from literature is illustrated in Figure 1. In this framework, effective use of social networks for recruitment by HR professionals is the main dependent variable, which was the primary interest of this research. The six independent variables that are process efficiency, passive talent attraction, reachability, company image enhancement, niche market target and quality of information were extracted directly from the factors identified through previous literature. Six hypotheses were developed based on the theoretical framework to find out the relationship between the effective use of social networks for recruitment and the six identified factors.

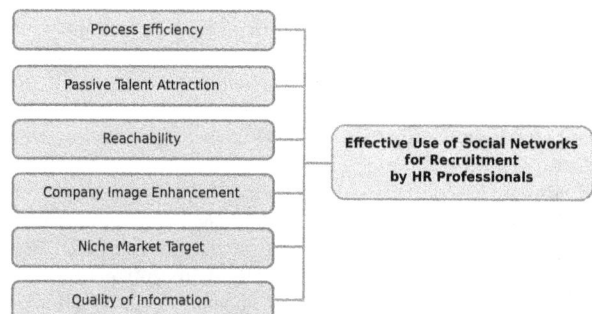

Figure 1: The Proposed Conceptual Framework

Measurements for each variable were identified through previous literature and the measurement devices (i.e. the questionnaire and interviews) were designed to record data along these measures. All the questionnaire items relating to each measure were designed based on five-point Likert Scale, whereas the interview questions relating to these measures were designed as semi-structured questions.

Among the measurements for **process efficiency** of recruitment activities, shorter recruiting cycle is considered in the literature as one of the most important attributes [5, 8, 9, 12, 17]. Other measurements include frequency of cycles and the level of control on the recruitment process [5, 6, 8, 9, 12, 17, 20, 22]. Therefore, this research adopted cycle length, recruitment cycle frequency, and level of control over recruitment process as dimensions of process efficiency.

Reachability is defined as the level of accessibility offered for applicants and this ability to cover a wide range of applicants is considered as a significant factor in social media based recruiting [5, 8, 18, 20]. Hence, questionnaire items relating to the coverage of applicants were included as the measure for reachability in measurement devices.

Company image enhancement is measured through the level of reputation increase [5, 8]. Therefore, questionnaire items relating to the level of company brand improvement were included as the measure for company image enhancement.

Niche market target is defined as the capability of locating a specialized skill set. The ability to target specialized professionals is one of the reasons why companies are moving more towards social recruiting [8, 12, 20]. Hence, niche market target is measured through level of locating specialized skill.

Passive talent attraction is defined as attracting highly competent passive job seekers who are not interested in job search. However, locating passive talent is important in gaining competitive advantage from expertise skills [8, 20]. Hence, questionnaire items relating to the level of attracting and locating passive talent were included as the measures in the measurement devices.

It is important to measure the **quality of information** aspect of social recruiting [5, 8, 20], because lower quality of information leads to dissatisfaction and loss of trust towards any system. Overload of information such as receiving high number of resumes and incomplete information affects the quality of information. Therefore, quality of information is measured through the two dimensions, which are quantity of applications and level of information richness.

Among widely used social networks, LinkedIn was chosen as the social networking tool for the present study in validating the proposed conceptual framework. Therefore, dimensions of **effective use of social networks for recruitment by HR professionals** were drawn mainly analyzing the features provided by LinkedIn and based on its benefits and drawbacks to HR professionals. Hence, the dependent variable includes six dimensions, which are passive talent attraction, active talent attraction, preserving candidate pool, specific niche targeting, recruitment efficiency and company expectation fulfillment.

This study has been conducted using both quantitative and qualitative approaches to gain a deeper insight on how HR professionals use social networks in recruitment activities. Quantitative approach was chosen to reach a larger sample to gather data on well-understood factors while qual-

itative approach was chosen to gather detailed data on HR practices and social media use that required greater elaboration. Furthermore, qualitative approach was chosen to cross validate the findings of quantitative approach, as this is an emerging research area that lacks a comprehensive trove of literature.

The quantitative research work was assisted with a structured questionnaire whereas qualitative work was assisted by semi-structured interviews. Both demographic and inferential questions were included in the structured questionnaire covering all the variables. The type of survey questions were closed end and are mostly based on five-point Likert Scale. The semi-structured interview questions were designed to capture data on variables as well as data on social networks in various aspects such as to which extent software companies use LinkedIn, the most popular features used, and the encountered drawbacks. The data collected through interviews were used to verify the consistency of data gathered via questionnaire as social media usage for recruitment is still emerging.

Recruitment of Sri Lankan IT professionals was chosen as the case study to validate above developed hypotheses. Therefore, HR professionals who are responsible mainly for recruiting software engineers in software organizations in Sri Lanka were chosen as the population. To broaden the population for the data collection, as many software organizations as possible were approached to obtain a representative sample.

5. ANALYSIS AND RESUTLS

An online questionnaire was used as the research instrument and was sent to HR professionals of 60 software companies in Sri Lanka, which included both software product and software service companies. The data collection process was conducted throughout a one-month period and more responses were received at the beginning of the data collection phase whereas at the later stage number of responses received was very less with a final 41 responses.

Furthermore, nine software companies that are highly sought after by job applicants in Sri Lanka were interviewed to gain deeper insights on recruitment methods used and the level of LinkedIn usage by HR professionals. Eight of the interviews were conducted in person visiting each company's HR Manager or Assistant HR Manager while one interview was conducted over telephone.

5.1 Demographic Analysis

A demographic analysis was performed to verify whether the sample is representative of overall population. The returned responses have ensured a representative sample of the IT industry in Sri Lanka and Figure 2 shows that about 60% of the responses are from companies that have 100 or more software engineers. Having more employees in a software company indicates that company undertakes significant recruitment activities. Thus, the sample represents data suitable for the purpose, because the data was sourced mainly from companies likely to have significant HR activities.

As a further demographic analysis, the importance of finding passive talents for HR professionals was also tested. It was observed that 88% of the HR professionals in the sample have said it is important or very important to find passive talent as depicted in Figure 3. As social networking sites facilitate locating passive talent, HR professionals who

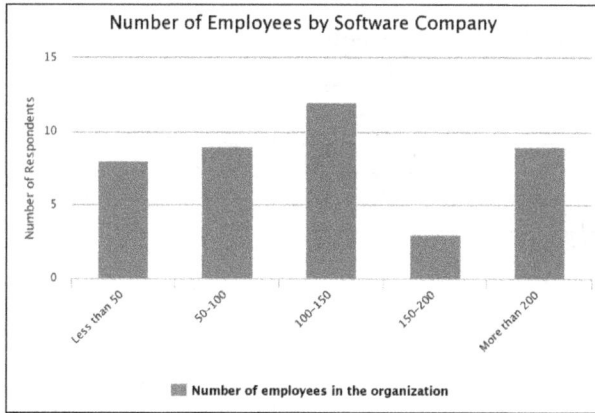

Figure 2: Company Size in terms of Number of Employees

stated it is important to seek passive talent could benefit from social networks. This also validates that sample data was collected from the right audience, who can benefit by social networks such as LinkedIn.

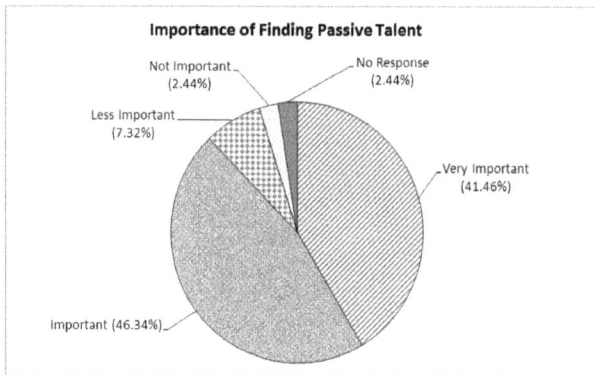

Figure 3: Level of Importance in Finding Passive Talent

5.2 Reliability Analysis

A reliability test on the experiment instrument, that is the questionnaire, was done by computing the Cronbach's Alpha Coefficient (CAC) for the 41 responses and is shown in Table 2 for each variable. The closer Cronbach's Alpha is to 1, the higher the internal consistency and thus the reliability of the research instrument with a value above 0.7 is generally accepted as reliable [21]. Therefore, data gathered were of good quality passing the reliability test.

5.3 Descriptive Analysis

This section provides an overview of the recruitment practices carried out to acquire software engineers and the extent to which social media based recruiting is utilized. The data for the analysis was the number of software engineers recruited by companies in 2014. The number of software engineers recruited in 2014 was analysed to get an understanding of the existing recruitment capacity. 20% have recruited 0 - 5 software engineers, another 20% have recruited 5 - 10, 17% have recruited 10 - 15, 10% have recruited 15 - 20 and 33% have recruited more than 20 software engineers in year 2014. Therefore, nearly half the HR professionals in the case study have recruited more than 15 software engineers during

the year indicating that the sample includes companies that undertake significant amount of recruiting activities.

The distribution of technologies and platforms used by software companies in advertising their vacancies is shown in Figure 4 with 68% of the HR professionals using company website, 92% using job-listing sites, 24% using email campaigns, 56% using social networks such as Facebook and LinkedIn, and 44% using other methods. This data from the quantitative approach shows that HR professionals are able to use a wide array of techniques as listed. The qualitative study was used to elaborate the "Other" methods depicted in Figure 4 and found to include traditional advertising methods such as newspaper advertisements, brochures etc.

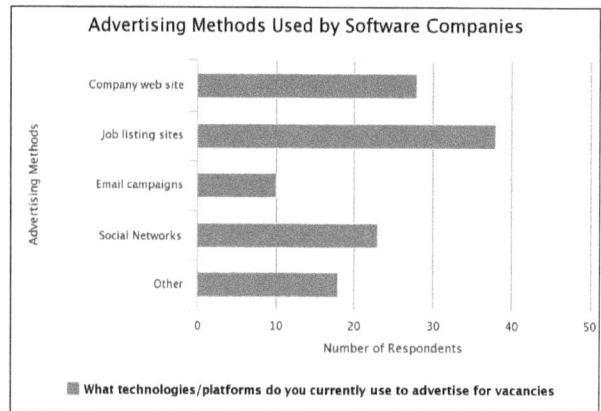

Figure 4: Methods Used for Advertising

When analysing various methods used for headhunting, it was observed that 18% of the HR professionals use employee profiles in company web sites, 59% use LinkedIn, 28% use other social networks such as Facebook, and 62% use other methods as shown in Figure 5. Through the data gathered via semi-structured interview questions, it was identified that "Other" methods includes referrals and recruitment agencies. Sample data showed that 87% of the HR professionals use social media for headhunting with LinkedIn as a major source of headhunting used by nearly 60% of the HR professionals in the sample.

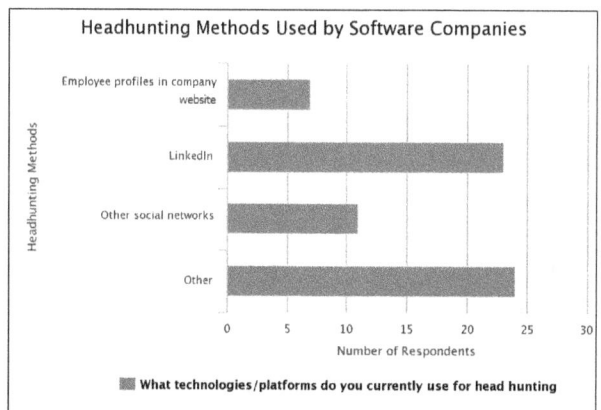

Figure 5: Methods Used for Headhunting

Analysis of different social media networks used for recruitments in software industry indicates that 80% of the HR professionals use LinkedIn, 49% use Facebook, 12% use Twitter, 2% use YouTube, and 22% do not use any of these

Table 2: Cronbach's Alpha Coefficient Values of Variables

Process Efficiency	0.820
Reachability	0.744
Company Image Enhancement	0.811
Passive Talent Attraction	0.615
Niche Market Target	0.732
Quality of Information	0.882
Effective Use of Social Networks for Recruitments	0.770

social networks as shown in Figure 6. According to sample data, LinkedIn and Facebook are the leading social networks that are involved in the recruitment process.

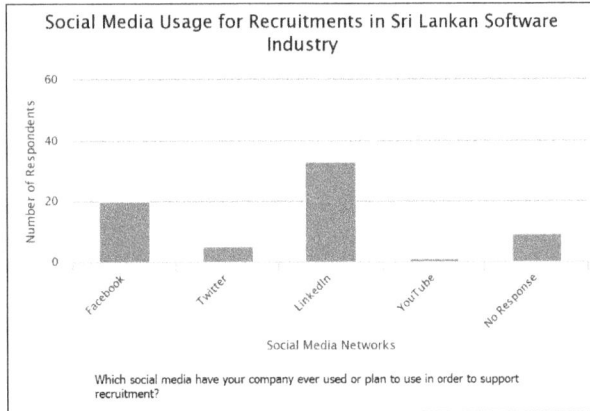

Figure 6: Distribution of Social Media Usage for Recruitment

The factors that motivate companies to use LinkedIn are summarized in Figure 7. The most often cited reasons for LinkedIn use includes it being a new trend, a preferred platform for professional talent, ability to participate in discussions and forums, ability to fill challenging positions, ability to build company brand, capability of utilizing employee contacts, ability to do direct search to reach passive candidates, and capability of advertising campaigns to reach active candidates.

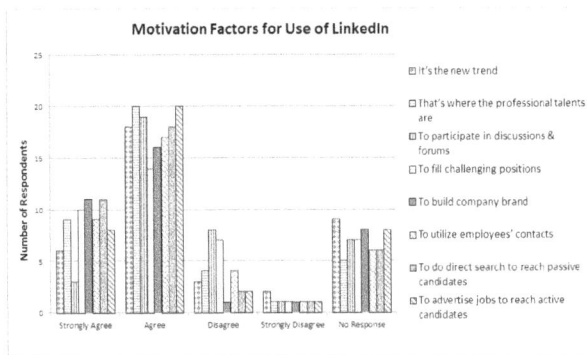

Figure 7: Motivation Factors of LinkedIn

Based on the analysis of data, majority of the respondents agree on the usefulness of LinkedIn in terms of company brand enhancement, utilization of employee contacts, passive talent reach, and active talent attraction with 60% of the respondents agreeing LinkedIn to be useful in terms of all four of these factors. Hence, it shows that a majority

of the HR professionals and their companies have benefited from the use of LinkedIn.

The duration of LinkedIn use by software engineering companies in the case study for recruitment is shown in Figure 8. 32% of the respondents have used for less than 6 months, 22% have used for 6 - 12 months, 10% have used for 12 - 18 and 18 - 24 months, and 26% respondents have used for more than 24 months. As data indicates nearly 55% of the respondents have used LinkedIn for less than 1 year, it can be derived that companies are new to the use of LinkedIn for recruitment activities.

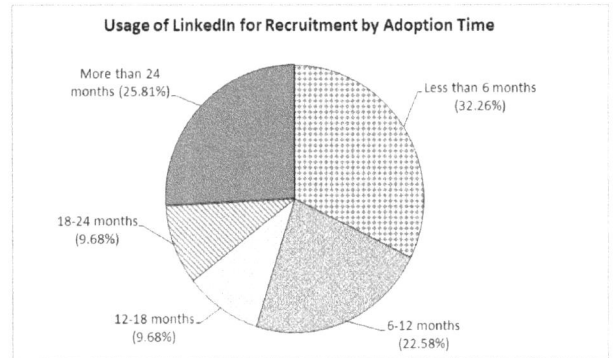

Figure 8: Usage of LinkedIn by Adoption Time

5.4 Inferential Analysis

Inferential statistics computed with *Pearson Correlation Matrix* was used to test the six hypotheses for the relationship between dependent variable and independent variables. According to the Pearson Correlation Coefficients obtained through the inferential analysis shown in Table 3, alternate hypotheses were accepted for $H1_A$, $H2_A$ and $H5_A$ while it was rejected for $H3_A$, $H4_A$ and H6A allowing the acceptance of corresponding null hypotheses.

The analysis shows that process efficiency, reachability and passive talent attraction exhibit a significant positive correlation with use of social networks by HR professionals. Therefore, it can be concluded that if HR professionals perceive process efficiency improvement in the recruitment process, reachability to a wider audience, and attracting of passive talent to be possible with social networks, then they are using those social media tools effectively.

As company image enhancement, niche market targeting, and quality of information did not exhibit a significant correlation with the use of social networks, it can be concluded that those factors have no impact on effective use of social networks. In conclusion, process efficiency, reachability, and passive talent attraction were identified as factors indicating effective use of social networks for recruitment.

Table 3: Inferential Statistics - Pearson Correlation Coefficients

Use of Social Networks by HR Professionals	Pearson Correlation	Sig. (2-tailed)
Process Efficiency	0.332*	0.034
Reachability	0.319*	0.042
Company Image Enhancement	0.220	0.167
Passive Talent Attraction	0.297	0.059
Niche Market Target	0.588**	0.000
Quality of Information	-0.130	0.418
*. Correlation is significant at the 0.05 level (2-tailed).		
**. Correlation is significant at the 0.01 level (2-tailed).		

5.5 Qualitative Analysis

To obtain a deeper insight into HR practices in the presence of social networks and to validate the findings from quantitative approach as this is an emerging research area that lacks comprehensive literature, nine HR professionals were interviewed from companies with employee numbers ranging from 80 to 2500. The nine companies were chosen from a popular set of software companies in the industry known to attract more candidates so that collected data can be used to understand the recruitment strategies of these companies and the level of social media usage including LinkedIn. The interviews were conducted using a set of semi-structured questions to obtain in depth data from HR professionals. Furthermore, all the interviews were conducted as in-person interviews except for one which was conducted via a telephone conversation.

It was observed that a majority of the HR professionals who were responsible for the recruitment activities out of the sample have started their career as software engineers themselves and have moved into HR and operations management later in the career. Agarwal and Ferratt [1] have stated that most of the success stories have a dedicated IT HR person who bridges the gap between HR and IT functions. As many HR professionals in the sample are from an IT background, the condition observed by Agarwal and Ferratt is satisfied.

The quantitative analysis showed the use of job listing sites to be the most popular method of *advertising* vacancies. This finding was collaborated by the results of interview data analysis as "topjobs", which is the most popular online job board in Sri Lanka, has become the most widely used job advertising method. Furthermore, interview data revealed advertising internally and via social media also plays a significant role. While the most popular employee *sourcing* method used by interviewed companies is referrals, other methods such as direct campus recruiting and job advertising (via job boards, social media, print media, corporate website etc.) also play a significant role in sourcing candidates by the companies interviewed for the case study.

The qualitative analysis showed that for the recruitment of fresh graduates the primary method is direct campus recruitment while for personnel with specific skill sets the method to be either LinkedIn or head hunting. Out of the interviewed companies, except for three with limited LinkedIn use all the others are using LinkedIn as a significant part of their recruitment strategy.

The interviewed HR professionals revealed that use of LinkedIn increases the quality of recruitment process supporting the relationship drawn for process efficiency through inferential analysis. The accessibility to a wider audience and a broader pool of passive talent with LinkedIn was substantiated by interviews. However, passive talent was searched mostly for specialized skills. It was also pointed out that the availability of more avenues for locating passive talent could lead to a collapse of the sustainability of the industry due to excessive poaching of talent from other companies. In addition, interviews revealed that some companies are making significant use of social media to position the company brand among software professionals.

Although it was found that, there is no relationship between niche market targeting and use of LinkedIn from the quantitative analysis, during the interview data analysis it was perceived LinkedIn to be widely used for locating specialized skills. This contradiction could have occurred due to having only one questionnaire item related to the variable that is niche market targeting.

Furthermore, HR professionals claimed social networks to be unsuitable for bulk recruitments, because it is time consuming to source large numbers during a hiring streak. In such situations, HR professionals do not get time and flexibility to research in different avenues, hence choosing options that are more convenient.

The perception of LinkedIn recommendations and endorsements was examined during the interviews. Although different companies had different viewpoints, overall majority are making use of recommendations. Endorsements were not seen as a highly value adding feature among the interviewed companies. However, companies claimed that they perform validation checks on both recommendations and endorsements, which is a position supported by prior research [3].

The most common reasons given by companies for their use of LinkedIn are features that give access to a wider audience, clear visibility of candidate profiles, as a platform to brand company image, to locate specialized skill and increased quality of recruitment process. Through the interviews, it was identified that recruiting passive talent via social networks has ethical concerns for industry sustainability as exposure to greater passive talent attraction methods result in greater difficulty in employee retention.

Furthermore, it was observed in the interviews that there is a trend of using data analytics for recruiting activities and some have been already using it. It gave a direction that more intelligence is required by software companies to attract right talent, which could be supported by LinkedIn, as it is able to collect vast amount of data and make deeper analysis.

6. DISCUSSION AND CONCLUSION

This study has identified process efficiency, reachability, and passive talent attraction as effective uses of social networks for recruitment activities. As per the prior studies, process efficiency [5, 6, 8, 9, 12, 17, 20, 22] and passive talent attraction [8, 20] play an important role in deciding selection of online recruiting methods. Through the present study, it is shown that HR professionals consider these factors in social networks based recruitment activities extending the prior research work. According to a research conducted by Galanaki [8] on identifying factors affecting the decision to adopt online recruitment using 99 IT companies listed in London Stock Exchange, worldwide coverage ranked as the least priority positive factor. However, through the findings of the present study, it was revealed that worldwide coverage plays a significant role in social recruiting.

Although previous literature indicates ability to target niche markets [8, 12, 20] as one of the concerns for online recruiting, through the present study it was found that, there is no relationship between niche market targeting and use of social networks for recruiting activities. However, during the interview data analysis it was perceived that social networks are widely used for locating employees with specialized skills. This study was focused on a very limited set of factors, as this is a new area lacking significant volume of in-depth research publications. A separate study is required to elicit more factors contributing to effective use of LinkedIn in recruitment process.

Furthermore, present study found that quality of information and company image enhancement has no impact on effective use of social networks. Although majority of previous studies have shown that HR professionals are concerned in quality of information [5, 8, 20], a study done by Chapman and Webster [5] shows that it is not a major concern for some HR professionals as there are other mechanisms to filter poor quality information. Thus, present study contributes to the findings drawn by Chapman and Webster. As the present study was conducted in a time during which HR professionals were starting to use social networks in Sri Lanka, company image enhancement via social recruiting may still be in a pre-mature state. However, this needs to be further studied.

Job boards, recruitment agencies, social media, referrals, campus recruiting and corporate websites are the more widely used methods from the spectrum of recruitment methods. Print media has not yet disappeared from the spectrum, because some companies are still using newsprint for attracting candidates. The findings of this research support the argument raised by Doherty [6] that social media should not be used as an exclusive recruitment tool, but must be part of a mix of methods to source right talent. Furthermore, HR professionals claimed social networks are not suitable for bulk recruitments, because it is time consuming to source large numbers during a hiring streak. In addition, they claimed hiring passive candidates is expensive compared to active job seekers.

The leading social networks that are involved in the recruitment process in Sri Lankan software industry are LinkedIn and Facebook. LinkedIn is being used in various stages of recruitment process such as advertising the vacancy, locating the candidate, initial screening, company branding etc. However, it was observed that currently social networks are add-ons to the existing recruitment process but not a re-

placement. LinkedIn recommendations are considered as useful in understanding candidate's background and capacities whereas endorsements are perceived to be less useful.

This research study showed that some HR professionals are still exploring how they could benefit from various social networks including Facebook, LinkedIn, Twitter, and YouTube. The reason why some software companies are still not using social media for locating candidates is that currently they are satisfied with the existing recruiting methods as they still get good candidates and are not facing difficulties in searching for talent. However, HR professionals from such companies concluded that when it becomes difficult to source right talent they would start using social media.

The best uses of social networks for recruitment process was identified as process efficiency improvement, passive talent attraction, reachability, understanding candidate background and capacities, locating specialized skills and recommendations. However, research showed social networks to be unhelpful when performing bulk recruitments and time critical recruitments as it consumes a considerable time span. Thus, based on the findings, as a final contribution, a framework was built to evaluate the usefulness of social networks as a recruitment tool that is shown in Figure 9.

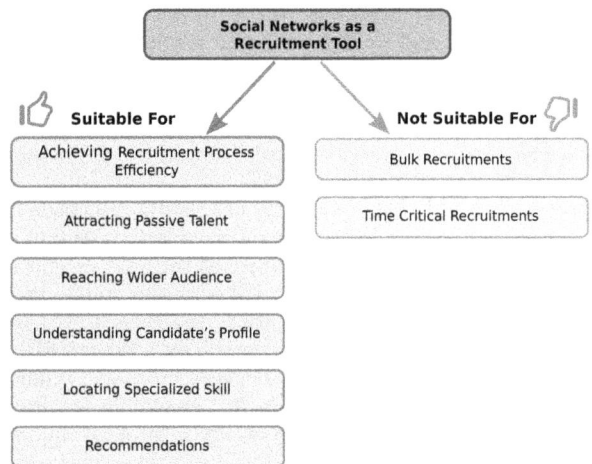

Figure 9: Framework for Evaluating Social Networks as a Recruitment Tool

7. REFERENCES

[1] R. Agarwal and T. W. Ferratt. Crafting an hr strategy to meet the need for it workers. *Communications of the ACM*, 44(7):58–64, 2001.

[2] R. Agarwal and T. W. Ferratt. Enduring practices for managing it professionals. *Communications of the ACM*, 45(9):73–79, 2002.

[3] V. R. Brown and E. D. Vaughn. The writing on the (facebook) wall: The use of social networking sites in hiring decisions. *Journal of Business and Psychology*, 26(2):219–225, 2011.

[4] A. Capiluppi, A. Serebrenik, and L. Singer. Assessing technical candidates on the social web. *Software, IEEE*, 30(1):45–51, 2013.

[5] D. S. Chapman and J. Webster. The use of technologies in the recruiting, screening, and selection processes for job candidates. *International Journal of Selection and Assessment*, 11(2-3):113–120, 2003.

[6] R. Doherty. Getting social with recruitment. *Strategic HR review*, 9(6):11–15, 2010.

[7] S. Gager, R. Bowley, S. Husbands, and M. Milam. Australian recruiting trends. Technical report, LinkedIn, 2015.

[8] E. Galanaki. The decision to recruit online: a descriptive study. *Career Development International*, 7(4):243–251, 2002.

[9] S. F. Gale. Internet recruiting: Better, cheaper, faster. *Workforce*, 80(12):74–77, 2001.

[10] Jobvite. 2014 social recruiting survey. Technical report, Jobvite, 2014.

[11] M. Lauraine. The advantages and disadvantages of using linkedin for job search. https://www.linkedin.com/pulse/advantages-disadvantages-using-linkedin-job-search-lauraine-mcdonald. Accessed: 2015-10-01.

[12] I. Lee. An architecture for a next-generation holistic e-recruiting system. *Communications of the ACM*, 50(7):81–85, 2007.

[13] LinkedIn. About linkedin. https://press.linkedin.com/about-linkedin. Accessed: 2015-01-10.

[14] LinkedIn. Linkedin talent insights: Talent pool report software engineers. Technical report, LinkedIn, September 2012.

[15] S. A. Madia. Best practices for using social media as a recruitment strategy. *Strategic HR Review*, 10(6):19–24, 2011.

[16] J. C. Meister and K. Willyerd. *The 2020 Workplace: How Innovative Companies Attract, Develop, And Keep Tomorrow's Employees Today*. HarperBusiness, 2010.

[17] S. M. Miller. Help wanted: is the online job market working for your business? *Office Solutions*, 18:27–29, 2001.

[18] R. Munger. Technical communicators beware: the next generation of high-tech recruiting methods. *Professional Communication, IEEE Transactions on*, 45(4):276–290, 2002.

[19] B. Munstermann, A. Eckhardt, and T. Weitzel. The performance impact of business process standardization: An empirical evaluation of the recruitment process. *Business Process Management Journal*, 16(1):29–56, 2010.

[20] A. Reger. The impact of the business networking site linkedin on private, large, multinational companies? recruitment process in ireland. Master's thesis, National College of Ireland, 7 2013.

[21] U. Sekaran. *Research methods for business: A skill building approach*. John Wiley & Sons, 2006.

[22] A. Tomlinson. Energy firm sharpens recruiting, saves money with in-house job board. *Canadian HR Reporter*, 15(20):7–8, 2002.

College-Based Career Experiences as Determinants of IT Labor Market Entry: A Survival Analysis Model

Tenace Setor
Nanyang Business School
Nanyang Technological University
tenacekw001@ntu.edu.sg

Damien Joseph
Nanyang Business School
Nanyang Technological University
adjoseph@ntu.edu.sg

ABSTRACT

Novice IT professionals are not well-endowed with experience and professional knowledge-*attributes gained in the course of IT work*-which could facilitate labor market outcomes such as entering the IT workforce immediately after completing college education. However, college-based career experiences such as job shadowing, mentorship, internships and cooperative education are valuable sources of human capital which can engender good future performance and productivity; and, thus, can often decide the employment fate of novice IT professionals. The current study draws on human capital theory and develops a set of hypotheses relating college-based career experiences to the likelihood of securing IT jobs. We test our hypotheses using data from the National Longitudinal Survey of Youth 1997 cohort. We find that hands-on forms of college-based career experiences such internships and cooperative education increase the likelihood of securing IT jobs immediately after completing college. We do not find support for vicarious forms of college-based career experiences i.e. mentorship and job shadowing. We discuss the implications of our results on research and practice.

Keywords
Human capital theory; Job shadowing; Mentoring; Cooperative Education; Internships

1. INTRODUCTION
Extant IT research have identified professional knowledge and experience, gained in the course of IT work, as attributes which facilitate individuals' labor market outcomes (Ang et al. 2002; Joseph et al. 2012; Mithas and Krishnan 2008). This stream of research (Ang et al. 2002; Joseph et al. 2012; Mithas and Krishnan 2008) examine professional knowledge and experience as determinants of IT compensation. IT employers value professional knowledge and experience because they engender good future performance (Ang et al. 2002; Mithas and Krishnan 2008). These studies have largely focused on samples of IT professionals in the mid-late stages (*i.e.* average of 7-13 years of IT experience and above) of their careers.

In contrast, comparatively few studies have been conducted on human capital of novice IT professionals (Aasheim et al. 2009; Joseph 2008). Joseph (2008) examined the role career-based interventions play in IT students' decision to choose IT as a

SIGMIS-CPR'16, June 2–4, 2016, Alexandria, VA, USA.
© 2016 ACM. ISBN 978-1-4503-4203-2/16/06…$15.00.
DOI: http://dx.doi.org/10.1145/2890602.2890606

career; and Aashiem et al. (2009) surveyed IT managers on the knowledge and skills required for entry-level IT professionals. Career-based interventions such as internship is positively related to IT graduates' choice of IT as a career because internship shapes career expectations and reduces uncertainties surrounding career decision making (Joseph 2008); and IT managers perceive interpersonal skills, organization skills and technical skills as the most important skills required for entry-level IT professionals (Aasheim et al. 2009). From a theoretical perspective, these studies remain silent on what indicates human capital for novice IT professionals; and how this human capital facilitates entry into the IT workforce. The current study proposes a research agenda that focuses on college-based career experiences such as mentorship, internship, job shadowing and cooperative education as sources of valuable human capital that could potentially facilitate novice IT professionals' entry into the IT labor market (Lent et al. 2002). We ask do college-based career experiences increase the likelihood that novice IT professionals will secure IT jobs immediately after completing college?

To answer the above research question, we draw on human capital theory which emphasizes that college-based career experiences are valuable because they engender good productivity and performance. We formulate a set of hypotheses that relates college-based career experiences to the likelihood of securing IT jobs.

2. THEORETICAL FOUNDATION & HYPOTHESES DEVELOPMENT
2.1 Human Capital Theory & Employee Selection
Human capital theory emphasizes the acquisition of professional knowledge and work experience (Becker 2009). Professional knowledge and experience embodies an employee's cognitive stock of value-creating capabilities. Professional knowledge can be directly acquired via formal education and on-the-job training. Experience, on the other hand, can be gained either via hands-on practice or vicariously (Miller and Jamieson 1991; Tesluk and Jacobs 1998). Vicarious experience involves individuals observing others, e.g. peers or superiors, while they perform complex work functions and execute their occupational roles (Miller and Jamieson 1991; Tesluk and Jacobs 1998). Through observation, positive work values, ethics, routines, and work attitudes are transmitted vicariously (Joseph 2008).

Professional knowledge and experience acquired either directly or vicariously raise employee productivity, which ultimately impacts firm productivity and performance (Bharadwaj 2000). Employers value productivity, and as such, they tend to select and hire employees with as much experience and professional knowledge as possible. (Becker 1962; Ehrenberg and Smith 1994; King et al. 2005).

2.2 College-Based Career Experiences and Early Entry into the IT Labor Market

In this study, college-based career experiences are job-shadowing, internship, cooperative education and mentorship experiences that provide opportunities for college students to learn the obligations of the world of work (Dillon and Lending 2014; Fifolt and Searby 2010).

Job Shadowing Experience

Job shadowing is a career intervention program which requires students to shadow experienced professionals and learn about what is required of the respective profession (Herr and Watts 1988). In the context of IT work, individuals observe experienced IT professionals perform work and thus acquire procedural knowledge, work shortcuts, values, ethics and behaviors that make experienced IT professionals productive (Burke and Ng 2006).

The acquired techniques, shortcuts, ethics and behaviors enrich individuals' understanding and knowledge of modern IT work (Joseph 2008). IT employers believe that novice IT professionals who know the shortcuts, values, ethics and technicalities of IT work tend to be productive on the job (Lee et al. 1995); and as such IT employers tend to hire novice IT professionals with job shadowing experience.

Accordingly, we hypothesize that,

H1: *The more the job shadowing experience, the higher the likelihood that IT professionals will secure IT jobs immediately after completing college.*

Internship Experience

Internships provide opportunities for individuals to gain hands-on experience in the real world of work (Chillas et al. 2015; Ciofalo 1992; Gold 2002). During IT internships, individuals- referred to as interns directly apply the knowledge and concepts of IT to solve real business problems (Raymond et al. 1993). Also, IT interns exchange ideas, communicate and build working relationships with colleague interns, experienced IT professionals and supervisors (Raymond et al. 1993). As such, IT students acquire a wide spectrum of skills such as problem-solving skills, communication and interpersonal (soft) skills and hands-on experiences.

The hands-on skills acquired by IT students via internship programs raises their productivity levels when they enter the IT labor market. Since IT employers value productivity, they are likely to recruit entry-level IT professionals with internship experiences (Fifolt and Searby 2010). Accordingly, we hypothesize that,

H2: *The more the internship experience, the higher the likelihood that IT professionals will secure IT jobs immediately after completing college.*

Mentorship Experience

Mentorship refers to an intense interpersonal exchange between mentees and experienced professionals (mentors), in which mentors share a wide-variety of career-related experiences with their mentees, over a sustained period of time (Chao et al. 1992; Russell and Adams 1997). In the context of IT work, experienced IT professionals serve as conduits through which professional knowledge, relevant to the world of IT work, is vicariously imparted to mentees (Hunt and Michael 1983).

Professional knowledge, imparted through mentorship experiences, is valued by employers because it contributes to employee productivity (Green and Bauer 1995; Scandura 1992). Thus, to increase overall firm productivity-via individual productivity-IT employers tend to recruit novice IT professionals who are equipped with professional knowledge gained through mentorship experiences (Fifolt and Searby 2010). Accordingly, we hypothesize that

H3: *The more the mentorship experience, the higher the likelihood that IT professionals will secure IT jobs immediately after completing college.*

Cooperative Education

Cooperative education offers individuals the opportunities to integrate college education with periods of employment in specialized fields of interest (Gardner and Kozlowski 1993; Jaeger et al. 2008). Whilst in school, future IT professionals develop both professional and industrial skillsets required for successful performance through cooperative education (Gardner and Kozlowski 1993; Gardner and Motschenbacher 1993). Further, experience gained via cooperative education better prepares novice IT professionals to cope with the challenging world of IT work post labor market entry (Joseph 2008).

Prior research has found that college-graduates with cooperative education experience learn the ropes of their jobs faster because of their prior hands-on learning experiences (Gardner and Kozlowski 1993). Another research found that at the entry-level, professionals with cooperative education experience received higher starting salaries (Gardner et al. 1992). This suggests that employers value cooperative education experience; and thus are likely to recruit novice IT professionals who have cooperative education experience (Fifolt and Searby 2010). Accordingly, we hypothesize that

H4: *Cooperative education increases the likelihood that novice IT professionals will secure IT jobs immediately after completing college.*

3. METHOD

This section begins with a description of our dataset, how we constructed the sample used in conducting the study and censoring of our sample. We follow with a description of the measures and the data analytical technique used in testing our hypotheses.

3.1 DATA

We used data from the National Longitudinal Survey of Youth, 1997 cohort (NLSY97). The National Longitudinal Survey of Youth 1997 survey is a nationally representative longitudinal survey conducted by the National Opinion Research Center (NORC) at the University of Chicago and sponsored by the U.S Bureau of Labor Statistics (U.S. Bureau of Labor Statistics 2014b). The NLSY97 survey follows the life of American youths born between the years of 1980 and 1984. The first survey was conducted in 1997 and consisted of 8984 individuals. The NLSY97 survey continues to run on an annual basis, and the most current survey was conducted in 2012.

3.2 SAMPLE CONSTRUCTION

Our initial sample consisted of respondents who declared computer/information science as a major during their enrolment in college. We subjected each respondent in our initial sample to the following sample inclusion criteria: one, respondents must have completed college i.e. provided the date of completion. Two, respondents must have reported actively searching[1] for a full-time job (worked at least 35 hours a week) in the civilian labor market, after completing college. After eliminating respondents who did not meet the inclusion criteria, the resulting (final) sample consisted of 318 respondents; representing 3.5% of the NLSY97 cohort.

Of our final sample, 68.9% are male and 31.1% females. The average age of our sample at the time individuals completed college was 24.4 years ($SD = 2.6$). In terms of ethnicity, 58.8% of the final sample is Caucasian and 41.2% is non-Caucasian, including African-Americans, Asians and Hispanics. Overall, 62.0% of the final sample graduated from public colleges and the remaining 38.0% graduated from private colleges; 33.6% of the sample attained associate's degrees and 66.4% attained bachelor's degrees.

We proceeded to construct a survival dataset from our final sample. Survival data is a longitudinal data designed to capture the occurrence of an event of interest (i.e. entry into IT labor market in the case of our study) and the time within which observations transition from one qualitative state to another (Allison 2010). It is worth mentioning that, it is not necessary that every respondent in a survival dataset experiences the event of interest. For our sample, we began observing respondents at the time they completed college; and recorded the *survival time* - the time it took an individual to secure a job after completing college.

3.3 CENSORING

Not all individuals in our sample entered the IT labor market when the study window closed. These individuals were treated as censored data. In our sample, right censoring could occur for any of the following reasons: one, individuals entered non-IT professions; two, individuals could not enter the labor market before the close of the study window in the last survey year and three, the loss of individual data due to survey attrition (missing data). Uncensored observations, however, consisted of individuals who entered the IT profession immediately after completing college. Table 1 shows the set of IT job titles which qualified an individual as an IT professional. IT jobs are identified by their Occupational Classification Codes (OCS) (U.S. Census Bureau 2000).

4. MEASURES

Dependent variable

Our dependent variable is the likelihood of securing an IT job immediately after completing college. We chose this specific period (i.e immediately after completing college) because we believe the effect of college-based career experiences on labor market outcomes will be strongest at the entry-level when individuals have no working or labor market history. We modelled the likelihood of securing an IT job immediately after completing college as an inverse function of the elapsed time, in

months, between college completion and job start dates, using a survival analysis technique[2].

Table 1: Occupation Classification Codes and their Corresponding Occupations in the NLSY97

OCS 2002 Code	Job Title
0110	Computer and Information Systems Managers
1000	Computer Systems Analysts/Computer Scientists
1010	Computer Programmers
1020	Computer Software Engineers
1040	Computer Support Specialists
1060	Database Administrators
1100	Network and Computer Systems Administrators
1110	Network Systems and Data Communications Analysts
1400	Computer Hardware Engineers

Source info: U.S. Bureau of Labor Statistics (2014) "2002 Occupational Classification Codes," at http://www.bls.gov/cps/cpsoccind.htm

Independent Variables

At the college level, the NLSY97 survey asks respondents about the types and number of college-based career experiences they are have participated in. We measured all college-based career experiences-job shadowing, internship, mentorship-except cooperative education, with continuous variables. Cooperative education was coded as a dummy (1 = Cooperative education Experience; 0 = No cooperative education experience). The continuous variables indicate the number of times individuals participated in the respective college-based career experiences.

Controls

Guided by prior research we included 12 control variables that could potentially influence the likelihood of securing IT jobs. To account for the potential influence of socioeconomic and demographic factors (Mouw 2003; Reimers 1983), we controlled for *household income*, measured as the logged value of the total household income (adjusted for inflation using 2011 as the baseline year) prior to the year the individual entered the labor market; *gender* (male = "1", female = "0"); *age*, measured in years, *ethnicity* (white = "1", non-white = "0") and region of residence in the U.S. (north east = "0", north central = "1", south = "2" and west = "3"). We controlled for other human capital variables (Heckman et al. 2006) such as *grade point average (GPA)*, measured on a 4.0 scale; and *education level* (associate's degree = "0", bachelor's degree = "1"). We accounted for school fixed effects by controlling for the *college type* (private = "0", public = "1"). We controlled for the logged *hourly rate of pay of job* (adjusted for inflation using 2011 as the baseline year), measured in USD per hour and *working hours* measured by the number of hours per week that a respondent spends on the job. Industry fixed effects were controlled for using dummy variables based on U.S. Census Bureau's four digit industrial classification codes. We coded *manufacturing* as "1"; *professional, business* or *finance* as "2"; *services* as "3" and *others* as "0", if a respondent reported a job in the respective industry. We followed the

---

[1] The National Longitudinal Surveys project, under auspices of the U.S. Bureau of Labor Statistics, describes an active job search as the type of search that may result in the offer of a job without a further action on the part of the job seeker (U.S. Bureau of Labor Statistics 2014a). Active job search includes contacting employers directly, contacting employment agencies and sending out resumes or filling out job applications.

[2] We elaborate on the survival analysis technique used in modelling the dependent variable later in the paper.

recommendations of Allison (2010) and controlled for year effects since there was no single entry time for all observations *i.e.* respondents completed college in different years. (Y2000-Y2003 = "0", Y2004-Y2008 = "1" and Y2009-Y2011 = "2").

5. DATA ANALYSIS

We used survival analysis to estimate the effect of college-based career experiences on the likelihood of securing IT jobs. Survival analysis is a class of statistical techniques for modelling the amount of time it takes for one to experience an event (Allison 2010). Thus, models estimated using survival analysis techniques take into account the "time to an event" (Hosmer et al. 1999, p. 2); which in the context of the current study is the time it takes an individual to secure an IT job immediately after completing college.

Cox Proportional-Hazard Regression Model
From the class of survival analysis techniques, we chose the Cox proportional-hazard regression for the following reason. the cox proportional-hazard regression is able to incorporate information from censored data in estimating the model parameters of interest (Allison 1984). Unless censoring is random *-censored observations are unbiased representatives of the remaining observations which are at risk of experiencing the event*, failure to account for the censored data could result in biased estimates (Allison 1984; Cook and Campbell 1979; Raffiee and Jie 2014).

The final cox proportional-hazard regression model is specified in equation 1. The dependent variable, $h_i(t)$, represents the *hazard function* which is the likelihood that an individual i will secure an IT job at a time t, observed within the study window, conditioned that the individual did not secure the job before completing college (Allison 1984).

$$h_i(t)=\lambda_0(t)\exp(\beta_{i1}X_{MentorshipExp}+\beta_{i2}X_{InternshipExp}+\beta_{i3}X_{JobShadowingExp}$$
$$+\beta_{i4}X_{CooperativeEdExp}+\beta_{i5}X_{GPA}$$
$$+\beta_{i6}X_{BachelorsDegree}+\beta_{i7}X_{PublicCollege}+\beta_{i8-9}X_{GraduationYear}+\beta_{i10}X_{Age}+\beta_{i11}X_{Male}+\beta_{i12}X_{WhiteEthnicity}$$
$$+\beta_{i13}X_{HrlyRateOfPay}+\beta_{i14}X_{WorkHour}+\beta_{i15}X_{RealHHIncome}+\beta_{i16-18}X_{Industry}+\beta_{i19-21}X_{RegionOfResidence})$$

The *baseline hazard function*, $\lambda_0(t)$, represents the hazard function for an individual when all the covariates $(\beta_{i1}...\beta_{i21})$ have a value of zero (Allison 2010). The baseline hazard function is analogous to the intercept term in standard regressions.

6. RESULTS

Hypothesis 1 predicted that novice IT professionals with higher job shadowing experience are more likely to secure IT jobs immediately after completing college. Results from the cox regression analysis do not provide support for hypothesis 1. The regression coefficient of job shadowing experience was negative and not statistically significant (β = -0.042, z = -0.291, *n.s.*).

Hypothesis 2 predicted that novice IT professionals with higher internship experience are more likely to secure IT jobs immediately after completing college. Results from the cox regression analysis provide support for hypothesis 2. The coefficient of internship experience was positive and statistically significant (β = 0.241, z = 1.991, p < 0.05). In terms of hazard ratio, novice IT professionals with high internship experience were 1.273 times more likely to secure IT jobs compared to novice IT professionals with low internship experience.

Hypothesis 3 predicted that novice IT professionals with mentorship experience are more likely to secure IT jobs

immediately after completing college. Results from the cox regression analysis do not provide support for hypothesis 3. Though the direction of the regression coefficient of mentorship experience is positive, it is not statistically significant (β = 0.323, z = 1.105, *n.s.*).

Hypothesis 4 predicted that novice IT professionals with cooperative education experience are more likely to secure IT jobs immediately after completing college. Results from the cox regression analysis provide support for hypothesis 4. The coefficient of cooperative education experience was positive and statistically significant (β = 0.307, z = 2.107, p < 0.05). In terms of hazard ratio, novice IT professionals with high cooperative education experience are 1.359 times more likely to secure IT jobs compared to novice IT professionals with low cooperative education experience.

7. DISCUSSION

In this study, we examined the implications of four forms of college-based career experiences on the likelihood of securing IT jobs immediately after completing college. The four forms of college-based career experiences examined were job shadowing, internship, mentorship and cooperative education. Using the human capital theory as our theoretical lens, we predicted that novice IT professionals with high college-based career experiences are more likely to secure IT jobs.

Human capital theory suggests that college-based career experiences build human capital for novice IT professionals (Becker 1962). Because human capital increases the productivity levels of novice IT professionals, novice IT professionals are more likely to be hired by IT employers. Consistent with human capital theory, we found that internship and cooperative education experiences increase the likelihood that novice IT professionals will secure IT jobs immediately after completing college. Our findings appear to be consistent with a 2008 survey report conducted by National Associations of Colleges and Employers (NACE). The NACE survey reported 36% of employers made hires from their established internship and cooperative education programs (Fifolt and Searby 2010).

In contrast, we did not find evidence to support our predictions that vicarious forms of college-based career experiences i.e. mentorship and job shadowing experiences increase the likelihood that novice IT professionals will secure IT jobs immediately after completing college. Findings from prior research by Joseph (2008) could provide explanations for the lack of evidence. Job shadowing and mentorship experiences are gained vicariously and as such these forms of college-based career experiences may not directly contribute to the building of self-efficacies and the requisite competencies required to secure IT jobs (Day and Allen 2004; Joseph 2008). Because job shadowing and mentorship experiences are not hands-on experiences, there is also the possibility that individuals may make highly subjective conclusions about the world of IT work; which may not necessarily be true (Joseph 2008). In addition, the bounded nature of job shadowing and mentorship restricts individuals from gaining richer and broader insights and experiences about the real world of IT work (Joseph 2008).

In sum, it appears that the conversion of vicarious forms of experiences *i.e.* mentorship and job shadowing into practical experiences valued by IT employers is moderated by quality dimensions, such as richness and scope of mentorship and job shadowing, and individual traits e.g. self-efficacy. We, therefore, call on future research to investigate the quality of vicarious forms of college-based career experiences as a potential moderator in examining the labor market outcomes of vicarious forms of college-based career experiences such mentorship and job shadowing.

8. IMPLICATIONS FOR RESEARCH

Our study contributes to IT research in two ways. First, to the best of our knowledge, our study is the first to have used human capital as the theoretical lens to examine the role college-based career experiences play in facilitating early entry into the IT labor market. Specifically, we examined the effects of job shadowing, internship, mentorship and cooperative education experiences - i.e. direct and vicarious forms of experiences-on the likelihood that novice IT professionals will secure IT jobs immediately after completing college. Prior IT research has mainly focused on the labor market outcomes of quantitative aspects of experience such as IT experience and tenure much to the neglect of college-based career experiences.

Two, our study extends prior research by focusing on labor market outcomes of novice IT professionals. Prior research has mostly examined the IT labor market outcomes using samples of IT professionals within the mid-late stages of their career (e.g. Ang et al. 2002, Joseph et al. 2012, Mithas and Krishnan 2008). IT professionals within the mid-late stages of their career are endowed with IT experience and professional knowledge gained in the course of IT work. Unlike IT professionals in the mid-late stages of their careers, who are endowed with accumulated IT human capital, novice IT professionals have little or no experience in the labor market; and thus may not have requisite IT experience and professional knowledge known to influence labor market outcomes.

9. IMPLICATIONS FOR PRACTICE

Our study contributes to practice in the following ways. First, our study provides implications for IT institutions in preparing IT talents for the job market. Our study informs IT training institutions about the specific forms of experiences that are more likely to facilitate novice IT professionals in finding IT jobs. Of the forms of experiences, IT training institutions should realize that hands-on experiences gained through internships and cooperative education are more likely to facilitate candidates' early entry into the IT labor market upon graduation. As such, when training institutions are faced with budget constraints they can make an informed decision regarding which forms of experiences to invest in, that would be useful to novice IT professionals on the job market.

Second, for novice IT professionals, our study puts to rest the questions about the requisite human capital required to make early entry into the IT labor market. Our study provides strong evidence for the importance of hands-on experience in influencing the likelihood of securing IT jobs at the entry-level. Our study suggests that though novice IT professionals may not have experience from participating in the IT labor market, experiential capital gained through internships and cooperative education could facilitate early entry into the IT labor market.

10. CONCLUSION

The current study examined the role that college-based career experiences play in facilitating entry into the IT labor market. In particular, we examined the influence of job shadowing, internships, mentorship and cooperative education experiences on

the likelihood that a novice IT professional secures an IT job immediately after completing college. The results show that hands-on forms of college-based career experiences such as internships and cooperative education increase the likelihood that novice IT professionals will secure IT jobs immediately after completing college. This suggests that hands-on forms of college-based career experiences play a significant role in determining the employment fate of novice IT professionals on the job market.

11. REFERENCES

Aasheim, C. L., Li, L., and Williams, S. 2009. "Knowledge and Skill Requirements for Entry-Level Information Technology Workers: A Comparison of Industry and Academia," *Journal of Information Systems Education* (20:3), p. 349.

Allison, P. D. 1984. *Event History Analysis: Regression for Longitudinal Event Data.* Sage.

Allison, P. D. 2010. *Survival Analysis Using Sas: A Practical Guide.* Sas Institute.

Ang, S., Slaughter, S., and Yee Ng, K. 2002. "Human Capital and Institutional Determinants of Information Technology Compensation: Modeling Multilevel and Cross-Level Interactions," *Management Science* (48:11), pp. 1427-1445.

Becker, G. S. 1962. "Investment in Human Capital: A Theoretical Analysis," *The journal of political economy*), pp. 9-49.

Becker, G. S. 2009. *Human Capital: A Theoretical and Empirical Analysis, with Special Reference to Education.* University of Chicago Press.

Bharadwaj, A. S. 2000. "A Resource-Based Perspective on Information Technology Capability and Firm Performance: An Empirical Investigation," *MIS quarterly*), pp. 169-196.

Burke, R. J., and Ng, E. 2006. "The Changing Nature of Work and Organizations: Implications for Human Resource Management," *Human Resource Management Review* (16:2), pp. 86-94.

Chao, G. T., Walz, P. M., and Gardner, P. D. 1992. "Formal and Informal Mentorships: A Comparison on Mentoring Functions and Contrast with Nonmentored Counterparts," *Personnel psychology* (45:3), p. 619.

Chillas, S., Marks, A., and Galloway, L. 2015. "Learning to Labour: An Evaluation of Internships and Employability in the Ict Sector," *New Technology, Work and Employment* (30:1), pp. 1-15.

Ciofalo, A. 1992. *Internships: Perspectives on Experiential Learning. A Guide to Internship Management for Educators and Professionals.* ERIC.

Cook, T. D., and Campbell, D. T. 1979. *Quasi-Experimentation: Design and Analysis for Field Settings.* Rand McNally.

Day, R., and Allen, T. D. 2004. "The Relationship between Career Motivation and Self-Efficacy with Protégé Career Success," *Journal of Vocational Behavior* (64:1), pp. 72-91.

Dillon, T. W., and Lending, D. 2014. "Using Professional Consultants to Mentor Cis Students on a Simulated Consulting Project," *Proceedings of the 52nd ACM conference on Computers and people research*: ACM, pp. 171-175.

Ehrenberg, R. G., and Smith, R. S. 1994. "Modem Labor Economics," *NY: Harper Collins College Publ*).

Fifolt, M., and Searby, L. 2010. "Mentoring in Cooperative Education and Internships: Preparing Protégés for Stem Professions," *Journal of STEM Education: Innovations and Research* (11:1/2), p. 17.

Gardner, P. D., and Kozlowski, S. W. 1993. "Learning the Ropes! Co-Ops Do It Faster,").

Gardner, P. D., and Motschenbacher, G. 1993. "More Alike Than Different: Early Work Experiences of Co-Op and Non Co-Op Engineers,").

Gardner, P. D., Nixon, D. C., and Motschenbacker, G. 1992. "Starting Salary Outcomes of Cooperative Education Graduates," *Journal of Cooperative Education* (27:3), pp. 16-26.

Gold, M. 2002. "The Elements of Effective Experiential Education Programs," *Journal of Career Planning and Employment* (62:2), pp. 20-24.

Green, S. G., and Bauer, T. N. 1995. "Supervisory Mentoring by Advisers: Relationships with Doctoral Student Potential, Productivity, and Commitment," *Personnel Psychology* (48:3), pp. 537-562.

Heckman, J. J., Stixrud, J., and Urzua, S. 2006. "The Effects of Cognitive and Noncognitive Abilities on Labor Market Outcomes and Social Behavior," National Bureau of Economic Research.

Herr, E. L., and Watts, A. 1988. "Work Shadowing and Work-Related Learning," *The Career Development Quarterly* (37:1), pp. 78-86.

Hosmer, D., Lemeshow, S., and May, S. 1999. "Applied Survival Analysis: Regression Modelling of Time to Event Data. John Wiley & Sons," *New York*).

Hunt, D. M., and Michael, C. 1983. "Mentorship: A Career Training and Development Tool," *Academy of management Review* (8:3), pp. 475-485.

Jaeger, A. J., Eagan, M., and Wirt, L. 2008. "Retaining Students in Science, Math, and Engineering Majors: Rediscovering Cooperative Education," *Journal of Cooperative Education and Internships* (42:1), pp. 20-32.

Joseph, D. 2008. "Increasing the Number of Entrants into the It Profession: The Role of Experiential Training," *Proceedings of the 2008 ACM SIGMIS CPR conference on Computer personnel doctoral consortium and research*: ACM, pp. 2-4.

Joseph, D., Boh, W. F., Ang, S., and Slaughter, S. A. 2012. "The Career Paths Less (or More) Traveled: A Sequence Analysis of It Career Histories, Mobility Patterns, and Career Success," *MIS Quarterly* (36:2), pp. 427-452.

King, Z., Burke, S., and Pemberton, J. 2005. "The 'Bounded'career: An Empirical Study of Human Capital, Career Mobility and Employment Outcomes in a Mediated Labour Market," *Human Relations* (58:8), pp. 981-1007.

Lee, D. M., Trauth, E. M., and Farwell, D. 1995. "Critical Skills and Knowledge Requirements of Is Professionals: A Joint Academic/Industry Investigation," *MIS quarterly*), pp. 313-340.

Lent, R. W., Brown, S. D., Talleyrand, R., McPartland, E. B., Davis, T., Chopra, S. B., Alexander, M. S., Suthakaran, V., and Chai, C.-M. 2002. "Career Choice Barriers, Supports, and Coping Strategies: College Students' Experiences," *Journal of Vocational Behavior* (60:1), pp. 61-72.

Miller, A., and Jamieson, I. 1991. *Rethinking Work Experience*. Taylor & Francis.

Mithas, S., and Krishnan, M. S. 2008. "Human Capital and Institutional Effects in the Compensation of Information Technology Professionals in the United States," *Management Science* (54:3), pp. 415-428.

Mouw, T. 2003. "Social Capital and Finding a Job: Do Contacts Matter?," *American sociological review*), pp. 868-898.

Raffiee, J., and Jie, F. 2014. "Should I Quit My Day Job?: A Hybrid Path to Entrepreneurship," *Academy of Management Journal* (57:4), pp. 936-963.

Raymond, M. A., McNabb, D. E., and Matthaei, C. F. 1993. "Preparing Graduates for the Workforce: The Role of Business Education," *Journal of Education for Business* (68:4), pp. 202-206.

Reimers, C. W. 1983. "Labor Market Discrimination against Hispanic and Black Men," *The review of economics and statistics*), pp. 570-579.

Russell, J. E., and Adams, D. M. 1997. "The Changing Nature of Mentoring in Organizations: An Introduction to the Special Issue on Mentoring in Organizations," *Journal of Vocational Behavior* (51:1), pp. 1-14.

Scandura, T. A. 1992. "Mentorship and Career Mobility: An Empirical Investigation," *Journal of organizational behavior* (13:2), pp. 169-174.

Tesluk, P. E., and Jacobs, R. R. 1998. "Toward an Integrated Model of Work Experience," *Personnel psychology* (51:2), p. 321.

U.S. Bureau of Labor Statistics. 2014a. "How the Government Measures Unemployment," *Current Population Survey Technical Documentation*).

U.S. Bureau of Labor Statistics. 2014b. "National Longitudinal Survey of Youth 1997," *U.S. Department of Labor*).

U.S. Census Bureau. 2000. "2000 Standard Occupation Classification." U.S. Government Printing Office, Washington, D.C.

Designing Games for Presence in Consumer Virtual Reality

Lewis Carter
Idea Lab, Griffith University
Kessels Rd, Nathan, 4111
QLD, Australia
+617 3735 5191
L.Carter@griffith.edu.au

Leigh Ellen Potter
Idea Lab, Griffith University
Kessels Rd, Nathan, 4111
QLD, Australia
+617 3735 5191
L.Potter@griffith.edu.au

ABSTRACT

With virtual reality technologies entering the consumer market this year, it is the task of those producing content for the virtual reality platform to ensure that users have an experience that lives up to expectations. Virtual reality comes with its own strengths and weaknesses, and these must be taken into account when designing applications to produce the best possible experience for interaction. This paper employs a qualitative case study to examine participants in sessions with a virtual reality game prototype utilizing the Oculus Rift. The game prototype was designed to investigate problem areas of virtual reality. Data was then analyzed through thematic analysis, and a preliminary set of game design heuristics specific to virtual reality were created. These heuristics are written so that virtual reality game designers can easily apply them.

Keywords
Virtual reality; consumer virtual reality; heuristic evaluation; video game; presence; game design; Oculus Rift

1. INTRODUCTION
Virtual Reality technology has traditionally consisted of cumbersome created environments and has often required complex sensors worn on the body for an individual to interact with the environment. The emergence of head mounted virtual reality devices is shifting the technology into the commercial consumer area. In 2014 Facebook purchased the Oculus VR company, and Mark Zuckerberg has stated that this form of virtual reality is the social platform of the future.

A range of virtual reality head mounted display devices, including the Oculus Rift and HTC Vive, have started entering homes as commercial products this year. These devices will provide people with a new form of interaction and engagement with both technology and their environment. It becomes imperative that applications are built to engage users and take full advantage of the uniqueness of the platform.

Often when a new platform is created developers rely too heavily on the design principles from previous generation of technology.

SIGMIS-CPR '16, June 02-04, 2016, Alexandria, VA, USA.
© 2016 ACM. ISBN 978-1-4503-4203-2/16/06...$15.00.
DOI: http://dx.doi.org/10.1145/2890602.2890626

These principles usually do not translate well, applying knowledge that was cultivated under different situations and pretenses. This was last exhibited when touch enabled mobile devices became prevalent. It took many years for developers to learn not to rely on old analogs that simply did not translate to meaningful interaction on the new platform.

If we are to develop meaningful social interactions facilitated by technology, then we must ensure that the applications we build are both suited to the attributes of that technology, and fill the needs of the people who will use it. This paper aims to support this through the exploration of the specific development needs of the new head mounted display virtual reality devices. Through a clear understanding of both the device and interaction with the device, we can consider guidelines to support the development of supportive and engaging applications.

In order to explore the nature of interaction with head mounted virtual reality devices, we developed a set of mini-game applications. Through observing people interacting with the device and applications, we were able to generate a set of high level guidelines to support the development of engaging virtual reality interaction. This paper presents the initial outline of heuristics to assist designers and developers when working with these devices, with an emphasis on creating presence. The idea of presence is of prime focus, as it is one of the principal points of interest in achieving communicable enjoyment in virtual reality.

We will first discuss the nature and needs for virtual reality, and of presence as it relates to virtual reality. An outline of heuristic generation will be given, together with a description of our research and research approach. After describing the virtual reality sessions we conducted, we will outline the initial set of heuristics for working with head mounted display devices for virtual reality.

2. CONCEPTS
2.1 Virtual Reality
Virtual Reality (VR) refers to computer-generated simulations or environments [2] that a user experiences through an array of different technological means [18]. The aim of VR is to mimic sensory information from the real world, such as audio, tactile and visual input, and deliver them to a user through artificial means [4]. While the degree to which systems can achieve this are varying, VR setups that exist today can deliver 'real feeling' experiences.

Work on VR has occurred over the last few decades. As more research was conducted in the area, different ways of creating and delivering VR were established. Computer assisted virtual environment (CAVE) systems allowed users to stand in a room and interact with projections on the walls, simulating being in a different location [10]. In contrast, Head Mounted Displays (HMDs) allow for the displays to be strapped to a user's head. Companies such as Oculus, Sony and HTC lead the current development of consumer grade HMDs. Initial commercially available models for some of these HMDs are currently shipping to consumers, and several companies sell or provide Development Kits to developers. These development kit products are usually early iterations that are missing technical or experience driven features.

One of the major issues with past attempts and iterations on VR was the lack of capable hardware to achieve the required results [1]. This absence of hardware caused the development of primitive implementations that were difficult to use [4] resulted in nausea or 'simulator sickness' [21], or were simply too expensive to be adopted for wider use [10]. However, the new wave of technology has had predominantly positive feedback, giving consumer grade VR a more optimistic future.

This paper will define VR as "a real or simulated environment in which a perceiver experiences telepresence" [32]. This definition highlights the importance of telepresence, more commonly referred to simply as 'presence' [30], as a key aspect of VR. While there are still hardware issues to solve [1], developers must now look to the actual programs they write for VR, and what they can do to ensure a user's interaction and sense of presence.

2.2 Presence

Presence is a concept that has been defined in a variety of ways. The most common definition of presence describes it as the subjective sensation of "being there" [12, 16, 28]. Slater [30] goes on to define this as 'reported presence', which looks at what users subjectively report back about their experience. Other sources seek to find a less subjective definition, and interpret presence as the indiscernible replacement of sensory feedback with an equivalent virtual version [29]. Some definitions rely heavily on the user's ability to interact in the environment using their entire body. We will use the definition of 'reported presence' when discussing presence due to the restrictions of available input types at the time of research. Should a user report they felt 'present' in VR, this would be enough to say the game scenario is creating a sense of presence.

Slater [29] outlines three conditions for achieving presence in VR: that there is a continual sensory motor loop, where the user is able to continually perceive the world, that this perception mimics how the user can perceive the real world, and that the world behaves in a consistent way over time. The first and second refer mostly to attributes that immersive hardware should facilitate. The third refers to prolonging the sense of presence. In essence these conditions refer to creating a world that acts consistently over time and predictably to the user. It should be noted that this does not imply that the environment must replicate the real world exactly, but that it conforms to set rules that the simulation defines.

Presence is considered the most important aspect for indicating an enjoyable or successful VR experience [27]. A sense of presence is associated with user engagement, and as such for this paper a user experience representing high levels of presence will be deemed positive, while less presence will be deemed as a negative. Beyond taking a user's reported presence as a measure, behavioral observation will also be used. Should a user act as they would if the simulated events were actually happen, it can be said that the user is experiencing a high level of presence [31].

2.3 Game Design and Virtual Reality

In this paper we are focusing on the use of games within VR, as games represent an accessible implementation of technology with social implications. Game design has been defined as "the act of deciding what a game should be" [26]. The term is quite open and all encompassing, and as a result can be difficult to define beyond basic decision-making. In many situations game design is frequently applied directly to a person, à la the 'game designer' and defined from there [9, 26]. This paper will define game design as a way to refer to the decisions that a developer needs to make when creating a game [26].

Through literature and industry discussion, areas of concern have been raised when designing experiences for VR. Those of most prominence are:

- Height disparity [35], where adverse effects can occur to the player when in game eye level does not match that of the player in real life. This is most commonly observed when a player is sitting while using a HMD, even though the gameplay has the player walking around from a standing position. Players have reported ranging issues with height disparity, from noticing the discrepancy and losing their sense of presence, to indicating simulator sickness [21].

- Grabbing techniques [5], where players expect to be able to use full body movement to interact with the virtual environment. Due to limited input capabilities of current HMDs, designers must find an appropriate kinesthetic metaphor that does not decrease a player's sense of presence.

- Depth perception [35], where players are not used to games being presented in stereoscopic 3D (in the same sense of '3D movies'). While often depth perception will help create a sense of presence, certain situations can cause sensory illusions and may confuse the player. Games have been designed to use this in positive ways [3], however the effects on presence and depth illusions occurring when players do not expect them are unknown.

- Movement in a vessel, where it is thought that players are far more comfortable when using HMDs from a seated position. Particularly, it is commonly thought that placing the player inside a vehicle in-game and matching their real life seated position will greatly decrease instances of nausea and simulator sickness [25]. More generally, how a player perceives and reacts to unexpected or different ways of traversing will be explored.

- Extreme situations, such experiencing great heights [14]. A Player's willingness to cooperate in such scenarios is still under examination, particularly when players have pre-existing fears of such environments.

- Computer Controlled AI [30], where tests have shown players are more aware of the subtleties and movements of computer generated characters. This can cause problems when attempting to make rich environments that require Non-playable characters (NPCs), as players are more likely to lose presence if the NPCs do not appear act and react in a life-like manner.

It is our intent to examine each of these areas and generate an initial set of thoughts on how developers may be able to solve these issues. These solutions will then have implementation implications in other development areas.

2.4 Heuristics

Heuristic evaluation was originally defined as the "informal method of usability analysis where a number of evaluators are presented with an interface design and asked to comment on it" [24]. While this definition relies on specialists in the given field to conduct analysis [23], it was later found that a set of heuristics could be evaluated and recorded to allow others to conduct the analysis with high success rates. To this end, we define heuristic evaluation as "a method of usability evaluation where an analyst finds usability problems by checking the user interface against a set of supplied heuristics or principles" [19], where heuristics simply refers to a "checklist of issues to consider" [23].

Heuristic evaluation has been attempted on video games before [8, 11, 13], looking at usability, engagement and/ or fun, and also applied to interface elements of VR [33]. With the obvious overlap between VR environments and traditional video games, this past research could be considered pertinent in certain situations. However, this research is yet to be applied to VR, and current knowledge suggests the majority of these heuristics would either be irrelevant, likely to cause false positives, cause nausea or a lapse in presence.

This paper will generate a preliminary set of heuristics that can be used by game designers to build better, more engaging experiences for VR. These heuristics can then be evaluated for use in other VR applications. Heuristic evaluation allows individuals to conduct their own analysis, and gives us a means to present academic work in a more digestible way. There is a divide between the work that academia does and the games that professional developers make. Much research is done in fields that have an impact on game development, and yet the research is very rarely applied or even seen by those who could best utilize it. In an effort to overcome these issues, we aim to deliver our findings through a set of heuristics, and that the approachability that comes intrinsically to heuristic evaluation may allow developers to better employ the research.

3. RESEARCH APPROACH

This paper will use a qualitative approach, as the purpose is to identify how a person feels and understands a situation. The objective is to "measure relationships between variables" [15], or more specifically, seek to understand "the experience of individuals, captured in its "lived" form, with a minimum of preplanned, imposed structure" [15]. We aim to identify a set of problem points in the design of VR applications, looking to recognize those that are intrinsically tied to current game design practices.

An interpretivist paradigm has been applied to the research. Interpretivists "seek to combine data into systems of belief whose manifestations are specific to a case" [20]. This is applicable to this research, as it relies on observation and context; being able to understand then analyze a participant's experience in VR will form the basis of our outlined heuristics. Context is an imperative part of this research, and to not analyze the findings with this in mind would greatly limit the research [36].

3.1 Research Methodology

This research will use a case study methodology, as it allows for data to be collected in various forms that lend themselves to the creation of heuristics. As game designers predominantly look to examine player's emotions and feelings towards a game as they play, we must employ similar mechanisms to those of play testing to be able to inspect those same areas.

A case study methodology allows for the examination of happenings within context [36], which as discussed previously is necessary to understanding all the conditions affecting the results.

While a case study allows for many data collection methods, this research will utilise questionnaires, behavioral observation and think-aloud protocol (TAP) [17]. A small sample size will be used as this is within the recommended quantities of participants when conducting a case study [36].

3.2 Case Study

Participants were asked to complete tasks in seven scenes within an application. The application was developed using Unity3D with models sourced from the asset store. Scenes were designed by the researcher to investigate the previously mentioned problematic areas of VR development. Each scene corresponded to a specific task, namely:

1. Walk around and get comfortable in VR.

2. Pick up a rock, and attempt to throw it in one of the basketball hoops.

3. Do a few laps around the (driving) course.

4. Look and move around the environment.

5. Move around the environment.

6. Find the persons that are in the scene.

7. Move around on the ice.

A more in-depth description of each scene will be given while discussing data and findings.

The Oculus Rift Development Kit 1 was used as the HMD for this case study. At the time of testing it was the only HMD available to the researchers. A PS3 controller was chosen as the input device as at the time of research it was the most accessible, and it was not known the type of gamepad or the style of input that would ship with consumer HMDs. The consumer version of the Oculus Rift will rely on gamepad input upon release, and thus was deemed appropriate for use in this research.

At the beginning of the testing participants were asked what platforms they use to play games, to determine how familiar they were with the devices. A total of 15 people participated in the case study (2 female, 13 male). Convenience sampling methods were conducted for the purpose of this research. Recruitment of students as participants were conducted through brief announcements in lectures and reminders in a subsequent tutorial class. Non-student participants were recruited via a Facebook post by the researcher, and those interested were asked to contact him. Participants who had not used the Oculus Rift HMD previously were given extra time in the first scene to become familiar with the technology.

3.3 Data Collection and Data Analysis

It is important to ensure that findings are recorded with equal respect to both negative and positive results. As a result, three different data collection methods were used to ensure as much data could be recorded, and that any preconceived notions would not influence data. This study implemented behavioral observation, think-aloud protocol (TAP) and questionnaires [17].

Thematic analysis [7] was employed in order to find recurrent themes in the data. This approach was chosen to allow "a method for identifying, analyzing, and reporting patterns (themes) within data". It also allows for context to be applied, permitting various aspects to be interpreted with regard to the research topic [6]. The attributes of designing for VR are not well known, and thematic analysis allows for those attributes to be extracted.

Before conducting the study participants were informed that parts of the experience may cause nausea. A consent package was given to participants, and required the signature of the participant in order for the case study to commence. The package outlined the risks of nausea, that participation was voluntary, and that the session could be concluded at any stage should the participant feel the need for any reason.

3.4 Focus Areas

As the goal was to explore the attributes of the VR technology that influence interaction with the device, the prototype was designed to invoke certain elements that have been noticed by VR enthusiasts or academia as possible issues for players, as well as keeping the gameplay open to find further instances that may be of note. Each of the seven scenes was created around an area of designing for VR that has raised questions in the community. To summarise, those were:

1. The disparity of height between the player in game and actual height of the player outside of the game [35]. In Scene 1, the player view was deliberately placed higher than the players 'real life' height.

2. Testing an implementation of tactile feedback and the player's acceptance of gaming metaphors in VR [5]. Scene 2 will mimic a common metaphor for picking up and throwing objects featured in games and evaluate its effectiveness in VR. Scene 2 also involves some depth perception tests [35]. Multiple basketball hoops for throwing objects into will be included, which will vary in size to see if players notice, and how they respond.

3. Faster movement when the proposed scenario includes the fiction of sitting in a car/ vessel, and the player's response to sitting in a vehicle [34]. Scene 3 will have the player drive around a track, with the possibility of crashing or flipping the vehicle.

4. The participant's reaction to extreme heights, and their willingness to participate in otherwise impossible feats, such as jumping off the building [1, 14]. Scene 4 will place the player at the top of an unstable building to gauge their reaction.

5. Faster movement in the form of heightened running speed, without the guise of being inside some kind of vessel. Scene 5 will give players the ability to run super fast.

6. Participant responses to Non playable characters (NPCs) and how they read their intent/ actions [30]. Scene 6 will contain three NPCs that exhibit differing characteristics.

7. Participant reaction to low friction surfaces that cause gliding, and how their physical body responds to this difference in movement. Scene 7 will allow players to glide around on the surface of an ice-rink.

3.5 Scene 1

In this scene the player's camera was raised above the ground to a level higher than what would be typical in a first person video game. The camera sat just over 2 meters off the ground, meaning it was higher than the participant's eye levels in real life. Scene 1 involved walking around in a spaceship themed environment. The player could walk on suspended platforms above a purple colored liquid. The area was broken up into two separate rooms, both of which were very similar in appearance. The player was tasked with wandering on the platforms to get used to wearing the HMD and interacting with the virtual environment. Players were asked to do this from both the standard seated position and also while standing and to note any differences.

While most players needed to be prompted, generally all players

noticed height discrepancies between how tall the in game character was and how tall the player was while traversing the scene. Most players felt they were too tall. When asked to stand, most players did note that this felt 'closer' to what they expected, however still felt like the in game character was quite tall. Most couldn't cite a particular reason, while just a few suggested it was because the side rails on the platforms were short.

The height of the player in the game can affect how they perceive the field of view. While the field of view never changes, participants showed that they were more receptive to noticing the differing heights from the seated position, where they unconsciously have expectations of how far they can see that differed from what was presented. Most players could tell that the camera was further off the ground than what they were used to in real life, with only a few believing they were instead shorter. It is important to note however that most players needed to be prompted in this scene before taking in and assessing the height discrepancy. Only 3 players ever commented on a height change beyond this scene, where in actuality the height of the player differed in each, notably in Scene 4 where the player was made shorter then in all previous scenes.

What this tells us is that while players can perceive variances in height, as long as it is in the general range of where the player's eye level is in real life, the difference is negligible. This is easily solved in games where the in game character is in a seated position, as a player will most likely also be seated to play the game. VR companies such as Oculus stated early on during development they were targeting a "seated experience" [22], which would have caused issues when creating an experience where the in game fiction has the player standing and walking around. In more recent times, Oculus and developers alike have been creating experiences utilizing both. The key for developers will be determining if users are likely to stand or sit while playing their game.

If the player is seated while the in game character is standing, the discrepancy between the two visual heights will be noticed more readily by the player. The closer the player's view within the scene is to their current position in the real world the less chance the player will notice any differences. While the chances are still slim, the findings suggest moving the camera lower to have it more closely match the player's current sitting height will likely alleviate the chance of the difference being noticed.

3.6 Scene 2

In this scene the player starts in the middle of a desert themed area, where there are small rocks scattered on the ground, and larger rocks as scenery in the surrounding area. Ahead of the player there were 5 basketball hoops, which ranged in size from standard to triple what is normal. The player was asked, using controls on the gamepad, to pick up the smaller rocks and attempt to throw at least one into any of the basketball hoops. Once close enough to a rock and looking in its direction, players could press a button to pick the rock up. The rock would then hover about 30cms away from the player's viewpoint, and would require a second button push to throw. The longer the player held the button, the further the rock would be thrown.

Players had difficulty throwing a rock into one of the hoops, with most only ever achieving this right before moving onto the next scene. Some players had difficultly picking up the rock, struggling with attempting to put the rock about centre of the screen so that their button pressing would be registered. After getting to know how long holding the button would throw the rock, most players misjudged the size of the basketball hoops, throwing short almost always. Players eventually learnt to move much closer to the hoops, with most aiming for the smaller ones thinking they would be easier. Only one player gave up before getting a rock into a hoop.

Player's impressions varied greatly to do with having the rock hover in front of them as a metaphor for holding something. While some participants were more than happy with the implementation, thoughts ranged from finding it slightly odd to outright weird. Those who were comfortable with it were almost exclusively people who play video games daily. Daily game players mentioned having seen this kind of metaphor at work in other games, and through previous experience they were more comfortable.

Those who were inexperienced with using a gamepad, or indicated they did not play video games often, were more likely to voice disapproval. In contrast, those who played video games every day indicated they enjoyed the level's mechanics. Those who stated they didn't mind the metaphor also had an easier time throwing the rocks and understanding the mechanic. This suggests that borrowing from classic video game design tropes or elements will be more willingly accepted if the intended audience are seasoned gamers.

Some players also commented on the annoyance of having to look at the rock to be able to pick it up. Because the player had to be quite close to the rock in order for the game to recognise the player's intent to pick it up, it often resulted in requiring the player to move their neck into uncomfortable positions. Doing such an activity for an extended period of time would be damaging to the player and most likely also cause them to stop interacting with the game.

These points suggest it is unwise to use the HMD's head tracking as a predominant control source. Head movement should be not be dictated by the game, as its intended purpose is to let the player look around in the environment. The player should be able to look around freely while moving through the environment, as opposed to being forced to look in a given direction to interact.

3.7 Scene 3

This scene involved driving a car, where should a player take a corner too quickly the vehicle would flip and the player would be involved in a crash. The flipping of the car was to see how participants would react to such an event in VR. This scene's results that pertain to speed need to be compared to those that came from Scene 5 to be fully understood. The discussion on fast movement will be had with the discussion for Scene 5.

Most participants moved their body in someway as a reaction to the car flipping. Those who moved their head with the flipping car were the ones who reported feeling the most present in the scene. Knowing a level of presence can be shown through kinesic movement, we can say the more pronounced the involuntarily reaction was, the higher sense of presence the player felt. Those who elected to experience the crash several times were more likely to experience discomfort that was not always nausea related. While a few players did indicate nausea due to this event, this may have been influenced by the suboptimal level of immersion the hardware being used delivered.

As has been previously stated, it is well known that taking away head tracking from the player and forcing the camera not to react to the player's head movement can cause severe discomfort or nausea. While during the crash the player did not lose the ability to look left and right in the environment, the camera orientation was being dictated by the orientation of the car. In situations where the player is in control of that orientation it is unlikely that discomfort would be experienced, such as what a flight simulator would present. In the situation presented in the prototype however, the player does not have control over the flipping car, and unless they were doing so purposefully, may not have instigated the crash willingly. Another influencing factor may have been if the player did not expect for a crash occur, or did not realize what was happening when their car begun to spin.

Repeated plays of an experience such as the car flip appear to cause more discomfort then pleasure. However, players were experiencing significant levels of presence during these moments, as proven by their involuntary head movements in real life. Many participants reflexively moved their head in reaction to the car flip, and as discussed in Chapter 2, this tells us they were experiencing presence during this moment. Given this, we can conclude that such "catastrophic" events could be used sparingly to heighten player experience and their overall sense of presence.

3.8 Scene 4

Several large buildings that were beginning to decay populated this scene. While they were still standing, flora had begun to grow within the buildings. The player was placed atop one of the buildings, where no guardrails were present to ensure they did not fall off. The entire building was on a slight slant, making the ground the player was walking on uneven.

This scene was designed to test participant's reactions to a scenario that would usually invoke some sort of emotion. This scene was one where participants were most likely to voice emotion during playing, and was also cited in the questionnaire as the most emotional. Many players voiced concerns of vertigo, where reactions ranged from willing to move to the edge and look down happily to edging towards the drop very slowly. What is interesting about this scene is that participants that voiced concerns of vertigo, said that the scene was 'scary', or reacted adversely in some way were also likely to say that the scene was the most real or that it was their favorite experience from the prototype.

This suggests VR may allow for more emotional games. Where traditional games tend to focus on action as a predominant force for creating 'fun', VR will allow for game design that is more focused on emotions. In much the same way people enjoy horror movies, Participants whom were noticeably taken aback from the scenario said that the scene was still very enjoyable. While both forms will still be possible, it may be wise for developers to aim for more emotional designs first, before expanding.

3.9 Scene 5

In this scene players were given the ability to run much faster than normal. The scene was set in Hong Kong at nighttime, and was made a little larger then the other environments due to the player's increased movement capabilities. This scene was created in stark contrast to Scene 3 looking to see the reaction of players when moving at high speeds when not contained within a vehicle in the fiction.

Reactions were fairly mixed; some found the speed too much, with several finding it induced nausea. Others really appreciated the bonus speed, finding it enjoyable. A few people once experiencing the faster movement speed found going back to the standard speed to be annoying and too slow. A couple of participants said it was their favorite type of movement, even though one of those people said it did cause some nausea.

The idea of the driving level was to see if participants were more comfortable moving at high speeds when placed inside a vehicle. This is supposed to allow the simulation to feel more "real"; walking around at high speed is not something that can be done in real life, whereas traveling in a car is done frequently. Comparing the results to those of Scene 3 suggests that this may not be the case. More participants said that they preferred the movement style in Scene 5 than they did of Scene 3.

While it is commonly thought that players are more comfortable when under the illusion of being transported inside a vessel, these results indicate otherwise. The belief that being placed inside a transportation vessel will increase presence for the player may be incorrect. It is possible that matching the player's height and body position in VR with their real world position was conflated with having the user placed within a virtual vehicle. The results indicate that these ideas may be separated.

3.10 Scene 6

This scene was set in Tuscany. Players were placed at the back of a small villa, where they could wander inside or around to the front and have a view of the water. Three NPCs were placed within the environment. One was making direct eye contact with the player's camera; the second was programmed to look off to the right of the player's camera, but always to a specific spot in space, while the third did not react. All the NPCs used the same character model, and exhibited subtle movements as though they were breathing. Each NPC was holding a weapon, which was purely cosmetic. They blinked occasionally. This scene aimed to look at how players interact with NPCs in VR.

There were mixed feels about the NPCs. A lot of the participants had adverse reactions to the NPCs, most citing some sort of emotional resistance to them. Most participants assumed some sort of hostility from the NPCs, likely due to their menacing stance and that they were holding a gun. The 3rd NPC was the best received; of participants who made comments on him, they were happy that he was enjoying the view, although some took the fact that he was ignoring them begrudgingly. Of those who spoke to what the NPCs may have been thinking, some were scared or concerned by the first as he was staring at them, while the second was allegedly hiding something. A notable amount of participants were not compelled to make comment on the NPCs. This indicates that they were likely uninterested with the NPCs, due to them not doing much in the scene beyond moving their heads.

To include NPCs in the game they should serve a tangible purpose. We can also see that players will project intentions and thoughts on the NPCs based on small or inadvertent movements and animations. This means that much more effort must be focused on ensuring NPC animations convey the intended emotions or motivations. Inadequate representations of NPCs appear to weaken a player's reported and observed presence. It is difficult based on the research to determine if the NPCs were influencing the player's sense of being in the environment or their sense of being with another person. Each would require different implementations to improve, and was not within the scope of this paper to explore.

We can state more generally that a level of realism is required for NPCs in VR. Players appear to more willingly accept NPCs as life-like, and thusly perceive non-verbal communications such as body language more readily. A dissonance may then occur if what a player perceives is not reflected through the actions or speech of the NPC.

3.11 Scene 7

This scene was themed to be an ice rink. A large ridge of land surrounded frozen water in a donut shape, which itself then surrounded a smaller mass of snow-covered ground. The ice changed how the player interacted with the ground; inertia was not lost straight away when the player stopped moving forward. Instead, their character would continue to slide for a distance before gradually coming to a complete stop. This scene intended to investigate how movement that was predictable but still out of the player's control would be received in VR.

Participants reacted as expected in this scene. They enjoyed sliding on the ice, and for the most part this did not cause any of the participants to feel ill. Several players tensed up while sliding on the ice, however this was not the norm, which suggests this scene did not create the sense of presence some of the other scenes did.

Of note was that several participants made comment on the friction levels of the ice. All of those who commented concurred that the ice was not as slippery as they felt it should be, and would have preferred if the distance the player slid were longer. While this is something that is easy to change, it does suggest that players in VR are more in tune with the experiences they are having. They are much more likely to notice if something that is intending on reproducing reality is achieving that goal. This may mean when designing for VR developers may need to be more precise when deciding on values where players are likely to have experienced something similar in real life.

3.12 Emergent Findings

While each of the scenes aimed to identify something particular, it was hoped that they were designed in a way that would result in some findings that were not expected, and could aid in the creation of new heuristics.

In Scene 1, some of the participants that noticed (without being prompted) they were taller then usual cited environmental cues as the reason they felt too tall. This speaks to a need to keep the scale of the world consistent. In traditional games certain elements have to be made bigger or smaller so that they actually look the correct size. A good example of this is in first person games, where objects that are more important to the player are often made larger to stand out. In contrast, out-of-scale objects in VR become very noticeable, and can have an adverse affect on presence.

On a similar note, the world needs to be consistent otherwise players will notice the parts that are not. From Scene 6, several players were noticeably taken aback when they saw that the NPCs had guns. In many first person traditional games this is not something noteworthy; many games revolve around shooting and seeing NPCs that carry weapons. But in the prototype the players had played through 5 previous scenes, which did not contain any violence or weapons. The Tuscany setting of the scene also leant itself to a peaceful play scenario, as a setting such as this is not often associated with guns and violence. To suddenly have NPCs who were carrying weapons was a surprise to a lot of the participants. In a similar vain to the concept of 'foreshadowing' in cinema and novels, if a character with a gun had appeared in the first scene, it is possible the players would not have reacted the way they did upon first seeing a weapon. The characteristics of a game are defined in the player's mind in the first moments of gameplay, and they hold these expectations throughout the session.

Many participants in the questionnaire highlighted the need to have an in game body to represent themselves while in the VR. What is interesting about this is that these same people had unfavorable opinions of the avatar in Scene 3. While this avatar was not very complete or complicated, players felt most comfortable in this scene when their body in real life matched the positioning of the in game avatar. As the avatar in the game didn't move, participants were putting themselves into the position of the avatar in order to get this feeling. This suggests that either an avatar should reflect the body position of the player entirely, or be left out entirely. As reflected in the results for Scene 3, players reacted adversely to noticing they had an in game avatar that did not respond to their movements. In contrast, before they realised they had any avatar at all, responses ranged from not noticing at all to undeterred.

In the questionnaire most players highlighted Scene 6 as the one that felt most real. Most associated this with the higher level of detail, as well as the additions such as butterflies, the boats in the water and the added sound effects. This scene was a modified version of the example scene that Oculus provide with the Unity SDK. Sounds and finer details much like the butterflies were outside of the scope for the other scenes that were created, but as this scene already included them they were left in. The however suggests to us that scenes that contain more details aid in creating presence.

It is also useful to note that in most of the scenes that were created players were not compelled to explore outside of the area they started in (A notable counter example here is Scene 5, where the faster movement allowed players to more easily traverse the map). In scenes where players were able to roam freely they almost exclusively did not, and stuck to the area they started in. Scene 2 included scenery that was hovering over the ground, but as participants chose not to explore behind them not one of them noticed. After jumping off the building in Scene 4, almost all players chose to stick to investigating the building they had just fallen from, as opposed to making their way across the level to one of the many other buildings that could be seen.

These points suggest that environments for VR do not have to be vast, but they do have to be detailed. Players will happily spend time investigating a small section of the environment if it is detailed enough instead of attempting to traverse large distances.

4. HEURISTICS
Based on the analysis of the data collected, we have outlined areas of interest that should be converted into heuristics for the purpose of heuristic evaluation. Below is an initial draft of those heuristics with a brief description.

- Camera height should be between player's eye level and expected avatar height. The player will notice if their height in game is too far from their eye level in the current position they are in. If the player is not going to be in the same position as the game avatar, then a middle ground will need to be found to avoid the player discovering the dissonance. Heuristic based on findings from Scene 1.

- Design metaphors to suit your audience. Players that are not as accustomed to gaming will expect game mechanics that resemble real life more then those who have more experience with traditional games. Only borrow metaphors from traditional games if your audience is seasoned gamers. Heuristic based on findings from Scene 2.

- Do not necessitate head tracking as an essential part of gameplay. Designing a game around constant head movement will quickly cause neck strain and pain to the player. Game essential controls should not be tied to the movement of the head. Give the player something to look at, but don't necessitate the action. Heuristic based on findings from Scene 2.

- Do not frequently repeat in game events that dictate player orientation. Gameplay that dictates the orientation of the in game character can be used for emphasis but should not be repeated frequently. Players will experience great discomfort from repeated incidents, but they can be enjoyable if used sparingly. Heuristic based on findings from Scene 3.

- Design first for an emotional response, then to create spectacle. Players respond most to slower, emotionally driven gameplay rather then fast action sequences. Designing an experience that creates an emotional reaction should be first priority, followed by adding additional layers. Heuristic based on findings from Scene 4.

- NPCs must be as lifelike as possible. The player will notice odd NPC behavior much more readily than in traditional games. If NPCs are to be included, they should serve a purpose and not be just background decoration, where they should be as realistic and as fleshed out as possible. Heuristic based on findings from Scene 6.

- Scenarios that the player may have experienced need to be fine-tuned. Greater care must be taken in designing experiences players can identify with. Subtle differences will be noticed more readily, which will take the player out of the experience. Heuristic based on emergent findings, as well as Scene 7.

- Don't diverge from the expectations set at the beginning without reason. Occurrences that do not conform to the rules of the environment as defined at the beginning of the gameplay will break presence. Changes should be introduced with reason and subtly. Heuristic based on emergent findings.

- Either the player avatar is complete or do not include one. Players will expect a fully functional body that mimics what they do in real life. If it does not, it is likely that they will be distracted and lose their sense of presence. Players cannot be distracted by something that isn't there. Heuristic based on emergent findings, as well as Scene 2.

- Design a small, detailed environment over a vast one. Players will choose to explore the environment in their general vicinity rather than traveling great distances to explore. Choose to create a smaller but interesting situation over creating a massive environment that looks mostly the same. Heuristic based on emergent findings.

5. CONCLUSION
This paper presents initial work on identifying a set of heuristics to aid developers in designing for presence in VR. A sense of presence has been associated with an enjoyable or successful VR experience [27], and as such is critical if our social interactions facilitated by this technology are to be positive and meaningful.

Head mounted display VR technology is a platform that is still evolving. Problematic designs can be damaging to emerging technologies when exposure and popular opinion are still being formed. The aim of creating heuristics outlining the current understandings of VR design is so developers have an easily applicable means to improve their practices. These heuristics represent a first pass in understanding VR design using game design as a social implementation. It was not within the scope of this initial project to test these heuristics. Future research will look to evaluate the heuristics academically to ensure they work to the advantage of both developers and people using the technology.

As time progresses more will be understood about designing for presence in VR. Through iterative design and trial and error developers will come to understand the differences in philosophy between traditional and VR application design. However these methods involve a great deal of commitment and often result in failed or unprofitable products. The creation of a prototype and subsequent analysis was done with the intent of making these issues more recognizable. Through the creation of these heuristics the hope is our findings can be applied to future VR projects with ease.

6. REFERENCES

[1] Abrash, M. 2014. What VR Could, Should, and Almost Certainly Will Be within Two Years.

[2] Biocca, F. and Levy, M.R. 1995. *Communication in the Age of Virtual Reality*. Lawrence Erlbaum Associates.

[3] Blaha, J. and Gupta, M. 2014. Diplopia: A virtual reality game designed to help amblyopics. *Virtual Reality (VR), 2014 iEEE* (2014), 163–164.

[4] Boas, Y.A.G.V. 2013. Overview of Virtual Reality Technologies. (Southhampton, 2013).

[5] Bowman, D.A. and Hodges, L.F. 1997. An evaluation of techniques for grabbing and manipulating remote objects in immersive virtual environments. *Proceedings of the 1997 symposium on Interactive 3D graphics* (1997), 35–ff.

[6] Boyatzis, R.E. 1998. *Transforming Qualitative Information: Thematic Analysis and Code Development*. SAGE Publications.

[7] Braun, V. and Clarke, V. 2006. Using thematic analysis in psychology. *Qualitative Research in Psychology*. 3, 2 (Jan. 2006), 77–101.

[8] Clanton, C. 1998. An Interpreted Demonstration of Computer Game Design. *CHI 98 Cconference Summary on Human Factors in Computing Systems* (New York, NY, USA, 1998), 1–2.

[9] Crawford, C. 1984. The art of computer game design. (1984).

[10] Cruz-Neira, C. et al. 1993. Surround-screen projection-based virtual reality: the design and implementation of the CAVE. *Proceedings of the 20th annual conference on Computer graphics and interactive techniques* (1993), 135–142.

[11] Desurvire, H. et al. 2004. Using heuristics to evaluate the playability of games. *CHI'04 extended abstracts on Human factors in computing systems* (2004), 1509–1512.

[12] Draper, J.V. et al. 1998. Telepresence. *Human Factors: The Journal of the Human Factors and Ergonomics Society*. 40, 3 (Sep. 1998), 354–375.

[13] Federoff, M.A. 2002. *Heuristics and usability guidelines for the creation and evaluation of fun in video games*. Citeseer.

[14] Freeman, D. et al. 2014. Height, social comparison, and paranoia: An immersive virtual reality experimental study. *Psychiatry Research*. 218, 3 (Aug. 2014), 348–352.

[15] Haldemann, V. 1993. Editorial Qualitative Methods: Why? *Canadian Journal on Aging/La Revue canadienne du vieillissement*. 12, 02 (1993), 129–138.

[16] Held, R.M. and Durlach, N.I. 1992. Telepresence. *Presence: Teleoperators and Virtual Environments*. 1, 1 (Jan. 1992), 109–112.

[17] Järvinen, P. 2004. *On Research Methods*. Opinpajan Kirja.

[18] Krueger, M.W. 1991. *Artificial Reality II*. Addison-Wesley.

[19] Lavery, D. et al. 1996. *Heuristic evaluation. Usability evaluation materials*. Tech. Rep. TR-1996-15. Glasgow, Scotland: University of Glasgow.

[20] Lin, A.C. 1998. Bridging Positivist and Interpretivist Approaches to Qualitative Methods. *Policy Studies Journal*. 26, 1 (Mar. 1998), 162–180.

[21] Lin, J.J.-W. et al. 2002. Effects of field of view on presence, enjoyment, memory, and simulator sickness in a virtual environment. *IEEE Virtual Reality, 2002. Proceedings* (2002), 164–171.

[22] Mitchell, N. et al. 2014. 2014 Oculus Connect - Fourth Keynote - Group.

[23] Nielsen, J. 1994. Heuristic evaluation. *Usability inspection methods*. 17, 1 (1994), 25–62.

[24] Nielsen, J. and Molich, R. 1990. Heuristic Evaluation of User Interfaces. *Proceedings of the SIGCHI Conference on Human Factors in Computing Systems* (New York, NY, USA, 1990), 249–256.

[25] Regan, C. 1995. An investigation into nausea and other side-effects of head-coupled immersive virtual reality. *Virtual Reality*. 1, 1 (Jun. 1995), 17–31.

[26] Schell, J. 2008. *The Art of Game Design: A Book of Lenses*. Taylor & Francis.

[27] Schubert, T. et al. 2001. The Experience of Presence: Factor Analytic Insights. *Presence*. 10, 3 (Jun. 2001), 266–281.

[28] Sheridan, T.B. 1994. Further musings on the psychophysics of presence. *Humans, Information and Technology* (Oct. 1994), 1073–1077 vol.2.

[29] Slater, M. et al. 2009. How we experience immersive virtual environments: the concept of presence and its measurement. (Jan. 2009).

[30] Slater, M. 2009. Place illusion and plausibility can lead to realistic behaviour in immersive virtual environments. *Philosophical Transactions of the Royal Society B: Biological Sciences*. 364, 1535 (2009), 3549–3557.

[31] Slater, M. 2007. The concept of presence and its measurement. *PEACH Summer School, Santorini, Greece*. (2007).

[32] Steuer, J. 1992. Defining Virtual Reality: Dimensions Determining Telepresence. *Journal of Communication*. 42, 4 (Dec. 1992), 73–93.

[33] Sutcliffe, A. and Gault, B. 2004. Heuristic evaluation of virtual reality applications. *Interacting with Computers*. 16, 4 (Aug. 2004), 831–849.

[34] van Veen, H.A.H.C. et al. 1998. Navigating through a virtual city: Using virtual reality technology to study human action and perception. *Future Generation Computer Systems*. 14, 3–4 (Aug. 1998), 231–242.

[35] Ware, C. et al. 1993. Fish tank virtual reality. *Proceedings of the INTERACT'93 and CHI'93 conference on Human factors in computing systems* (1993), 37–42.

[36] Yin, R.K. 2013. *Case Study Research: Design and Methods*. SAGE Publications.

New Product Diffusion: The Role of Sentiment Content

Tung Cu
SUNY Plattsburgh
101 Broad Street
Plattsburgh, NY 12901
(518) 564-2777
tcu001@plattsburgh.edu

Helmut Schneider
Louisiana State University
E. J. Ourso College of Business
Baton Rouge, LA 70803
(225) 578-2516
hschnei@lsu.edu

James Van Scotter
Louisiana State University
E. J. Ourso College of Business
Baton Rouge, LA 70803
(225) 578-4792
jvanscot@lsu.edu

ABSTRACT

The current study is focusing on diffusion and adoption of new digital artifacts. The goal is to explore the social role of user-generated content (UGC) during the diffusion process of digital products in the context of online social networks. Data collection is conducted on 154 new digital products during a two-year timeframe. Results of the study provide a deeper insight into the influence of textual UGC sentiment on new product diffusion and how such a web system (i.e.: online social networks) can help to enable a process of value co-creation. The overall finding shows that Volume of Post and UGC Sentiment have a dynamic impact on Diffusion (Adoption Rate) of digital products.

The study sheds light on the crowding power and the long-tail effect in online social networks. Findings also offer valuable implications for organizations to set up their strategic vision in terms of digital marketing, customer relationship management, and information dissemination.

Keywords

User-generated content, new product diffusion, sentiment analysis, video game, information retrieval.

1. INTRODUCTION

It has become clear that Online Social Networks (OSN) have grown to be one of the most prominent forms of communication of our time. OSNs are notable in that they allow the creation and exchange of User Generated Content or UGC [26], and as such have become a tool for bringing together small contributions from millions of people, making their contributions matter (Time Magazine, 25 December, 2006). This trend is no longer limited to teenagers, but now also includes older generations. It is therefore reasonable to say that UGC is an important subject for many individuals and organizations who want to make profitable use of OSN which is a collective power that will "change the way the world changes". John Rendon, the president of Rendon Group, a global strategic communications consultancy, said that "the game changer" is "user-created content."

SIGMIS-CPR '16, June 02-04, 2016, Alexandria, VA, USA.
© 2016 ACM. ISBN 978-1-4503-4203-2/16/06 $15.00
DOI: http://dx.doi.org/10.1145/2890602.2890627

A number of scholars across different disciplines have investigated various aspects of UGC social influence such as reviews and movie revenue [14, 29]; review and sales or sale ranking [12, 22, 40]; affective content and sales conversion [27, 30]; user rating and software market share [15]; Twitter sentiment, public mood, and voting behavior [7]; and chatting and stock performance [38].

The literature shows that typical UGC variables such as volume of chatter (Volume of Post), richness of content (Depth of Post), and product rating (Rating) have revealed their role of social influence. Although the effects of UGC on organizational performance has widely received attention from the academic community, it is a surprise that little, if any, research has been done to explore the dynamic relationship between sentiment and diffusion. Therefore, the purpose of the current study is to fill this gap by integrating UGC variables into the original diffusion model to explain dynamic patterns of the relationship between sentiment and new product diffusion.

In the current study, we aim to empirically document the role of sentiment content in shaping dynamic patterns of digital product diffusion in online social networks. This study is concerned with the following research questions: *How does UGC sentiment shape dynamic patterns of digital product diffusion in OSN?*

2. SENTIMENT AND DIFFUSION

When it comes to deciding whether or not to adopt a new product, people may rely on their own knowledge when comparing benefits against costs and risks. However, when facing a certain level of uncertainty, they can also look to external sources to help make their decision. The literature on social media networks suggests that peer-to-peer influence is one of the strongest influences on users' behavior [6]. This form of social influence can occur when UGC, usually in a textual form, is used as a medium to transfer ideas from one individual to another. In such cases, users' emotional states can be evoked when they are reading product feedback or comments containing sentiment content [28]. This is congruent with psychological research in which people rely on feelings when making judgments [21]. In addition, affective content can influence their thoughts and behaviors which lead to changes in their judgment of products [3, 39]. Thus, sentiment about a new product can effect an online user's decision to use that product. Sentiment could predict the diffusion of a new product for several reasons:

First, past research on UGC has shown that the intensity of textual sentiment (valence) can have a significant impact on review helpfulness and eventually on the sales of physical goods, a proxy of diffusion [17, 30, 34]. Second, unlike organization-created information, UGC can be collected at a relatively fast pace and even up-to-the-minute, as shown in the data collection section of the current study. Thus, UGC sentiment could represent hot news and rich information about the product performance and it could make the digitalized product more viral [5]. Third, in the information age, potential adopters are increasingly overwhelmed with the amount of information they receive every day. They usually look for helpful summaries or evaluations on the pros and cons of the product [10, 33]. Moreover, a previous study regarding review-length data suggests that online users read comment text rather than relying only on summary statistics [12]. Fourth, past research has shown that users rely more on information from other users' rather than from the company's official channel. Consumers have developed a general tendency to disbelieve or be skeptical toward marketing messages. The reason is that UGC is more up-to-date, objective and real because it is provided by other users [6, 19].

The above reasons clearly indicate that UGC sentiment is a good candidate for predicting the diffusion of a new product. However, the impact may not be instant, but delayed and can have feedback from the diffusion process. Unlike traditional word of mouth that is faded out in voicing communication, online UGC in social networks are recorded and presented for anyone who is interested in the new product. Thus, the UGC posted after the product's introduction can stay for a long time and could have an impact on a potential adopter weeks after the posted date [12]. Moreover, existing adopters who have bought the product might chat about it on the social network they are a member of. Other potential adopters who are uninformed or who are undecided about which brand to buy may consult UGC sentiment before finalizing their decision. The online reviews and discussion could subsequently affect their decision. At the aggregate level, these decisions would translate into adoption rate. However, it might take anywhere from a few days to a few weeks for UGC sentiment to reflect in the adoption rate because of several reasons. First, online users have to develop trust towards online reviews from strangers whom they have never met before. They need time to extract and digest the information they can count on. Second, usage complexity, especially in the case of high involvement products, might cause uncertainty, risk, and unforeseen costs for adopters. UGC sentiment itself has to take time to diffuse among social network users, and thus slow down the diffusion process.

Reverse impact of new product diffusion on UGC sentiment may also happen. This process begins with the first group of adopters when available information does not yet exist. Usually, the majority of early adopters are active members of the social network. They are motivated to post their reviews and discussions about the new product. Depending on how viral these reviews are, UGC sentiment can evolve strongly or weakly. Some potential adopters might be impressed by the overwhelming sentiment and quickly adopt the new product. Other potential adopters might take time to search for more product reviews from different sources enabling them to compare their anticipation of new product perception with the external sentiment before making their decision. Other innovation characteristics such as relative advantage, compatibility and availability also contribute to a voluntary acceptance or a delay adoption of the new product [2]. Therefore, we believe that *Sentiment has a dynamic relationship with Diffusion (Adoption Rate) and that it might take time for Sentiment to truly effect Diffusion and vice versa.*

3. DIFFUSION MODEL

To propose a new model for our study, we first rely on a traditional diffusion model which well depict the influence of past

adoptions of a new product innovation on diffusion [4, 16, 35]. The Bass model shows that Diffusion (dY/dt) at time t is a function of Past Adoption (Yt-1) in both level and square formats. In addition to Past Adoption, the literature indicates that Sentiment, Volume of Post, Depth of Post and Rating related to multiple product attributes are good predictors of Diffusion [9, 31]. Therefore, the below equation (1) mathematically describes the relationship between Diffusion and its predictors:

$$\text{Diffusion}_t = Y_t - Y_{t-1} = \alpha_0 + \alpha_1 Y_{t-1} + \alpha_2 Y_{t-1}^2 + \beta_1(\text{Sentiment})_{t-i}$$

$$+ \beta_2(\text{Volume of Post})_{t-i} + \beta_3(\text{Depth of Post})_{t-i} + \beta_4(\text{Rating})_{t-i} +$$

$$\xi_{,t}$$

Where:
Diffusion $(Y_t - Y_{t-1})$: Adoption Rate (weekly) is defined as the number of new adopters who adopt a new digital product at time t.
Past Adoption (Y_{t-1}): The accumulative number of adopters at t-1
Sentiment: Weekly sum of the positive valence and negative valence of the product in a week.
Volume of Post: The weekly total number of reviews, messages, or comments posted about the product
Depth of Post: The weekly average number of words of reviews about the product
Rating (of Community): The weekly average rating score of the product

4. METHODOLOGY

In our research design, we select the study industry and site on several criteria to ensure the feasibility, validity, and reliability of the study. That being said, the video game industry was selected for several reasons. First, video games are one of the most popular digitalized products. More than 150 million Americans play video games, according to the newest report's ESA Group. The video game industry is currently growing much faster than any other entertainment industry such as music and movies. Second, a video game can be classified as high-involvement product. Thus, the role of reviews is potentially greater for video games than for other types of digitalized products. Moreover, video games generally contain rich content because it usually takes up to the whole week for a player to conquer one. Therefore, reading game reviews is quite important for gamers to avoid bad purchases and wasted time from playing a boring game. To select the study site, we follow the [11] framework using several criteria. First, the website must have rich data on textual UGC across the time period of investigation. Second, users' adoptions over time should be countable. Third, players' reviews and discussion which signal the product's diffusion, have to be retrievable. Using these criteria leads us to select the gaming website suggested by [40].

Traditionally, past research relies on survey data to study diffusion-related topics. While this kind of informed data may take some advantages to serve for a deductive approach, its unresolved limitations of data quality and availability prevent us to use the method in an online setting. Survey sampling and confirming individual source of data might not possible. Unlike survey, Chau and Xu's approach uses a real website for a field experiment to control data quality and enrich data availability.

Regarding the sampling design, we choose a one year round, from February 2012 to October 2012, to extract a list of targeted video games. Note that the actual time for data collection extended to two years to cover one-year span for games released in October 2012. Unlike previous studies, we apply a systematic sampling method to extract a list of gamers to count the number of adoptions over time. We use the search engine provided by the website to search for all usernames starting with all numeric and alphabet letters. We then randomly select a starting username of each 0-9 and a-z list of usernames. Using a step of 10, we finally obtain a subject sample consisting of video gamers who has adopted at least one game.

Since the study uses panel data for the model, the database includes three different data sets. While the first data set yields data for video games as the main unit of analysis, the second data set yields data for diffusion variables; and the third data set yields data for UGC variables. The first data set consists of 282 games. However, to avoid result bias, some game titles released on multiple consoles were dropped, narrowing the sample further to 260 games. Since at least 6 data points are required to apply a time-series analysis, 106 games were dropped. The final sample consists of 154 game titles for time-series analysis. The second data set provides individual information of gamers' adoption behavior. The data set consists of 105,454 gamers. To obtain the number of adoptions overtime, we follow the procedure proposed by [18]. An adoption is recorded if a new game title appears in the gaming list of a video gamer. To construct the third data set, we collect all reviews of each video game posted on the website. In total, the UGC database sample contains 93,879 posts between February 2012 and October 2012. We used SAS Sentiment Studio software to quantify sentiment of reviews and followed the procedure proposed by [1]. The combination of the three data sets yields a complete panel data (weekly) of 7,183 records for 154 video games in the time range between February 2012 and October 2012.

5. EMPIRICAL RESULTS

5.1 Unit Root Test

The unit root tests are very consistent. The results show that all panel unit root tests, except Breitung's linear trend [8], are significantly rejected at an alpha level of 5% or lower. These tests also indicate that all variables of interest, except Rating, can be considered weak stationary[1].

5.2 Endogeneity Test

A series of Granger causality tests are performed on each pair of variables [20]. We use lags up to 12 (a quarter) as a rule of thumb for a weekly event having some sort of cyclical effects. The Granger Causality tests indicate substantial endogeneity among the variables analyzed. Especially, at a level of lags < 4, all hypothesized exogenous variables except Rating show a Granger causality on Diffusion and vice versa. In contrast, when the lag level is larger than or equal to 4, except Rating (first difference), Diffusion does not cause a significant Granger on any other three variables. Only Sentiment and Volume of Post have Grange Causality with Diffusion. Dual causalities between Diffusion and other exogenous variables, when lag is less than 4, explain the dynamic relationships among these variables during the first 4 weeks (one month). See Table 1.

We can infer that during the initial stage some active members, game advocators or pre-adopters who added a game of interest into their wish lists might start to post some comments or reviews about the game, which motivates early adopters to adopt and play the game. A number of them are also active members.

They then would come back to the game page and post what they might experience with the game. Depending on the level of accumulated sentiment, this loop will evolve more or less. Thus, there is a dual causality between Diffusion and Sentiment. Note that one month is also the average time for a gamer to play and finish a game. With lags larger than 4, while Sentiment and Volume of Post still show some motivation for new adopters, a number of previous adopters did not come back to post on the game page since they did not want to comment on the game that already receives a number of posts [13]. Thus, after a few weeks, Diffusion in the previous time period does not indicate any signal about changing UGC levels of the next period. Therefore, we only have a cause from UGC to Diffusion during this time. In addition to 12 lags tested, the study also performs Granger Causality Tests for lags of 13 to 16 and found that the lags of 14 and 15 tests indicate some unstable causality, while the lag of 16 test shows no causality among variables. The extending summary of Granger tests for lags of 13 to 16 was not presented here because it does not affect the outcome of our research.

Table 1: Summary of Granger Test Results

IVs	Granger	DV	Significant	Optimal
Sentiment	→	Diffusion	Sig. @ lag = 1 ÷ 12	Lag = 2
Sentiment	←	Diffusion	Sig. @ lag = 1 ÷ 3; NS @ lag = 4 ÷ 12	Lag = 2
Volume of Post	→	Diffusion	Sig. @ lag = 1 ÷ 12	Lag = 2
Volume of Post	←	Diffusion	Sig. @ lag = 1 ÷ 3; NS @ lag = 4 ÷ 12	Lag = 2
Depth of Post	→	Diffusion	Sig. @ lag = 1; NS @ lag >1	Lag = 1
Depth of Post	←	Diffusion	Sig. @ lag = 1 ÷ 3; NS @ lag = 4 ÷ 12	Lag = 1
D(Rating)	→	Diffusion	NS @ lag = 1 ÷ 12	NA
D(Rating)	←	Diffusion	Sig. @ lag = 4 ÷ 11; NS @ lag = 1 ÷ 3	Lag = 11

Note: "→" means a lagged effect, while "←" a feedback effect.

A previous study found that 50% adoptions occur within 4 months after a video game was released [40]. The 4-month period is almost equal to 16 weeks (16 lags). This means that reciprocal effects among variables are more likely to occur in the first half of the diffusion process than in the second half. The result shares a common agreement with past research and gives positive support on the idea that UGC has a dynamic relationship with diffusion in the early stage than the late stage of the diffusion process.

5.3 Cointegration Test

The cointegration test can be done with a procedure developed by [24, 25]. As shown in the section of panel unit root test, Sentiment, Volume of Post, and Rating are non-stationary in one of the test procedures. Thus, the panel cointegration model will consists of these variables. The cointegration results show that the tests do not detect any long-term equilibrium among the evolving variables, even when the dependent variable, Diffusion, is added into the model. The Johansen Fisher Statistics values from both trace test and max-Eigen test are significantly higher than Chi-square critical values in all cases of hypothesized number of cointegrations. Therefore, we can conclude that these variables can be included in an autoregression model. However,

---

[1] Test details will be provided as if requested.

Pedroni and Kao test shows a cointegration among Sentiment and Volume of Post.

6. MODEL SPECIFICATION

6.1 Vector Autoregressive Model

According to the above Johansen test, no cointegration was found among variables of interest. Thus, a VAR model can be used in this case. The above Granger-Causality (endogeneity) test indicates that there are dual causalities among variables in some points. Based on the result, the vector of endogenous variables includes Adoption Rate, Sentiment, and Volume of Post. The vector of exogenous variables for each endogenous variable consists of an intercept, Past Adoption, Square of Past Adoption, Sentiment, Volume of Post, Depth of Post, and Rating. Before a full VAR model is analyzed, it is necessary to conduct a buffer step in which we can exam a partial VAR model which only includes Diffusion and Sentiment. Since the Granger tests show dual causalities between them for the lags less than 4 and optimal at 2, the parameter for the lag intervals of endogenous variables will be 1 to 2. To analyze the reciprocal effects between Diffusion and Sentiment, we perform two VAR models. In the first one, Diffusion is modeled to depend on Sentiment and its one and two lags. Note that by nature, the level and square of past adoption variables are added into the model. In the second model, Sentiment is assigned as the endogenous variable, whereas Diffusion as the exogenous variable. By default, the one and two lags of both Sentiment and Diffusion are added into the model.

On one hand, the result from the first model shows that there are lag effects on both Diffusion and Sentiment. Specifically, Sentiment positively stimulates instant adoption, after one week and after two weeks. Likewise, Diffusion (adoption rate) can impact on Sentiment in the same week or after two weeks. This is consistent with previous studies which propose lagged effects of online word-of-mouth on a retail store's online traffic [36]. See Table 2.

Table 2: Dynamic Model of Diffusion and Sentiment

DV = Diffusion	Model 1	DV = Sentiment	Model 2
Past Adoption Y_{t-1}	0.0164		
Past Adoption Y_{t-1}^2	-9.29E-07		
Sentiment	1.617	Diffusion	0.0025
One-lagged Sentiment	0.697	One-lagged Diffusion	5.02E-05*
Two-lagged Sentiment	-0.047*	Two-lagged Diffusion	0.0015
One-lagged Diffusion	0.151	One-lagged Sentiment	0.044
Two-lagged Diffusion	0.188	Two-lagged Sentiment	0.012
Adj-R^2	0.278	Adj-R^2	0.204
Akaike AIC	10.96	Akaike AIC	4.71
Observations	7183	Observations	7183

On the other hand, Diffusion shows some weak effects on Sentiment, reflecting some consistency with the previous causality tests. The two-lagged Diffusion has a strongly positive effect on Sentiment, whereas the one-lagged Diffusion does not. Sentiment has positive relationships with its one and two lags. Some

previous studies also confirm the positive signs when they exam the relationship among past reviews and current reviews [13, 32]. Therefore, we can conclude that a reciprocal relationship has occurred between Diffusion and Sentiment. However, the causality from Sentiment to Diffusion is much stronger than that from Diffusion to Sentiment.

To estimate the full VAR model, we first apply two lags to reach a balance of an acceptable forecasting power and modeling parsimony for an initial model. Besides, from the Granger-Causality test, majority of variables of interest have their highest significance of F-statistics for one or two lags. The procedure to specify the VAR model step by step adds exogenous variables for one or two lags into the VAR model. Following the theory of new product diffusion, the level and square of Past Adoption at t-1 are always added into the VAR model. See Table 3.

Table 3: Estimated Parameters of Full VAR Models

DV = Diffusion	Model 1	Model 2	Model 3
Past Adoption Y_{t-1}	0.0164	0.0164	0.0164
Past Adoption Y_{t-1}^2	-9.29E-07	-9.26E-07	-9.26E-07
Sentiment	1.617	1.559	
One-lagged Sentiment	0.697	0.749	
Two-lagged Sentiment	-0.047*	0.582	
Volume of Post			1.237
One-lagged Volume of Post			0.406
Two-lagged Volume of Post		-0.398	-0.033
Adj-R^2	0.278	0.279	0.279
Akaike AIC	10.96	10.96	10.96
Observations	7183	7183	7183

The results indicate that Sentiment and Volume of Post have some sort of effects on Diffusion, while Depth of Post and Rating are not significant as explanatory factors of Diffusion. Specifically, model 1 shows that only UGC Sentiment and its one lag have a positive relationship with diffusion. Like the dynamic model in the previous section, model 1 implies that Sentiment can instantly stimulate people's adoption behavior. It also causes a one-week delay effect on the adoption rate. In contrast to model 1, model 3 points out that Volume of Post is the sole UGC metric to explain Diffusion. Besides, among UGC metrics, Volume of Post and its one and two lags indicate the strongest impact on Diffusion as their coefficients have the highest t-value except that of Past Adoption. This finding is consistent with past research regarding the relationship between Volume of Post and organizational performance [38].

Model 2 shares a common outcome with model 1 in terms of the positive relationship between UGC Sentiment and Diffusion. However, results from the model 2 show that both two-lag UGC Sentiment and two-lag Volume of Post are significant to influence people's adoption behavior. While UGC Sentiment still has some positive impact after a two-week delay, Volume of Post causes a negative rather than a positive effect. Although it seems to cause a conflict between Sentiment and Volume of Post, the result reflects an agreement with past findings. If a review had some good sentiment, it would receive helpfulness and thus stimulate adoption behavior. At the same time, people prefer to post reviews for products that are less available and less successful in the market [13]. Thus, at one point, posting rate would decrease significantly and negatively impact on the overall adoption rate as shown in the model 3.

In all three models, the finding is consistent in a way that Diffusion at time t is strongly dependent on the level and square of Past Adoption at time t-1. It also shows a strong consistency with the theory of diffusion as the VAR model becomes significantly stronger when the level and square of Past Adoption at t-1 are added in the model. Actually, the largest variance of Diffusion can be explained by Past Adoption because they are directly related to adoption behavior. The AIC values, which reflects the parsimony of a model, are comparable among the three models. However, the Adj. R^2 values of model 2 and 3 are slightly better than that of model 1. In practice, we can use all three models to explain the variance of Diffusion because their modeling indices are not much different and both Volume of Post and Sentiment can be converted to a very good explanatory power for Diffusion. Although exogenous variables show a significant relationship with the dependent variable, its explained variance is rather low, just approximately 27 percent. Note that Sentiment and Volume of Post are highly cointegrated because, as shown in the above table, two variables are not significant together. They stands alone to explain Diffusion. The cointegration between the two variables causes their explain power eclipsed and thus shrunken the amount of DV explained variance.

6.2 Vector Error Correction Model

Unlike the outcome of the Johansen test, the result of the Pedroni and Kao cointegration test shows that there are cointegrations among variables. And in some panel unit root tests, some variables do not contain a linear deterministic trend. Thus, a VEC can be used in this case [23].

Table 4: Estimated Parameters of VEC Models

DV = Δ Diffusion	Model 4	Model 5	Model 6
Past Adoption Y_{t-1}	0.0135	0.0135	-0.006
Past Adoption $Y_{t-1}{}^2$	-6.29E-07	-6.77E-07	5.12E-07
One-lagged Δ Sentiment	-1.45	-1.397	-1.098
Two-lagged Δ Sentiment	-0.04	-2.809	-0.042*
One-lagged Δ Volume of Post	-2.22	-1.688	0.856
Two-lagged Δ Volume of Post	-0.88	-0.016	0.028*
Adj-R^2	0.55	0.54	0.4
Akaike AIC	10.67	10.68	10.95
Observations	7029	7029	7029

In the VEC model 4 with an assumed cointegration between Diffusion and Sentiment, the results with no trend in data show that both the difference of Sentiment (one and two lags) and the level of Volume of Post (one and two lags) have a significant relationship with the difference of Diffusion in the presence of the second order of one-lagged Diffusion. When we estimate the VEC model with either a linear trend in data or a quadratic trend in data, both the difference of Sentiment (one and two lags) and the level of Volume of Post (one and two lags) still indicate a

significant impact on the difference of Diffusion. Moreover, the modeling indices of Adj. R-square and Akaike AIC are improved and have the values of 0.54 (10.69) and 0.55 (10.67). In the VEC model 5 with one cointegration rank for Volume of Post, when no trend in data is chosen, the results show that both the difference of Volume of Post and the level of Sentiment have a significant relationship with the difference of Diffusion in the presence of the one and two-lagged Diffusions. When a linear trend in data in cointegrated equation is assumed, we have a similar result. But, both Adj. R^2 and Akaike AIC indices are slightly improved from 0.53 (10.69) to 0.54 (10.68). Note that when the quadratic trend in data is considered, the VEC model is slightly improved. The explained variation of the difference of Diffusion is almost the same and the Adj. R^2 increase with a small amount from 0.53 to 0.54.

In the VEC model 6 with multiple cointegrations (rank more than two) among Diffusion and Volume of Post and Sentiment, the results show that both differences of Volume of Post (one lag) and Sentiment (one lag) are significant predictors of the Diffusion difference when we assume no linear trend in data and in the presence of the differences of Diffusion (one and two lags) and the second order of Diffusion at time t-1. However, compared with previous models, the model performance is not good. Its indices significantly decrease from 0.550 to 0.402 for Adj. R^2 and from 10.67 to 10.95 for Akaike AIC. When linear and quadratic trends in data are taken into account, the results are similar and the performance of the VEC model is not significantly improved.

A combination of all VEC results indicates that the VEC models considering a linear trend in data, in general, perform better than those VEC models with an assumption of no trend in data. In all three models, Diffusion is strongly dependent on the level and square of Past Adoption. Among significant VEC models, model 4 has the highest Adj-R^2 and the lowest Akaike AIC values. Thus, model 4 is considered the best one to explain dynamic patterns of Diffusion. Moreover, the adjusted R-square value is significantly improved from 0.279 (model 2) to 0.55 (model 4). This means that when we use a VEC approach to correct cointegrations among time-series variables, the proposed model performs much better and is able to explain more than half of the Diffusion variance.

Considering results of VAR and VEC models, we learnt that sentiment content or, in another word, pros and cons comments can be very viral to instantly trigger adopting behavior. The effect might also be delayed over time and it could strongly spill over in the Internet for one or two weeks.

7. CONCLUSION

This study is focusing on diffusion and adoption of digital artifacts. The goal is to explore the social role of user-generated content during the diffusion process of digital artifacts in the context of online social networks. The study spans a wide range of analytic methods and tools such as predictive modeling, latent sentiment analysis, data retrieval, and other tools for network analysis and visualization.

Results of the study provide a deeper insight into the influence of user-generated content (UGC) on IT diffusion and how such a web system (e.g.: online social networks) can help firms enable a process of value co-creation. The study sheds light on the crowding power and the long-tail effect in online social networks. Findings also offer valuable implications for organizations to set up their strategic vision in terms of targeted marketing, customer relationship management, and information dissemination. The overall finding shows that the amount of discussions (Volume of Post) and their valence (Sentiment) toward a new digital product have a dynamic impact on diffusion of the digital product. But, the relationships depend on certain situations.

Specifically, we do find dynamic relationships between Diffusion and UGC metrics including Sentiment and Volume of Post. Consistent to previous studies, among UGC metrics, Volume of Post is the strongest predictor of Diffusion, so does the Business Performance. Although past research has discussed the relationship between Sentiment and Business Performance, the current study is the first one to look inside the dynamic relationship between Diffusion and Sentiment. Sentiment has a positive and dynamic relationship with Diffusion (Adoption Rate).

Moreover, both Sentiment and Volume of Post were found to induce a higher short-term response and a longer carryover effect on Diffusion in the early stage than in the late stage. In addition, we also find that a response of Diffusion to a shock of Sentiment can last longer for a single-generation product than for a multiple-generation product. Unlike previous studies, however, our study did not confirm significant impacts of information richness (Depth of Post) and game rating (Rating) on Diffusion, although Granger tests show moderate causalities among them.

The study sheds light on the crowding power and the long-tail effect in online social networks. Findings also offer valuable implications for organizations to set up their strategic vision in terms of digital marketing, customer relationship management, and information dissemination.

7.1 Contributions

Our research offers several potential contributions for advancing knowledge and understanding of the diffusion literature and user-generated-content effects. First, to the best of our knowledge, the study is the first one to claim a dynamic relationship between sentiment and new product diffusion. By tracking the number of new adopters over time and quantifying textual sentiment, our work provides a new method to collect a measurable link between UGC activities and adoption behavior. Second, the classic diffusion model is extended to include UGC terms reflecting social influences of innovators toward potential followers via online textual communication. Third, this study makes a methodological contribution by demonstrating a systematic sampling approach to collect an unbiased sample. Fourth, unlike past research which assumes a constant role of UGC during the diffusion process and among various product generations, this study indicates that the contagious role of UGC is much more important during the early stage of diffusion, especially for a brand new product rather than an extension of an existing product.

In addition, our investigation of UGC dynamic effects on new product diffusion can help managers to gain practical benefits in some ways. Sentiment aggregation can play as a proxy to predict new product success. Managers can apply techniques in our study to have better measures of UGC metrics, especially sentiment scores. The strong link between sentiment scores and adoption rate of a new product can help to predict if the new product is successful during the early stage. Besides, managers can also apply the proposed model to forecast sales and demand because, when combining with spatial data of UGC metrics, managers can cluster new product demand of different markets and thus are able to control their inventory and manage their supply chain systems.

Finally, our research may help firms manage their customer relationships. An increasing number of firms have offered beneficial and/or financial incentives to existing OSN members (customers) to provide helpful new product reviews. Traditionally, customer lifetime value (CLV) or member lifetime value (MLV) is the most important metric for managers to implement a strategic move targeting different groups of customers. CLV describes the amount of revenue or profit a member (customer) generates over his or her entire lifetime. With a new approach to track UGC, managers can add customers' UGC contributions into the firm's CLV portfolio. By that way, firms are able to maintain customers' loyalty and motivate them to participate in disseminating new product information.

7.2 Limitations

Along with academic and practical contributions, we also acknowledge several limitations in the study. First, we collect data from only one video game networking site, but not other comparable sites. Thus, data limitation prevents us from generalizing the results to different product categories. Second, UGC metrics and reviews collected could be manipulated by the site owner. Since the data collection is conducted in one website, it is hard to validate if the data is reliable or not. Third, we use SAS software to conduct sentiment analysis of new product discussions. The software is designed to analyze unrelated messages. However, a number of reviews and discussions used in the study are linked to each other. Thus, sentiment scores could be biased due to this problem. Finally, our model does not include interaction terms between UGC metrics and past adoption as suggested in the literature. This can reduce the power of the tested model to explain variance of diffusion.

7.3 Future Research

This work could be extended in several directions. First, due to data source limitation, we could not gather data of diffusion breadth and diffusion depth. Further research could explore the relationship between the three diffusion dimensions and UGC metrics. Second, most of past studies use historical data to forecast sales and demand of a new product. Future research could develop a new model of real-time forecasting based on spatial UGC metrics in different social media networking sites. Third, social influences of social network hubs on diffusion are different in each stage of the diffusion process [37]. Little has been known about how these hubs use UGC to influence on their followers' adoption behavior. Finally, diffusion of a new product in an online setting is actually formed by two parallel processes. The first is the diffusion of viral information about the new product. The second is the diffusion process of the new product itself. Further research should be conducted to get insight into this duo diffusion.

8. ACKNOWLEDGMENTS
Our thanks to ACM SIGMIS for allowing us to present our study to the conference.

9. REFERENCES
[1] Abbasi, A. and Chen, H. Cybergate: A Design Framework and System For Text Analysis of Computer-Mediated Communication. *MIS Quarterly*, 32, 4 2008), 811-837.

[2] Agarwal, R. and Prasad, J. The role of innovation characteristics and perceived voluntariness in the acceptance of information technologies. *Decision Sciences*, 28, 3 1997), 557-582.

[3] Andrade, E. B. Behavioral Consequences of Affect: Combining Evaluative and Regulatory Mechanisms. *Journal of Consumer Research*, 32, 3 2005), 355-362.

[4] Bass, F. M. A New Product Growth for Model Consumer Durables. *Management Science*, 15, 5 (January 1, 1969 1969), 215-227.

[5] Berger, J. and Milkman, K. L. What Makes Online Content Viral?? *Journal of Marketing Research (JMR)*, 49, 2 2012), 192-205.

[6] Bickart, B. and Schindler, R. M. Internet forums as influential sources of consumer information. *Journal of interactive marketing*, 15, 3 2001), 31-40.

[7] Bollen, J., Mao, H. and Pepe, A. Modeling Public Mood and Emotion: Twitter Sentiment and Socio-Economic Phenomena. *Proceedings of the Fifth International AAAI*2011).

[8] Breitung, J. The local power of some unit root tests for panel data. *Adv Econometrics*, 152000), 161-177.

[9] Brynjolfsson, E. and Kemerer, C. F. *Network Externalities in Microcomputer Software: An Econometric Analysis of the Spreadsheet Market*. Institute for Operations Research and the Management Sciences, City, 1996.

[10] Cao, Q., Duan, W. and Gan, Q. Exploring determinants of voting for the "helpfulness" of online user reviews: A text mining approach. *Decision Support Systems*, 50, 2 (1// 2011), 511-521.

[11] Chau, M. and Xu, J. Business Intelligence In Blogs: Understanding Consumer Interactions And Communities. *MIS Quarterly*, 36, 4 2012), 1189-1216.

[12] Chevalier, J. A. and Mayzlin, D. The Effect of Word of Mouth on Sales: Online Book Reviews. *Journal of Marketing Research (JMR)*, 43, 3 2006), 345-354.

[13] Dellarocas, C., Gao, G. and Narayan, R. Are Consumers More Likely to Contribute Online Reviews for Hit or Niche Products? *Journal of Management Information Systems*, 27, 2 (Fall2010 2010), 127-157.

[14] Dellarocas, C., Zhang, X. and Awad, N. F. Exploring the value of online product reviews in forecasting sales: The case of motion pictures. *Journal of Interactive Marketing*, 21, 4 (// 2007), 23-45.

[15] Duan, W., Gu, B. and Whinston, A. B. Informational Cascades and Software Adoption on The Internet: An Empirical Investigation. *MIS Quarterly*, 33, 1 2009), 23-48.

[16] Fichman, R. G. and Kemerer, C. F. Toward a Theory of the Adoption and Diffusion of Software Process Innovations. In *Proceedings of the IFIP Working Conference on Diffusion, Transfer and Implementation of Information Technology* (1993).

[17] Garber, T., Goldenberg, J., Libai, B. and Muller, E. From Density to Destiny: Using Spatial Dimension of Sales Data for Early Prediction of New Product Success. *Marketing Science*, 23, 3 2004), 419-428.

[18] Garg, R., Smith, M. D. and Telang, R. Measuring Information Diffusion in an Online Community. *Journal of Management Information Systems*, 28, 2 (Fall2011 2011), 11-38.

[19] Goh, K.-Y., Heng, C.-S. and Lin, Z. Social Media Brand Community and Consumer Behavior: Quantifying the Relative Impact of User- and Marketer-Generated Content. *Information Systems Research*, 24, 1 (March 1, 2013 2013), 88-107.

[20] Granger, C. W. Investigating causal relations by econometric models and cross-spectral methods. *Econometrica: Journal of the Econometric Society*1969), 424-438.

[21] Greifeneder, R., Bless, H. and Pham, M. T. When Do People Rely on Affective and Cognitive Feelings in Judgment? A Review. *Personality and Social Psychology Review*, 15, 2 (May 1, 2011 2011), 107-141.

[22] Gu, B., Park, J. and Konana, P. The Impact of External Word-of-Mouth Sources on Retailer Sales of High-Involvement Products. *Information Systems Research*, 23, 1 (March 2012 2012), 182-196.

[23] Hill, R. C., Griffiths, W. E. and Lim, G. C. *Principles of econometrics*. Wiley, Hoboken, NJ, 2011.

[24] Johansen, S. Statistical analysis of cointegration vectors. *Journal of economic dynamics and control*, 12, 2 1988), 231-254.

[25] Johansen, S., Mosconi, R. and Nielsen, B. Cointegration analysis in the presence of structural breaks in the deterministic trend. *The Econometrics Journal*, 3, 2 2000), 216-249.

[26] Kaplan, A. M. and Haenlein, M. Users of the world, unite! The challenges and opportunities of Social Media. *Business Horizons*, 53, 1 2010), 59-68.

[27] Kozinets, R. V., de Valck, K., Wojnicki, A. C. and Wilner, S. J. S. Networked Narratives: Understanding Word-of-Mouth Marketing in Online Communities. *Journal of Marketing*, 74, 2 2010), 71-89.

[28] Lau-Gesk, L. and Meyers-Levy, J. Emotional Persuasion: When the Valence versus the Resource Demands of Emotions Influence Consumers' Attitudes. *Journal of Consumer Research*, 36, 4 2009), 585-599.

[29] Liu, Y. Word of Mouth for Movies: Its Dynamics and Impact on Box Office Revenue. *Journal of Marketing*, 70, 3 2006), 74-89.

[30] Ludwig, S., de Ruyter, K., Friedman, M., Brüggen, E. C., Wetzels, M. and Pfann, G. More Than Words: The Influence of Affective Content and Linguistic Style Matches in Online Reviews on Conversion Rates. *Journal of Marketing*, 77, 1 2013), 87-103.

[31] Mahajan, V., Muller, E. and Wind, Y. *New-product diffusion models*. Springer Science & Business Media, 2000.

[32] Moe, W. W. and Trusov, M. The Value of Social Dynamics in Online Product Ratings Forums. *Journal of Marketing Research (JMR)*, 48, 3 2011), 444-456.

[33] Mudambi, S. M. and Schuff, D. What Makes a Helpful Online Review? A Study of Customer Reviews on Amazon.Com. *MIS Quarterly*, 34, 1 2010), 185-200.

[34] Pan, Y. and Zhang, J. Q. Born Unequal: A Study of the Helpfulness of User-Generated Product Reviews. *Journal of Retailing*, 87, 4 (12// 2011), 598-612.

[35] Rogers, E. Diffusion of innovations. *New York*1983).

[36] Stacey, E., Pauwels, H. and Lackman, A. Beyond Likes and Tweets: Marketing, Social Media Content, and Store Performance. *The Center for Measurable Markting*2013).

[37] Susarla, A., Oh, J.-H. and Tan, Y. Social Networks and the Diffusion of User-Generated Content: Evidence from YouTube. *Information Systems Research*, 23, 1 (March 2012 2012), 23-41.

[38] Tirunillai, S. and Tellis, G. J. Does Chatter Really Matter? Dynamics of User-Generated Content and Stock Performance. *Marketing Science*, 31, 2 (March 1, 2012 2012), 198-215.

[39] Wood, S. L. and Moreau, C. P. From Fear to Loathing? How Emotion Influences the Evaluation and Early Use of Innovations. *Journal of Marketing*, 70, 3 2006), 44-57.

[40] Zhu, F. and Zhang, X. Impact of Online Consumer Reviews on Sales: The Moderating Role of Product and Consumer Characteristics. *Journal of Marketing*, 74, 2 2010), 133-148.

Author Index